Shakespeare
as
Political Thinker

Shakespeare

as

Political Thinker

Edited by

John E. Alvis and Thomas G. West

ISI Books
Wilmington, Delaware
2000

Cataloging-in-Publication Information

Shakespeare as political thinker / edited by John E. Alvis and
      Thomas G. West.—2nd ed., rev.—Wilmington, Del. :
      ISI Books, 2000.

      p.   ; cm.

      Includes bibliographical references and index.
      ISBN 1-882926-50-1
      1. Shakespeare, William, 1564-1616—Political and
social views. 2. Politics and literature—England—History—
16th Century. 3. Political Plays, English—History and
criticism. I. Alvis, John. E. II. West, Thomas G., 1945-

PR3017 .S5 2000   00-100745
822.3/3—dc21   CIP

Published in the United States by:

ISI Books
P.O. Box 4431
Wilmington, DE 19807-0431
800-526-7022 • www.isibooks.org

Manufactured in the United States of America

In reverent memory of our parents

Irvin Clement Alvis

Ruth Catherine Alvis

Irving Parmelee West

Marjorie Ergmann West

Contents

FOREWORD

The essays collected in this volume proceed from the common conviction that Shakespeare's poetry conveys a wisdom concerning political things commensurate with the charm and vigor that distinguish his artistry. From various vantages the authors have attempted to bring to light the principles of this wisdom. Addressing a range of plays inclusive of *Richard II, 1* and *2 Henry IV, Henry V, Measure for Measure, The Tempest, Timon of Athens, Troilus and Cressida, The Merchant of Venice,* and the major tragedies, as well as the sonnets, the essays inquire into the significance of politics for Shakespeare's characters and for the poet as thinker.

Most of the contributors will be found to regard Shakespeare as a poetic exponent of the great tradition of classical political philosophy stemming from Socrates, a tradition whose thoughtfulness has recently been recovered and displayed by such scholars as Leo Strauss. In particular, their essays reveal a general sympathy with the approach developed in a work that is the nearest progenitor of this book, *Shakespeare's Politics* by Allan Bloom with Harry V. Jaffa (both of whom have contributed to the present collection, and both of whom were students of Strauss). This predominant grain is brought out by the inclusion of some essays—notably those of Louise Cowan and Robert B. Heilman—which cut across it.

The themes explored here concern the nature and limits of political life; the origins of Shakespeare's understanding of politics in Christianity, Machiavelli, and the ancients; perfect and imperfect statesmanship; England, Rome, and the best polity; the link between individual character and political regime; and the relationship between poetry, politics, religion, and philosophy.

Some of these issues have been all but ignored in previous Shakespearean criticism, and many academic custodians of Shakespeare might contest the propriety of setting poems to answer political and philosophical questions. In some degree, then, these interpretations are provocations, or rather new entries in a continuing controversy.

JEA

ACKNOWLEDGMENTS

The authors of this collection were participants, as speakers or discussants, at a conference on "Poetry and Politics in Shakespeare" held at the University of Dallas in October 1978. About half of the essays were presented at the conference; the rest were written especially for this volume.

The conference was co-sponsored by the Intercollegiate Studies Institute, Inc. (ISI), through the kind offices of its then Western Director, Peter W. Schramm, who now directs the Ashbrook Center for Public Affairs at Ashland University in Ohio. We are grateful for ISI's generous support.

The Intercollegiate Studies Institute also made possible the publication of this second edition. We thank Jeff Nelson, Publisher of ISI Books, and Christopher Briggs, ISI Senior Editor, for bringing the book back into print.

The editors also wish to thank Andrew Moran of the University of Dallas (UD) English Department for major help with proofreading. Thanks also to proofreaders John Grant, Jeff Elmendorf, and Kathryn Martin, all students in UD's Institute of Philosophic Studies.

TGW

NOTE ON THE REVISED EDITION

The second edition differs from the first in these particulars—there are two new chapters: Alvis's on *Hamlet*, and Cantor's on *Macbeth*. Berns, de Alvarez, Flannery, Platt, and West have revised their chapters, but only in minor respects. The "Introductory" chapter and other front matter have been updated. The remaining chapters were reprinted without change, except for corrections of typographical errors.

TGW

THE EDITORS AND AUTHORS

John E. Alvis is Professor of English at the University of Dallas and a member of the faculty of the Institute of Philosophic Studies. He presently serves as Director of American Studies at Dallas. He is the author of *Shakespeare's Understanding of Honor* (Carolina Academic Press, 1989); *Divine Initiative and Heroic Response: The Political Plan of Zeus* (Rowman and Littlefield, 1995); and editor of *Areopagitica and Other Political Writings of John Milton* (Liberty Fund Press, 1999). He has published articles on Virgil, Ghiberti, Shakespeare, Milton, Melville, O'Neill, Caroline Gordon, and Derek Walcott, as well as writings on American politics, constitutional issues, the political thought of Willmoore Kendall, and controversies in contemporary American higher education. His present interest is completing a series of full-length plays about the statesmen Hamilton, Lincoln, and Wilson.

Laurence Berns has been teaching at St. John's College, Annapolis, since 1960. He is the author of "Gratitude, Nature and Piety in *King Lear*" (*Interpretation*, 1972); "Aristotle's *Poetics*" (in *Ancients and Moderns*, Basic Books, 1964); "The Relation between Philosophy and Religion: Reflections on Leo Strauss's Suggestion Concerning the Source and Sources of Modern Philosophy" (*Interpretation*, 1991); "Aristotle and Adam Smith on Justice: Cooperation Between Ancients and Moderns?" (*Review of Metaphysics*, 1994); and "Our Political Situation: Good Government, Self-government and American Democracy" (in *The Great Ideas Today: 1997*, Encyclopaedia Britannica, Inc.). He is completing an amply annotated translation of Aristotle's *Politics*.

Allan Bloom was a professor in the Committee on Social Thought at the University of Chicago. His best-seller, *The Closing of the American Mind: How Higher Education Has Failed Democracy and Impoverished the Souls of Today's Students* (Simon and Schuster), appeared in 1987. He is also the author of *Shakespeare's Politics* (with Harry V. Jaffa, Basic Books, 1964); *Giants and Dwarfs: Essays 1960-1990* (Simon and Schuster, 1990); *Love and Friendship* (Simon and Schuster, 1993); and translations of *The Republic of Plato* (Basic Books, 1968) and Rousseau's *Emile* (Basic Books, 1979).

Paul A. Cantor is Professor of English at the University of Virginia. He has written *Shakespeare's Rome: Republic and Empire* (Cornell University Press, 1976); *Creature and Creator: Myth-making and English Romanticism* (Cambridge University Press, 1984); and *Shakespeare: Hamlet* (Cambridge University Press, 1989).

Louise Cowan received her Ph.D. in 1953 from Vanderbilt University. She served for many years as the Graduate Dean and chairman of English at the University of Dallas, and as Director of its Institute of Philosophic Studies. With her husband, Dr. Donald Cowan, she pioneered the University's lauded core curriculum based on classic texts. She is a Founding Fellow of the Dallas Institute of Humanities and Culture, established in 1980, and the creator of its Teachers Academy, an intensive continuing education program that has allowed hundreds of secondary school teachers to renew their vocations and pursue graduate study in literature. She is the recipient of numerous awards, grants, and professorships, including the National Endowment for the Humanities' Charles Frankel Prize for her work in advancing the study of the humanities. Dr. Cowan's publications include *The Fugitive Group* (1959, 1968); *The Southern Critics* (1971); *The Terrain of Comedy*, ed. (1984); *Teaching the Teachers* (1986); *The Epic Cosmos*, ed. with Larry Allums (1992); *Classic Texts and the Nature of Authority*, ed. with Donald Cowan (1993); and, most recently, *Invitation to the Classics* (1998), ed. with Os Guinness. In addition, she has published numerous articles on Faulkner, Coleridge, Homer, Aristophanes, Shakespeare, Eudora Welty, Toni Morrison, and others.

Leo Paul S. de Alvarez is Professor and Chairman of the Department of Politics at the University of Dallas. His most recent work is *The Machiavellian Enterprise: A Commentary on* The Prince (1999).

Christopher Flannery is Professor of Political Science and Chairman of the History and Political Science Department at Azusa Pacific University.

Robert B. Heilman is Professor Emeritus of English at the University of Washington, where he chaired the Department of English from 1948 to 1971. He has written about Shakespeare in studies of *King Lear* (*This Great Stage*, Louisiana State University Press, 1948) and *Othello* (*Magic in the Web*, University of Kentucky Press, 1956); in various chapters of his volumes on genre (*Tragedy and Melodrama*, University of Washington Press, 1968, and *The Ways of the World: Comedy and Society*, University of Washington Press, 1978, winner of the Christian Gauss Prize of Phi Beta Kappa); in essays in various quadricentennial volumes (1964); and in his editions of *Cymbeline* (Penguin, 1965) and *The Taming of the Shrew* (New American Library, 1966). In 1974 he gave the Second Annual Shakespeare Lecture to the Shakespeare Society of America, of which he has since been a trustee. Retired since 1976 (and a widower since 1985), he produced two volumes of essays in 1991, *The Southern Connection* and *The Workings of Fiction*. Another volume of essays, *The Professor and the Profession*, was published by University of Missouri Press in 1999.

Harry V. Jaffa is a Distinguished Fellow of the Claremont Institute. Before his retirement he was Henry Salvatori Research Professor of Political Philosophy, Claremont McKenna College and Claremont Graduate University. His essay on *King Lear* is in Bloom's *Shakespeare as Political Thinker* (1964). Jaffa's books include *Thomism and Aristotelianism: A Study of the Commentary by Thomas Aquinas on the* Nicomachean Ethics (1952); *Crisis of the House Divided: An Interpretation of the Issues in the Lincoln-Douglas Debates* (Doubleday, 1959); *Liberty and Equality: Theory and Practice in American Politics* (Oxford, 1965); *The Conditions of Freedom: Essays in Political Philosophy* (Johns Hopkins, 1975); *How to Think about the American Revolution* (Carolina Academic Press, 1978); *American Conservatism and the American Founding* (Carolina Academic Press, 1984); and *Original Intent and the Framers of the Constitution: A Disputed Question* (Regnery, 1994). His most recent book is *A New Birth of Freedom: Abraham Lincoln and the American Civil War*, vol. 1: *Why the War Came* (Rowman & Littlefield, 2000).

Michael Platt has taught literature, political science, and philosophy, here in America, at Dartmouth and the University of Dallas, where he directed the literature program of the Institute of Philosophic Studies, and abroad, at the University of Heidelberg. His *Rome and Romans According to Shakespeare* first appeared in 1976 (2nd ed.: University Press of America, 1982); his "Falstaff in the Valley of the Shadow of Death" is in *Major Literary Characters: Falstaff*, ed. Harold Bloom (Chelsea House, 1991); and his *Seven Wonders of Shakespeare* is forthcoming. His essays on Nietzsche will be found in the *Journal of Value Inquiry*, vol. 22, and *Nietzsche Studien*, vol. 17 and 22. And his essays on learning and teaching the young today in America are in "Souls without Longing," *Interpretation*, 1991; "What Student Evaluations Teach," *Perspectives on Political Science* (Winter, 1993); and "The Young, The Good, and the West," in *America, The West, and the Liberal Arts*, ed. Ralph Hancock (Rowman & Littlefield, 1998). Dr. Platt lectures for ISI, writes for *Practical Homeschooling*, and is headmaster of the Friends of the Republic, the family home school in East Wallingford, Vermont, and Albany, Texas.

Barbara Tovey taught in the Departments of Philosophy and Humanities at the University of New Hampshire until her retirement. She is the author of "Shakespeare's Apology for Imitative Poetry: *The Tempest* and the *Republic*" (*Interpretation*, 1983); "Portia's Suitors" (with Richard Kuhns, *Philosophy and Literature*, 1989); and "Wisdom and the Law: Thoughts on the Political Philosophy of *Measure for Measure*" (in *Shakespeare's Political Pageant*, ed. Joseph Alulis and Vickie Sullivan, Rowman & Littlefield, 1996). At present she is engaged in a study of Boccaccio and Chaucer.

Dain A. Trafton is Professor Emeritus at Rockford College. He has published articles on various topics in Renaissance and modern literature. He is the author of *Tasso's Dialogue on the Court* (*English Literary Renaissance Supplements*, 1973); co-author of *Tasso's Dialogues: A Selection with the "Discourse on the Art of the Dialogue"* (University of California Press, 1981); and co-editor of *The Legacy of Benedetto Croce: Contemporary Critical Views* (University of Toronto Press, 1999). He published his first short story, "Jeremiah's Wrath: A Tale from the Indian Wars in Maine," in *Boulevard* (Spring, 1999), and he is currently working on others as well as a novel set in sixteenth-century Naples.

Thomas G. West is a Senior Fellow of the Claremont Institute and Professor of Politics at the University of Dallas. He is the author of

Plato's Apology of Socrates: An Interpretation (Cornell University Press, 1979). A revised edition of *Four Texts on Socrates: Plato's* Euthyphro, Apology, *and* Crito, *and Aristophanes'* Clouds (co-translated with Grace West) appeared in 1998. His latest book is *Vindicating the Founders: Race, Sex, Class, and Justice in the Origins of America* (Rowman & Littlefield, 1997). Several of his essays are on the Claremont Institute website, at www.claremont.org.

INTRODUCTORY:

SHAKESPEAREAN POETRY AND POLITICS

John E. Alvis

Shakespeare owes his pre-eminence among poets to the power that allows his art to charm spectators but equally to the comprehensiveness of his wisdom regarding human things, a wisdom which invites and sustains inquiries into its grounds. The essays here collected presuppose that the charm exists for the sake of the wisdom. The contributors presume that Shakespearean poetry affords something more determinate and responsible than the personalized fabrication of an imagined world answerable only to the requirements of self-coherence. If Shakespeare composes a supreme fiction, its supremacy rests upon its singular comprehensiveness as an image of truth. The poems and plays propose a series of vantages upon the one preconstituted world to which all men share access according to the varying capacities of their intelligence and heart. Shakespeare's acknowledgment that his images subserve truth—"minding true things by what their mock'ries be"—opens his art to interpretation while imposing the office of critical judgment. Because we know something about the same world he knows, we can interpret his poems and make discriminations between the various claimants to knowledge depicted in his poems. Because we evidently know appreciably less than he knows, the task of interpretation and judgment must proceed under his guidance. Criticism develops as an inquiry, a conversation of non-catechetical query and reply wherein the questioner seeks instruction from his superior even as regards the questions he should ask. For the peculiarly unequal character of this conversation requires that the questioner learn from the poem what questions he should set it to answer. Here too Shakespeare provides guidance.

From the pointed comments which obtrude from time to time in his

Prologues, as well as from the remarks regarding dramatic poetry contained in *Hamlet* and *A Midsummer Night's Dream*, one may gather that Shakespeare anticipates two distinct audiences for his work.[1] The distinction seems to amount to rather more than the familiar matter of the disparity between jostling base mechanics and place-keeping gentry. A quibble in one late prologue appears to hold out the hope of a rare "understanding friend" silent among the impecunious clustered at the lip of the stage.[2] Committing the company's playbooks to print ensures that the plays can be ruminated under circumstances that permit leisured reflection, even among those not of the leisured class. Yet the availability of printed texts does not remove another sort of distinction between attentive auditors and oblivious groundlings. Experience attests that readers can consume years in blear-eyed confrontation with folio facsimile and concordance without relinquishing their naïveté as mere spectators. The serious student of Shakespeare's poetry has occasion to reflect upon his own naïveté each time he returns to a play he once may have thought he had grasped. A difference in the reach and depth of attentiveness distinguishes those who are merely spectators from those capable of entering into conversation with the dramatist. Shakespeare's chances of acquiring understanding friends are made better by print only to the extent that his readers possess those virtues of the art of reading that are identical with those recognized for the art of close conversation. The enabling virtue for conversation would seem to be the concern on the part of the listener to understand what the poet is concerned to understand. Shakespeare indicates the more important concerns by giving prominence throughout his poetry to certain recurrent topics.

One of the foremost of these topics is politics. The plays offer a political surface inasmuch as their action is public action. Shakespeare's stage supports only enactments which have a public extension. To first discern the prominence of politics, it suffices to note the arrangements of *dramatis personae* by reference to social station. We know that the bulk of the characters are public men before we know anything else about them, and we know that their numbers will be ample enough to convey a sense of the richness of public affairs. The surface of action bears out the surface of characterization. The plot of a Shakespearean play usually turns upon a changeover among those who exercise political power (the tragedies and histories) or upon complications arising from political exile or from problematic enforcement of a law (the comedies). Since dramatic poetry almost necessarily requires public settings and social activities, the bald fact that the surface of the plays is political does not carry us far toward conclusions regarding Shakespeare's understanding of politics. However, our flat-footed observation is not without significance. Modern audiences are familiar with dramas which attempt to confine their subject to the inwardly turned experience of individuals or which restrict their scope to a portrayal of relationships within one family. Shakespearean drama passes beyond the private lives of particular men and beyond the incompletely public life of families. Every Shakespearean character lives within a political regime governed by laws and shaped by distinctive institutions. How a character acts and how he perceives his deeds is affected, sometimes crucially affected, by his participation in the corporate life of a city or a realm. We might infer from his political focus that Shakespeare conceives the political context as a necessary condition for displaying, and hence also for understanding, human nature. Quite apart from the instinct of sexual love that brings man to woman or the need to exchange affection that keeps men and women together and extends to kindred, and perhaps apart from the innate sociability that causes men to congregate on any terms, Shakespeare presents human beings seeking their completion within associations that maintain community by combining affection and compulsion. Shakespeare provokes his serious readers to consider in what sense this propensity to live in political community is natural to human beings. Is it natural merely in the sense of instinctual, habitual, or given; or is it natural in the sense of proper to the realization of the essential? The omnipresent political bearings of the plays invite, one may say, this first question of political philosophy. To pursue it at all satisfactorily, one is obliged to consider other questions relating to the view of human nature that appears to underlie the poetry. Politics does not exhaust Shakespeare's subject. We see political life transacted within horizons that enfold other human activities; principal among these are sexual love, friendship, divine worship, the interactions of kinsmen, personal combat, and, in rare instances, the pursuit of private contemplation. We may discern the place of the political theme within Shakespeare's subject by gauging the weight of politics in relation to the other ends the dramatist allots to his characters. The estimate depends upon an assessment of what for Shakespeare constitutes a human life. Do his plays and poems imply a view of what essentially defines human beings?

The subject which for Shakespeare subsumes all others and which appears to be the distinctively human province is the activity of making choices. His characters deliberate toward choice, implement their decisions, and reflect upon the consequences of having chosen one possibility in preference to another. Every play builds toward, then moves from, an important act of choice which stands as a fulcrum transferring momentum of complication to momentum of resolution. The same holds true for the non-dramatic works. *Venus and Adonis* and *The Rape of Lucrece* center upon moments of decision; the sonnet sequence imparts a sense of dramatic urgency by reflecting upon the eligibility of alternate courses of action. Will the young man marry or guard his bachelor autonomy? Can the poet-lover resolve the division of his affection and liberate himself from his dark lady? It appears that for Shakespeare the distinctively human mode of being—though not necessarily man's highest mode of being—reveals itself in acts of choice. Men are what they elect to do.

Election "makes not up," as Burgundy reminds us, upon just any conditions. If they are not predetermined, Shakespearean characters are yet predisposed to certain choices by the bent of their personalities and by the influence of circumstances. Their decisions never occur in a void but always within a world partly of their own making, partly not. With his first appearance a Shakespearean personage bespeaks an ordination to a certain purchase upon life compounded of his individual proclivities modified by sexual identity, blood heritage, and circumstances of social station. He also finds himself born into an order of authoritative opinion supported by political power. His neighbors share a public creed, declaring themselves hospitable to a given view of human and divine affairs and unfriendly to others. Prior to any volition, therefore, Shakespeare's characters are men or women; are attached by birth to a set of kinsmen; are born Englishmen, Italians, Romans, Greeks, or Danes; possess as their birthright a station and occupation; are pagan, Christian, or Jew. Every character thus shares a public world with other citizens or subjects, even though he takes his place within the particular sector of that world claimed by his individuality. A Shakespearean character can be seen as a gathering of motives, feelings, and thoughts which by their dual origin constitute a meeting ground where individual personality conjoins with political formation.

Considering that the era during which the plays were conceived was a time when fundamentally opposed conceptions of civil society contended for dominance, we should not be surprised to discover that Shakespeare's poetry conducts an inquiry into issues connected with political formation—an inquiry commensurate in scope with that pursued by political philosophers. If we take note of the principal alternative views upon this theme available to an educated man of the Renaissance, we may suppose that Shakespeare found himself confronted with a choice between three rival teachings. We can imagine him standing at a juncture from whence three roads diverge. One way leads back to classical antiquity and the foundations of political philosophy in the thought of the Greeks. The route terminates in Athens, but to arrive there one goes via Rome. Another way would take the poet to Jerusalem (Davidic or Christian) and a view of the city conceived under the auspices of scriptural religion. The third fork leads to a state shortly to be named, in one of its imagined versions, New Atlantis, a novel regime built on a conception of political community avowedly modern and opposed to classical and Judaeo-Christian traditions by a purpose that envisions the relaxation of the moral standards upheld by classical and scriptural education for the sake of releasing energies required for the effort of liberating human beings from such naturally imposed limitations as scarcity, insecurity, and bodily ills.

A review of the intellectual sources evident in the plays or readily accessible to the playwright allows us to extend the figure. We may imagine several guides posted on the three roads to solicit travelers. Stationed about midway, we should say, on the route to Athens, Virgil invites traffic towards Rome, and somewhat beyond, Plutarch urges the traveler who has toured the Roman Republic to continue his journey on to Greece. Further on the peregrine dramatist can discern Aristotle and, vague in the distance near the vanishing point, he can just distinguish Plato. Commanding intellectual authorities also mark the route to the Holy City. Close to the crossroads Hooker, Fortescue, More, and John of Salis-bury might be posted, in the distance Aquinas and various schoolmen, then Augustine. At a further distance Paul and the Evangelists would beckon, while most remote, like Plato poised at the horizon, there might stand the austere figure of Moses, author of the Pentateuch. The third road is under construction. A knot of unrecognizable workers set paving stone for the thoroughfare that will carry men to the modern city. They move to the orders of two master engineers who are known to the traveler. Machiavelli and Bacon urge him to join in the direction of the highway project.

Shakespeare could know these political guides through their writings. He incorporates Plutarch verbatim in his Roman plays, constantly alludes to Virgil's *Aeneid*, quotes Paul and the Evangelists, refers to Aristotle and Plato, and appears to adapt a portion of one of Plato's dialogues.[3] Concerning his knowledge of the later Christian writers we know little, but scholars think he collaborated on a play about More (he mentions More in *Henry VIII*) and there is some evidence that Shakespeare knew John of Salisbury's chief political work, the *Policraticus*.[4] In any event he would know something of the principles that inform the writings of these thinkers from sermons or from the retail work of Elizabethan literary middlemen. Concerning his acquaintance with the early architects of modernity we can hardly be certain, but there are three references to Machiavelli by name, and, if Shakespeare was not Bacon, he presumably knew something of Bacon's early thought. Just how much Shakespeare may have read in authors other than Plutarch is a matter of conjecture. However, one does not require a listing of his personal library to sense a kinship of the philosophical themes evident in the plays with the concerns of the writers in these three rival traditions. The themes are decisively political. They turn upon the questions that motivate all political thought: what is the best life for man and what public arrangements are most conducive to this life? We might reasonably hope to find in Shakespeare's plays some guidance for our own inquiries into the three traditions and hence some direction for our own attempts to reflect on this perennial question. Yet one does not find direction if one does not seek it, and few contemporary authorities on Shakespeare seek political guidance from his writings.[5] Literary critics who attribute wisdom to Shakespeare's art—a group by no means co-extensive with those who ascribe excellence—are rather inclined to say that his wisdom "transcends" politics altogether. Their opinion is misfounded, I think, but perhaps not inexplicable.

It may be that the political inquiry which animates Shakespeare's plays can capture the interest of only those modern readers who, after a conscious effort of self-displacement, can think themselves back to the juncture of the three roads. For most readers of Shakespeare the rivalry between the three traditions is no longer alive. If they know of it at all, they think of it as a past controversy which has been settled in favor of modernity. But if they know the rivalry merely as something past, we may suspect they do not really know it. I do not mean to say that every member of the contemporary audience considers himself a partisan of the project begun by Machiavelli and Bacon and completed, at least in principle, in the modern technological state. Yet in one disabling respect modern readers of Shakespeare come to his plays as more or less unwitting captives of a technological regime which encourages a view of politics essentially technological in its conception of ends.

A thinker distinguished for his protracted inquiry into the grounds underlying modernity finds the distinctive character of machine technology in its "challenging" or "setting upon" nature. To the challenger bent on setting upon its resources, the physical world reveals itself as a "standing-reserve" awaiting the challenger's demands.[6] Presently regnant doctrines of political order comport with the peremptory bearing of technology. Modern politics envisions the state as an engine for exploiting the standing-reserve of nature and distributing the gains thereof. This conception of political life as an enterprise in human mastery directed against a grudging but indefinitely malleable cosmos once had to earn a hearing in opposition to the teaching of classical philosophy and scriptural religion, a teaching which located the end of civil society in the cultivation of character. The success of the modern premise in securing custodianship over public education has caused modern readers to be put at an unsympathetic distance from older poets whose political understanding was formed by the classical or scriptural traditions. Ancient, medieval, and Christian-humanist moralists were aware of the powers of moral suasion possessed by poets generally, and especially by dramatists. They could see that every dramatic performance was a political event inasmuch as every play disposes its audience to share its author's view of human character and human ends. By virtue of its influence over the moral education of the citizen, dramatic art was once considered to be subject to the comprehensive educative art of the legislator.[7] Its potential of co-operating with or, for that matter, of subverting the shaping effect of the laws was once thought inseparable from its essence: its making of compelling images of human beings enacting moral choices. Men are disposed to imitate what the artist disposes men to admire. Of necessity, then, the charming images presented in plays compete with the imperative voices of the laws. Even if it should aim at encouraging law-abidingness, each work of the dramatic poet conveys through its imagined life possibilities of conduct which offer alternatives to the regime the audience has come to know through the laws. Within the understanding of politics that prevailed prior to modernity, poetry is in principle political because it pursues indirectly the end of character formation which political constitutions pursue directly through their legislative instruments.

Modernity leaves unchanged the educative property of drama. The modern reader can sense that Shakespeare's plays move their audiences to respond with love or disgust to the actions wrought on the stage. He can guess that the habits of moral discrimination promoted by Shakespeare's guided spectacles may cohere to provide a sort of wisdom. However, because modern readers tend uncritically to accept the moral confinement of modern politics, they incline to think of this wisdom as having nothing to do with politics and are therefore predisposed to over-look the centrality of politics, in its ancient sense, to Shakespeare's subject.

To perceive the political character of Shakespeare's plays, one may be compelled to recover a vantage upon political things that sees the essential political act less in terms of power and more in terms of educa-tion, manners, morals, religion, and ethics.[8] Such a recovery might begin by reviving the ancient and Socratic understanding of regimes as images of certain dominant types of the soul. According to this conception, par-ticular cities encourage the development of distinct human characters and reflect in their institutions, laws, educative customs, and arts their sponsorship of a particular view of human nature and of the best life. A reading of the dramas informed by this pre-modern view of the political can better understand the oligarchic excesses of Shakespeare's Venice, the timocratic drive of Shakespeare's Rome, and the shaping effects of royal rule upon the character of life in Shakespeare's England. The re-cidivist critic must soon realize, however, that the Socratic and Aristote-lian analysis of regimes is not altogether sufficient as a model by which one may approach Shakespeare's thought on man and the city. The view underlying the ancient classification of regimes comports well enough with the plays' emphasis upon varieties of ways of life, but in at least one important respect the classical types do not fit the world portrayed in the plays. The distance between Christian Venice and pagan Rome cannot be accounted for simply by referring to the differences Aristotle noted between oligarchic and timocratic constitutions. Shakespeare also de-picts a kind of *politeia* which Aristotle does not envision at all. Duke Theseus and Richard II are both autocrats, yet classical notions of mon-archy will not prepare us for the most important difference between a Theseus who governs by natural virtue and a Richard who rules by ap-peal to his people's endorsement of a special political theology thought to derive from scriptural religion. One must supplement the ancient classi-fication of constitutions with an understanding of the way regimes derive their form from communal opinions concerning divinity and divine law. In the plays set before the advent of Christianity, human lives take shape from individual propensities responding to the laws of cities. In the plays set within Christian times, Shakespeare's characters consult not only their native inclinations and the laws of their state, but, concurrently, certain transcendent prescriptions decreed by the scriptural God. To follow Shakespeare's reflections upon human beings and citizens, one must re-flect upon the political consequences of Christian belief. The political subject necessarily embraces the religious subject.

A reader who comes to the plays equipped with some awareness of the pre-modern horizons of politics will likely find more significance in the dramatic settings than an audience which does not relate politics to character formation. One who has retrieved an older understanding of the varieties of regimes may see in the diversity of settings an indication of Shakespeare's attempt to explore the alternative conceptions of the best civil life offered, respectively, by classical antiquity, Christianity, and modernity. For example, the classical method of distinguishing regimes by reference to the ethical type that a regime fosters may provide a rationale for the sequence of plays set in Greece. The Grecian dramas appear to rehearse the range of forms one encounters in the Platonic-Aristotelian classifications of constitutions. *Troilus and Cressida* presents a heroic timocracy, *Timon* an ancient oligarchy, *Pericles* ancient monarchy and tyranny, *A Midsummer Night's Dream* monarchy and the origins of antique democracy.[9] From the same vantage the Roman plays and *The Rape of Lucrece* appear to coalesce in another sequence wherein Shakespeare considers in Republican and Imperial versions a regime animated by the conviction that the best life equates with the attainment of superlative public honors. The Roman poems seem also to present a community that seeks to arrange its affairs virtually without reference to the divine. The absence of gods serves to intensify the Romans' dependence upon securing the approval of other men.[10] By relating setting to the understanding of the regime as a way of life, we may get a new purchase upon the dramas Shakespeare assigns to his Englishmen and Renaissance Italians. England and Venice appear to serve as locales for inquiries into the problems specific to Christian societies and, at the same time, to offer public situations appropriate for confronting some of the issues posed by modern politics. The ten dramas set in England and, especially, the continuous action of the two tetralogies, depict the transition from a Christian monarchy based on assumptions of divine providence to a more modernly conceived sovereign for whom authority depends exclusively upon the ability of the prince to cultivate a reputation for piety while finding his final guidance in principles consistent with the anti-Christian statecraft of a Machiavelli. Richard II stands at the beginning of this transition, Richard III at its completion. Henry V is the necessary bridge between the Christian Richard II and the imperfect Machiavellian, Richard III. In its corporate deeds and standards the English people reflect the change evident in their rulers. The last of Shakespeare's English plays, *Henry VIII*, resolves a problem central to the first, *King John*, and marks the appropriate culmination in the development implicit in the entire sequence. With Henry VIII the Christian church becomes formally subordinate to the English king. Shakespeare's England comes to resemble Shakespeare's Rome, with the addition of a queasy conscience.

Venice offers the most distinctively modern setting. The mercantile Venetian republic represents modernity in three respects. It dedicates itself to capital venture (distinguished from the capital consumption of Timon's Athens); it encourages the mingling of races and religions; it seeks to promote the utmost liberty compatible with laws promoting speculative commerce. More than any other Shakespearean regime, Venice depends upon luck. Venetian tragedy (*Othello*) turns upon a moment of extraordinary bad luck, whereas Venetian comedy (*The Merchant of Venice*) finds its resolution through a number of instances of wondrous good luck. Venice appears to be extraordinarily dependent upon chance because it lacks corporate means for resolving conflicts bred by its three dominant civic attributes. The city is incompletely modern to the degree that its technical resources are rudimentary compared with the science and inventions enjoyed by subsequent modern commercial regimes. Yet, with respect to achieving a providence over human affairs it is difficult to see that a more competent technology should lessen rather than increase the Venetian dependence upon fortune.

An often repeated half-truth has it that Shakespeare portrays all his dramatic personages, whatever their nominal differences of country, as Elizabethan Englishmen.[11] The truth tacit in this observation is that Shakespeare presents perennial modes of the soul which appear virtually the same in all ages and express their typicality in a perennial idiom. Athenian craftsmen share a common manner of speech with Roman shoemakers and London workingmen. Similarly, men who exercise authority will settle into styles of thought, gesture, and diction appropriate to persons of consequence and therefore can be expected to manifest common traits regardless of their local habitations as Athenian notables, Roman senators, or English dukes. An inordinate preoccupation with exactitude would dwell upon pedantic historicity at the expense of obscuring these continuities of human nature. Yet Shakespeare does make discriminations of essence between regimes. His Romans may wear hats and refer to clocks, but they do not bare their heads for a king, nor do they measure time by reference to the birth of Christ. The distance between the Roman republic and the English monarchy becomes evident from a comparison of the Roman plays with the English histories and proves demonstrably consequential for Shakespeare's portrayal of two distinct ways of life. When we pass from Rome to Britain we perceive a difference in the terms of public existence which coincides with differences in the conception of the supernatural, of death and the afterlife, of the grounds of moral and political obligation, of the ends of ethics, and of the hierarchy of human virtues. Shakespearean characterization thus seems to proceed from an understanding of human being as manifested in perennial types accommodated to the usages of regimes and further specified by personality.

Shakespeare's depiction of a variety of constitutions invites us to inquire into the problem of their comparative rank. From observing the diversity in the ways men conduct their public affairs, we are led to think about what political arrangement best consists with the requirements proper to man's essence. The plays' parallel emphasis upon the continuity of human types across national boundaries and historical epochs may provide bearings for an approach to the question of the best regime. According to a venerable teaching of traditional political philosophy, the city writes in larger characters the logos of the individual soul, and the proper constitution of the individual soul establishes a standard for judging the constitutions of regimes. Shakespeare's dramas appear to develop an elaborately detailed rendition of this ancient theme. We may apprehend something of the standard in regard to which the various regimes can be ranked by considering Shakespeare's portrayal of the range of human types and, within that range, those models which seem to constitute his version of the complete soul. Each of his general types distinguishes itself from the others by its emphasis upon one aspect or possible disposition of the soul. The political subject of the plays and their implied standard for political well-being begins to emerge when we take into account the types of the soul that figure most centrally and consider the hierarchy that seems to obtain among them.

Shakespeare's commoners emphasize the embodied character of human being. Although they resemble blocks and stones only from the partisan viewpoint of ambitious men who fail to capture their will (a Marullus or a Buckingham), they do confine themselves, for the most part, to confronting the world on grounds dictated by bodily necessities and localized affections. Their speech moves purposefully when it employs fleshly expressions but staggers when it attempts abstractions. They are unreflective; general ideas come upon them with the jolt of novelty. Their desires also bespeak a short tether. Left to their own initiatives they display few aspirations, preferring, usually, to rest secure in possession of modest and homely gratifications. Shakespeare's common men do not ordinarily desire to rule simply for the sake of ruling, although they may invoke the power of their numbers to come by the means of subsistence or safety. They tend to be more aware of their obligations than their rights. The commoner is the creature of his generally benign but ever transitory emotions. He values warm fellowship over austere singularity and holds ingratitude the worst of crimes. Consistent with their closeness to the body, Shakespeare's ordinary men are not far-sighted, although they can be shrewd. Consequently, they are fairly immune to visionary schemes, yet prove vulnerable to rhetoricians who may appeal to their passions and immediate interests. Demagogues can capture their will but fail to hold it for any dependable duration. Whether pagan or Christian, Shakespeare's populace inclines towards the sentiments favored by Christian teaching. Pity, kindliness, humility, forbearance, mercy, patience, ingenuousness comport easily with the native temperament of these bodily men. The same qualities make the populace remarkably deliquescent. Because their virtues grow from feelings rather than from settled convictions they give way to opposed vices under the pressure of opposite emotions. Within rather extensive limits the commoners allow their affections to be directed by emotional provocations deployed by patricians or lords.

Shakespeare's plebs, servants, and citizens display the liveliness of vigorous senses rather than the spirited dispositions of men who live for honor. Spiritedness requires the persistent self-awareness that dominates the consciousness of minds who enjoy or aspire to privileges of rank. Shakespeare's nobles constitute a second order of human character distributed across the lines demarking specific political arrangements, a perennial estate of the soul composed of men and women whose conduct brings to prominence the soul in its spirited, we may say, its self-determined aspect. If the commoner inhabits a world of immediate satisfactions, the Shakespearean notable lives by and for his aspirations. He desires more amply than the commoner, and the good he most intensely desires is almost beyond the comprehension, certainly beyond the reach, of the populace. The aristocratic soul receives definitive expression in characters such as Coriolanus, Hotspur, and Henry Monmouth, men who consider bodily enjoyments and security insipid compared with the all-sufficing delights afforded by public recognition. English lords, Italian grandees, and optimates of Greece and Rome contend with their fellow noblemen for public attention, while their ladies compete for titles in husbands and sons.

In his quest for honor the spirited man will espouse virtually any means to win admiration. The usual paths to celebrity are conspicuous wealth, birth, position, beauty, valor, or services rendered to the state. These may be combined with more peculiar claims to distinction; a noble may want to be known as a lover, a subtle diplomat, a mirror of fashion and manners. Whatever their accomplishments, Shakespeare's nobles expect that virtue will be ratified by fame. The fallen Wolsey can even announce his desire to become renowned for scorning renown. But the most favored proof of honor is the ability to check and overbear the will of someone else. Hence the aggressive baiting and high-stomached irascibility that mark men of birth. A meeting between Shakespeare's aristocrats signals a commencement of hostilities between the meeting parties or leads to their alliance against some other noble. English peers vie for court positions, wealth, warriorly supremacy, the favors of ladies, the ear of the king; Roman patricians quarrel with plebeians if they lack matter for controversy among themselves. Their ingenuity in discovering causes for factional agitation recalls the famous maxim propounded by Madison: "so strong is this propensity of mankind to fall into mutual animosities, that where no substantial occasion presents itself, the most frivolous and fanciful distinctions have been sufficient to kindle their unfriendly passions...."[12] The inclination toward virulent factionalism that Madison ascribes to mankind at large Shakespeare confines to the higher classes wherein considerations of prestige are the first concern. Spiritedness overlaps national boundaries but takes on a specific political character when channeled into particular politically sanctioned activities. Every Shakespearean regime features a range of spirited men, but regimes differ in the avenues to honor which each publicly encourages.

A third dimension of the soul becomes evident when we consider a grouping of figures who strive primarily neither for the bodily ends of the commoner nor for the honor desired by the aristocrat. Characters such as the Princess of Aquitaine, Theseus, Edgar, Kent, Cordelia and the chastened Lear, Duke Vincentio, Belmont's Portia, Viola, Hermione, and Prospero all appear to live for the sake of guiding others to conduct consistent with an elevated understanding of human nature which only the guides themselves possess. Most of these sponsors of the commonweal voice convictions concerning the ultimate character of human being. They seem to be more reflective than Shakespeare's other personages. Whether they possess official political power or not, these prudent men and women suggest Shakespeare's view of the statesman. They represent the soul in its activity as an ordering principle embodying the powers of speculative and practical intelligence which offer at least the possibility of governing the soul in its two other aspects of unreflective sentiment and self-conscious but insufficiently reflective spiritedness. The superior person understands the other orders and possesses an impressive degree of self-knowledge, whereas the other orders understand neither him nor themselves. Because these natural aristocrats of the spirit are depicted always in their relatedness to others as lovers, children, parents, liegemen, or rulers, one hesitates to identify their common excellence simply with contemplative intelligence. Hamlet, Prospero, and Vincentio give themselves on occasion to solitary study, but from the difference in their plight it appears that statesmanship requires putting speculative virtue in the service of practical ends. Hamlet is tragic precisely because he cannot make this transit, whereas the comic Prospero and Vincentio *are* comically fortunate because they successfully accommodate the contemplative to the practical life. Speculative virtue of itself does not seem sufficient to encompass wisdom regarding human things and, as the examples of Hamlet and Prospero suggest, the withdrawal that accompanies the speculative life may even work at odds with the intelligence required to order human affairs. The sort of intellectual excellence Shakespeare attributes to the superior human being consists of a blending of theoretical principle with intuitive tact responding to particulars.[13] The plays do make us aware of a more exclusively contemplative possibility available to the speculative poet, but this awareness is conveyed by reminders of the presence of the dramatist overseeing his creations rather than embodied in any of the staged characters. The consequence of seeing the limits of politics by reference to this fourth estate of the soul may be felt in many of the plays.

Our survey of Shakespeare's range of perennial types should note two other human dispositions which fall outside the array of bodily, spirited, and prudent men. Besides these three orders, Shakespeare depicts lovers and saintly characters. The lovers appear everywhere except in Republican Rome. All other regimes afford the possibility of a private enclave within the public life reserved for men and women who desire to cultivate erotic friendship with a particular beloved while oblivious to the wide world. Erotic love in Shakespeare embraces all the colors of passion ascending from feral lust (Goneril, Regan, Tarquin, Angelo, Demetrius and Chiron) to romantic vertigo (Hermia and Lysander, Helena of *All's Well*, Viola, Bassanio, Orlando, Valentine and Proteus, Desdemona, Romeo and Juliet) to glamorous exaltation (Antony and Cleopatra), to high courtesy and spiritual mutuality (Berowne and the

Princess of Aquitaine, Benedick and Beatrice, Ferdinand and Miranda, Theseus and Hippolyta, Florizel and Perdita). Whatever its species, love can present a special problem for the polity because it points up one of the limits of politics: the city, as city, cannot satisfy the lover. The most the city can hope for is that it may harmonize erotic attachments with citizenship by encouraging marriage. Marriage gives love a public character and provides lovers with public interests which suffice to tame somewhat the uncivil privateness of erotic energy. Shakespearean comedies end in marriage for the sake of the community as much as for the happiness of the lovers. Desire and romantic hyperbole diminish by several gradations with the domestic contract. Once marriage prospects seem firm, the Princess can set Berowne his task of emptying bedpans; once Ferdinand is publicly espoused to Miranda, he can begin to cheat her at chess.

Two other dispositions have the effect, like erotic love, of making the city seem contemptible and altogether insufficient as a guide to the most eligible purposes of life. The ontological disgust of a Timon, Thersites, or Hamlet cannot keep company with a city that falls short of an association composed of human beings incapable of ingratitude, pretense, or frailty. Hence the type of the soul exemplified by these misanthropes appears unsuited for life in any human city. It is difficult to see these men as other than nihilists since they envision no positive purpose for themselves. While rejecting the corporate ends pursued by other men they can offer no alternative focus that might sustain spiritual integrity. Thus, they tend, like Hamlet, to identify felicity with death, finding their completion only in the most definitive negation. The malcontent affords a contrast with Shakespeare's other apolitical type, the saint, who does embrace a positive alternative to public life. Shakespeare's pious human beings—notably Henry VI, Vienna's Isabella, and (possibly) Katharine of Aragon—seek their end in a sanctity which imposes public obligations but which cannot be fulfilled by any arrangement of the public order. Given his otherworldliness, Henry VI presumably cannot find his happiness in kingship even were his temperament more spirited. Pious men and women fix their attention upon another world which promises felicity through intimate relatedness to a personal God. Only Christians are pious in this sense; Shakespeare's pagans know nothing of an afterlife or of communing with their gods in this existence. The possibility receives dramatic treatment only in the touchingly comic episode of Bottom's enchantment which, although comic, apparently disturbs Theseus to such a degree that he manages to exclude Peter Quince's ballad of "Bottom's

Dream" from the court masque. Bottom "discourses wonders" but precisely on that account is "no true Athenian" (IV.ii.26-27). Religion in Shakespeare's pagan world is either inertly nominal (in Rome) or a constituent ingredient of the *politeia* (Athens). In the Christian regimes of Venice, Vienna, England, Denmark, and the Italian cities, religion may be in tension with politics and, thus, may offer an alternative to political life. An important theme of the histories is the attempt of the English monarchy to make Christian piety amenable to political purposes. The failure of this attempt is a major cause of the disorder that plagues England, whereas the partial successes of Henry V and Henry VIII appear to secure an imperfect harmony though probably at the expense of justice. The histories may suggest that the problem of subordinating Christian piety to political authority is insoluble in England and, perhaps, anywhere.

From his portrayal of the scale of human types we may gather some intimation of Shakespeare's understanding of the best life available to man. If the characters possessed of prudential wisdom and care for the commonweal constitute for Shakespeare authoritative models of excellence, then we may suggest an answer to the question of the best regime as well as a resolution of the problem of political power. The best regime would be that order of public affairs which produces this highest sort of character; power and authority would belong by natural right to those who can make best use of it. If the superior soul includes as a dimension of his excellence the kind of virtue that comports with the exercise of political power, then that soul ought to rule. This appeal to theoretical right bears out the cumulative argument of the plays. At the same time, the histories and tragedies record the usual adjustments of natural rights to be expected from a world which offers resistance to any theoretical standard.

Shakespeare seems to acknowledge this tension between sound principle and the limits imposed upon its application by confining his portrayals of the best regimes to the comedies. One way of defining the difference between the comedies, on the one hand, and the histories and tragedies, on the other, is by reference to the relaxation of limiting conditions upon natural right which obtains in the comic actions. We can appreciate the political significance of this relaxation if we consider the plight of the naturally superior man when he must work within a tragic context. Edgar may enjoy a *de jure* claim to authority equal to the claims of Theseus, Duke Vincentio, Portia, and Prospero; but chance favors the comic group. Edgar does not possess the power *de facto* which the members of the comic group possess by happenstance or by preternatural art. Moreover, several other limitations upon success are artfully ignored in the comedies. Men do not die and time seems never to run out, although both death and insufficient allowances of time would destroy the complicated web spun by the comic architects. By making artifice conspicuous in the comedies Shakespeare appears to limit their connection with the given world. Finally, even with the benefit of their artfully liberated premises we may feel that the resolutions achieved in the comedies are still decidedly provisional. The good government of Theseus lays down no foundations whereby good government may continue after he is gone, yet it has undermined one of the important laws of the city. His is a victory for youth, but in a real world there would remain accounts to be settled with Egeus and the other fathers who may think the prerogatives of age have been rather presumptuously dismissed. The providence of fairies does not seem to offer a trustworthy court of appeal for resolving public problems. The massive artifice paraded in *A Midsummer Night's Dream* serves to remind the audience of the play that real political resolutions require an art similar, it may be, in its purposes but necessarily different in detail and execution. Prudential tact enables such a recognition. Shakespeare assumes this capacity in his understanding friends and nurtures the virtue by presenting comedies which require delicate adjustments of perspective to be grasped. We begin to understand the comedies after we learn how and when to say hold, enough!

Theseus, Vincentio, Portia, and Prospero stand for the highest reach of excellence that is ordinarily available to human beings. Their excellence has a political character in that they are pre-eminently suited to the task of harmonizing diverse human beings through the arts of speech, law, and deliberation. Because they understand human nature they are capable of guiding others in such a way as to realize what is best in their characters, to moderate (though they cannot and do not seem to transform) what is worst, and to provide for their incorporation in a decent polity. The comic heroes take cognizance of the laws, institutions, and customs that prevail in the countries of their habitation but do not take their bearings from the usages of a particular regime. Rather, they seem to locate their ways and aims by reference to standards known through natural reason. Neither do they appear to be religious souls, although they take care not to offend against the pieties of their fellow citizens. They apparently regard religion as they regard political institutions, making intelligent use of pious beliefs by putting these in the service of ends they have determined on the grounds of the naturally just and reasonable. Shakespeare's superior men are political but not simply the products of their cities. We see them finally as superior human beings, not as good Athenians, good Viennese, good Italians, good Venetians. If they are fundamentally reverent towards some higher Being (and this I think is not certain) they are not adherents of a distinctly pagan nor of a distinctly Christian view of divinity. In principle these characters point to the fulfillment of human beings within the limits of politics. Their lives *are* the fulfillment, and their political activities show the way men should be ruled. However, the limits of politics, as such, begin to emerge when we take account of the special character of their achievement and when we begin to appreciate how difficult, if not impossible, would be the extension of their achievement to historical regimes.

The comic statesmen do not found utopias. Prospero enjoys the disposal of an impressive techne which, presumably, he could employ for such a purpose. But if Gonzalo's idea of establishing the perfect commonwealth occurs at all to Prospero, he chooses not to pursue the project.[14] Just barely and by prodigious efforts, he does manage to arrange conditions that could promise a decent public life for Milan and Naples (if, that is, we leave out of account the fact that the two cities are separated by a distance comparable to the distance separating either place from Prospero's isle). By similarly remarkable and presumably unrepeatable efforts, Theseus and Vincentio secure moderate expectations of decency for their cities. It is not clear that Portia's modestly benign association of wealthy friends can extend its sway from Belmont to Venice. Not only do the exemplars of statesmanship found no ideal polity; it could be said that, allowing a doubtful exception in Theseus, they found nothing we could properly call a complete and actual political entity. They introduce no comprehensive public modes and orders as a Moses, Cyrus, David, Romulus, or Theseus (Plutarch's or Machiavelli's) would. They invent no constitutions, nor do they introduce new religions. They do not shape a distinctive way of life for a people, nor do they work toward installing a new national purpose. Shakespeare comes close to depicting a national founding in his portrayals of Henry V and Henry VIII, but these political creators seem not to possess a wisdom commensurate with the epic scope of their enterprise. We may doubt that the English kings understand as deeply as the comic statesmen do. That the architects of communal decency in the comedies disavow utopian projects further commends their prudence and suggests that Shakespeare casts a cold eye on schemes that would promise from political contrivances something on the order of salvation.

Yet at one remove from actuality, the comedies do suggest a special sort of political founding. We may say they present us with a distilled image of the political act, an image which offers a paradigm through which we can grasp the essential character of political virtue and in terms of which we may evaluate the fully articulated regimes embodied in the non-comic plays. Insofar as they offer a touchstone for assessing the health of political constitutions the comic societies resemble the paradigms of the best city worked out discursively in such works of political philosophy as Plato's *Republic*, More's *Utopia*, John of Salisbury's *Policraticus*. Shakespeare's model differs from those offered by the treatises in that it aims at a more modest reconstruction of the given in accord with an end which, in comparison with, say, Socrates' project for setting philosophers over the city, is also much more modest. Shakespeare's paradigmatic regime requires only that those who possess authority also possess a high degree of practical wisdom and devotion to promoting the public good.

We may doubt that Shakespeare envisions the likelihood of discovering even these relatively modest conditions realized in actual historical regimes. Beyond the little group of Theseus, Vincentio, and Prospero we are hard put to think of any prominent character dedicated to fostering the good of the polity in preference to any other end. I have earlier mentioned Edgar as an example of such a will, and one might add Cominius and Henry IV. Edgar has the will and prudence but lacks the authority; Cominius has the will but insufficient authority and, in view of his support of Coriolanus for consul, may be doubted to possess the requisite prudence; Henry, once crowned, possesses some authority but not enough, and his prudence, if not his will, is doubtful.[15] The intriguing but obscure images of potential statesmen such as Alcibiades and Richmond are— intriguing but obscure.[16] Shakespeare elects not to portray the reign of Richmond as Henry VII, although the first Tudor appears propitiously at the end of *Richard III*, and enjoys an honored memory in *Henry VIII*. Both Caesars are rendered enigmatic but unprepossessing; Elizabeth receives occasional tributes but not a dramatic presentation that might make intelligible the high portentousness which attends the announcement of her birth in the last of the histories. Both Rome and England, the most carefully articulated of Shakespeare's historical regimes, seem to fail in the attempt to produce a decent political life, if by decency we understand the lively concords and just arrangements of diverse souls and of the various social orders achieved at the conclusion of some of the comedies. It may not be merely adventitious, therefore, that no Shakespearean comedy of the political sort is set in England[17] and no

comedy of any sort in Rome. We may wonder whether it be not a principal of Shakespeare's political understanding that the very enlargement of
the scope of politics in England and Rome precludes a complete political
life and imposes austere limits upon statesmanship. The complete public
life and fully competent statesmanship may be possible only within communities small enough to allow for face-to-face contact between rulers
and ruled.

The differences between the various historically certifiable regimes
reduce to different conceptions of what should be honored. Shakespeare
appears to share Aristotle's view that "roughly speaking, honor is what
politics is concerned with."[18] In the absence of prudent men endowed
with official authority, the crucial political consideration turns upon the
relationship between the numerous bodily men and the relatively few
but powerful spirited souls. The decisive issue seems to be the disposition of the spirited class. Men of spirit will, in any event, seek honor; but
a society takes its distinct form by promoting a certain path to honor in
preference to others. It thereby provides for a national character and, at
the same time, brings upon itself a distinct set of problems. Because
Rome believes that "valor is the chiefest virtue" and identifies nobility
with the manliness exhibited, first, in war, and, analogously, in contention of any sort, the republic finds itself vexed by continual intramural
battles between patricians and plebeians. The two orders recognize their
community only when they must come together in the face of an external
threat. For Shakespeare, Rome ceases to be as a distinct ethos when
Octavian's epoch of "universal peace" calms the world.[19] Because the
Venetian republic honors opulence generated by mercantile venture it
promotes the freedom and cosmopolitanism that enable a wide-ranging
and vigorous commerce. The city then discovers that to defend itself it
must engage foreigners who value courage and generalship more than
wealth, or that to meet its need for capital to support their ventures the
citizens must accommodate men who do not share their religion.[20] Moreover, the habits required for successful commercial venture do not keep
good company with Christian benevolence. Either charity suffers from
the exigencies of commercial calculation or commerce suffers from charity.

The principle that underlies the British ethos is more difficult to
formulate. Shakespeare's Englishmen yearn for distinction as fervently
as do his Romans, Athenians, and Venetians; but it is not so clear what
they commonly hold to be deserving of honor. When we attempt to say
what Englishmen revere, we may note first their attachment to their own.
They revere their island. The soil of England is dearer to the Englishman

than the soil of Rome or Athens to Romans or Athenians (it sounds anomalous to speak of the soil of Venice). The sense of esteeming what is properly one's own extends to language. Only Englishmen love their native tongue, whereas no Shakespearean Athenian speaks of his reverence for Greek, no Roman of his devotion to Latin, no Venetian of his delight in Italian. The affectionate consciousness of place and racial identity evident in the Englishman is only faintly echoed by Shakespeare's Romans and Frenchmen and hardly at all by anyone else. This sense of belonging to a place can be detected in the pagan Britishers of *Cymbeline* and *Lear* but seems more pronounced in the England of the Christian era. Shakespeare's Englishmen espouse Christian doctrine, yet they seem to conceive of themselves as constituting an enclave of pagan nobility within Christendom. In his famous patriotic testament Gaunt does not clearly distinguish "Christian service" from a manly valor that recalls pagan Rome. Shakespeare's greatest Englishman can admit (or boast?) that if it be a sin to covet honor he is the most sinful of souls. From the teachings of Christianity it would seem to be a grave sin not only to covet but even to desire earthly glory, not to speak of making aggressive war for the sake of honor. Yet Henry Monmouth's English soldiers are edified rather than shocked by their king's honest battle speech. They are not shocked, perhaps, because, as it seems to be with all Englishmen, they cannot believe that Christianity truly interdicts the life of conspicuous outdoing cherished by every English gentleman. Intermittently, however, and usually after setbacks have diminished their chances for gaining greater worldly prestige, they experience doubts. A Shakespearean Englishman is compounded of native spiritedness troubled but rarely controlled by an imperfect Christian conscience. He lives chiefly to enhance his position within a social hierarchy determined by secular considerations of blood, landholding, valor, and royal favor while, in the interstices of this fevered court life, in moments of disgrace or near death, he hopes for heaven. Shakespeare's England does not suffer so intensely as his Rome from conflicts between the few and the many. Its equally grave public disorder proceeds rather from the opposition of nobles to king and king to Church. Beneath these institutional conflicts one may sense the remote source of the social unease in the moral fissure caused by the rivalry of two incompatible views of human purpose and human excellence. Christian conscience undermines Anglo-Saxon resolve to dominate, whereas the native will to power constantly erodes integrity of conscience. The English soul wars against itself to no conclusion while the natural virtues of prudence and justice become the principal casualties of the national psychomachia. We are reminded of C. S. Lewis's conclusion regarding the tragic predicament of Arthur's Camelot: the effort to found a decent earthly city is caught between the upper millstone of Galahad and the nether of Mordred.

Shakespeare's apparent skepticism regarding the possibility of realizing his model of the decent regime should not be interpreted as an indifference to the task of understanding the diverse characters of imperfect historical constitutions. If happy polities are all alike, each unhappy regime is unhappy in its own particular way, and it is important to grasp the particular causes of a particular defect. More positively, even defective regimes offer some access to the good life, if only by emphasizing unduly one necessary dimension of the soul. They exhibit the virtues of their defects. Oligarchic Venice and Athens promote beauty and leisure as the by-products of their love of wealth; timocratic Rome produces noble instances of courage from its cultivation of war and general belligerence; England torn by a divided allegiance to counsels of Christian perfection contending with recipes for secular success breeds men who are aware, however imperfectly, of transcendent standards. The dramatist can maintain a reverent care for his images of human imperfection because he sees in the most imperfect of them some qualities which could be incorporated in an image of the whole. Shakespeare's portrayals of incomplete polities resemble Aristotle's accounts of partisan regimes. Aristotle's oligarchs, democrats, and aristocrats are partisans in the negative sense that they unjustly equate a part of political good with the whole, but also in the positive sense that they do recognize a constituent dimension of the natural whole. Somewhat similarly, Shakespeare's readers may come to understand the natural whole of politics—the best practicable or least indecent regime—by working through the sequence of partisan regimes that takes shape over the entire course of the Shakespearean canon. The essays presented in this volume suggest some ways for beginning such an inquiry.

Considered in terms of its capacity for fulfilling human nature, politics, as such, reveals a further limitation. All Shakespearean personages are political in the sense that they live out the consequences of having been born into and nurtured by a particular regime. In a different sense, few characters are political. Most do not rise to the life of political endeavor, electing instead to serve ends which cannot in and of themselves produce the public weal but only, at best, contribute to it if directed to that purpose by superior men who do espouse politics as their existential justification. Still other characters live outside politics (the great naysayers) or claim to live *beyond* the political (the otherworldly Christians and the early Prospero). We wonder how it stands with the creator of these dramatic personages. Where does Shakespeare, as poet, locate his own activity with respect to politics?[21] Is Shakespearean wisdom and Shakespearean art a political thing or something beyond politics?

The ending of *A Midsummer Night's Dream* suggests a movement from the play's world to the real world of the audience, as though the wedding of Theseus and Hippolyta were one with an actual wedding party.[22] The concluding plaudite of *The Tempest* announces a similar blending of the fictive with the actual wherein Prospero seems to embrace the audience in his design for achieving modest civil concord. His plea for indulgence and prayer may encourage the audience to feel capable of entering into partnership with Prospero and perhaps with the dramatist who has been so closely associated, if not identified, with the magus. These post-dramatic flourishes make emphatic a possibility of interchange between art and life which one may sense in the performances of all Shakespearean plays. The plays invite their audiences (in theaters or studies) to continue the action of the plays by applying the moral principles affirmed in the fiction to their own existence. Insofar as these principles are political, Shakespearean drama performs a political function. Somewhat like Prospero, Vincentio, and Theseus, the dramatist arranges spectacles that may have a beneficial effect upon the public life. However, although the art is political in content and in effect, the wisdom which informs the art may suggest a life beyond politics. Shakespeare's wisdom certainly does not appear to owe its final character to the fact that he is an Englishman. Although his plays do encourage patriotism in Englishmen, he does not encourage his understanding friends to revere England as the best conceivable nor even, it seems, as the best practicable ordering of human affairs. Shakespeare's wisdom includes but goes beyond the wisdom available to any citizen as citizen. We may doubt that Shakespeare's wisdom exists, like Prospero's, for the sake of a political end or indeed for the sake of any end beyond itself. Reflection upon the character of the soul's seeking simply to know may lead us conclude that a life devoted to that end is truly a life beyond politics. To know what extends beyond politics, it helps to know the full scope of the political realm. Shakespeare's poetry assists us in understanding what surpasses politics by allowing us to grasp how far politics extends in the determination of human lives.

Notes

1. Compare *Hamlet* II.ii.423-514, and III.ii.1-43; *A Midsummer Night's Dream* I.ii.1-97, and V.i; the Induction to *The Taming of the Shrew*, especially ii.12-138; the "Preface" to *Troilus and Cressida* and Prologue 22-25; *Henry V* II.31-32, 39-40, III.34-35, IV.46-53, V.1-6, and Epilogue; Epigraph to *Venus and Adonis*; the Induction to *2 Henry IV* 1-22; and the Prologue to *Henry VIII*. All references to the plays are to the Penguin *Complete Works* (New York: Viking, 1969), Alfred Harbage, general editor.

2. *Henry VIII*, Prologue, 22. Editors generally gloss the "understanding" as a jibe at the expense of the "understanders" or groundlings, but the context allows a serious twist to the trite jest.

3. The exchange between Brutus and Cassius that turns upon the phrase "the eye sees not itself" (*Julius Caesar* I.ii) seems to be modeled upon Socrates' conversation with Alcibiades in Plato's *First Alcibiades*. The same dialogue provides the reference for Ulysses' allusion to a "book" written by "a strange fellow" in *Troilus and Cressida* (III.iii.95-111). Aristotle is mentioned by name in *Troilus and Cressida* (II.ii.166) and in *The Taming of the Shrew* (I.i.32).

4. Roy Battenhouse, *Shakespearean Tragedy: Its Art and Its Christian Premises* (Bloomington: Indiana University Press, 1971), pp. 345-348, has argued rather convincingly that Menenius's belly fable in *Coriolanus* depends upon the elaboration of the body-city analogy worked out in the *Policraticus* V.2.

5. Among those who have contributed to the study of the political implications of the plays are Allan Bloom with Harry V. Jaffa, *Shakespeare's Politics* (New York: Basic Books, 1964); Michael Platt, *Rome and Romans According to Shakespeare* (1976; 2d ed., Lanham, Md.: University Press of America, 1982); Howard B. White, *Copp'd Hills Toward Heaven: Shakespeare and the Classical Polity* (The Hague: Martinus Nijhoff, 1970); George Anastaplo, "Prudence and Mortality in Shakespeare's Tragedies," I *University of Pittsburgh Law Review*, 40 (Summer 1979), 730-745, and *The Artist as Thinker: From Shakespeare to Joyce* (Chicago: Swallow Press, 1981). The publication in *American Political Science Review* (*APSR*) of an essay by Bloom on *Othello* and Jaffa's interpretation of *Lear* touched off something of a controversy in which the literary critic Sigurd Burckhardt quarreled with Bloom through the next issues of *APSR* (see Burckhardt, "English Bards and *APSR* Reviewers," 54 [1960], 158-166; Bloom, "Political Philosophy and Poetry," 54 [1960], 457-464; Burckhardt, "On Reading Ordinary Prose: A Reply to Allan Bloom," 54 [1960], 471-473). Burckhardt attacked some of the particular readings proposed by Bloom and Jaffa, but Bloom's complaint notwithstanding, I cannot see that Burckhardt questions the validity of an approach that emphasizes political implications. In any event, Burckhardt's book

Shakespearean Meanings (Princeton: Princeton University Press, 1968) offers valuable interpretations of political themes in Shakespeare. Other works which bear on Shakespeare's politics without taking the subject as their formal focus are J.F. Danby, *Shakespeare's Doctrine of Nature: A Study of King Lear* (London: Faber and Faber, 1954); Robert B. Heilman, *Magic in the Web: Action and Language in "Othello"* (Lexington: University of Kentucky Press, 1956) and *This Great Stage: Image and Structure in "King Lear"* (Baton Rouge: Louisiana State University Press, 1948); Northrop Frye, *Fools of Time: Studies in Shakespearean Tragedy* (Toronto: University of Toronto Press, 1967); Reuben Brower, *Hero and Saint: Shakespeare and the Graeco-Roman Heroic Tradition* (Oxford: Oxford University Press, 1971); J.L. Simmons, *Shakespeare's Pagan World: The Roman Tragedies* (Charlottesville: University Press of Virginia, 1973); L.C. Knights, *Some Shakespearean Themes* (Stanford: Stanford University Press, 1959); J. Leeds Barroll, *Artificial Persons: The Formation of Character in the Tragedies of Shakespeare* (Columbia: University of South Carolina Press, 1974).

Subsequent to the first edition of *Shakespeare as Political Thinker* in 1981, several studies of Shakespeare's politics have appeared, notably: Jan H. Blits, *The End of the Ancient Republic: Essays on Julius Caesar* (Durham, N.C.: Carolina Academic Press, 1982), and his *The Insufficiency of Virtue: Macbeth and the Natural Order* (Lanham, Md.: Rowman & Littlefield, 1996); Larry Peterman, "The Failure of Henry V," in Thomas B. Silver and Peter W. Schramm, ed., *Natural Right and Political Right: Essays in Honor of Harry V. Jaffa* (Durham, N.C.: Carolina Academic Press, 1984), pp. 83-102; George Anastaplo, *The Constitution of 1787: A Commentary* (Baltimore: Johns Hopkins University Press, 1989); John E. Alvis, *Shakespeare's Understanding of Honor* (Durham, N.C.: Carolina Academic Press, 1990); Allan Bloom, *Love and Friendship* (New York: Simon and Schuster, 1994); Joseph Alulis and Vickie Sullivan, ed., *Shakespeare's Political Pageant: Essays in Literature and Politics* (Lanham, Md.: Rowman & Littlefield, 1996); David Lowenthal, *Shakespeare and the Good Life: Ethics and Politics in Dramatic Form* (Lanham, Md.: Rowman & Littlefield, 1997). *Interpretation: A Journal of Political Philosophy*, edited by Hilail Gildin, regularly publishes articles bearing upon political issues in the plays. See further the publications of Paul Cantor and Michael Platt cited in "The Editors and the Authors," in this volume.

6. Martin Heidegger, "The Question Concerning Technology," in *Basic Writings*, ed. David Farrell Krell (New York: Harper and Row, 1977), pp. 297-298.

7. The classic arguments in support of this view are developed in Plato's *Republic* and *Laws*, Aristophanes' *Frogs*, Augustine's *City of God*, and Rousseau's *Letter to d'Alembert on the Theater*. Compare Milton's

Areopagitica (especially the section dealing with Plato) and Goethe's *Faust* (33-242).

8. See Bloom, *Shakespeare's Politics*, pp. 10-12.

9. See White, *Copp'd Hills*, especially pp. 25-64.

10. Perhaps Shakespeare's most notable departure from his sources in Plutarch's *Lives* consists in his elimination of Plutarch's numerous examples of Roman piety. He declines to give dramatic treatment to supernatural marvels that Plutarch attests on his own authority and passes over those instances in which, according to Plutarch, Romans allowed their political fortunes to be determined by their piety. Compare, for example, Plutarch's and Shakespeare's accounts of the circumstances that precede the banished Coriolanus's attack upon Rome and the details of the embassy scene.

11. T.J.B. Spencer, "Shakespeare and the Elizabethan Romans," *Shakespeare Survey*, 10 (1957), 27-38, makes some sensible observations regarding the neglect of Shakespeare's fidelity to Roman history occasioned by this popular view.

12. *The Federalist Papers*, No. 10, p. 59, Cooke edition. As documentation for his remarks, Madison could have cited the Temple Garden scene of *1 Henry VI*, where the factions of York and Lancaster grow out of a school dispute over an unspecified legal quiddity.

13. Compare Aristotle's discussion of *phronesis* in the sixth book of the *Nicomachean Ethics*.

14. Howard White carefully distinguishes Prospero's government from traditional island utopias and from Bacon's version of Atlantis in his *Peace Among the Willows: The Political Philosophy of Francis Bacon* (The Hague: Martinus Nijhoff, 1968), pp. 93-107. See also Paul Cantor's chapter on *The Tempest*, below.

15. Dain Trafton also questions Bolingbroke's good will. See his essay in this volume.

16. On the political qualifications of Alcibiades, see the remarks of Leo Paul de Alvarez in his chapter on *Timon of Athens*, below.

17. *The Merry Wives of Windsor* does afford a singular demonstration of middle-class domestic competency. However, the winning shrewdness of Ford, his wife, and Mrs. Page neither achieves nor is meant to achieve a political end. Nevertheless, we may wonder whether the play does not glance at an important dimension of England's public life in its suggestion that tightly knit local communities continue to achieve justice in their casual way, despite the turmoils that beset the monarchy and court.

18. *Politics*, 1095b.

19. The Rome of *Titus Andronicus* can readily accommodate Goths and Moors because it has ceased to think of citizenship in terms of a choice of a distinct way of life. Whereas Coriolanus cannot bring himself to lead a for-

eign force into Rome, Titus's son does not hesitate to install himself Emperor on the strength of his support from the Goths. In fact, Titus himself—the last of the Romans—commands Lucius to raise an army among his former Gothic enemies to revenge himself upon his native city.

20. See Bloom's comments on Othello, Shylock, and Venice in *Shakespeare's Politics*, pp. 14-74.

21. Michael Platt considers Shakespeare's understanding of his own activity as dramatic poet in his analysis of Sonnet 94, below.

22. See James L. Claderwood, *Shakespearean Metadrama* (Minneapolis: University of Minnesota Press, 1978), pp. 127-148.

The Unity of Tragedy, Comedy, and History:
An Interpretation of the Shakespearean Universe

Harry V. Jaffa

At the end of the *Symposium*, when all the company had either departed or were sunk in drunken slumber, Socrates was still engaged in conversation with Aristophanes and Agathon. As to most of this discussion, Aristodemus (who related the story to Apollodorus) had no recollection. He had missed its beginning and was too sleepy to have remembered well what he did hear. The substance of it was, however, that Socrates was driving them to the admission that the same man could write both comedy and tragedy and that it belonged to the same art to write tragedy and comedy. It was now the dawn following the evening on which the drinking party had begun, and presently Aristophanes dropped off to sleep, and then Agathon. Socrates, after making his friends comfortable, arose, washed himself, and went off to spend the day in his usual pursuits.

We do not have any of this dialogue, in which Socrates compelled a tragic poet and a comic poet to admit that the art of each was also the art of the other. We do know, however, that such admissions would have been entirely paradoxical in the Athens of their day. Tragedies were not written by comic poets, and comedies were not written by tragic poets. Indeed, we do not know, to this day, of any great poet who has written both tragedy and comedy. That is to say, we do not know of any such poet except William Shakespeare. Shakespeare is the greatest—perhaps he is the only—poet to have practiced the art referred to by Socrates at the end of the *Symposium*.

It is entirely conventional to speak of Shakespeare's Platonism, since something called Renaissance Platonism is held to have characterized much literature of the sixteenth and seventeenth centuries. We have no direct evidence—or at least no more than anyone else—of an influence upon Shakespeare resulting from Socratic writings. That Shakespeare deliberately set out to become the poet of the *Symposium* may be taken as no more than a fancy. Yet it is this fancy that we shall take with utmost seriousness. For it is one that we think makes Shakespeare's work as a whole more intelligible than any other single hypothesis.

Shakespeare did indeed write both tragedy and comedy. He also wrote something called history, for which there is no evident anticipation in what Socrates is reported to have argued at the end of the *Symposium*. However, the reduction of comedy and tragedy to a single art may well have prepared the way for a third *genre* of drama, one which may at once be both tragic and comic. To guess by what argument Socrates drove Agathon and Aristophanes to admit that comedy and tragedy belonged to a single art, we must ask what art it is that produces the Socratic conversation or dialogue. Certainly that art is akin to what we now call a Socratic, as distinct from a pre-Socratic, view of the universe.

Socrates himself, we are reminded, was a subject of Aristophanean comedy. The *Clouds*, we also remember, ends with the burning of the *phrontisterion*, the Socratic "think-tank." It is set afire by Strepsiades, the old farmer who had come to Socrates, to learn how to make the weaker argument the stronger one, so that he could go into the law courts and defeat his creditors. But he was too old to learn well, and so he sent his son in his stead, the same son who had incurred the debts that had led to the crisis in his affairs. We learn from the *Clouds* the connection between sophistry and what we presume is pre-Socratic philosophy: that philosophy teaches that Zeus does not exist ("God is dead"), that Whirl is King, and hence that justice is merely conventional. It is because justice—and morality in general—is merely conventional that those skilled in nature—the philosophers—are the ones most apt for dealing with convention. For they know that there are no sanctions for morality beyond mere utility or expedience. But Strepsiades' son, Pheidippides, learns his lessons too well. Having become detached from, or emancipated from, traditional morality, he learns to beat his father. He learns to hold in contempt those sacred prohibitions upon which the family and the city have hitherto subsisted. Indeed, we can see in the ending of the *Clouds*, the beginning of the story of a different Oedipus, a comic Oedipus. The burning of the *phrontisterion*—the death of Socrates—becomes a great joke, wherein we see the revenge of the city upon Socratic skepticism. Aristophanes is a comedian, because he chooses to make us laugh at this matter. He could have been a tragedian, had he chosen to regard the death of Socrates as catastrophe, one which evoked pity and terror. Yet the *Phaedo,* a different but parallel account of the death of Socrates, is equally without passion, equally without pity or terror. If it does not evoke our laughter, as does the *Clouds*, it nonetheless evokes Socrates' laughter.

Leo Strauss often quoted Sir Thomas More, that in the Gospels, "Our Lord" never laughs, but that he weeps "twice or thrice." To this, Strauss would add that in the Socratic dialogues, Socrates never weeps, but that he laughs "twice or thrice." Among the instances of Socrates' laughter, one comes near the end of the *Phaedo*, when Crito asks Socrates, "How shall we bury you?" The entire burden of the long dialogue in the prison, on the day of the execution, is that the soul is immortal and that death is no more than a separation of the soul from the body. It is a separation that emancipates the soul from the bondage of the body and permits its return to the regions of intelligible reality, for which it has yearned throughout its term of imprisonment in the flesh. The soul is "each man himself" in a sense in which no man is his body. Hence the burial of Socrates' body cannot be a burial of Socrates. At Crito's question of "How shall we bury you?" Socrates replies that he must catch him first! Surely, we are invited to laugh—with Socrates—at Crito.

Are we invited to laugh at the death of Jesus? Certainly we must contrast the apparently painless death of Socrates, with the agonizing death of Jesus on the cross. Jesus' prayer to his Father, to forgive his persecutors—for they knew not what they did—reminds us of the Platonic-Socratic thesis that, since virtue is knowledge, wrongdoing is ignorance, and hence involuntary. The death of Socrates is not tragic, because there is no catastrophe—indeed, no suffering either—and hence neither pity nor terror in the spectacle of his trial or execution. But neither is there catastrophe in the death of Jesus, if we take his death to be a necessary means to the glorious end of his resurrection. If, through his death, Jesus is united with the Father, even as Socrates is united with the Idea of the Good, death is for both a consummation devoutly to be wished. In the case of both, we are bound to ask, "Death, where is thy sting? Grave, where is thy victory?" If tears are shed at Jesus' death, they must become tears of joy when the resurrection succeeds it.

"It must needs be that offenses come; but woe unto that man by whom the offense cometh." This seems to be the formula *par excellence* for tragedy. Tragedy subsists upon the necessity of human error, combined with the acceptance of human responsibility. Oedipus is the quintessential tragic hero. In attempting to escape from his fate, he runs into it. Perhaps more important, he discovered the fate he had run into, by demanding to know what it would have been better for him not to have known. His fate lay in his character, in his impetuous (and hence flawed) nobility. Had he been less impetuous, and less noble, he might have escaped that fate. In demanding the truth at all costs, he represents philosophy. Yet he is not a philosopher. He lacks self-knowledge. Had he sought the meaning of his fate in thought, and not in action, that fate would never have transpired. We only mention in passing—now—that a full inquiry into the meaning of tragedy would compare the impetuosity of both King Lear and Coriolanus with that of Oedipus.

Had Oedipus been capable of self-knowledge, by philosophic, and not by tragic action, he would not have been a hero. Or, to put it somewhat differently, an Oedipus reasoning out his problems, instead of acting them out, would have been a comic, and not a tragic, figure. The strength of his flawed soul is visible to ordinary mortals, who look up to Oedipus, sympathize with him, and feel pity and terror at his catastrophe. In the case of neither Socrates nor Jesus, is it possible for the "audience" to make that kind of identification which makes Oedipus a tragic hero. Both of them are too much above ordinary humanity. We do not really understand what it is to be a lover of wisdom or a lover of God in the sense that they are either the one or the other. Both Socrates and Jesus inspire wonder, because the distance between them and ordinary mortals is so great. Neither is a flawed character. Neither is seen as a cause of the catastrophe which befalls him. Neither, in fact, suffers a catastrophe in the proper tragic sense. For each, there is ascent, rather than descent. The fate of each—or both—partakes in the decisive sense more of comedy than of tragedy.

Tragedy, we observed, subsists upon the necessity of human error. The Socratic thesis, that virtue is knowledge, has as its obverse Socrates' assertion that he knew that he knew nothing. Is Socrates' knowledge of ignorance an affirmation of virtue, or of lack of virtue? Socrates does in fact lay claim to wisdom, a kind of "human" wisdom, he says. For this reason, Socrates' knowledge of his ignorance must be said to partake more of knowledge than of ignorance, for it is the condition of the quest for genuine knowledge, and hence of genuine wisdom or virtue. If Socrates had said that he knew that he knew nothing, and moreover that he knew that he could never know anything except nothing, he would have been a different Socrates. Then he might have been Meno, or perhaps the Socrates imagined by Nietzsche. But Socrates is forever exhorting men to virtue. Unless Socrates was consciously and deliberately devoting himself to an absurdity, he must have believed virtue—and hence knowledge—to be intrinsically possible, however difficult. Still, the disproportion between Socrates' knowledge of his ignorance, and the ignorance of their ignorance, by the generality of mankind, is comical in the extreme. Since the typical Socratic dialogue is a conversation between Socrates and someone ignorant of his ignorance, the typical Socratic dialogue is comical in the extreme. Hence the dialogue—the Socratic art—is typically and essentially comic. At the end of the *Phaedo* we will laugh, with Socrates, at Crito. The death of Socrates will nonetheless induce in us a certain sadness, just as it did in Crito. If Socrates' instruction had succeeded—perhaps, we should say, had his instruction been more perfect, or we better learners—neither we nor Crito would have been sad. But then neither we nor Crito would ask, "How shall we bury you?" The teaching of the *Phaedo* culminates in the doctrine of the eternal separation of soul from body, for those who have been purified by philosophy. For those for whom the prospect of such a separation is unsatisfying, there is the eternal reunion of soul and body in the Gospels. Nietzsche called Christianity Platonism for the masses. Certainly it is more democratic, since a life of willing suspension of disbelief is more accessible to the many than one of relentless inquiry. Yet Crito loved that union of soul and body called Socrates, and it is not clear to us how he could have loved a disembodied soul. Perhaps we all have more of Crito in ourselves than of Socrates. Perhaps then Christianity is better called Platonism with tears, the Platonism of those who cannot abandon their love of individuals in their quest for universals. Perhaps it refers also to those who, recognizing the priority of comedy, are not for this reason less inclined to weep at the ineluctable tragedy of merely human things. Certainly in Shakespeare, the causes of laughter, and the causes of tears, are never far removed from each other. Nearly every comedy could have become a tragedy, and nearly every tragedy has that in it which points towards a non-tragic possibility. In Shakespearean tragedy, there is always that which points toward comedy; in Shakespearean comedy, there is always that which points toward tragedy.

In Shakespeare's universe comedy has a certain priority. This may be seen by the unique place, within that universe, of *The Tempest*. This play is the only one that may be said to have Shakespeare's art as its explicit subject. Prospero is an impersonation of Shakespeare himself. The island is the stage. On this island Prospero exercises absolute rule. The instrument of this rule is Ariel. Ariel is Prospero's magical power over his subjects: these nominal subjects are the actors in the play. The real subjects are the audience: ourselves (the Epilogue emphasizes this). In the theater, on the stage, it is the magic of Shakespeare's poetry that controls our passions, by controlling our access to reality. But the island is more than the stage. In a deeper sense, it is the cave. Shakespeare is the puppeteer who fashions the images, whose shadows (images of images) become our reality. *The Tempest* is also the relationship of the city and the soul. There are the three classes corresponding to the three metals—or three parts of the soul. Prospero and Miranda are joined by Ferdinand, to form the first part of the triad. There are six in the "court" party. And Stephano and Trinculo join Caliban, to represent the "third" class. According to Plato, the arrangement of the marriages is the central mystery of philosophic rule. The arrangement of the marriage between Ferdinand and Miranda is the culmination of Prospero's exercise of that wisdom he has gained by making "the liberal arts...all my study."

Prospero is presented to the vulgar as an Italian renaissance stage Magician, as indeed he is. But the illusions by which he governs have no effect off the stage—except as they remain with his audience. As Duke of Milan he was victim of a plot, by which his brother, Antonio—to whom he had deputed his authority—usurped his name and place. We are struck by the fact that Prospero's studies of the liberal arts unmanned him for the government of Milan. His brother, who might be described as a student of Machiavelli, usurped that government from him, and thereon cast Prospero and Miranda adrift in the tiny boat—intended for their coffin—that carried them to the island. But the fate that carried Prospero to the island, later cast Antonio and his confederates upon the same island. There Prospero could practice his art of government upon them, as he never could in Milan or anywhere else.

The Tempest is one of those Shakespearean comedies called "dark." In truth, all Shakespearean comedies—with the exception of mere farces, like *The Merry Wives of Windsor*—are dark. The typical Shakespearean comedy is a tragedy that does not happen, a tragedy prevented from happening by the improbable presence within the play of a wise man, or wise woman. The corruption of the Dukedom of Milan and the Kingdom of Naples is prevented from having its proper consequence, only because Prospero can command the wind and the water to obey him (Luke 8:25).[1] (Is he, in this, a Christian Socrates, or a pagan Jesus?) This coincidence of wisdom (or, more precisely, of philosophic poetry) and political power has no greater probability than in Plato's *Republic*. In *Measure for Measure*, a man like Prospero's brother is handed political power by a reigning Duke who, like Prospero's brother (but not like Prospero) should hold power. But it is as improbable that the tragic consequences of Angelo's rule should have been averted, by Vincentio's "invisible" rule, as that Prospero should rule by his command of the wind and the waters. In *The Merchant of Venice*, we have every element of tragedy present, but the agency of a wise woman, Portia, assuming a disguise like Vincentio's, thwarts the tragic denouement. In *Midsummer Night's Dream* there is a plot in which the lovers seem to be doomed, as in *Romeo and Juliet*. But the enchanted forest and the magic of Oberon (with Puck playing a role similar to Ariel's) prevent the tragic circumstances from having their tragic effect.

*M*acbeth is surely a prototypical Shakespearean tragedy. It is a play about a man of extraordinary valor and devotion, a man of heroic stature. He has achieved greatness and is destined for even greater greatness. Whether his fate will be a good or evil one, somehow lies in his own hands. Yet an overweening ambition, aiming beyond itself, causes him to fall. The spectacle of Macbeth's fall from grace, is perhaps the most terrifying in the annals of tragedy. *Lear, Hamlet,* and *Othello* evoke mixtures of pity and terror. But for sheer terror, nothing equals *Macbeth*.

"I think nothing equals Macbeth," wrote Abraham Lincoln to the Shakespearean actor, James Hackett, in 1863, amidst the most terrible tribulations of the Civil War. In 1865, on the boat returning to Washington, after his visit to the fallen Confederate capital, Richmond, Lincoln read at length from *Macbeth* to the party with him. To the end of their days, those who were present never forgot Lincoln's reading of the lines,

> Duncan is in his grave,
> After life's fitful fever he sleeps well
> Treason has done its worst. Nor steel, nor poison,
> Malice domestic, foreign levy, nothing,
> Can touch him further.

Some three days later, Lincoln was dead.

What did Lincoln see in *Macbeth*? In his letter to Hackett he ventured somewhat diffidently at a "small attempt at criticism." This was that he thought "the soliloquy in Hamlet commencing 'O, my offense is rank,' surpasses that commencing 'To be or not to be.'" The soliloquy which Lincoln preferred was that of the King, in which Claudius kneels in prayer, but knowing that his prayer cannot be accepted, because he does not know how to surrender the fruits of his crime. It is the articulation of the sense of moral responsibility or, rather, of the sense of the reality of a moral universe that is inexorable in its demands.

In Lincoln's Lyceum speech of 1838, he anticipated in his imagination not only the role he was one day to play, but that of John Wilkes Booth as well. Booth cried out "Sic semper tyrannis" (the motto of the State of Virginia, recalling also Patrick Henry's famous speech in the Burgesses), as he leaped onto the stage of Ford's Theatre. But Lincoln had long ago written that the destroyer of the republic might be one who, thirsting and burning for distinction, "will have it, whether at the expense of emancipating slaves, or enslaving freemen." Lincoln had, so to speak, written Booth's apology, because he knew how ambiguous must be the action of that man who, while emancipating slaves, might be thought an enslaver of freemen. Of course, that is how Lincoln's enemies, then and now, regarded him. (See, for example, M. E. Bradford's extraordinary comparison of Lincoln to Hitler, in *A Better Guide Than Reason*.[2]) That slavery produced a sense of guilt in Lincoln himself is unquestionable, as it is certain that he experienced the tragic catharsis in Shakespeare's articulation of the meaning of guilt, both in Claudius's soliloquy in *Hamlet*, and in the portrayal of Macbeth's self-destruction.

Macbeth is moreover a parable of a parable, re-enacting as it does the story of the Fall. The attraction of *Macbeth* for Lincoln must also have had much to do with the assimilation within the American political tradition of the idea of the American Paradise with slavery as the forbidden fruit. Here is how that idea came to be expressed by Lincoln, in his argument with Douglas, in an addition to the Peoria speech of 1854.

> In the course of my main argument, Judge Douglas interrupted me to say, that the principle of the Nebraska Bill was very old; that it originated when God made man and placed good and evil before him, allowing him to choose for himself, being responsible for the choice he should make. At the time I thought this was merely playful; and I answered it accordingly. But in his reply to me he renewed it, as a serious argument. In seriousness then, the facts of his proposition are not true as stated. God did not place good and evil before man, telling him to make his choice. On the contrary, he did tell him there was one tree, of the fruit of which, he should not eat, upon pain of certain death. I should scarcely wish so strong a prohibition against slavery in Nebraska.

Despite the disclaimer in the last sentence, Lincoln taught the American people, some eleven years later, that "every drop of blood drawn by the lash" had to be "paid by another drawn by the sword" because "'the judgments of the Lord are true and righteous altogether.'" Lincoln read the Bible very much in the light of Shakespeare's reading of the Bible, considering *Macbeth* in the light of Biblical interpretation.

Macbeth's tragedy is different from Oedipus's. Macbeth's character is not his fate. Macbeth does indeed have the power to choose between good and evil, and the contest between the two principles is tremendous. The catastrophe of Macbeth's fall (or Fall) is all the more terrible for the fact that he might (unlike Oedipus) have chosen differently. In Act I, scene vii, in his soliloquy, Macbeth argues conclusively that it is both wrong and inexpedient for him to murder Duncan. Until now, the claims of ambition and virtue have coincided in his life. Now they diverge. So powerful is ambition that, he would not be held back by fears of what would happen to him in an afterlife. "We'd jump the life to come," he says. However, he continues.

> in these cases
> We still have judgement here, that we but teach
> Bloody instructions, which being taught return
> To plague the inventor. This even handed justice
> Commends the ingredients of our poisoned chalice
> To our own lips.

This, be it remembered, was included in Lincoln's reasoning, when he wrote, "As I would not be a slave, so I would not be a master." A man who enslaves others, teaches others to enslave him. A man who murders his way to the throne is apt to be murdered on the throne. Yet this lesson, taken by itself, is merely utilitarian. It argues against the successful appropriation of the fruits of crime. It does not argue against the crime itself. Above all, it does not argue against the inner effects of crime, what it does to the wrongdoer. Lady Macbeth is successful in persuading her husband to change his mind, because she persuades him that the assassination will indeed

> trammel up the consequence, and catch
> With his surcease, success.

This will happen because she will drug the drink of Duncan's chamberlains, leaving the king unguarded in the night. Moreover, their apparent drunkenness will make plausible an accusation against them, of having committed the murder. Finally, she asks,

> Who dares receive it other,
> As we shall make our griefs and clamor roar
> Upon his death?

That is to say, having gained power by the murder, that power will safeguard them from those who might be their accusers.

Macbeth knew, or believed, that he could not escape detection by God. He had willingly surrendered his "immortal jewel" to the "common enemy of man." Until Lady Macbeth came forward with her plot or plan, he did not think he could escape detection by human accusers, either. The serpent, we must remember, told Eve that "You will not die," after she had told him of God's prohibition of eating the forbidden fruit, upon pain of death. But Eve and the serpent were wrong, because they failed to comprehend what God meant by "death." Lady Macbeth, in offering the forbidden fruit to her husband, failed to comprehend all that was needed to escape detection. She did not know that her soul, and her husband's, would begin to die from the moment that their guilt became a fact. She did not know that their guiltiness would betray them, without any external detection being necessary. She did not know that the forbidden fruit, so fair to the eye, and so apparently good to eat, would turn to dust and ashes. Lady Macbeth is in the end herself apparently a suicide. Yet the physical act of self-destruction is but incidental to the greater suicide she committed when, in the role of Eve, she tempted her husband to the Fall.

Lincoln's letter to the Shakespearean actor, James Hackett, in which he expressed his admiration for *Macbeth*, ended by saying that he looked forward to hearing Hackett "pronounce the opening speech of Richard the Third." Perhaps this association of *Richard the Third* and *Macbeth* in Lincoln's letter was merely fortuitous; but the relationship between the two plays is anything but that. They are the two Shakespearean plays concerned above all with the phenomenon of tyranny. Both are called tragedies in the canon, although they are radically different, both as tragedies, and as treatments of tyranny. We will question whether *Richard the Third* is properly called a tragedy. We would observe, however, that it is part of Shakespeare's art to persuade us that no metaphysical necessity required Macbeth to follow Lady Macbeth's advice, and that had he not done so, the play could have become a farce about a hen-pecked husband! We must remember that wise men are not the stuff of tragic heroes, but that philosophers—like Socrates—may indeed be hen-pecked.

The difference between *Macbeth* and *Richard the Third* corresponds closely to the difference between the choiceworthiness of tyranny, as represented in either the *Republic* or *Gorgias* of Plato, and as represented in *The Prince* of Machiavelli. In the Platonic dialogues, Socrates is challenged to maintain the thesis that the just man, stripped of every external advantage, and loaded with every external evil, is nonetheless better off than the successful tyrant, the perfectly unjust man. We are shown the just man, his family and friends murdered before his eyes, his eyes then burnt out, and he himself finally crucified. (He seems to suffer all—or even more than all—the misfortunes of Job and Jesus.) He is possessed of every good thing, except justice. Yet, Socrates maintains, it is better to be just than to be unjust.

Macbeth can be looked upon as a dramatization of Socrates' argument. For in it we see a just man transformed into an unjust man. And we see that unjust man deprived of every enjoyment that he might have had from the goods of fortune. We see the actions by which he became, and maintained himself in his tyranny, to be self-defeating: for in the process of becoming a tyrant, he lost every reason for being a tyrant. His death in the end is merely episodic in his real tragedy, which is the inner destruction of his soul. *Richard the Third* is in this respect the very opposite of *Macbeth*. Richard *enjoys* both becoming and being a tyrant. Richard the Third is a conscienceless Macbeth. Macbeth—and, still more, Lady Macbeth—are destroyed by their consciences. But Richard has no conscience. Macbeth's guilty conscience betrays him at every turn. Richard easily deceives nearly everyone. Macbeth is misled by a woman. Richard specializes in deceiving women. For him there is little or no pleasure in consummating a seduction. His joy is in the process of seduction, which is inseparable from the conquest with which it ends. One cannot imagine Richard as a husband or father. No "act of love" in any proper sense is possible for him. Yet Macbeth is in love with his wife. Indeed, his fidelity to her is inseparable from his being. His ambition to be king is an ambition he possesses as head of a family. He is a family man, even though he has no surviving children. Yet it is for the children he expects to have, that Lady Macbeth is to bear, that he does everything, however wicked.

Richard is a wonderful liar. He lies with grace, boldness, enthusiasm, and conviction. He is a master of fraudulent piety which (in the spirit of his master) he would teach us is the only genuine piety. No one who believed that God existed could abandon himself so wholeheartedly to such a public exhibition of piety. Since Richard is not restrained by any shame before God, he has no reason to be restrained in his hypocrisy before man. It is because he himself believes nothing, that he can concentrate so successfully on making others believe him. Macbeth must bribe men into becoming his henchmen and his minions. But Richard manipulates others into becoming voluntary accomplices. Such manipulation becomes a high art, and we are led to admire him as we would admire any great performing artist. His victims are enticed into becoming his agents. They are led to assist him to destroy others, and then are destroyed in turn. It is part of Richard's art that his victims are made in the end to curse themselves rather than him for their fate.[3] Macbeth's victims—Duncan, Banquo, Lady Macduff—excite an exquisite pity in us, and there is a tragic grandeur in their deaths. Macbeth does not destroy his victims' dignity. But Richard's victims are first made into fools, and then into corpses. Richard enjoys being king, more for the opportunities it provides for treachery and deception than because treachery and deception enable him to become king.

Macbeth is a man of overpowering political ambition. He seeks immortality by founding a dynasty, which is why he does not fear—or greatly fear—Hell. Hell does not restrain him, because he thinks that, even in Hell, he will take satisfaction from what transpires on earth, and he does not think that either God or the Devil can deprive him of this. In this, he is quintessentially political. Richard, believing nothing, has no fears or hopes in an afterlife. Nor is he ambitious, as Macbeth is. He has no family and no interest in having a family, and hence he has no interest in posterity, or his reputation with posterity. If Macbeth is the quintessentially political man, Richard is the quintessential individualist. He cares for nothing besides himself, not even for the name or office of the king. It is simply one of those things that fools worship, and for Richard, Macbeth would have been a great fool. What fascinates him is the folly of those who care for these symbols of belief in immaterial things. For Richard, politics becomes an end in itself, because it has no ends. His death is no more tragic than the burning of the *phrontisterion* at the end of the *Clouds*. He is a nearly perfect symbol of Machiavellian modernity.

I have said that Shakespeare is the poet who, according to Socrates, would write both tragedy and comedy. But Shakespeare's historic fate placed his writing of tragedy and comedy within a context created by both Platonism and Christianity. Still further, it placed him in a context created by the Machiavellian critique of Christianity, no less than by Christianity itself. The Machiavellian critique of Christianity transformed Christianity into modern science, including modern social science. Christianity, transformed by Machiavelli, meant Christianity in which man's estate was to be relieved, not by salvation in the next world, but by security in this one. That Machiavellianism would be changed into Hobbism and Lockeanism is something Shakespeare could not have anticipated in detail, but he certainly anticipated it in principle. Falstaff's catechism on honor—to mention only one of many evidences of this—anticipates that critique of honor which is central to Hobbes's teaching (and, after him, to that of Locke and Marx). The denigration of honor is central to modernity, which in its final form is devoted above everything to comfortable self-preservation. (By this we distinguish modernity from post-modernity.) On the surface, Machiavellianism appears concerned with honor. This is because Machiavelli appears as a critic of Christianity, which depreciates pride (whose object is honor) and elevates humility. Closer examination however shows that Machiavellianism is as hostile to magnanimity as is Christianity. Aristotle's great-souled man, although laying claim to all the honor that is rightly his, yet holds even honor in contempt. He knows that those who give honor are not his equals, and hence cannot truly honor him. Hence he cannot be tempted into a base act for the sake of honor. In Shakespeare, we see the emergence of a line of political men—notably Henry IV and Henry V—who are partly Machiavellian, and partly Christian, and whose Christianity and Machiavellianism subsist in a certain kind of harmony. They are certainly not great-souled men, in that there is no act from which they would abstain, where their political interests are involved. Political ambition has certainly displaced salvation, as the moving principle of their souls. Yet they are not tyrants—like Macbeth—doing everything merely for personal or dynastic reasons. Their self-interest has taken on a patriotic cast, and they expect that God will forgive their sins. They think He will recognize the merging of this self-interest with a new, national conception of the common good.

Henry V, on attaining the throne, banishes Falstaff. Yet Falstaff—or what he represents—will not stay banished. For Henry, the art of politics is very much the art of war, in the Machiavellian sense. Henry does not risk his life, like Hotspur, "to pluck bright honor from the pale faced moon." He makes a cold-blooded calculation of when he must enter hot-blooded combat. But he would never face an enemy he could cut down from behind. He does not act for honor as an end in itself any more than Falstaff. In the first book of Aristotle's *Politics* the classical view of war and commerce (including usury) as alternative means of acquisition is set forth. According to this view, war is a nobler means than trade, and the qualities of warriors are looked up to, while those of traders are looked down upon. But in the Machiavellian and Christian perspective, both of which depreciate magnanimity, the opposition between war and trade as modes of acquisition, tends to wither away. The Machiavellian prince aims at security, and no means are too base for him to gain it. Hence trade, should it prove equally or more effective than war, in gaining this security, will not be ruled out because of its baseness. The transformation of the art of war into the art of trade, of Machiavellianism into Hobbism and Lockeanism, was destined from the outset. One might go further and say that the transformation of Falstaff into the merchant of Venice (or of Amsterdam or of London) was destined from the outset. Falstaff will do anything for the sake of the comfort and preservation of his body, whether robbing at Gadshill or shamming at Shrewsbury. And he will do either or both with a pious expression and a sacred text. He will re-emerge some centuries later, as Babbitt and Elmer Gantry.

Shakespeare shows us the emergence of post-Christian modernity most clearly in his Venetian plays. The *Merchant of Venice* displays for our approval nearly every vital element of John Locke's political teaching. It demonstrates the impossibility of a successful commercial republic's enjoying the "luxury" of religious prejudice. While Shylock is "converted" to Christianity, this happens after his daughter has married a Christian (and he has eaten dinner with one, against the laws of his religion). But the Christianity to which he is converted will not be that of a Spanish Marrano, but that described in Locke's *Reasonableness of Christianity*. It is a Christianity which will reject the Inquisition and adopt the principles of the *Letter on Toleration*. In the same way, *Othello* demonstrates the impossibility of racial prejudice: if the citizens of Venice are preoccupied with making money, they must hire the best mercenary soldier their money can buy. Othello happens to be such a one. Of course, *Othello* is a tragedy, but it is such because the outsider cannot believe he has been accepted as fully as he has been accepted. This disbelief underlies his jealousy. But modernity will eventually dissolve the inner as well as the external obstacles to the inter-racial as well as to inter-faith marriages. The equality of all before God, which in medieval Christianity had been promised in the city of God, will now be established as the rule upon earth. No one has marked this transformation more clearly than Shakespeare.

Shakespeare's work, seen as a whole, comprehends what today would be called a history of western civilization. Only in the light of this "history" can Shakespeare's deepest intention—to be the poet-philosopher of the English-speaking peoples, the teacher of its citizens, statesmen, and legislators—be comprehended. This does not mean that each play can be fitted in some mechanical fashion into this historical scheme. Perhaps there are some plays that cannot be fitted into it at all. Certainly plays like *Cymbeline* and *Winter's Tale* and *Pericles* are so difficult to understand that we cannot be certain where they fit. But if we proceed from the main line of the plays that have a distinct chronological and historical setting, we can perceive a structure that is perfectly distinct, to which we can refer what is less distinct, and what is indistinct. The Shakespearean universe anticipates Montesquieu's account of political things, in the *Spirit of the Laws*, an account which turns on the comparison of the Roman and British constitutions. The Roman plays and the English plays are the axis upon which Shakespeare's account of political things turns. Of the Roman plays, we will briefly consider the three famous tragedies, *Coriolanus, Julius Caesar,* and *Antony and Cleopatra.* These not only form a trilogy, but have an inner relationship to each other, which enables us to conjecture that they form a single whole within the larger whole of Shakespeare's universe. Certainly they may be compared with the English sequence that begins with *The Life and Death of King John*, followed by the series, *The Tragedy of King Richard the Second, The First Part of King Henry the Fourth, The Second Part of King Henry the Fourth,* and *The Life of King Henry the Fifth.* If one takes into account the three parts of *King Henry the Sixth, The Tragedy of King Richard the Third,* and *The Famous History of the Life of King Henry the Eighth,* one can say that Shakespeare has presented the pageant of English history, from the end of the fourteenth century, through the Wars of the Roses, until the foundations of the Tudor dynasty, and the break with Rome. In *King John* there is an aborted break with Rome. One can then look upon the entire cycle or sequence of English history plays as extending from an aborted break in the thirteenth century until the final break in the sixteenth. Oddly enough, that strange and complex "comedy," *Cymbeline,* which is set at about the time of the birth of Jesus, may be seen as a "British Roman" play, and hence as the link between the two great series, Roman and British. As an element in the main plot, we see an attempt by the successor of Julius Caesar to collect the tribute that had been levied by his great predecessor. We see a Roman army invade Britain and be defeated. We then see the British monarch paying voluntarily the levies he had refused to pay under compulsion! This is a mystifying parable of the Roman-British relationship. The sovereignty of Julius Caesar seems to be acknowledged in a Dantean sense. The questionable sovereignty of his successors seems also to be hinted at. The continuation of the Roman regime seems to be the desirable outcome, although apparently no longer in the imperial sense originally associated with the great Julius.

One thing we may take as certain: that the latter end of the Roman-British relationship is somehow implicit in Rome's beginnings. It is implicit in that career toward greatness which is rendered intelligible to us by *Coriolanus*. We are meant to compare the victory of Caius Marcius, fighting alone within the gates of Corioli, with the victory of Henry V at Agincourt. We are meant to compare this mirror of a Christian prince— in which respect Henry is another Hamlet—with this supreme epitome of republican pre-Christian heroism. Henry's story, unlike Coriolanus's, ended in personal triumph. But Henry's reign was brief and was followed immediately by the Wars of the Roses, England's greatest disaster. Shakespeare's audience, however much they may have enjoyed the patriotic spectacle of Henry's victory, knew that it was an illusion. The union of France and England under the crown of England had substantial existence only in Shakespearean speeches. Such a union would be again proposed in 1940 by Winston Churchill, with the same effect. Coriolanus's story, ending in personal tragedy, laid the foundation of the most powerful, and powerfully successful regime, the world had seen. To this we must now turn: ending in the beginning.

Machiavelli, in his *Discourses*, had taken issue with those who, while praising the Roman constitution, had criticized the unending strife between the plebs and the patriciate. This conflict, which endured throughout the history of the republic, so far from being a weakness in the regime, was, according to Machiavelli, the source of its greatest strength. (This Machiavellian thesis, somewhat revised, has reappeared in our times as the case for a permanent contest between two parties, as the foundation of free government.) In *Coriolanus*, we have a Shakespearean dramatization of this Machiavellian understanding of the secret of Rome's success.

Coriolanus hates the plebs. He does so because they are preoccupied with the safety and comfort of their bodies. They care much for their freedom, but little for honor. They will fight if they must—to preserve their freedom, or for booty—but not for the honor of victory or the glory of conquest. Coriolanus, however, thinks that they do not deserve their freedom. Their freebooting in the hour of victory fills him with contempt. Freedom belongs only to those who can use it well, and he thinks using freedom well requires virtue. He cannot understand those who want freedom without caring for virtue. He does not think that the people deserve to be free. His policy would lead to their enslavement, something the people themselves well understand. Although the tribunes are deceitful, the people follow them because they sense that the argument against Coriolanus is a sound one. Coriolanus is indeed the enemy of the plebs, and it is his policy to deprive them of political rights. Had the tribunate not been instituted, they would have been subjected. The institution of the tribunes represents a decisive turn in Rome's history, towards that mixed regime which became the essence of Roman republicanism, and which enabled—or caused—Rome to conquer the world. Had this turn not taken place, and had the plebs been subjugated as Coriolanus wished them to be, Rome would have become Sparta: an oligarchic military republic, whose army could not have fought abroad, because it was needed to maintain slavery—or helotry—at home.

Nevertheless, Coriolanus needs the plebs. He needs them because he can understand himself only in relationship to them. More precisely, he needs them *and* Aufidius for his self-understanding. He must have someone who he thinks is or might be his equal, with whom he can fight. If there was no one with whom he could fight as an equal—no worthy challenger for the championship, so to speak—Coriolanus would not know how to think well of himself. His virtue is not intrinsic, it does not consist in habituation, but in his passion, his passionate negations. Hence he both loves and hates Aufidius. He loves him as someone more like himself than anyone else in the world. Yet he hates him as one whose just pretensions stand between Coriolanus and that godlike unchallengeable superiority which he passionately desires. There is nothing in the plebs, as there is in Aufidius, which commands his respect. Yet the plebs are Romans, and Aufidius is a Volscian. Coriolanus's whole being points toward a transpolitical standard of human excellence, toward the distinction between a good man and a good citizen. Yet his passion for victory, blinds him as to what that good might be. In this sense, Coriolanus resembles Oedipus more than any other Shakespearean character. His passionate character largely determines his fate. Yet a larger fate than that of Coriolanus is at stake in his tragedy. The real hero is not Coriolanus himself, but Rome. And the embodiment of Rome is not Coriolanus himself, but Rome. And the embodiment of Rome is not Coriolanus, but Volumnia. The Roman matron, typified by Volumnia, is the secret of Rome's success. Being a woman, she understands the plebs' absorption in their bodies, even as she projects her fiery spirit onto her son.

In a brilliant essay on *The Rape of Lucrece*, in *Rome and Romans According to Shakespeare* (Salzburg, 1976), Michael Platt has pointed out that the beginning of Shakespeare's account of Rome begins properly with this epic poem. It is, so to speak, the prologue to Coriolanus, since Coriolanus won his fighting spurs in the fight against Tarquin.

> At sixteen years,
> When Tarquin made a head for Rome, he fought
> Beyond the mark of others.
> ....
>   He bestrid
> An o'erpressed Roman, and in' the Consul's view
> Slew three opposers. Tarquin's self he met,
> And struck him on his knee.

Professor Platt also points out that Lucrece's rape is not altogether properly described as such. It is what Aristotle called a "mixed" action, being compounded of the voluntary and the involuntary. Tarquin gives her the choices, of submitting to him voluntarily, with the promise of her unchastity remaining secret, or being killed by him. In the latter case, he will accuse her to the world of being unchaste, having caught her *in flagrante delicto* with a slave (whom he will also have killed). The resemblance of Tarquin's proposal to the plot of Lady Macbeth against Duncan is notable. So Lucrece really does have the choice, of remaining chaste, while losing the reputation for chastity; or losing her chastity, while keeping the reputation of it. She chooses in fact to lose her chastity, and then to commit suicide, after accusing her traducer. Her suicide will be the pledge of the truthfulness of her accusation. In the end, the passion that dominates her—and that comes to dominate the republic she founds thereby—is the passion of revenge. This passion of revenge becomes in turn a passion for honor. In a monarchy, honor belongs intrinsically to the king, who is the fountain of honor for others. Hence a maid or matron does not become unchaste with a king—or a god. In a republic, honor belongs to the citizen or, strictly speaking, to the citizen as member of a family. The republican Rome comes to light then as a collection of honorable families. Since the honor of a family is peculiarly a matronly honor, the Roman matron becomes the heart and soul of the Roman family, and thus of Rome itself.

Professor Platt has observed that, had Lucrece been a Christian, she would have decided the choice offered her by Tarquin differently. She would have preferred to keep her chastity intact in the eyes of God, rather than her reputation before men. Moreover, she would have been forbidden by God to take her own life. Her passion for revenge and honor moreover stand in stark opposition to Christian suffering and humility. The Lucrecian foundation of republicanism, considered as a dialectical principle, is the dialectical negation of Christianity. Lucrece's suicide, defines the spirit of Roman patriotism. This is the spirit embodied in Volumnia and transferred by her to Coriolanus.

Yet in Shakespeare's presentation, Lucrecian paganism becomes the originating cause of Christianity. For it is the originating cause of that military virtue by which Rome conquered the world and, in so doing, prepared the vehicle of Christianity. For Shakespeare is also the bearer of a tradition usually associated with Dante. By this tradition, the history of Rome was also sacred history, even before Rome had become the center of Christianity. This thesis seems to have developed out of the long struggle for supremacy between Popes and Emperors in the Christian Middle Ages. The imperialists, denying the Pope's right to absolve subjects from obedience to their secular rulers, and thus to meddle in secular government, claimed a divine sanction for secular authority. In the service to such claims, they declared that the conquest of the ancient world by Rome, which made Rome into the capital not only of Italy but of the world, laid a necessary foundation for Christ's universal mission. In short, there had to be a catholic polity, before there could be a catholic church. (The Greek word *katholos* means universal.) Rome under Caesar conquered the world. But in becoming the imperial city, Rome was obliged eventually to extend its citizenship to the world. As Roman citizenship became universal, Rome ceased to be a city. For a city is a particular, and a universal particular is an absurdity. Yet the parochial bonds of Roman citizenship had to be broken, before the parochial bonds of Jewish monotheism could be broken. The twofold process had to go forward in a kind of reciprocal relationship: hence Dante (and Shakespeare) could see God's providence at work, as much in the history of Rome, as in the history of the Jews. Dante put Brutus and Cassius into the innermost circle of Hell, along with Judas. As the three arch-traitors, together they comprise—in his view—the soul of treason. Although Shakespeare seems certainly to have shared Dante's thesis that the history of Rome was providential, he did not share his unambiguous preference for monarchy. Nor did he abhor the cause of Brutus and Cassius. Indeed, Shakespeare's *Julius Caesar* is perfectly ambiguous, in its perfectly sympathetic presentation of the points of view of the Caesarian party and of the republican party, together with an equally critical appreciation of the shortcomings of both. What is certain, however, is that Shakespeare saw the cause of Caesar triumphing for what seem to be almost supernatural reasons.

> O Julius Caesar, thou art mighty yet!
> Thy spirit walks abroad, and turns our swords
> In our own proper entrails.

Here is the root of Richard II's doctrine, that God keeps legions of heavenly angels in service for the cause of legitimate monarchs. Julius Caesar would not take upon himself the name and title of a king. But "Caesar" became the ground of a title better than any king could claim. As Rome, because of Caesar, became the ruler of all cities, and of all kings, the name Caesar came to denote "King of Kings." Thus Jesus Christ was to inherit the name of Caesar, along with a dominion that Caesar had prepared for him. All this is made luminous in Shakespeare's account of Rome.

The transition from the intensely pagan origins of Roman republicanism to its Christianity in post-Caesarian Rome can be seen to have its very causes in *Coriolanus*. Marcius Brutus's ambition will drive him to feats of unimaginable heroism upon the battlefield. By these feats, Rome will conquer its enemies. Because of these feats, Coriolanus will be offered the highest honors and offices of the city. He will stand for consul. But to stand for consul, he must have the votes of the plebs. This is required by the Constitution. To court their votes, he must stand in the Forum, wearing the robes of humility. He must show the wounds (the stigmata) he has received in the service of the city. But Coriolanus does not know how to wear robes of humility. His very being is constituted by his pride. How can he be asked to ascend by descending?

> A beggar's tongue
> Make motion through my lips, and my armed knees,
> Who bowed but in my stirrup, bend like his
> That hath received alms! I will not do't,
> Lest I surcease to honor mine own truth,
> And by my body's action teach my mind
> A most inherent baseness.

To become consul, according to Coriolanus's account, seems to have meant becoming (at least for the moment) a Christian. The knees must bend, not in warlike action but in humility, and one must become a beggar, in order to become a ruler. "He has put down the mighty from their thrones, and exalted those of low degree." Perhaps the most revealing sentence Coriolanus speaks is the one above, when he declares he cannot do that by which he will dishonor his truth. Coriolanus in this reveals something philosophic in himself. He would lead a consistent life. But he is unphilosophic in thinking that a consistent life is possible on the level of action, of deed as distinct from speech. He thinks, moreover, that his body's action can teach his mind. In truth, however, it is the action of the mind that must teach the body. In reversing the proper order of the relationship of mind and body, he has reversed the proper order of the relationship of understanding and action. Winston Churchill, writing in the classical tradition, has declared that

> a Statesman in contact with the moving current of events and anxious to keep the ship on an even keel and steer a steady course may lean all his weight now on one side and now on the other. His arguments in each case when contrasted can be shown to be not very different in character, but contradictory in spirit and opposite in direction: yet his object will throughout have remained the same.... The only way a man can remain consistent amid changing circumstances is to change with them while preserving the same dominating purpose.

Volumnia has already expressed similar thoughts to her son asking

> If it be honor in your wars to seem
> The same you are not, which, for your best ends,
> You adopt your policy, how is it less or worse
> That it shall hold companionship in peace
> With honor, as in war, since that to both
> It stands in like request?

For Volumnia, all politics is war, and deception may be practiced in both peace and war. Volumnia, no less than Churchill, would have distinguished honorable from dishonorable deception. It was clear to her that Coriolanus could direct the policy of Rome from the office of consul, as he did from the office of general. She saw that if the plebs were not to be subjugated and enslaved, they must be mollified. And she saw that as they cared for freedom based upon equality, and not for honor based upon virtue, their "voices" must be secured by a display of humility, and not of pride. But the pride she felt as a Roman, who wanted her city to conquer the world, demanded this sacrifice of pride.

What Coriolanus wanted is shown by the character his old friend Menenius gives him, as he returns form exile at the head of the Volscian army, and Rome lies at his mercy.

> The tartness of his face sours ripe grapes. When he walks, he moves like an engine, and the ground shrinks before his treading. He is able to pierce a corslet with his eye, talks like a knell, and his hum is a battery. He sits in his state as a thing made for Alexander. What he bids be done is finished with his bidding. He wants nothing of god but eternity and a Heaven to throne in.

Coriolanus does not understand that distinction between theory and practice upon which statesmanship rests. Consistency in thought and consistency in action are different. Because Coriolanus does not understand this, he wants to be a god rather than a wise man. Or, to put the matter somewhat differently, he would be a god like that of Israel, rather than like that of Aristotle. Not his mind, but his will, is the core of his being. And not to have anything stand between his will and the accomplishment of his will is the consistency he seeks. In fact, Coriolanus achieves his goal, at least momentarily. He does so as an enemy alien, and not as a citizen. But he has contradicted himself far more profoundly, in becoming an alien to Rome, than he would have done by wearing the robes of humility with an affected humility.

I have said that the true hero of *Coriolanus* is Rome itself. Rome is embodied in Volumnia rather than her son. It is her spirit that sends him out to conquer for Rome, and it is she who breaks him when he ceases to be the servant of Rome and returns as its destroyer. Yet there is a Rome even greater than Volumnia that governs its fate. For had Coriolanus understood what we have found him unable to understand, he would have been a different man. He would have been one who, understanding the subordination of body to mind, of action to thought, of the practical life to the theoretical life, would have held victory in war to be a lesser goal. He would not have been driven as he was to display his military virtue, as if it was the highest virtue. The enormous power of his soul was driven through a narrower channel than it would have been, had his soul been of a greater breadth and elevation. Had Coriolanus been more prudent, he would have gained the consulship: but by wearing the robes of humility in the manner for which they were destined, he would have brought to an end that internecine war, which Shakespeare—following Machiavelli—sees as the engine of Rome's dynamic expansionism. The providence which superintended Rome's destiny thus kept alive the hostility between plebs and patriciate, until there was no world outside of Rome. This completion of the Roman *telos* was achieved under Julius Caesar. And so it was Caesar who in the end wore the robes of humility with humility, thus symbolizing the end of the Roman republic. With Caesar, political life proper comes to an end. The internecine war between plebs and patriciate ends simultaneously with the end of the conflict between Rome and the world outside Rome.

In *Julius Caesar* we see the relationship between Coriolanus and the plebs, and Coriolanus and the patriciate, reversed. Caesar's defeat of Pompey meant the end of that Senate that Coriolanus wanted to rule without the participation of the plebs. Now the plebs, which loves freedom and equality, but not virtue, comes into its own. Shakespeare never shows us the "real" Julius Caesar, at least not in the aging, failing, vain, superstitious character he brings on stage. The genius of Caesarism is shown in all its glory in the person of Mark Antony. Antony's speech over the dead body of Caesar is the quintessence of democratic rhetoric. Perhaps we should call it the quintessence of the rhetoric of Christian democracy, however anachronistic that might seem. Antony whips the people into a frenzy, as they see the wounds Caesar suffered, and are taught to believe that those wounds were suffered for their sake. The Caesar Antony conjures before them did all that he did do, because he loved the people. Caesar, Antony tells them, saw Rome *as* the people, not as people and patriciate. Rome's conquests were all for them. Now the people can live forever on Caesar's conquests. There will be no more famines, as there were when the Senate ruled, for the whole world, paying tribute to Rome, will be paying tribute to the people. But Rome is now the world. And thus the people—the poor—are the world. Indeed, the lowly are now exalted. That is to say, they are exalted by Caesar, and can remain exalted, so long as Caesar, or the cause of Caesar, is not betrayed.

M ark Antony leads the Caesarian party to victory over the conspirators. The party of ancient republican virtue, the party once symbolized by Coriolanus, is dead. Perhaps nothing symbolizes this fact so much as the reduced role of women in the play. Caesar himself is hen-pecked, and goes to his doom, in part, out of an irritable desire to show that he is not hen-pecked. But Brutus's wife, Portia, is the last of the line represented by Volumnia. By leaving her out of the conspiracy, Brutus shows how little he himself understands of the Roman republican tradition he is vainly trying to preserve. For the political capacity of Rome had its source in the Roman matron.

Notwithstanding Antony's genius, it is chance, or providence, or the ghost of Julius Caesar, which proves decisive at Philippi. Brutus and Cassius both commit suicide, each thinking the other has been defeated, when he has not. Had they been Christians they would not have killed themselves. They might then have discovered their errors and gone on to victory. In short, had they been Christians, Caesar would not have triumphed, and Christianity would not have been politically possible! Their paganism, like that of Lucrece before them, was necessary for the victory of Christianity.

The Antony we see in *Antony and Cleopatra* is the same one—albeit older—as the Antony who made the speech over the dead body of Julius Caesar. Although he does not know it, his political career is over. He represented the political genius that made Caesarism triumphant, but that genius was exhausted in its triumph. He will prove impotent in the new era that he himself has done so much to usher in. "Impotence" may seem like a strange word to apply to the lusty Antony, yet it does in fact fit him in more ways than one. His political incapacity is a cause of grief not only for his supporters; it is mourned by no one more eloquently than by Octavius. Octavius knew that if Antony but put forth his strength, even for a moment, he was no match for him. Octavius needed Antony—up to a point. He both feared and admired him, and moved against him only when he saw that he must. He turned against Antony, because Antony would neither rule nor be ruled. The challenge of Brutus and Cassius had called forth all of Antony's genius. Now that the world is ruled in the name of Caesar by a triumvirate, the government of men has in substance been replaced by the administration of things. The new era will call forth the cold-blooded, calculating administrator. Octavius is perfectly fitted for it. Antony is not. He cannot be a chairman of the board, because he cannot be chairman of the bored. The business of the triumvirate bored him. Roman matrons, however beautiful and virtuous, will bore him. Cleopatra will not.

Octavius is described by his messenger to Cleopatra, after the victory at Actium, as "the universal landlord."[4] Shakespeare thus reminds us that this Roman empire will become the Holy Roman Empire and be a feudal empire, in which the Emperor will indeed be regarded—at least in theory—as the universal landlord. We are reminded of John of Gaunt's dying speech, in *Richard II*, in which he denounces the king for leasing out England, "like to a tenement or pelting farm." Feudalism, in which the landlord might "lease" his estate, stands in opposition to patriotism.

It would require more than a thousand years, after the victory of Caesarism at Philippi, for the political spirit of ancient patriotism to reappear in the world.

Antony is a Roman. He is one of the three supreme fighting men portrayed by Shakespeare, three men who are *three personae* of one essential character. They are, as we have already noted, Coriolanus, Antony, and Macbeth. In *Macbeth*, the hero remarks at one point,

> My Genius is rebuked, as it is said
> Mark Antony's was by Caesar.

This is Shakespeare's clue to the continuity of this theme. All these three great fighting men represent, in ways which differ as their circumstances differ, the conjunction of Venus and of Mars. Both Coriolanus and Macbeth are political men, in part because they are family men. We have argued in the interpretation of *Measure for Measure* that Coriolanus is in the end unable to fight against Rome because he cannot trample upon the womb that bore him, nor that which bore his son, to keep his name living to time. There is no more erotic moment in Shakespeare than that in which Coriolanus catches the eye of the wife from whom he has been separated by exile, and we become aware of the desire with which he is filled. Her last kiss, which "his true lip hath virgin'd," throughout that exile, expresses his fidelity. Had Coriolanus been able to take a wife or mistress from among the Volscians, he might have been able to lead the Volscian army to the sack of Rome. Shakespeare here expressed with all the poetic genius that only he could command the inner connection between virtue and republics, between the family and the city, between marital fidelity and political loyalty. Caesar, abetted by Antony, at once ended Rome's contest with the world, and the plebs' contest with the patriciate. In the universal homogeneous state, politics proper is at an end. If there is no anti-Rome, there can be no Rome. There are no conflicting claims to rule within Rome, as between freedom and equality, or honor and virtue; nor is there any contest between Rome and Corioli (or Rome and Carthage), as to which city should rule. In fact, there is no contest proper between Antony and Octavius, since Antony's abilities are so clearly pre-eminent. The contest comes about only because of the vacuum of power created by Antony's withdrawal, the withdrawal of the best political man, from the active life. But it is not the contemplative life to which Antony turns. That, we know from Prospero, would also have been dangerous. He is still the lusty warrior, whose love-making will be divorced from the family, because the family will no longer be the ground of the city. But it is dangerous to make love at the pinnacle of power, while neglecting power. Antony and Cleopatra enjoy each other because their enjoyment is illicit, and because it is dangerous. The lawful and secure enjoyment of husbands and wives in a republican regime will be replaced by a new kind of erotic relationship. Republican marriage involved perpetuation of a particular family within a particular regime. Marriage in a homogeneous world state must differ according to this difference. Depriving the family of its political nature will require an art to replace that nature.

Antony is unable to be faithful to a Roman wife as Coriolanus is unable to be unfaithful to his Roman wife. Fulvia leads a revolt against the Caesarian party while Antony dallies with Cleopatra. We see in this that even the breakup of a Roman family manifests its political nature, as we see the husband's alienation from his wife cause the wife's revolt against the husband's party. But when Antony, in the service of Caesarism, ended the political independence of the Senatorial class, he ended the political function of the Senatorial family, and of the Roman matron. It is against this that Fulvia rebels.

Caesar and Antony have ended the political *eros* of Roman republicanism, by donning the robes of humility with an enthusiasm impossible for Coriolanus. For Coriolanus, the act of love which preserved his name to time, linked him by an eternal link, to his wife, his family, and Rome. For immortality was intrinsic to political ambition, and his fidelity to the ground of political life—in his mother, wife, and son—was thereby assured. Antony—another Coriolanus, in a difference time, and a different political world—has no possibility of a dynastic interest in Rome. The "home-bred and prescriptive" has lost its charm. The exotic takes its place. Cleopatra was the quintessence of the exotic.

Octavia, Augustus Caesar's sister, to whom Antony is briefly married, after Fulvia's death, resembles Coriolanus's Virgilia. She is young, beautiful, and virtuous. Cleopatra, we should note, is long past the prime of her beauty. The basis of her attraction is not nature, but art. She can attract Antony, and keep him ensnared in the toils of her attractions, as Octavia cannot. Octavia represents constancy. Cleopatra represents change. "Age cannot wither, nor custom stale, her infinite variety," Enobarbus says of her, in perhaps the most famous line in the play. She is the courtesan of courtesans, hers is the art of pleasing by the unexpectedness of her moods, her willfulness, and her mastery of novelty in the art of love. When the family is no longer the vehicle of political ambition, the constancy and chastity of a wife loses its erotic along with its political charm. In Coriolanus's Rome, immortality was sought in the linking of the generations. In post-Caesarian Rome,

> The nobleness of life
> Is to do thus, when such a pair
> And such a twain can do 't....

The act of love becomes an end in itself, abstracted from all other relationships. When Antony qualifies his assertion, by reference to "such a pair," he thinks, of course, of the fact that his mistress is Queen of Egypt, and he himself (in his own eyes) the emperor of the world. Yet their preoccupation with pleasure separated from any function that the pleasure enhances or perfects, will unfit and unsuit them for these lofty positions. Having reached the summit of the world, they will amaze the world, not with the story of their rule, but with the story of their kissing and their coupling.

Cleopatra repeatedly betrays Antony. He is defeated by a lesser man, because of his alliance with her. The "wrangling Queen...whom everything becomes" carries her arts of fascination into the deadly serious business of war, where it is fatal. Yet in the end she is faithful to him: in death and after death. But the Antony to whom she is faithful is a giant, a hero, and a god.

> I dreamed there was an Emperor Antony.
> Oh, such another sleep, that I might see
> But such another man!
> ....
> His legs bestrid the ocean. His reared arm
> Crested the world. His voice was propertied
> As all the tuned spheres, and that to friends.
> But when he meant to quail and shake the orb,
> He was as rattling thunder. For his bounty,
> There was no winter in 't, an autumn 'twas
> That grew the more with reaping. His delights
> Were dolphinlike, they showed his back above
> The element they lived in. In his livery
> Walked crowns and crownets, realms and islands were
> As plates dropped from his pocket.

As Octavius is inheriting the Caesarian title upon earth, Antony is becoming the Emperor of Heaven. Cleopatra will endow him with all, and even more than all, that he lost by losing the contest with Octavius because of her. Coriolanus before Rome wanted "nothing of a god but eternity and a Heaven to throne in." Antony will have that eternity and that throne, having (unlike Coriolanus) abandoned earthly power for love.

Early in the play, when Charmian remonstrated with Cleopatra for constantly opposing Antony's moods and wishes, Cleopatra asked, "What should I do I do not?" Charmian replied, "In each thing give him way, cross him in nothing." To this, Cleopatra answered, "Thou teachest like a fool the way to lose him." Cleopatra knows her business. Her relationship with Antony, through most of the play, is best expressed in those words of Antony's, in the opening scene, which we repeat: "Fie, wrangling Queen! Whom everything becomes...." Through most of the play, Cleopatra is struggling to gain and keep Antony's affections, in her struggle with Rome, and Rome's representatives: Fulvia, Octavius, Octavia, and his own fading sense of duty and political self-interest. In that struggle, she cannot play his wife. Hers are the arts of the mistress. Only when Antony is dead and she herself is dying, can she, addressing him who is now Emperor of Heaven, say: "Husband, I come." She has destroyed every earthly interest of Antony's. She has been his dearest enemy, but also his most deadly. But now she claims the title which she herself had scorned on earth. In time she had been faithless, but in eternity she will be faithful. Here we have the pagan paradigm of the prostitute turned saint, the tradition of Mary Magdalene. We see here another stage in the transformation of Caesar into Christ, as we see also in Cleopatra, declaring her eternal marriage to the Emperor of Heaven, the prefiguration of a bride of Christ.

Antony and Cleopatra's time upon the summit cannot last. They are doomed lovers, but their doom is also their salvation. Danger and novelty are both wearing, and they would have become bored with each other. Clinging to love, abandoning worldly power, and defying worldly power, the moment of their love has an intensity to match its brevity. But that brief moment—as paradigm of man's earthly existence—is transfigured at the end, into something different and lasting. The pleasures of their earthly love will not be the end of their love. In their tragic fall will come transfiguration. But that tragic fall implies as well a joyful consummation, in which the grave will not have victory. For they will be united in eternity, in a final resurrection. "Husband, I come."

The Shakespearean political universe displays a cycle of regimes, be-

ginning in the republicanism that results in the overthrow of Tarquin,
and ending in the establishment of Caesarism. From *Antony and
Cleopatra*, until *Macbeth*, from the extinction to the revival of that heroic political passion founded in the family, is a period of well over a
thousand years. Shakespeare's understanding of Roman republicanism
follows closely Machiavelli's account. It may be that his understanding of
the periodicity of the political cycle also follows Machiavelli's. No attempt will be made here either to apply or test this hypothesis. The sequel to *Antony and Cleopatra* may well, however, be *Measure for Measure*, no less than *Macbeth* (All three are Jacobean, rather than Elizabethan plays). In *Measure for Measure* the arts of holy and profane love—
both of which Antony and Cleopatra present—have become completely
separated. Their reunion becomes the task of the philosophic statesman,
represented by the Duke Vincentio. Could Vincentio have succeeded—
and the very form of the comedy tells us that he could not—the Roman
cycle might have been reinstituted. From *Antony* to *Measure* is within a
century of that 1,666 years that Leo Strauss says is, according to
Machiavelli, the minimum period of Christianity.

The two Venetian plays can be understood as the extension of the
English history cycle. Shakespeare knew that the commercial regime taking form before his eyes would in time become democratic and republican. This he could present in a Venetian setting, as he could not present
it in an English setting. The Venetian plays present us the principles and
nature of bourgeois democracy. Henceforth Christianity, Judaism, blacks
and whites, the family and the regime, must find their place within a
framework consistent with the terms of trade, with comfortable self-preservation. But *Antony and Cleopatra* marks not only the end of the ancient political world: it marks no less the end of modernity as well. For
the end of the ancient world and the end of the modern world have this
in common: they are accompanied by the prospect of the universal homogeneous world state, in which political life, properly so called, will be
at an end. The pursuit of private pleasure, without public spirit, is the
mark of the bourgeois, properly so called. But it is also the mark of communist man, as described by Karl Marx in the *German Ideology*. The
man who fishes, hunts, paints, or plays, according to his whim, is also
pursuing private ends. Communism sees the perfect solidarity of the
human race consummated in the release of all public energy in private
pleasure.

Shakespeare has not presented to us the vision of the whole of western man's political universe in order merely to consign us to our place

upon the cycle. The very possibility that that cycle can be made the object of contemplation, as he has made it, indicates that we are in some sense free to accept or reject our historic fate. We need not repeat in action the history of Rome, after we have partaken of it, with our passions no less than our understanding, thanks to the genius of the philosopher who is also the supreme poet. We can see in Shakespeare's characterization of the different actual and historic regimes, the defect in each man who embodied a regime, and which made him a tragic figure. We are enabled to enjoy the tragic catharsis, as we contemplate the greatness inherent in the shortcoming. We would not give up Coriolanus to the wisdom that would have averted his tragedy. But neither do we wish to repeat that tragedy in our own lives. Shakespeare thus teaches us to moderate our own expectations to the level that Coriolanus did not level his. For Coriolanus is no longer necessary to us. We have something infinitely greater: the art and wisdom of William Shakespeare.

Notes

This is a revised and enlarged version of a lecture delivered to the George Washington Society, at Harvard University, April 14, 1980.

1. This was pointed out to me, some thirty years ago, by Leo Strauss.
2. LaSalle, Ill.: Sherwood Sugden, 1979, p. 56.
3. I owe this observation to Mr. Grant Mindle.
4. I owe this observation to Edward Erler.

RICHARD II

Allan Bloom

Shakespeare not only presents us with the spectacle of a man be-coming a god (Julius Caesar) but in *Richard II* also permits us to witness a god becoming a man. As a consequence of what one might call political logic, Richard was thought to be, and thought himself to be, somehow divine: to have the right and the capacity to rule men, a king ought to have a superior nature, must be a god or the representative of a god; because he must be, he is. The play tells the tale of Richard's unkinging and his agony as he faces the human condition for the first time.

Richard II is also the tale of Henry Bolingbroke's grasping of the crown and thereby his loss of innocence. He thought he would purge the throne of a stain left on it by Richard's having committed the sin of Cain, but he is constrained to commit the same sin in order to found his rule. Instead of becoming a god, he becomes a murderer. The king he became could never be the king Richard was.

Thus these two tales join to tell a third tale, that of kingship in its divine claims and criminal foundations.

In spite of what some critics say, there can be little doubt that Shakespeare teaches us that Richard is a sort of legitimate tyrant who deserves to be deposed. Moreover, he chooses to present the divine right of kings as the underpinning of Richard's rule and thereby teaches that the principle is responsible for his tyrannical deeds. Richard never understands the real conditions of rule and believes that he is unaccountable. This does not mean that Shakespeare holds there to be nothing divine in kingship; nor does it mean that Shakespeare believed that once Richard's undisputed title to rule vanishes, there could ever be an unproblematic legitimacy in this world. But that is precisely the burden of the play: legitimacy is a problem, and Richard, God's vicar, is an artificial contrivance which disguises rather than resolves the problem.[1]

Similarly, the fact that Bolingbroke's accusations are true does not mean that his motives are good or that he understands what he is about. He entertains the baseless certainty of a tribunal beyond the king's to which he can appeal, which will vindicate him and give him ground on which to stand. And he wants rule; his accusations are pretexts for supplanting the king. He does not wish to reform Richard but to replace him. Strangely, though, Shakespeare seems to have more sympathy with Henry's ambition than his indignation, for the perfect justice demanded by the latter passion has no foundation in politics and the quest for it is even pernicious, while the former passion is an expression of the manliness so lacking in this regime and so necessary to political virtue. Such manliness—to be found in the Roman heroes and in Henry's son Henry—rebels against rule by others and, properly educated and channeled, is the surest foundation of freedom. Richard becomes manly only for a moment at the very end when it is too late. And Henry, who began by being manly, loses his nerve when he realizes the consequences of what he has done. He cannot bear to accept the responsibility, tries to return to the old pieties, and becomes humble. But his pride has set in motion tendencies which are to culminate in a wholly new world, one in which the pride of noble men will have its place and rule will require prudence and courage as well as birth.

In keeping with the purely conventional character of a regime where the ruler is absolute and his title is only birth supported by a fiction of divine right, the atmosphere of *Richard II* is suffused with artificiality of speech and deed. This artificiality is particularly to be remarked in the relationships among human beings. At the outset it is taken for granted that the just man is to be proved in trial by combat and that God, just as He is immediately present in the king, will directly indicate where the truth lies by the victory in arms. Divine action and brute force preempt entirely the field properly governed by prudence. God is just and provides a law behind which He stands, but human reason cannot penetrate to His reasons and plays no role in the system of justice. Richard, despite his fears that the result of the combat will inculpate him, is constrained by the rules of honor to permit it. But this aborted combat on St. Lambert's Day in the lists at Coventry is the last trial by combat England will ever see. When Richard II recognizes that the risks are too great for him and halts it, he unwittingly brings the era of chivalry, the era of Christian knights inaugurated by the first Richard, the Lion-Hearted, to its end. By Act IV the challenges of the lords have become empty bluster and a parody of what they had been. They will never be committed to a test. New ways of settling disputes and determining the right will have to be found.

Thus at the outset we see "medieval" England, but we also see that it is moribund. A criminal king against whom there is no recourse is opposed to an ambitious potential successor who comes ever closer to challenging the sacred person of the king himself. And the supports of the old order—represented by the Dukes of Lancaster and York—are themselves old and have lost conviction. Lancaster passively leaves the issue to heaven and dies, while York, who is really a comic figure, provides the transition to the new order. The principle of the old order is enunciated by Gaunt in his discussion with the Duchess of Gloucester (I.ii), and he embodies its dignity. One must bear with insults and apparent injustices in this world in the conviction that they are expressions of God's infinite goodness. Unswerving loyalty and faith against all the evidence of the senses and merely human reason is the subject's proper posture.

> God's is the quarrel; for God's substitute,
> His deputy anointed in his sight,
> Hath caus'd his death; the which if wrongfully
> Let heaven revenge, for I may never lift
> An angry arm against his minister. (I.ii.39-43)

But the Duchess represents the problem in Gaunt's principle and the countervailing principle. Her husband has been murdered, and he was Gaunt's brother. Outraged family feeling ought to seek vengeance. The ordinary sentiments, directly experienced by all normal human beings, are suppressed in favor of a purely arbitrary duty to obey the king. Whereas all the principal men in *Richard II* are artificial, and none particularly admirable, the three women in the play (Richard's queen and the Duchess of York in addition to the Duchess of Gloucester) are all both natural and admirable. They love their husbands and their children. Humanity, banished by the men, seems to have taken refuge in the women. For varying but related reasons these women cannot depend on the men in their families; and in their sufferings they do not appear to hope in God. They endure, and in their fortitude they provide a measure for the failings of the men to whom they are most nearly related—the Duchess of

Gloucester to Gaunt, the queen to the king, the Duchess of York to the Duke of York. In the scene under discussion the audience cannot but side with the Duchess of Gloucester against Gaunt, nor can one help but feel that if Gaunts are the subjects, the rulers will be Richards. Disarming good men is equivalent to arming evil men.

Moreover, there is no doubt that the first two acts are intended to establish Richard as an evil king who deserves to lose his throne. He is shown to be a murderer, a thief, a wastrel surrounded by flatterers, lacking in all the familial pieties—a monarch without care or conscience. He is convicted before our eyes of all the accusations made against him, and this portrait is relieved by no charming features. Bolingbroke's schemes are thereby given the color of justice. By the end of Act II power and loyalty have slipped away from Richard as a rightful consequence of his crimes. But even if Bolingbroke is right in deposing Richard, that fact alone does not suffice to make him king. He has justice on his side, as well as the talent to govern in these troubled times, a secondary title of inheritance,[2] the consent of the nobles, and the adherence of the people. But all of this does not quite add up to Richard's indisputable family title and the sense of divine right apparently attached to it.

Henry's problem is posed and solved in comic fashion by York, the last remaining son of Edward III and the last remaining fragment of the old regime. Although he has reproved his nephew Richard for depriving Henry of his inheritance, as Lord Governor in Richard's absence he loyally forbids Henry entry into England and treats him as a rebel. But he possesses no power and certainly lacks the energy or the conviction to be a martyr to Richard's cause. So he declares himself neuter and invites the rebels to spend the night at his place. York's neutrality symbolizes the exhaustion of the old order. He solves his own problem by ending up a fanatic adherent of the new king, acting as though Henry were the old king. The example of Henry's change from subject to ruler teaches a lesson which York desperately tries to suppress, one from which other subjects will nonetheless profit.

Suddenly, at the beginning of Act III, Richard, who is no longer really king and is beginning to realize it, becomes interesting. As he descends to the estate of mere man, his soul is inspired by the poetic muse. It is as though Shakespeare wished to tell us that the most divine in man is man. He provides Richard with the play's most beautiful lines to allow him to voice questions about what he might really be when he discovers he is not what convention told him he is. He never succeeds in finding himself, but we see the articulation of his soul as he gropes toward his goal. We do not find that Richard is ever good, but we do find him touching.

Richard returns to England from the Irish wars to find his neglected country torn by rebellion. He speaks confidently to the earth of England which he takes to be animate and loyal, reminding it of his expectation that its flora and fauna will take up the cause of its rightful king. When chided by his episcopal advisor Carlisle, who tells him that God helps those who help themselves, he responds by comparing himself to the sun and announces that for every rebel soldier God provides Richard with a fighting angel. But when he hears that his Welsh troops have departed, he becomes disconsolate, only to regain confidence when he thinks of his uncle York's troops. Again his mood wavers when he expects to hear bad news from Scroop. Now he takes the tack of resignation. Of what value are human things? They are nothing when seen in the perspective of God's power or in that of the bleakness of death. All men are equal in both perspectives. Richard is ready piously to accept the vicissitudes of life. Being a king was nothing but a care to him. As he was confident in being everything, he professes himself resigned to being nothing. But, suddenly, he suspects that he has been betrayed by his friends, and now he is the man-God, Jesus, abandoned by all, surrounded only by Judases. And finally, when he learns that the man about to become king had executed his close associates, Richard collapses in despair:

> let us sit on the ground
> And tell sad stories of the death of kings. (III.ii.158-159)

Then once more he responds to the chidings of Carlisle and remembers York's troops. But, when he learns that York is with Henry, he knows he is no longer king and abandons all hope. He had hoped in God's arms, the Welsh arms, and York's arms. He has no arms of his own, nor does he imagine trying to get them. Richard is night, Henry day. A new sun has risen.[3]

As is evident, Richard's moods are mercurial. But what is most striking about them is that they move between two poles and never point to another alternative. He is either hopeful or despairing, arrogant or humble, the glorious king or the poor man menaced by death. There is no middle ground.

> I'll give my jewels for a set of beads
> My gorgeous palace for a hermitage,

My gay apparel for an almsman's gown,
My figur'd goblets for a dish of wood,
My sceptre for a palmer's walking staff,
My subjects for a pair of carved saints,
And my large kingdom for a little grave,
A little little grave, an obscure grave. (III.iii.155-162)

The little piece of time between the two eternities—God and death—that comprises human life has no status for Richard. Yet it is only in this interval that political life is to be found, somewhat independent, and perhaps a bit forgetful, of God and death. The statesman must not be overwhelmed by the power and glory (not to mention the high moral demands) of God nor disheartened by the shadow cast over his concerns by death. He must trust in his own efforts and take seriously the goals of life, liberty, and glory. He must respect this world. But just as Richard's reign is founded on the God of the Christians, he has a Christian view of the world. He is either like God, or like Jesus, or like a monk or a hermit. He is never a political man. He is imprisoned in Julius Caesar's tower[4] but has no other connection with such men.

Richard has frequently been compared to Hamlet, for both possess histrionic natures. They are also alike in that Hamlet too views things in extremes, extremes which derive from a Christian's perspective. The Hamlet who is unwilling to kill the usurper while at prayer for fear that his soul will be saved and who thus loses his chance to right things in the realm is akin to Richard. They are both actors of their parts rather than being what they are, and they see this world through the optic of another world and thus transform it. And these two characteristics are probably effects of a single cause.[5]

Richard, like Gaunt, is able to see only divine justice or brute force, God's pastorate or a tyrant's arbitrariness. A world in which men are responsible for the defense of justice and provide for its rewards and punishments is unknown to him. This is underlined in III,iv, which immediately follows the two scenes on which the foregoing reflections are based. Richard's sweet queen wanders in the Duke of York's gardens and overhears the conversation of the gardener and his assistant. They are humble men; but for that very reason, in a world where everything high is conventional and artificial, Shakespeare makes them speak the language of nature and reason. They, like the women in this play, help to supply what cannot be gotten from the high-born, convention-ridden men. These two artisans compare their garden to the state and explain what should have been done by Richard and why his failing to do it has caused his downfall. They ascribe to an absence of art what others understand to be a result of God's will and men's sins. One cannot help being reminded of *Prince* XXV, where Machiavelli interprets what men call fortune or God's action in politics as a lack of prudence or foresight. Floods, he says, injure men not because they are sinners but because they did not build dams. These two workers suggest that art, in cooperation with nature, can make states as well as gardens grow. The founding of political science requires only a clear vision of things. But it is precisely that natural vision which is hard to achieve, for the prospect is clouded over by myths which must first be dispelled. The queen angrily reproaches the gardeners for committing the sin of Adam, for eating of the fruit of the tree of knowledge and thus bringing about a second fall. The only defense she can contrive for her husband is to view this not as nature's garden, given over to the control of rational men who can make it produce fruit for their sustenance, but as God's garden, the Garden of Eden, ruled directly by God, producing what God wills without the cooperation of man, whose inquiries into the mysterious ways of the ruler would be a sin. As gardeners should not put their hands to God's garden, rational subjects should not question Richard's state. This vision makes political science impossible and renders the attempt to establish it a sin, the sin of disobeying the ruler and of attempting to replace him. Piety, not art, is the foundation of Richard's state, and the emancipation of art requires the overturning of that state.

The case for Richard's rule is made by the finest or at least the most disinterested man among the principals, the bishop of Carlisle. (It goes without saying that Richard's touching eloquence does not make a case for his remaining as king.) Carlisle stands up before Henry and warns him not to depose the king. With his "if you rear this house against this house,"[6] he accurately prophesies the horrors of the Wars of the Roses. The overturning of one monarch provides argument for the overturning of another. There must be established authority and agreed-upon legitimacy. He believes that only divine right can establish such legitimacy, and an attack on the king is an attack on God. The dire consequences of such an attack Carlisle evidently attributes to God's wrath, although civil war would appear to follow naturally from the absence of a recognized sovereign. We would conclude that if Richard's rule is a failure, then some other source of legitimacy must be sought for. The king in his nation, according to Carlisle, is the image of God in the world. And everything that Richard is or is not derives from that vision of the whole. God's rule of the whole is the source of Richard's rule in England, and the latter seems to be the necessary consequence of the former. If there is something wrong with the order in England, it is probably related to something wrong with the cosmic order on which it is modeled.

This order is one in which prophecy takes the place of foresight, and Carlisle's prophecy is the supplement to Gaunt's earlier prophecy.[7] Gaunt treats England as a living being, its constitution, like that of a body, inseparable from it and unchangeable. Richard will be purged like a disease. Gaunt's indignation does not lead to rebellion, and none seems possible. Country and constitution are identical; rulers are produced out of its womb; one is oneself a part of one's country and one must love it. Carlisle, on the other hand, sees England's Christianity as something separable from it and knows the possibility of rebellion and change. Christianity is universal, and a nation can either participate in it or not. His loyalty is to Christianity. For him Christianity is represented by Richard. If England is to be purged of Richard, an element of that purgation must be a change in the nation's relation to Christianity, most specifically to God's representatives, the king and the priests. Carlisle forces us to correct Gaunt's vision. If England is to be free from the danger of Richards, there must be a change in the constitution and the spirit informing it. To render England unto itself the elements of the nation must be separated out and certain alien matter be removed. Only at the end of the history plays is there a king, Henry VIII, who is himself really the high priest and interprets the divine in such a way as to serve England. The eighth Henry is truly at home; Richard was only a stranger; and this he learns when he looks at himself in the mirror. A long and bloody path leads from Richard to Henry VIII, a path on which Englishmen learn that kingship is founded on nobles and commoners as well as on God. This mixture is perilous but through it wisdom can at least occasionally peep without being sinful or causing civil war. Carlisle shows us both the greatest dignity and the greatest weakness of the old order. God is supposed to rule; Richard actually rules. Without his faith that God protected him, he would have taken more care.

In the final act, York completes his comedy, Richard completes his tragedy, and Henry begins his career as a guilt-ridden, world-weary man, insecure and plotted against, distrusting even his own son.

Old York, the crumbling pillar of both the old and new orders, tries madly to persuade himself that they are identical by accusing his son of treason and demanding his death. His son was loyal to Richard and thus is disloyal to the usurper. York abandons Richard and, aping a Roman citizen, demands his own son's death as a punishment for disloyalty. The Roman's deed inspires awe because it proves firmness of soul and is done for the unquestioned common good and in the name of the most ancient and unquestioned authority. But after what has already transpired, nothing York could do would prove his firmness of soul. And Aumerle's adherence to Henry would imply the abandonment not only of his sovereign but his friend. It is ridiculous to suppose that Henry can command instinctive loyalty. That is exactly his problem. Attachment to him must be born of his wisdom, beneficence, and strength, for he is beginning afresh without the sanctions which were available to Richard. York's conduct merely puts that problem in relief and strikes us as horrible or absurd. The Duchess of York wins the sympathy of everyone, including the new king, with her defense of her son, springing as it does from a mother's natural affection. Such sentiments are taken more seriously now that the old structure of obligations has collapsed, and they must become part of the new structure if it is to hold. Henry's clemency is a start in that direction.[8]

Richard, despised and abandoned, having suffered the insults of the crowd, no longer looks to his divine Father for special protection. He surveys his situation and finds only his loneliness and vulnerability. He compares his prison to the world and populates it with his thoughts representing the different alternative lives, none of which can satisfy him. The life lived in the hope of the afterlife is contradicted by the demands of greatness on this earth. The king's glory and wealth are opposed by the commandments of humility and poverty. The Christian king imitates God while God calls the "little men." Being a king seems to preclude hopes for eternal bliss. The life of ambition cannot succeed, for it demands powers beyond those available to man. And the life of Stoic contentment does not work. Richard does not quite say why, but he indicates that such a posture only makes the best of a bad business and would be abandoned once out of misfortune: there is no true self-sufficiency. This is the popular view of philosophy, as expressed when one says, "he's taking it philosophically," a phrase never used when good things happen. Of the three alternatives it is fair to say that Richard has only thought through and experienced the first. Here at least he breaks out of its constraints but gives only a hasty glance at the other two. It is too late to consider them seriously. Richard's life and fall are marvelously illustrative of the first, which is the Christian alternative and is the one which dominated his world. Others would have to investigate the other ways of life, for Richard himself immediately slips back into his old choice between being a king or a beggar, or the synthesis of the two—nothing. At the last moment, tired of acceptance and drawing on an instinct of which he has hitherto been unaware, he rises to his own defense and fights his attackers. He dies like a man and as a man.[9]

When Henry learns that his wishes are fulfilled, that his rival, the question mark after his legitimacy, has been slain for him, just as Gloucester was slain for Richard, he is stricken with remorse. He accuses himself of the sin of Cain, as he had accused Richard, and vows to go on a crusade. He salves his conscience by trying to return to the chivalric tradition which he has just uprooted. This crusade will never take place because business at home is too pressing. His conscience takes his heart away from home, but home preempts his action. He is split. He cannot bear to face the possibility that the sin of Cain, as Machiavelli teaches, may play a role in the establishment of earthly justice. In deposing Richard he was halfway to the realization that he was committing a crime but that such crimes are sometimes necessary for the common good. However, so strong is his faith or his fear of hellfire, he prefers to brand himself a guilty man and cripple his political sense and dedication rather than admit what his deed has shown.[10] His son returns to his father's original impulse and with healthy self-assurance abandons crusades in favor of unjust wars with France which serve the evident interests of England instead of serving his conscience, using the priests as his political ministers rather than as the masters of his beliefs. He thus unifies England and himself. The Henriad as a whole shows the limits of conscience. Henry V provides a contrast to his predecessors not unlike the contrast between Hamlet and Fortinbras in a play that seems to bear a similar message. The exquisitely refined souls do not belong to the best political men.

There are two sins mentioned in *Richard II*: the sin of Adam and the sin of Cain. They seem to be identical, or at least one leads to the other. Knowledge of political things brings with it the awareness that in order for the sacred to become sacred terrible deeds must be done. Because God does not evidently rule, the founder of justice cannot himself be just. He cannot be distinguished from the criminal by his justice or anything else accessible to vulgar eyes. This capital problem was addressed long ago by Sophocles who showed that the hero who solved the riddle of the Sphinx and thereby discerned man, killed his father and slept with his mother. Machiavelli later repeated the teaching, perhaps in perverting it. I do not suggest that here Shakespeare stopped, but here he surely began. The universal problem of kingship is played out in the particular events of England by Shakespeare, who in his histories could be more philosophic than the historian because he was a poet. He gave England a mirror in which it could recognize itself as it ought to be, one which England would not have to smash as Richard smashed the mirror which reflected his image.

Notes

1. Henry IV does not affect us as a usurper whose crime is the cause of his misery. The presentation of Richard and Henry is too carefully banked with extenuating consideration to allow for simple blame of the latter or respect for the former. The play's impact is not such as to induce reverence for the king (either the old one or the new); rather, there is a subversive element in the detachment it induces. We pity the toothless descendent of Richard the Lion-Hearted; he is shown to possess neither divine nor human strength, and he no longer inspires awe. We experience no horror at what Henry does, but on the other hand, he does not inherit Richard's former sacredness. Moreover, the reader of the Histories as a whole can hardly believe that Shakespeare thought John or Richard to be rulers superior to Henry V or Henry VIII. Shakespeare's view of kingship and legitimacy is subtle and cannot be reduced either to reverence for tradition or bald rationalism. But one thing is certain: Henry V and Henry VIII face up to their priests as neither John nor Richard II does; and this seems to be at the core of the teaching of these plays.

2. Bolingbroke is next in line to the succession after the infant Earl of March, grandson of the Duke of Clarence, Edward III's second son. Cf. *Richard II* I.i.120-121; iv.36-37, New Variorum edition, ed. Black (Philadelphia: Lippincott, 1955).

3. Act III, scene ii.

4. V.i.4.

5. Mowbray is an interesting example of the political man living in this kind of world. He is a scoundrel, capable of all kinds of crimes. But he is also a believing Christian, praised as a defender of the faith against the infidels. He is a Christian knight from the times of the Crusades. He is a great sinner and a great repenter. He has a conscience and confesses. Although he takes political things seriously, they are for him apparently low. His Christianity affects him primarily, if not solely, insofar as it debases his view of human life and politics. All the great things are somewhere else, beyond this sphere, but he is still involved in politics. He is treacherous without any of the great justifications one finds in great political men. And his treachery is compromised by his conscience. (I.i.83-150; IV.i.91-100.)

6. IV.i.115-150.

7. II.i.33-70.

8. Act V, scenes ii-iii.

9. Act V, scene v.
10. Act V, scene vi.

GOD WILL SAVE THE KING:

SHAKESPEARE'S *RICHARD II*

Louise Cowan

God save the king! will no man say amen?
Am I both priest and clerk? well then, amen.
God save the king! although I be not he;
And yet, amen, if heaven do think him me.[1]
                                    (IV.i.172-175)

Despite the attention given to *Richard II* in recent years, it remains a puzzling and enigmatic work. Careful studies by political
and historical scholars have established its importance in Shakespeare's
canon, along with that of the other histories.[2] Even so, granting the intellectual seriousness of the play, the reader is none the less hard pressed—
if he relies on either of the views of it now dominant—to account for its
haunting and unforgettable power. One tendency is to see Richard as a
kind of *exemplum* demonstrating the misuse of kingly office. The successive plays of the second tetralogy, according to this view, work through
the resultant upheaval in the realm until finally Henry V, Richard's
conqueror's son, learns sufficient prudence to handle the intricacies of
royal authority. The other tendency is to interpret Woodstock's and
Richard's assassinations as crimes against the commonwealth, their ex-
piation requiring centuries and several different regimes—and hence the
placement of the other nine history plays in the order of their sequence
in time rather than composition. In this accounting, the moral disorder
ends with the triumphant founding of the Tudor dynasty.

Yet neither of these readings, for the most part sound and even illuminating in their close attention to the text, can account for the disturbing element of the drama: Shakespeare's portrayal of Richard's interior-

ity with such intensity that the audience must share his humiliation and devastation. Did Shakespeare, in writing one of a series of history plays, simply realize that, among the other materials provided him, the chronicle of this murdered king could most effectively be presented as biography, as Peter Ure suggests?[3] If so, this choice would of course necessitate the employment of artistic devices for gaining sympathy from the spectators. What seems more likely is that Shakespeare as poet is doing here precisely what he does in *King Lear, Hamlet,* and the other tragedies: drawing the audience into the magnetic field of suffering and causing his viewers, along with the protagonist, to enter that realm where humanity confronts the mystery of divine order.

But if attention is shifted from the state of the polity to the state of Richard's soul, can the play still be read as having a predominantly political intent? It is quite true, of course, that its subject matter is the politics of statecraft; but its central concern seems to lie with human destiny itself, touching upon metaphysical and spiritual regions that far transcend the political. Nor is its issue primarily historical; for to place *Richard II* within the structure of the "Tudor Myth" hypothesis, "by which events evolve under a law of justice and under the ruling of God's Providence, of which Elizabeth's England was the acknowledged outcome,"[4] is to run the risk of reducing the complexity of Shakespeare's tragic vision and, in this instance, his view of history. Surely the play itself hardly justifies the assumption that Shakespeare, along with Hall and Holinshed, equated the workings of Providence with temporal reward or punishment. But, further, even apart from the question of whether English history as Shakespeare depicts it shows any genuine moral advance (a serious question indeed, which one must eventually attempt to answer), there are in *Richard II* too many images of anguish, too much regret at something lost, to allow us to regard it as a mere way station along the road to political progress. We complete the play with compassion for Richard and with terror at the sacrilege committed against his person. Prophecies throughout the play (spoken by Gaunt, York, Richard's Queen, Glendower, Salisbury, Carlisle, the gardener, and Richard himself) have prepared us for a dire and terrible end; and finally even Exton, Richard's murderer, and Bolingbroke, his usurper, are granted a moment of appalled foresight into the consequences of their crime. The play, finally, makes us see the contradictory and unthinkable: that Richard has been a bad king who abused his power, but that his deposing is an offense that could destroy all England—and that, in fact, the royal "balm" cannot be removed. Richard and his murderer, as well as we, the readers, all at his death acknowledge his kingship: "Exton," the dying monarch charges, "thy fierce hand/ Hath with the King's blood stain'd the King's own land" (V.v. 109-110). And Exton replies, "As full of valour as of royal blood./ Both have I spill'd; O would the deed were good!" (V.v. 113-114).

The difficulty in the play, then, centers on its protagonist. But any effort to analyze Richard's character seems futile as an attempt to account for the "meaning" of the play. For Richard appears in so ambiguous a light that he has provoked almost as widely diverse interpretations as has Hamlet; and certainly one may say that *Hamlet* criticism reached a point of near-exhaustion in its virtually exclusive focus on the idiosyncratic personality of the Danish prince. One is almost tempted to declare of *Richard II* what T. S. Eliot said of *Hamlet*: that it has an inadequate "objective correlative," containing, as it seems to, a mass of feelings insufficiently accounted for by the plot and characterization.[5] Eliot's critical judgment that *Hamlet* is a "failure" stemmed from his frustration at finding Hamlet the person unbelievable. But the real question is one that C. S. Lewis raises in asking whether it is after all "the prince or the poem" with which we should be concerned.[6] *Hamlet* is not, he says, the study of a peculiar temperament so much as the depiction of a situation: a man is given a task by a ghost. And for Shakespeare "the appearance of the spectre means a breaking down of the walls of the world and the germination of thoughts that cannot really be thought." We are interested in Hamlet, then, because he describes for us "a certain spiritual region through which most of us have passed...rather than because of our concern to understand how and why this particular man entered it."[7]

It is the universality of Hamlet's (and Richard's) experience by which we are captured and which we are consequently obligated to understand. Aristotle is helpful in elucidating the relation between character and the general experience. He makes quite clear in the *Poetics* that poetry "tends to express the universal," that the kinds of poetry (epic, tragedy, comedy, and "dithyrambic") are all "modes of imitation," that tragedy (and therefore the other genres) is the "imitation of an action," that an action "implies personal agents, who necessarily possess certain distinctive qualities," that plot "is the first principle and, as it were, the soul of a tragedy."[8] It is not then that character is revealed in action, but the reverse: character is the *agent* of the action. The action is revealed through the character, with the end of our concern being what it is that happens rather than who it is that it happens to. The governing form of the entire drama, in other words, is the action, of which the plot is only the imitation. The action must necessarily be some archetypal movement of the soul, we might add, else it could hardly evoke the pity and terror which must be its final purpose.

In his remarks Aristotle is implying what later critics will call the "symbolic imagination," which, as Allen Tate has said, conducts an action from one level to another by means of analogy.[9] Plot, character, thought, language, spectacle, and song—all the elements of the play, as Aristotle names them, imitate in their own way this hidden and seminal action, which is what the play is "about." Everything within the play works by the obliquity of metaphor and the condensation of symbol to engage in the process of lifting the mind to that philosophical contemplation which makes poetry "a higher thing than history."[10]

What the literary reader has as his task in contributing to an interpretation of *Richard II* is thus indicated within the *Poetics:* first, he should attempt to ascertain the action behind the play, remembering that the plot best imitates that action and that characters are agents of it. This process in itself will necessitate some sense of "polysemousness," of several senses in which the text may be taken, these meanings contained within and implied by the literal sense.[11] Second, the literary reader ought to satisfy himself about what kind of poetry he is dealing with—tragedy, comedy, epic, or lyric, for the tone of the work is governed by its genre; and, third, he needs to address himself to the universal embodied within the poem, keys to which are to be found in dominant metaphors, or symbols, expressing the action. For the critic these operations should be undertaken in an effort to ascertain the unity of the play and should be used to overlay the careful analysis of the literal level of plot and character that has been provided by historians and political philosophers.

The plot of *Richard II*—the deposing of a king—imitates a larger, transcendent action of which Richard's temperament and character are only agents. That action is the attempt by a mortal being to remove from his soul an indelible mark placed there by God—an act of gross impiety, indeed of sacrilege, regardless of his own merit or lack of it. For Richard believes that, sacramentally, he is a king forever; and we must grant him the dignity of that conviction, even if his conception of the invulnerability of his kingship is naive and presumptuous. For instance, when he returns from Ireland to be greeted by the Bishop of Carlisle and Aumerle with the sobering news that Bolingbroke has returned from exile and is gathering around him a strong force, Richard speaks with pious disdain of any attempt to unseat him:

> Not all the water in the rough rude sea
> Can wash the balm off from an anointed king;

The breath of worldly men cannot depose
The deputy elected by the Lord.
For every man that Bolingbroke hath press'd
To lift shrewd steel against our golden crown,
God for his Richard hath in heavenly pay
A glorious angel: then, if angels fight,
Weak men must fall, for heaven still guards the right. (III.ii.54-62)

In the first four lines of this speech Shakespeare means to express, I think it may be argued, the generally accepted medieval and Renaissance understanding of the sacramental nature of monarchy.[12] He is interested in establishing the difference between man and office. The "balm" of an "anointed king" is not material, cannot be removed. One cannot depose God's "deputy" without incurring moral guilt. Others in the play besides Richard seem also to take the sacral nature of his office for granted. John of Gaunt, speaking to the widow of his slain brother Gloucester, staunchly opposes any vengeance to be exacted of the royal monarch:

God's is the quarrel—for God's substitute,
His deputy anointed in His sight,
Hath caus'd his death; the which if wrongfully,
Let heaven revenge, for I may never lift
An angry arm against His minister. (I.ii.37-41)

Can a king be deposed? Gaunt would say not. Yet old Lancaster hardly holds the king in such awe as to fear rebuking him for having conceived of his office as privilege rather than responsibility. He warns Richard that "a thousand flatterers sit within [his] crown," playing the part of poor physicians in concealing from him the seriousness of his illness. In his alienation from the people, Richard is "sick," Gaunt insists; and in leasing out his realm he has become "landlord of England," not king. These are the sins with which Richard is charged throughout the play: of being ruled by "favorites" rather than by truth and justice, of separation from the commons, and of using the lands and goods of the realm for the king's benefit rather than the commonwealth's. For a royal monarch, these are incapacitating flaws, as most of the lords well know. Yet Gaunt, for one, would not lift a hand against the king, however unworthy he might be.

The Bishop of Carlisle shares Gaunt's horror at those who would rebel against God's deputy and like Gaunt unsuccessfully attempts to lesson Richard. But later, after Bolingbroke has taken Richard prisoner and charged him in Parliament with crimes against the state, Carlisle speaks in defense of the king's "noblesse": "What subject can give sentence on his king?" he asks. "And who sits here that is not Richard's subject?"

> And shall the figure of God's majesty,
> His captain, steward, deputy elect,
> Anointed, crowned, planted many years,
> Be judg'd by subject and inferior breath
> And he himself not present? (IV.i.125-129)

If in criticizing Richard, Gaunt has emphasized piety toward England and the Bishop piety toward that which God has ordained, the Duke of York speaks up boldly to the king in defense of property rights and due succession:

> Take Hereford's rights away, and take from time
> His charters, and his customary rights;
> Let not to-morrow then ensue to-day;
> Be not thyself. For how art thou a king
> But by fair sequence and succession? (II.i.195-199)

The entire order of things will collapse, he implies, if Richard appropriates Bolingbroke's property. And, after Henry's return, ostensibly to reclaim his inheritance, the lords of the realm must in fact choose between the consecrated king and his challenger, whom most of them consider justified. York clearly states the dilemma:

> Both are my kinsmen:
> Th'one is my sovereign, whom both my oath
> And duty bids defend; th'other again
> Is my kinsman, whom the king hath wrong'd,
> Whom conscience and my kindred bids to right. (II.ii.111-115)

York has familial obligations to both Richard and Henry, and he must balance his sense of justice against his "oath and duty." Left in charge of Richard's kingdom during the king's absence and confronted by Henry's strength, he speaks out vigorously against "rebellion" but finally, acknowledging his own powerlessness, declares himself "neuter." York will later describe the piteousness of Richard's plight when the dethroned monarch follows in the triumphal procession of Bolingbroke; but in a quick turn of loyalty to the new king he will report his own son for treason. Quite obviously York's allegiance is more conventional than that of Gaunt or Carlisle. If we see in Richard some of the lineaments of the Hamlet to come, then York is a kind of Polonius, adapting himself to whatever regime is in power. But even he has spoken out, when he can, in favor of the anointed king and has called those who oppose him "rebels all."

Several other characters in the play share this view of Richard's spiritual kingship and the consequent moral offense of the rebellion against true authority. It is not a question of whether the king can do no wrong; no one in the play considers Richard above the law. The issue at stake is what to do with a monarch who has committed serious and habitual offenses. The play does not advance a belief in the "Divine Right of Kings," a theory which is not to be encountered, strictly speaking, until the seventeenth century.[13] It sets forth instead a thoroughly traditional English concept of the sacredness and authority of the office, with the king deemed answerable not only to parliament and law but to the higher powers of justice and love. Yet Shakespeare is neither advancing a political theory nor depicting a factually accurate account of fourteenth-century legal and political writings on the limitations of kingly power. He is instead exploring things that are eternally true, as they manifest themselves in specific situations. If a man has been anointed king, and both he and his people have recognized the analogies between the sacerdotal and the royal office, then within the given outlines of history the inner shape of events will be as Shakespeare here depicts them.

It is the work of the entire play to show that, rather than illustrating any particular theory of kingship, Richard commits the sin of *hybris*. For, if the first four lines of his boastful speech on the coast of Wales express the general understanding of monarchy, the last five, by their presumption, come dangerously near to being belief in the "divine right." They imply that the king is always, because of his office, right. Even further, they maintain that God will necessarily protect his deputy on earth. Other characters do not so oversimplify the situation. The Bishop of Carlisle acknowledges God's sovereignty but avoids the sin of presumption when he says to Richard, "that Power that made you king/ Hath power to keep you king in spite of all"; still, "the means that heaven yields must be imbrac'd/ And not neglected" (III.ii.27-30). Aumerle interprets the Bishop in terms that have no reference whatever to divine protection: "he means, my lord, that we are too remiss;/ Whilst Bolingbroke, through our security,/ Grows strong and great in substance and in power" (III.ii.33-35). Even Carlisle in his dire prophecy of internecine strife for England does not pretend to speak for God: "The blood of English shall manure the ground," he laments, "And future ages groan for this foul act."

> O, if you raise this house against this house,
> It will the woefullest division prove
> That ever fell upon this cursed earth.
> Prevent it, resist it, let it not be so,
> Lest child, child's children cry against you woe. (IV.i.145-149)

It is from his moral wisdom that the Bishop gives this impassioned warning rather than from a religious conviction that God will punish the sinners who oppose Richard. Raising "this house against this house" will prove the "woefullest division" that man has ever known—because of the nature of man and of society, not because of God's vengeance. Richard's speech, in contrast, boasts of God's certain retribution. In his vanity he implies that a king will always be victorious. He knows better; he is not quite a hundred lines away from his melancholy meditation on the death of monarchs:

> For God's sake let us sit upon the ground
> And tell sad stories of the death of kings:
> How some have been depos'd, some slain in war,
> Some haunted by the ghosts they have depos'd,
> Some poisoned by their wives, some sleeping kill'd,
> All murthered—for within the hollow crown
> That rounds the mortal temples of a king
> Keeps Death his court. (III.ii.155-162)

Richard has not been so naive as he has pretended; he knows the king's office to be a dangerous business. His presumption has come from having assumed to himself the timeless, permanent invulnerability of kingship; the dark hidden side of this "mystical" elevation is a heightened awareness of death. Here the crown, in being the obviously immortal part of sovereignty, serves to emphasize the pitiably mortal body of the king who wears it.[14] From this point on throughout the play until after his deposition, what we shall see in Richard is a fluctuation between his "two bodies," his identification with the one promoting presumption, with the other, despair.

But for all his pride, for all his vacillation and self-glorification, Richard bears the unmistakable mark of royalty. As M. M. Reese has commented, "Shakespeare's royalty is an essence that clings inalienably to failures like Richard II and Henry VI, even when they have forfeited the right to rule, and it is never attainable by usurpers like Bolingbroke."[15] Reese sees this essence as more than a kingly dignity: "It is the voice of a common consciousness of the mystery in the soul of state." The sacrilege committed against this sacramental order is the action of *Richard II*, and royalty is its dominant symbol. Shakespeare portrays this quality in two later "kings" who are separated from their royal power: Lear and Hamlet. All three testify to the anguish induced by royalty, to the virtually unbearable burden placed on their souls by the contrast between the dignity of their station and the dishonor in which they are held by others. Erich Auerbach has likewise written of Shakespeare's portrait of indestructible royalty, pointing out that this quality is accompanied in the plays by a medieval mixture of styles, so that the tragic and comic shift back and forth in the language and style of the kingly characters. Of Hamlet he writes:

> He jumps from the obscene to the lyrical or sublime, from the ironically incongruous to dark and profound meditation, from humiliating scorn leveled at others and himself to the solemn assumption of the right to judge and proud self-assertion.[16]

Auerbach comments similarly on Lear's "bitterly grotesque histrionics," in which he humiliates himself in front of others by conduct unbecoming his dignity. Yet "his nature is so unconditionally royal," Auerbach maintains, "that humiliation only brings it out more strongly."

Like Hamlet and Lear, Richard shifts from the lyric and exalted to the self-pitying or the brutally callous. He engages in theatricality, mocks himself and others with exaggerated irony, and like Lear and Hamlet, conducts himself in an unpredictable and inconsistent manner until he comes to understand the true nature of his royalty. It is this "antic disposition," marking a double vision, that is the plague of kings, as though the grace of office propels them in their vicissitudes away from the normal path, toward wildness and the borders of the irrational.

Richard's royal dignity is apparent at the beginning of the play, public and iconic, his "upright soul" manifest until, on hearing of John of Gaunt's illness, he drops his public manner to utter his base and unworthy prayer: "Now put it, God, in the physician's mind/ To help him to his grave immediately!" The prodigal and unfeeling king would appropriate "the lining of his coffers" to "make coats/ To deck our soldiers for these Irish wars" (I.iv.59-62). Richard's lack of piety for the bonds of kinship as well as of common humanity has already been foreshadowed in his implication in the death of his uncle, Woodstock. His callousness and irresponsibility are progressively revealed in his response to the news of Gaunt's death, his confiscation of the old man's goods, his lack of prudence in placing the weak York in charge of the realm during the king's absence, his theatrical return from Ireland to Welsh soil. When he hears of the threat to his reign, he reacts in wildly melodramatic fashion to whatever is said to him by his followers, alternating between hope and dejection. It is as though he is acting out before heaven, with his companions merely overhearing, the discrepancies between the way things ought to be and the way they are. His two soliloquies are poetic posturings in which he titillates his fancy with the possibilities of death and renunciation and yet is not truly touched by them.

By the time he appears in stark and brooding majesty on the battlements of Flint Castle, however, Richard is apparently undergoing an interior change. His mystical claim to inviolable kingship has been challenged; his temptation to self-pity and despair has been confronted; neither of these postures has represented his true identity, which he is just beginning to discover. Bolingbroke compares him to the "blushing discontented sun" when he sees the "envious clouds are bent/ To dim his glory." And York replies: "Yet looks he like a king. Behold, his eye,/ As bright as is the eagle's, lightens forth/ Controlling majesty" (III.iii.68-70). Richard is haughty and proud in his greeting to Bolingbroke; but his threat this time makes no mention of divine protection for himself; he has relinquished his invulnerability and speaks instead of divine retribution:

> Yet know, my master, God omnipotent,
> Is mustering in his clouds, on our behalf,
> Armies of pestilence, and they shall strike
> Your children yet unborn, and unbegot,
> That lift your vassal hands against my head,
> And threat the glory of my precious crown. (III.iii.85-90)

In the scenes immediately following, Richard alternately threatens, yields, rages, raves, holds himself up for pity, and engages in bitter irony. The significant transformation begins in him, however, after he is requested by Northumberland to come down to the base court. "Down, down I come," Richard says, "like glist'ring Phaeton." Something equivalent to the sun's being removed from its course in the heavens is happening to Richard, something so incredible and outrageous that he is impelled to race toward it, taking a perverse joy in debasing his "highness." He has been speaking fantastically, "fondly, like a frantic man," as Northumberland says. But when he appears "in the base court," he is again majestic, terse, straightforward, anticipating Bolingbroke's demands. When Henry would pretend that he has come but for his "own," Richard's reply is curt: "Your own is yours, and I am yours, and all" (III.iii.197).

Richard's true *agon* begins when he is summoned by Bolingbroke to a meeting of Parliament in Westminster Hall, where he is expected publicly to abdicate his office and name Henry his successor. He enunciates the key to the play in the lines, "Alack, why am I sent for to a king/ Before I have shook off the regal thoughts/ Wherewith I reign'd?" (IV.i.162-64). The mystery of how one can still be, within, a king while confronting, without, the person now considered to hold that office raises the most painful questions of identity. Neither of the king's "two bodies" with which he has been familiar is now available to him. He has "no name, no title." And yet, ironically, in being deprived of the power of the crown, he begins to feel himself all the more genuinely a king in the hidden recesses of his soul. The difference between being and doing occupies Richard's thoughts all through this scene. It is not merely levity and mockery that animate his ironic comments, but an anguish that gives him a strange detachment from events, so that he seems not to know where reality lies:

> God save the king! will no man say amen?
> Am I both priest and clerk? well then, amen.
> God save the king! although I be not he;
> And yet, amen, if heaven do think him me. (IV.i.172-175)

What Richard comes to in this apparent verbal quibbling is the realization that it is not man's power but "heaven's" that determines kingship. If he is not the king, then he assents to the honor and protection of whoever holds the office; if he is still the king in the eyes of God, then he is able to utter a *fiat mihi* to the martyrdom his position will entail. What he is certain of is that kingship is not a mere name, as it is being made out to be; it is an interior reality, a mark set upon one who becomes God's steward on earth. If at his accession the change in the king's soul is permanent, as Richard has before carelessly assumed and as he is now beginning to perceive in earnest, then it cannot be revoked, even when the outward habiliments are taken from him. To Bolingbroke's "I thought you had been willing to resign," Richard replies, "My crown I am, but still my griefs are mine./ You may my glories and my state depose,/ But not my griefs; still am I king of those." Richard is unmistakably the master in this abdication scene, unpredictable in his speech and action and no doubt acutely embarrassing to Bolingbroke, who has hoped for a peaceful transition. Yet there is a genuine dignity to Richard's demeanor and an authentic suffering, the most acute aspect of which comes from discovering himself a traitor along with the others:

> For I have given here my soul's consent
> T'undeck the pompous body of a King;
> Made glory base; and sovereignty a slave;
> Proud majesty a subject, state a peasant. (IV.i.249-252)

Does one have the right to resign a kingship? Is it not taking part in the treasonable act of deposing a king, even if that king be oneself? All Richard's banterings posit a deep self-division in this scene, along with his growing awareness that he can never change his larger royal identity. The analogy to a marriage is pointed out by Richard in the next act, when he takes leave of his wife:

> Doubly divorc'd! Bad men, you violate
> A two-fold marriage—'twixt my crown and me,
> And then betwixt me and my married wife. (V.i.71-73)

No more than he can cease being his wife's husband, even if the two are separated, can he leave off the kingship.

But before the abdication scene is over Richard takes part in a further bit of pageantry: he asks for a mirror to see what face he has, "since it is bankrupt of his majesty." Here, before the entire assemblage, he ponders his face, marveling at his unchanged visage, in which a "brittle glory shines." Afterward, he throws the glass down, breaking it into "a hundred shivers." It is not glory he seeks in its surface but some sign of his diminishment, some reflection in his outward visage of the "sorrow" that has struck "so many blows upon this face of mine,/ And made no deeper wounds" (IV.i.277-279). This mirror scene is not an indication of Richard's narcissism, as some have indicated. It is, rather, his searching examination of the external show of things and final renunciation of glory. Bolingbroke with a casual remark provides Richard with a way of understanding his situation: "The shadow of your sorrow hath destroyed/ The shadow of your face." Richard suddenly sees that, just as the mirror was but the outward reflection of his face, so his posturings, his "external manners of laments" are only "shadows to the unseen grief,/ That swells with silence in the tortur'd soul" (IV.i.296-298).

Taken from Westminster Hall, where he has renounced all of the kingly *potestas*, he is alone, finally, in Pomfret Castle, his solitude at this point merely a literalization of his previous alienation, when he had conceived of his kingly prerogatives for himself and not his people. His degradation and debasement have given him access—of a kind he has not had before—to the psychic reality which has governed his destiny. Enclosed in prison, unkinged, stripped of every luxury by which he has defined himself, he engages in the tragic search for identity and responsibility which will later occupy Lear. For it is not merely a matter of the "king's two bodies," the office persisting, the individual holder of office passing away. Richard was and remains in some sense king, just as a priest, even when removed from his ecclesiastical duties, is a priest forever. There is a moral bond between king and subjects that cannot be broken, even if the one has ignored it and the others wish to be rid of it. In desperate awareness that he is now cut off forever from any actual relationship with his people, Richard turns inward. But whereas, in the earlier part of the play, his thought has been prescriptive, pictorial, rhetorical, histrionic, it is now fertile and generative, not with the dialectic of philosophy but with the dynamic of the imagination:

> I have been studying how I may compare
> This prison where I live unto the world;
> And, for because the world is populous,
> And here is not a creature but myself,
> I cannot do it. (V.v.1-5)

What Richard has learned by now is that there can be no king without community. "Yet I'll hammer it out," he declares:

> My brain I'll prove the female to my soul,
> My soul the father, and these two beget
> A generation of still-breeding thoughts,
> And these same thoughts people this little world;
> In humours like the people of this world. (V.v.6-10)

He finds within himself the fullness of both the masculine and feminine actions: his mind, which previously dominated his soul, moving as it did from thought to thought with a superficial facility, now becomes passive and receptive to the secret part of himself, the soul, wherein lies his royal largesse. Hence his soul can engender in his brain offspring that, "still-breeding" (ever-breeding), beget others and so "people this little world," in the way that Adam and Eve first peopled it. Richard here is far from the attitude which at first glance he resembles, that expressed by Sir Edward Dyer in "My Mind to Me a Kingdom Is," wherein the speaker rejoices in the happiness of a mind that can rise above adversity. The title of Richard's "poem" would have to be "My Soul to Me a Kingdom Is," since, deprived of his realm, he fills his prison cell with soul-begotten images of human life, images which speak not of man's triumph over circumstances but of his implication in search, failure, and death. What Richard discovers in this dark psychical engendering is the paradoxical nature of human life. Both "beggars and kings" suffer the same calamities. Even "the better sort" of thoughts, those of "things divine," are contradictory, setting "the word itself/ Against the word." One is commanded, "Come, little ones," and yet is told how hard it is to enter. In all the modes of human life which he ponders, the imperative call to blessedness and the impossibility of achieving it have equal force:

> Thus play I in one person many people,
> And none contented.... But whate'er I be,
> Nor I, nor any man that but man is
> With nothing shall be pleas'd, till he be eas'd
> With being nothing. (V.v.31-41)

He has come to the limits of mortality: whether king or beggar, he is "but man" and, as man, cannot rest until he becomes "nothing."

What is beginning to happen to Richard in this prison scene is a participation with the body of humanity, accomplished through the imagination. The imaginative act occurs in times of disjunction, threshold situations, transitions. Richard is moving from one state of being to another. He knows now that he has taken too little thought of the subjects to whom he is bound in charity and duty. It is this communion with a reality outside himself that readies him for love and death. He moves from an image of the communal body to an image of time: someone is playing music for him, that Shakespearean symbol of harmony and the divine life. It is apparently played badly, for Richard comments:

> Ha, ha! keep time—how sour sweet music is
> When time is broke and no proportion kept!
> So is it in the music of men's lives.
> And here have I the daintiness of ear
> To check time broke in a disordered string;
> But for the concord of my state and time,

Had not an ear to hear my true time broke:
I wasted time, and now doth time waste me. (V.v.42-49)

Since he did not "hear the concord of [his] state and time," did not keep
the proper harmony and measure in his realm, he has become, as he goes
on to say, the "numbering clock" of time. He has missed the opportunity
for living *in* time, organically and harmoniously, with the measure and
proportion of music, and now must by "sighs and tears and groans/ Show
minutes, times, and hours." He has become, in the new time now organized around the usurping monarch, Bolingbroke's "Jack of the clock,"
time's fool. He has not, as a king should have, "redeemed the time."

"This music mads me," he cries out; "let it sound no more." But
though he would like it to cease, he blesses the heart that provides it for
him, "For 'tis a sign of love; and love to Richard/ Is a strange brooch in
this all-hating world" (V.v.65-66). This is the first occasion, one senses, on
which Richard has acknowledged his kinship with the rest of humanity,
his first instance of blessing anyone for anything. This strange jewel—
love and music—in its incongruity with the rest of the world enables him
to see that, in a fallen state, charity and benevolence are gifts rather than
one's rights. Richard's recognition of love heralds the *peripeteia* of the
drama: the appearance in his cell of a member of his former entourage,
the groom of his Barbary horse, who slips in to see him just a few moments before his murderers are to arrive. The groom brings with him not
only devotion and sympathy but also the reverence that Richard's subjects should feel for their king. "Hail, royal Prince," this anonymous and
humble fellow greets his unfortunate sovereign, just as Cordelia greets
her broken father with "How does my royal lord? How fares your majesty?" In each of these instances the salutation is directed toward the
restoration of dignity, addressed not to the private person but to that
larger self which each still is. "I was a poor groom of thy stables, king,"
the visitor declares, "when thou wert king." He has thus skilfully distinguished the two realms of authority and power by saying in effect, "King,
you were once king" (you were once in power), and so restores his moral
kingdom to the powerless monarch. The two grieve together that the
horse nurtured so carefully for Richard pranced under Bolingbroke "so
proudly as if he disdained the ground." Richard at first lashes out, "Would
he not stumble? Would he not fall down,/ Since pride must have a fall,
and break the neck/ Of that proud man that did usurp his back?" (V.v.87-
89). But then, after establishing the analogy between himself and the
horse, the new Richard softens:

> Forgiveness, horse! why do I rail on thee,
> Since thou, created to be aw'd by man,
> Wast born to bear? I was not made a horse
> And yet I bear a burthen like an ass,
> Spurr'd, gall'd and tir'd by jauncing Bolingbroke. (V.v.90-94)

Richard's momentary outrage that the horse did not display the loyalty that human sentiment would desire is quickly dispelled at the recognition that the horse behaved according to his station in the hierarchy of existence. In contrast, he, Richard, has behaved not at all like a king but responded to Bolingbroke's goading like a lesser beast than the horse. With his kingship confirmed, no longer can he play the ass; he responds as a man to the fresh insult that follows immediately, striking his keeper and killing two of Exton's servants who enter, armed, with their master. Richard rushes to his death as he has rushed to his abdication; but now his impulsive action is to right the previous wrong, knowing that only in death can his royalty, which cannot be removed in life, be preserved. He is able at this moment to separate the king's two identities properly: "Mount, mount, my soul! thy seat is up on high;/ Whilst my gross flesh sinks downward, here to die" (V.v.111-112).

Richard's death completes the action of the play: the attempt by mortal hands to erase an ineradicable mark on the soul. Plot, character, thought, language, spectacle, and even music depict that action. But the power of the drama lies in its ability to engage the successively higher dimensions to be found in the greatest poetry. Its literal sense, as we have indicated, is the deposing—and disposing—of a king. The other three senses are all analogical, the second concerning the loss of the medieval order and the movement to modernity; the third, the inevitable loss of innocence that is entailed in moral growth; the fourth, the painful death to the things of this world to prepare the soul for its ultimate destiny. The symbol of royalty encompasses all these meanings and of course on its highest level signifies the divine presence in man, the *imago dei*, which cannot be obliterated.

But all these analogies point to an archetypal parallel. Behind Richard's story of irresponsibility and presumption lies the dominant Western myth: the Fall of Man. Imaginatively, England is a garden: "This royal throne of kings, this sceptered isle, this earth of majesty...this other Eden, this demi-Paradise,...this happy breed of men, this precious stone set in the silver sea/ This blessed plot, this earth, this realm, this England" (II.i.40-50), as John of Gaunt on his deathbed expresses his piety.

To be exiled from England is to breathe English air in a strange land, as Bolingbroke asserts; to "engaol one's tongue," making it an "unstringed viol or a harp," according to ill-starred Mowbray. Richard is aware of the sacredness of English soil, even if he interprets that sacredness possessively and subjectively, as he is wont to do at lest throughout the first part of the play. Springing from the genuine love of the land which permeates the play is a piety for the bonds established between men: and the severity of the loss of these bonds can be realized only when one views the loss by means of the typology of the Fall.

Richard's Queen and the gardeners are familiar with the analogy; and, with the simple wisdom of the folk, the gardeners know that even a paradise needs pruning and care. The Queen, in her distress, speaks more sharply than is her probable custom, addressing the gardener as "Old Adam's likeness" and demanding of him "What Eve, what serpent, hath suggested thee/ To make a second fall of cursed man?/ Why dost thou say King Richard is depos'd?" (III.iv.75-77). The gardener answers her gently, pitying her anguish. If Richard does become symbolically an Adam figure, as I think likely, then with his fall also occurs the fall of nature and of England. The folk are no longer unified by a common purpose; they can be flattered into consent by an ambitious monarch; faction rises against faction among the lords; what finally ensues is cousin against cousin and father against son. This general decay has been occurring all along during Richard's reign, marked by the murder of Woodstock, the gradual falling away of the people, the alienation suggested between Richard and his wife, the extravagant expenditures of the court, the appropriation of private property by the king, the intrigues between proud and arrogant leaders. But, as the Bishop of Carlisle knows: once Richard is deposed, once a new king is crowned, England is exiled from the garden, from royalty. What the next three plays will present is the struggle to regain the authority of the king's identity.

That the kings Richard II and Henry V are entirely different sorts of rulers almost every reader will acknowledge; but that kingship itself is a very different thing in the two plays is less often argued. The world of Richard is ceremonial, chivalric, medieval, poetic, essentially static; whereas the world of Henry is pragmatic, modern, competitive, dynamic. The king in one is God's steward, in the other a man among men. Richard is the last of the medieval kings; Shakespeare, looking back on that time from his own day, imaginatively portrayed the England of John of Gaunt as the happy "Edenic" time, with Richard the first offender against blessedness. In Richard's "fall" into egotism and presumption lies the beginning of modernity; for Bolingbroke's coup is a response to a possibility already prepared for him. Indeed, it is in apprehending in *Richard II* the re-enactment of the Fall that we are given a clue to its relation to the other plays of the second tetralogy. The entire series comprises an almost complete cycle of genres, depicting the recurrent quest for right order in a fallen world. *Richard II*, though in itself a tragedy, is largely lyric in mood, as though the England of the Garden, the true state of happiness, is still fresh in men's memories. The cycle moves from Richard's abuse of royalty and his fall, which leads to the usurpation of the kingdom by a man of ruthless will; through the nocturnal world of *1 Henry IV*, where no real authority welds the people together and dark comedy reigns; through the diseased state of a regime in *2 Henry IV*, wearing itself out in insurrection and moving toward purgation with the "old" man rejected; to the energy and purposiveness in *Henry V* of a new king, ready for the epic task of establishing order, able to bring his people together in common cause, victorious in battle, wooing in the style of high comedy a French wife who will aid in the annexation of France for England and hence enlarge the kingdom.

Shakespeare's "history plays," then, have indeed a historical significance: they present a carefully worked out vision of history, showing the way in which divine providence operates in the world of human affairs. Certainly this pattern is presented in the second tetralogy, beginning with the fall of Richard. The pattern is the endless cycle of human action, repeated in time, with no apparent moral progress being made, since the same human imperfections exist and the same wrongs are committed in different circumstances. Yet in the move from order to chaos and back again to order Shakespeare has seized upon the fundamental figure of history which, in enacting a constant death and resurrection, impels man, in all his imperfection, toward that final end to which all things tend in the fullness of time. Alvin Kernan has noticed this enormous "motion" underlying the plays, seeing in *Richard II* "in political and social terms a movement from feudalism and hierarchy to the national state and individualism." He continues outlining the dimensions of this movement:

> In psychological terms it is a passage from a situation in which man knows with certainty who he is to an existential condition in which any identity is only a temporary role. In spatial and temporal terms it is a movement from a closed world to an infinite universe. In mythical terms the passage is from a garden world to a fallen world. In the most summary terms it is a movement from ceremony and ritual to history.[17]

I should maintain even more: in this second tetralogy Shakespeare has envisioned the story of mankind, as repeated in the history of the English people. We are not meant to be dismayed by the loss of royalty or by Hal's democratic pragmatism. No man is able to perform his task perfectly; in the Biblical tradition within which Shakespeare's imagination works, all earthly things are flawed and yet all are carriers of something flawless. Shakespeare sees the human enterprise as a series of catastrophes, brought about by the clash of human wills; yet within this turbulent and painful chronicle he testifies to the gradual mysterious growth of the kingdom.

Shakespeare shows us that human communities and political regimes exist in order to further what Allen Tate has called the "one lost truth that must be perpetually recovered—the supratemporal destiny of man.[18] It is in the constant rediscovery of shared love—between all sorts and conditions of men—that the true meaning of human history lies concealed. In *Richard II* it is in John of Gaunt's suffering and his love for his land, in Richard's Queen's love and loyalty, in the gardener's compassion for the tears of a queen, in the Bishop of Carlisle's courageous defense of a monarch, in the Duchess of York's impassioned plea for her son, in Bolingbroke's kindness to the Duchess and his respect for Carlisle. Between the interstices of events, so to speak, men perform virtuous actions in a creative response to each other and so do not merely discover but augment blessedness among men. It is Shakespeare's genius as dramatist to depict the invisible "by the things that are seen." He demonstrates in the brief shared moment of love and loyalty between the dispossessed monarch and the groom the re-establishment, on another level, of Richard's kingdom.

Notes

1. William Shakespeare, *Richard II*, Arden Edition, ed. Peter Ure (London and Cambridge, Mass.: Harvard University Press, 1956). Citations will be indicated in the text by act, scene, and line.

2. The most influential study of *Richard II* in the context of the other history plays is of course E.M.W. Tillyard's *Shakespearean History Plays* (London: Macmillan, 1944). This, along with Lily B. Campbell's *Shakespearean Histories: Mirrors of Elizabethan Policy* (San Marino, Calif.: Huntington, 1947), established the relation of the history plays to Elizabethan providential theories of history. More recent studies of importance considering the same issues are Henry Kelly, *Divine Providence in the England of Shakespeare's Histories* (Cambridge, Mass.: Harvard University Press, 1970), Robert Pierce, *Shakespeare's History Plays: The Family and the State* (Columbus: Ohio

State University Press, 1971), and Moody Prior, *The Drama of Power* (Evanston, Ill.: Northwestern University Press, 1973).

3. Introduction, *Richard II*, p. lxiii.

4. Tillyard, p. 321.

5. "Hamlet and His Problems," *Selected Essays* (New York: Harcourt, 1950), p. 125.

6. Lewis, "Hamlet: The Prince or the Poem?" *Proceedings of the British Academy* (London: Oxford University Press, 1942), 38:147-52.

7. Ibid., p. 151.

8. Aristotle, *Poetics*, trans. S.H. Butcher (New York: Dover, 1951), pp. 7, 25, 27.

9. "The Symbolic Imagination," *Essays of Four Decades* (New York: William Morrow, 1968), p. 427.

10. Aristotle, p. 35.

11. This analogical thinking, implied in Aristotle, was worked out only later in the Christian Middle Ages by biblical exegetes and expressed for students of literature most clearly in Dante's famous letter to Can Grande della Scala: Letter 10, *Translations of the Later Works of Dante*, trans. P.H. Wicksteed (London: J.M. Dent, 1904).

12. Fritz Kern makes clear that in the early Middle Ages consecration of the monarch was considered a sacrament: "Consecration, which according to the early mediaeval Church, was a vehicle of supernatural virtue, brought results, expressed in symbolical form, which were both psychological and religious on the one hand, and ecclesiastical and legal on the other. Its external symbols were seen in the ministrations of the priest who crowned and anointed; its inner efficacy was in the soul of the princely recipient; its outward efficacy was manifested in the 'character' that it conferred upon the person of the crowned and anointed prince." (*Kingship and Law in the Middle Ages*, trans. S.B. Chrimes [New York: Frederick A. Praeger, 1956], p. 36). Later, Kern points out, after the kingly anointing was no longer defined by the Church as a sacrament, the idea of the sacramental character of consecration persisted on into the Renaissance and even, to some degree, into modern times (pp. 50-58). See also Ernst H. Kantorowicz, *The King's Two Bodies: A Study in Medieval Political Theology* (Princeton: Princeton University Press, 1957); Edward Peters, *The Shadow King* (New Haven and London: Yale University Press, 1970); and Edna Zwick Boris, *Shakespeare's English Kings, the People, and the Law* (London: Associated University Press, 1978).

13. See Kern, pp. 1-145; as well as John Figgis, *The Divine Right of Kings* (Gloucester, Mass.: P. Smith, 1970), first published in 1896; and J.W. Allen, *A History of Political Thought in the Sixteenth Century* (London: L. MacVeagh, The Dial Press, 1928).

14. In his impressive study *The King's Two Bodies* Kantorowicz has assembled documents tracing the growth of a concept, encountered in Tudor times, that the king has two bodies, the body politic and the body natural, the one being immortal, and the other mortal. "The legal concept of the King's Two Bodies cannot," he maintains, "be separated from Shakespeare. For if that curious image, which from modern constitutional thought has vanished all but completely, still has a very real and human meaning today, this is largely due to Shakespeare" (p. 26). In a brilliant analysis of *Richard II* (pp. 24-41) Kantorowicz seems to equate Richard's thinking with Shakespeare's. I should like to suggest that the idea of an immortal *character angelicus* associated with kingship but existing apart from the individual king is, as Kantorowicz himself indicates in his citation of sources, a Renaissance doctrine. What Shakespeare is concerned with is the sacramental nature of monarchy, which is a quite different matter.

15. *The Cease of Majesty* (New York: St. Martin's Press, 1961), p. 121.

16. *Mimesis: The Representation of Reality in Western Literature* (Princeton, N.J.: Princeton University Press, 1953), pp. 316-317.

17. "The Henriad: Shakespeare's History Plays," *Modern Shakespearean Criticism*, ed. Alvin Kernan (New York: Harcourt, 1970), pp. 245-256.

18. "The Man of Letters in the Modern World," *Essays of Four Decades*, p. 16.

SHAKESPEARE'S HENRY IV:
A NEW PRINCE IN
A NEW PRINCIPALITY

Dain A. Trafton

Between the richly colored and dramatically imposing figures of Richard II and Henry V—at the very center, as it were, of Shakespeare's second tetralogy of plays about English history—stands the sober, curiously drab figure of Henry Bolingbroke. A mere outline of his career suggests a portrait that might have been composed almost entirely of highlights, both lurid and brilliant. Having seized the throne and murdered his cousin the king, Henry holds his prize against all comers, destroys his enemies at last, and bequeaths his conquests intact to his son. What this outline suggests, however, Shakespeare's art avoids. Throughout three plays notably filled with characters who dominate the stage, Shakespeare withholds from Henry the vividness that his story seems to warrant. Unlike other Shakespearean characters who commit outstanding crimes in the pursuit of thrones—Richard III, Macbeth, or Claudius—Henry has not been granted the moments of high dramatic intensity, the triumphs and the agonies, that make a hero. His is a study in grey. Moreover, as the tetralogy progresses from *Richard II* to the plays that bear his name, Henry literally recedes from view. A progressive diminishment of his presence on the stage occurs. In *Richard II* he is on stage about half the time; in the first of the plays named for him, however, his role is reduced by half, and in the second a further reduction leaves him with only three scenes, which amount to less than one sixth of the work. One might conclude that Henry's character simply never engaged Shakespeare's full interest, but such a conclusion would miss the point. The sobriety of tone befits the special intention of Henry's portrait. That intention is neither tragic nor heroic, but essentially political. In the curiously muted presentation of Henry can be discovered one of

Shakespeare's most searching political portraits—his most extended and also his profoundest political investigation of (to use the language of Machiavelli) a new prince in a new principality.[1] Other Shakespearean characters present the type in greater psychological and moral depth, and with greater dramatic power; none displays with such clarity and thoroughness the political implications of regicide and usurpation. Ultimately, moreover, the lusterless tones in which Henry is drawn point to Shakespeare's judgment upon the first Lancastrian king. As we shall see, the tetralogy's analysis of Henry's politics leads to a revelation of his essential deficiency.

According to Shakespeare, Henry's usurpation represents more than a simple change of dynasty. In defying, deposing, and eventually murdering Richard, Henry subverts not only the rule of a particular king, but also a fundamental principle of the realm. He violates, and thus undermines, the sanctity of monarchy itself, the belief that kings are God's deputies and that rebellion is a sin. Through the figures of Gaunt, Carlisle, York, and Richard himself, Shakespeare articulates this principle in all its religious dignity, and identifies it as an essential source of order in the traditional regime that exists at the beginning of the tetralogy. When the Duchess of Gloucester seeks revenge upon Richard for the murder of her husband, Gaunt sternly refuses to take action against "God's substitute,/ His deputy anointed in His sight."[2] When Henry is on the point of taking the crown itself from "plume-pluck'd Richard," Carlisle steps forward to deplore "so heinous, black, obscene a deed." If "the figure of God's majesty" is deposed, Carlisle warns,

> The blood of English shall manure the ground,
> And future ages groan for this foul act. (IV.i.137-148)

Henry must be presumed as familiar with the weighty significance of these views as are his father and Carlisle; yet neither the memory of the former nor the eloquence of the latter turns him from an act of profound impiety against the regime. Noting the ambiguities and contradictions in his statements, and the fact that he is not depicted clearly as a villain, most critics have concluded that Shakespeare intended to present Henry as a rebel who drifts into his radical course without quite knowing, or quite admitting to himself, what he is doing.[3] At heart, these critics argue, Henry is more of an opportunist than a schemer; his maneuvers finally leave him no choice except to make himself king, but he is not the kind of man to have reflected much along the way. That Henry's statements are often ambiguous and that he is an opportunist cannot be denied. However, to conclude that he drifts into rebellion, that he has not reflected upon the implications of his deeds, is to credit him too much or too little. In fact he is more thoroughly a rebel in thought than in action. He does not blink his own impiety; on the contrary, he guides his career consistently by a view of the world that is totally opposed to the one on which the traditional politics of the realm are grounded. Only when the extent of Henry's intellectual rebellion has come to light can the nature and cause of his deficiency as a new prince be perceived.

Interpretation of Henry's character is complicated by his evident prudence. Observation and his own admission inform us that he is an extremely politic man, constantly concerned with manipulating others and cultivating a public image:

> And then I stole all courtesy from heaven,
> And dress'd myself in such humility
> That I did pluck allegiance from men's hearts.
> (*1 Henry IV*, II.ii.50-52)

Unlike Richard, who makes a parade of his thoughts and feelings, Henry is a man of masks. Yet masks, too, reveal—especially when they are recognized as masks; and we shall see that Shakespeare has designed Henry's so that they point to the reality they partly hide. In one scene, moreover, near the end of Henry's life, Shakespeare allows us to see him momentarily divested of his disguises and speaking with shocking openness. Act III, scene i, of *Henry IV*, part 2, which contains Henry's only soliloquy, represents a spiritual crisis brought on by illness and the burden of a troubled reign. To his closest advisor, Warwick, Henry seems at times unbalanced during this scene, but his words provide an unusually clear insight into a mind that has discarded orthodox political ideals and has not flinched from deposing and murdering "the figure of God's majesty."

At the beginning of the scene Henry waits for Warwick and Surrey, whom he has just summoned to an impromptu midnight council, and soliloquizes on his insomnia. He wonders why he should suffer while the poor who lie in "smoky cribs" and the sailor on "the high and giddy mast" sleep soundly. "O sleep, O gentle sleep,/ Nature's soft nurse, how have I frighted thee?" (5-6), Henry asks, but finds no cause in himself. Sleep is simply a "dull god" and "partial"; it is the general lot of kings to suffer. What is striking here is that Henry does not impute his troubles to his own deeds. A more traditional mind might have invoked Carlisle's proph-

ecy at this point, but Henry has turned away from that vision. For him
there is no moral or religious significance in events; the god that governs
sleep manifests no rational pattern of cause and effect. As the scene
progresses, moreover, Henry's unorthodoxy becomes clearer. Warwick
and Surrey arrive, but instead of attending immediately to the business
at hand, Henry interrupts their advice with a long discourse upon the
nature of things:

> Oh God, that one might read the book of fate,
> And see the revolution of the times.   (45-46)

He begins by calling on God, but the account of "the revolution of the
times" that he goes on to give leaves God out entirely. Periodic cata-
clysms level mountains and dissolve coasts; the oceans themselves at times
withdraw; and Henry sees in such events not the providential hand of
God, but rather "how chance's mocks/ And changes fill the cup of alteration" (51-52). To Henry, obviously, his father's and Carlisle's views of
kingship are nothing more than pious myths. If the world is ruled by
"chance's mocks," traditional religious restraints possess no more force
than credulous minds are willing to give them.

In his present mood, however, Henry's view of the world seems more
cause for despair than confidence. He has avoided one dread—the dread
of sin—to discover another—the dread of meaninglessness as one drains
"the cup of alteration." "O, if this were seen," he laments,

> The happiest youth, viewing his progress through,
> What perils past, what crosses to ensue,
> Would shut the book and sit him down and die. (53-56)

What motive to great actions can there be in a world subject to pattern-
less change? As Henry rouses himself from depression one idea emerges
as predominant in his mind—the idea of necessity. Turning from universal disorder to the infidelity of friends, he recalls Richard's accusation of
Northumberland as the "ladder by the which/ My cousin Bolingbroke
ascends my throne," and interjects an apology—the only one he ever
offers—for his usurpation: "necessity so bow'd the state/ That I and greatness were compell'd to kiss" (70-74). And when Warwick seizes upon the
idea, urging Henry to recognize the "necessary form" in his present difficulties, he responds with vigor:

> Are these things then necessities?
> Then let us meet them like necessities;
> And that same word even now cries out on us. (92-94)

For Henry, there is a necessity that compels in spite of "chance's mocks." To learn exactly what necessity means to him and how it operates in the world he envisions we must examine his earlier career.[4]

The earliest clear indication of the necessity that Henry recognizes occurs in the first act of *Richard II*, in Henry's response to his father's efforts to persuade him to accept his banishment patiently. On the surface, Gaunt argues simply that a wise man makes the best of everything. Beneath his stoicism, however, lies his belief in the sanctity of kingship. From Gaunt's point of view, a kind of necessity obliges Henry to submit to Richard's sentence; not to submit would be a sin:

> Teach thy necessity to reason thus—
> There is no virtue like necessity. (I.iii.277-278)

Henry replies with a string of revealing rhetorical questions:

> O, who can hold a fire in his hand
> By thinking on the frosty Caucasus?
> Or cloy the hungry edge of appetite
> By bare imagination of a feast?
> Or wallow naked in December snow
> By thinking on fantastic summer's heat?
> O no, the apprehension of the good
> Gives but the greater feeling to the worse. (I.iii.294-301)

No moral dimension complicates the three examples of simple physical pain that Henry employs; in each, the only conceivable "good" consists in alleviating the pain rather than in patiently bearing it. By implying that being banished is analogous to holding fire in one's hand or suffering from hunger or wallowing naked in snow, Henry makes it clear that the only good he apprehends is the end of banishment. He reduces what his father regards as a moral issue, involving a necessity imposed by divine law, to a matter of avoiding personal pain. Gaunt's advice violates nature as Henry understands it. Gaunt assumes a world informed by divine purpose, but Henry takes his bearings by the body. Just as physical necessity compels men to avoid fire, hunger, and cold, so the psychological pain of banishment will compel Henry to end it. A great deal has been written about the motive of Henry's actual return to England, but critics have failed to perceive the importance of this speech. To those who pay attention, Henry's words are a warning that he has already determined to come home as soon as he can. His later claim "I come but for mine own" (III.iii.196) must be considered a politic lie; Northumberland's revelations immediately after the death of Gaunt (II.i.277-298) inform us that Henry has set out from Brittany even before the confiscation of his estate. Of course he wants his inheritance, but land is not what pricks him on. Not acquisitiveness but spirited self-assertion—an impulse that is strictly personal, and as compelling as the most powerful physical drive—impels Henry to violate the doctrine of kingship in which he does not believe, and to brave the mockery of chance in which he does. In a world bereft of the divine, the only necessity that obtains for a man derives either from his body's needs or from individual inclination; what but the sheer assertion of individuality leads one man to make himself king and another to "shut the book and sit him down and die"?

Obviously other possibilities exist—possibilities that lie somewhere between the violent course of usurpation and passive withdrawal from all effort—but they do not occur to Henry. Partly, of course, they do not occur to Henry because they do not occur for him. His condition precludes moderate courses. Given the necessity that brings him back illegally from banishment, he has no choice except to destroy Richard or be destroyed by him. Having defied the king, Henry can never be safe in England until he sits upon the throne himself, and until the old king lies dead. In a personal sense, at least, Henry's assertion that he and greatness "were compell'd to kiss" is true. At the same time, Shakespeare makes it clear that Henry considers the violent necessities of his own life to be not merely personal but also consistent with the design of nature as a whole. Indeed, Henry seems convinced that usurpation and regicide accord with "the revolution of the times." Logically, of course, there is no reason why "chance's mocks/ And changes" should foster usurpation and murder any more than loyalty; under fortune, nature is promiscuous, but procreative as well as abortive, constructive as well as destructive. As we have seen, however, Henry's meditation on the nature of things focuses on destruction and disorder—on the vast calamities that alter the very face of the earth. In the minds of those who hold the world to be empty of God and governed by chance or fortune, the violent and destructive side of things tends to become ascendant. Lucretius reveals this subtly, Machiavelli emphatically. Henry conforms to the pattern.[5]

At Flint Castle, for example, Henry envisions his meeting with Richard in images of elemental struggle:

> Methinks King Richard and myself should meet
> With no less terror than the elements
> Of fire and water, when the thund'ring shock
> At meeting tears the cloudy cheeks of heaven. (III.iii.54-57)

Here the violence upon which Henry bases his own career appears to reflect a universal disorder. Although he goes on to claim that in the coming confrontation he will be "the yielding water," the fact remains that Henry would not even have come to Flint Castle if he identified himself with the yielding elements. Earlier, indeed, he presented himself more frankly as a kind of natural force that might create a rain of blood:

> I'll use the advantage of my power
> And lay the summer's dust with showers of blood
> Rain'd from the wounds of slaughtered Englishmen. (III.iii.42-44)

And the image of a bloody rain recurs at the end of the play in a context that makes clear Henry's sense that one must live in accord with a violence that is essentially natural. Speaking of Richard's murder to the assembled court, Henry protests, "my soul is full of woe/ That blood should sprinkle me to make me grow" (V.vi.45-46). Whether Henry really feels sorrow or not, and if so how much, remains a matter of doubt; what cannot be doubted is that no scruple of conscience ever prevents him from pursuing the harsh course that his personal needs dictate. When he imagines himself a plant sprinkled with Richard's blood, Henry implies that Richard's murder must be seen as a necessary part of a natural process: just as a plant naturally requires rain, so Henry in the nature of things required the blood of the king whom he deposed.

In *Henry IV*, part I, nothing illustrates Henry's view of life more clearly than his praise of Hotspur. Commenting on Hotspur's victory over the Scots at Holmedon, Henry describes him as "amongst a grove the very straightest plant" and "sweet Fortune's minion and her pride" (I.i.81-82). The best man, it seems, the man most likely to prosper in Fortune's capricious eyes, is the best soldier. Like Henry himself, Hotspur lives by the needs of his own aggressive nature; and it is fully consistent with Henry's deepest convictions that his admiration increases when Hotspur's self-assertion aims at the throne. Having summoned Hal to the palace in order to rebuke him for his neglect of harsh necessity, Henry holds up the rebel Hotspur as an example of princely virtue:

> Now, by my sceptre, and my soul to boot,
> He hath more worthy interest to the state
> Than thou the shadow of succession;
> For of no right, nor colour like to right,
> He doth fill fields with harness in the realm. (III.ii.97-101)

According to Henry, who swears by his sceptre before his soul, the measure of Hotspur's worthiness for rule consists in his will and ability to take by force what he wants. In one contemptuous line, Henry dismisses the standards of legal and moral "right"; the only right he recognizes is the right established by might. "[E]ven as I was then is Percy now," he remarks, recalling his rebellion against Richard. No doubt Henry sees his own and Hotspur's careers as responsive to the same basic necessity—the need to assert oneself violently in a violent world, to use violence against others lest it be used against oneself.[6]

After Henry becomes king, of course, his admiration for men of similar virtue is necessarily restricted: his personal interests and the interests of the kingdom coincide. As exiled Henry Bolingbroke, he was fully prepared to "lay the summer's dust with showers of blood/ Rain'd from the wounds of slaughtered Englishmen"; as King Henry IV, he abhors civil strife and seeks to bring order to the land. Nevertheless, the opening speech of *Henry IV*, part I, reveals that the same views that confirmed him in rebellion now inform his scheme for restoring order. Henry comes on stage "shaken" and "wan with care," but expressing optimism. Insurrection has plagued his reign from the outset, but he perceives at last an opportunity to transform domestic enmity into a foreign war. An expedition to the Holy Land will serve Henry's turn. Ostensibly the expedition is to be a crusade. Henry describes himself as a soldier of Christ and alludes to his original intention of journeying to the Holy Land in atonement for the murder of Richard. However, close attention to Henry's words reveals the wholly political motives that lie behind his religious professions:

> No more the thirsty entrance of this soil
> Shall daub her lips with her own children's blood,
> No more shall trenching war channel her fields,
> Nor bruise her flow'rets with the armed hoofs
> Of hostile paces; those opposed eyes,
> Which, like the meteors of a troubled heaven,
> All of one nature, of one substance bred,
> Did lately meet in the intestine shock

And furious close of civil butchery,
Shall now, in mutual well-beseeming ranks,
March all one way, and be no more opposed
Against acquaintance, kindred, and allies.
The edge of war, like an ill-sheathed knife,
No more shall cut his master. (I.i.5-18)

That Henry considers war abroad a proper preventive for war at home illustrates his conviction that violent courses conform to nature and are more likely to win the favors of Fortune. His imagery suggests that bloodshed is inevitable. The very earth thirsts for her children's blood, and if "this soil"—England—is to be denied what it longs for, the result will be an abundance for the soil of foreign lands. Men resemble meteors, conventional symbols of cosmic disorder; "all of one nature, of one substance bred," they nevertheless—or therefore—butcher each other. Civil war is an "ill-sheathed knife," but the obvious remedy of sheathing the knife correctly never arises; the only possible course, it seems, is to draw the knife completely and employ it on others. Later, Henry claims that his subjects "were moulded in their mothers' womb/ To chase those pagans in those holy fields" (I.i.23-24). Men were born to fight; they carry from the womb an impulse to destroy. Just as Henry does not try to restrain that impulse in himself, his political program aims not at restraining his subjects but rather at channeling their violence outward toward foreigners. Peace is not his goal but rather a "well-beseeming" foreign war which will remove the destruction from England, and from Henry himself.

This political reading of the motives behind Henry's crusade is confirmed in *Henry IV*, part 2, during the king's final interview with Hal. There Henry analyzes his difficulties with the unruly noblemen of the realm who first helped him and now oppose him, and explains the policy by which he sought to check them:

I cut them off, and had a purpose now
To lead out many to the Holy Land,
Lest rest and lying still might make them look
Too near unto my state. (IV.v.209-212)

According to Henry, Hal too must find a way "to busy giddy minds/ With foreign quarrels." Of all Henry's references to a crusade, this one stands out as providing the most trustworthy account of his aims. Whereas earlier—in the presence of the court both at the end of *Richard II* and at the beginning of *Henry IV*, part I—public consideration precluded frankness, nothing inhibits him here. He knows that he is on his deathbed, and he has no object beyond offering his political wisdom to his heir. The lesson that he conveys has nothing to do with religious atonement or any other sacred duty. He wants to teach Hal how to save his throne, not his soul. Although Henry mentions the "indirect crook'd ways" by which he obtained the crown (*2 Henry IV*, IV.v.183-185), and concludes with a nod toward the traditional doctrine of kingship—"How I came by the crown, O God forgive" (IV.v.218)—the rest of his long speech expresses no guilt. On the contrary, most of what Henry say amounts to a recommendation of his "indirect crook'd ways," and makes clear his opinion that success in politics depends upon them. One must grasp the potential for violence in things and wield it to one's own advantage. Even one's "friends" have "strings and teeth" (IV.v.204-205).

Occasionally, as in these last words of counsel to Hal, Henry's religious expressions seem merely perfunctory or ironic; characteristically, however, as in his proclamations of a crusade, he appeals to religion for obvious political reasons.[7] Having established his rule by force, Henry apparently hopes to render it more secure by arrogating to himself the religious awe of a traditional monarchy like Richard's. The crusade is the main device by which Henry attempts to throw a veil of piety over his deeds, but he is careful to identify his kingship with convention from the very moment of his accession. In order to maintain the illusion of an unbroken succession, he does his best to present Richard's deposition as an abdication; and when York arrives to announce that Richard has agreed to step down, Henry promptly announces, "In God's name, I'll ascend the regal throne" (*Richard II*, IV.i.113). Carlisle revolts at this brazenness and rebukes it; most of the court, however, seems prepared to accept, at least initially, Henry's assumption of divine favor along with the crown. York makes an extravagant show of loyalty in denouncing his own son's plot against Henry; and after Henry, yielding to the Duchess of York's pleas, pardons Aumerle, the Duchess thanks him with a phrase that seems to acknowledge his legitimacy in traditional terms: "A god on earth thou art" (V.iii.134).

Even before the end of *Richard II*, however, it becomes clear that Henry's efforts to make himself a sacred king in the old style cannot succeed. In spite of his follies and delusions, Richard's claim to be a kind of "god on earth" commands the loyalty of respectable men like Gaunt and Carlisle; Henry will never enjoy such dignity. The kingdom he has seized rises in arms against itself:

the latest news we hear,
Is that the rebels have consum'd with fire
Our town of Ciceter in Gloucestershire. (V.vi.1-3)

His son and heir defies him. Contemptuous of his father's authority, Hal plays at robbery and beats the king's watch. Upon being informed of the royal "triumphs" to be held at Oxford, he is said to have promised to appear wearing the "favour" of a prostitute. And these are but the portents of worse disorders. As many critics have pointed out, the *Henry IV* plays anatomize a kingdom split into factions, each seeking its particular ends and lacking the common bond of loyalty that shapes a regime: "this house is turned upside down since Robin Ostler died" (*1 Henry IV*, II.i.9-10), remarks the Second Carrier, unwittingly turning a wretched inn into a symbol for the realm. Falstaff's cynical comment on Justice Shallow—"If the young dace be a bait for the old pike, I see no reason in the law of nature but I may snap at him" (*2 Henry IV*, III.ii.325-326)—expresses the ethos that, through Henry's example, has contaminated the land. Under the circumstances, even the religious values that Henry tries to appropriate in his rhetoric turn against him. Appealing to "the blood/ Of fair King Richard, scrap'd from Pomfret stones," deriving "from heaven his quarrel and his cause," the Archbishop of York "[t]urns insurrection to religion" (*2 Henry IV*, I.i.201-206). Rebellion engenders rebellion; the awe that protected Richard cannot protect his murderer.

Henry's effort to usurp the traditional sanctity of the throne along with the throne itself lays bare the fundamental defect of his policy. According to Machiavelli, a new prince in a new regime must make everything new; he must have the wisdom, skill, and courage to introduce an entirely new order that will obliterate even the memory of the old one. Left intact, or only impaired, the old order will return to haunt him. It furnishes a ready pretext and provocation to rebellion.[8] The truth of this teaching comes home to Henry with a vengeance. By attempting to resurrect in himself the principles of the old regime, by failing to exorcise Richard's ghost, Henry renders his usurpation abortive: he dooms himself to unceasing struggle, and afflicts both his dynasty and his kingdom. He and his direct heirs survive only by repeating his original violence over and over—first in England, then in France, then in England again. Both Henry and Hal spill blood continually and with considerable success; the reign of Henry VI, however, reveals the precariousness of their achievement. When the sword fails, the dynasty falls. As Shakespeare's contemporaries were aware, and as his earlier tetralogy of English history plays had already indicated, peace and stability return to the land only when the founder of a new dynasty—Henry VII, first of the Tudors—is able to revive the claims of traditional legitimacy and present himself plausibly as God's deputy on earth.[9]

Ironically, it is the revolutionary boldness of Henry's thought that betrays him in the end. Having thrust him on to regicide, his radically new vision of the nature of things fails to provide him with the ground on which to create a new regime. He recognizes that stable political rule cannot be based on force and cunning alone, yet his view of life as essentially egotistical, violent, and governed by chance offers no principle of order that can replace the divine right that surrounded earlier English kings. A doctrine of individualism and violent necessity has no power to bind men together. As a result Henry is forced outside the characteristic range of his mind, and this necessity confounds him. He possesses one part of what is needful in a new prince in a new principality—an understanding of, and ability to use, violence—but he wants an even more important part—the creative qualities of a founder who is both armed and a prophet. The personal sense of necessity that drives him to make himself king finally traps him in the narrowness and harshness of his vision. Henry proves incapable of the extraordinary *virtù* attributed by Machiavelli to a Moses or a Theseus; we may consider him a type of Cain, but not of Romulus.[10]

England and Henry suffer for his sins, but they are not the sins of which Carlisle thought. Shakespeare's dramatization of Henry's career focuses not on the unfolding of God's judgment, but rather on the strictly political consequences of a usurpation only half achieved.[11] By the light of Shakespeare's analysis, we perceive that Henry misses the greatness that alone could redeem the heinous crimes of usurpation and regicide. He remains a usurper rather than a founder. It is to this deficiency, above all, that his drabness points.

Notes

1. Machiavelli defines the kinds of principalities in the first chapter of *The Prince*: "Principalities are either hereditary, in which case the family of the prince has been ruling for generations, or they are new. And the new ones are either completely new, as was Milan for Francesco Sforza, or they are like members joined to the hereditary state of the prince who acquires them, as is the kingdom of Naples for the King of Spain" (trans. Mark Musa [New York: St. Martin's Press, 1964], p. 5).
2. *Richard II*, I.ii.37-38. Act, scene, and line references are to the Arden editions of *Richard II*, ed. Peter Ure (Cambridge, Mass.: Harvard Univer-

sity Press, 1956), of *The First Part of King Henry IV*, ed. A.R. Humphreys (London: Methuen, 1961), and of *The Second Part of King Henry IV* (London: Methuen, 1966).

3. For expressions of the prevailing view that Henry is basically an opportunist, see John Palmer, *Political Characters of Shakespeare* (London: Macmillan, 1948) pp. 135-138; Brents Stirling, "Bolingbroke's 'Decision'," *Shakespeare Quarterly* 2 (1951), pp. 27-34; Ure's Introduction to *Richard II*, pp. lxxiv-lxxv; A.L. French, "Who Deposed Richard II?" *Essays in Criticism* 17 (1967), 411-433; and Robert Ornstein, *A Kingdom for a Stage* (Cambridge: Harvard University Press, 1972), pp. 114-116.

4. The importance of Henry's idea of necessity has been recognized but never adequately studied: see, for example, Harold C. Goddard, *The Meaning of Shakespeare* (Chicago: University of Chicago Press, 1951), p. 162; Humphreys' note on III.i.72-74 in *The Second Part of King Henry IV*; and John C. Bromley, *The Shakespearean Kings* (Boulder: Colorado Associated University Press, 1971), p. 71. For more general remarks on the theme of necessity in the second tetralogy, see Humphreys' Introduction to *The Second Part of King Henry IV*, pp. xlv-xlvi; and Derek Traversi, *Shakespeare: From Richard II to Henry V* (Stanford: Stanford University Press, 1957), pp. 135-136.

5. On Lucretius, see Leo Strauss, "Notes on Lucretius," in *Liberalism Ancient and Modern* (New York: Basic Books, 1968), pp. 76-139 (esp. pp. 76-85, 133-135). For other examples of Machiavelli's usefulness in analyzing Henry's career, see Irving Ribner, "Bolingbroke, A True Machiavellian," *Modern Language Quarterly* 9 (1948), pp. 177-184; John F. Danby, *Shakespeare's Doctrine of Nature* (London: Faber and Faber, 1949), pp. 81-101; and Moody Prior, *The Drama of Power* (Evanston, Ill.: Northwestern University Press, 1973), pp. 219-248.

6. Near the end of *Henry IV,* part I, it is true, Henry upbraids Worcester in terms that suggest a rather different view of man and nature:

> Will you again unknit
> This churlish knot of all-abhorred war?
> And move in that obedient orb again
> Where you did give a fair and natural light,
> And be no more an exhal'd meteor,
> A prodigy of fear, and a portent
> Of broached mischief to the unborn times? (V.i.15-21)

Contrary to Henry's praise of Hotspur, these lines imply that peace and obedience rather than war and rebellion are natural, but we must understand them in the light of the dramatic situation. Talking to Worcester, Henry has an obvious reason to stress the virtue of obedience, but there is no evidence that it is part of his private morality. Although he condemns Worcester for being a "meteor," earlier Henry compared himself complacently to a "comet" (III.ii.46-49).

7. Some critics have contended that Henry's expressions of guilt are sincere; see, for example, John Dover Wilson's note on I.i.1-28 in *The First Part of the History of Henry IV* (Cambridge: Cambridge University Press, 1946); Traversi, *Shakespeare: From Richard II to Henry V*, pp. 48, 51, 81; and M.M. Reese, *The Cease of Majesty* (New York: St. Martin's Press, 1961), p. 286. Such a view seems to me incompatible with everything else that Shakespeare shows us about Henry. If Henry's religion is sincere, it never restrains his political actions in any way.

8. See *The Prince*, chapter 6.

9. See Shakespeare's presentation of Henry VII throughout the last act of *Richard III* (especially scenes ii, iii, and v).

10. See *The Prince*, chapter 6. Henry's final speech in *Richard II* suggests the analogy between himself and Cain (V.vi.43-50). He condemns Exton as a kind of Cain, but recognizes his own guilt as well.

11. Cf. Machiavelli's comment on "the present ruin of Italy": "And he [Savonarola] who said that our sins were the cause, said the truth; but they certainly were not the sins he thought, but rather the ones I have just recounted [military and political failures]; and since these were the sins of princes, they have come in turn to suffer the penalty for them" (Trans. Mark Musa, p. 101). That Shakespeare's second tetralogy departs from the moralized religious view of history favored by some of the Tudor chroniclers seems generally accepted by recent critics: see, for example, Alvin B. Kernan, "The Henriad: Shakespeare's Major History Plays," in *Modern Shakespearean Criticism*, ed. Alvin B. Kernan (New York: Harcourt, Brace, and World, 1970), pp. 245-275; and Moody Prior, *The Drama of Power*, pp. 14-33.

SPECTACLE SUPPLANTING CEREMONY: SHAKESPEARE'S HENRY MONMOUTH

John E. Alvis

The extended scope of Shakespeare's histories calls to mind ancient and Tudor biographies of princes, works such as Xenophon's *Cyropaedia*, Plutarch's *Lives*, or Bacon's *Henry VII*. Unlike the heroes of the tragedies and comedies, the central figures of the histories—Henry Bolingbroke, Henry Monmouth, Richard of Gloucester—are known through a career rather than a revelatory crisis. The greater amplitude of the histories allows the portrayal of a character's development from youth to maturity. Their leisure permits such vast growths by vegetable gradations as the terrific empire of Falstaff's belly, which once would have fit, if we are to trust his recollection, into an alderman's ring. The tetralogy form can also accommodate the gradual unfolding of a political project from its moments of conception, through stages of adjustment and revision, to completion and valedictory flourish. That we may appreciate the daring and momentous project espoused by Henry Monmouth, Shakespeare allows us to see how the goal he reaches in the last play of his tetralogy is conceived in the first. We might characterize Henry's purpose as the depreciation of traditional ceremony in favor of innovative spectacles.

The young prince makes his first appearance in connection with that particular ceremony which brackets the deposition of England's most ceremonious king. *Richard II* begins and ends with elaborate formal jousting. Bolingbroke's abortive joust with Mowbray at the beginning leads to the overthrow of a king who has placed his trust in received beliefs proclaiming the inviolability of his office. At the conclusion, the tourney of Oxford in honor of Henry IV's coronation represents one in a series of efforts by Bolingbroke to reestablish respect for the monarchy after hav-

ing all but destroyed the traditional basis of respect by deposing a legitimate king. Once he has assured himself of adequate power, the new king
devotes himself to good words and the cultivation of an awe-inspiring
decorum. He is now concerned to promote lawful forms and conserva-
tive custom. By contrast, his son's early concerns seem to be illegal and
studiously unconventional. Hal embarrasses his father by frequenting
taverns and by associating with outlaws who, under his protection, beat
the king's officers and rob travellers. To add to Bolingbroke's chagrin,
Hotspur relates a conversation that introduces a note of self-conscious
calculation on Hal's part, a note which will become throughout the plays
the unmistakable Monmouth leitmotif. When he had told Hal of the coronation tourney, the young prince had replied that he intended to pluck a
glove from the commonest whore in the brothels, and, wearing that as
his favor, unhorse any challenger. Hal's boast looks forward to the climax
of his career when he will again wear a glove for his chivalric favor and
answer a challenge to it. The glove by which Harry reveals his identity to
Williams at the end of *Henry* V is intended to demonstrate his responsibility and magnanimity. This early reference to heraldic favors also anticipates the midpoint of the career when Hal will make use of another
prop of chivalric ceremony. He will place the plumes betokening his station as Prince of Wales upon the face of the vanquished Hotspur. A first
impression may be that the sequence of the three favors lends support to
the widely held view that Hal progresses from rakish prodigal to courteous and responsible king. However, a closer inspection of the four plays
which develop Henry's career reveals another principle of continuity in
Hal's life causes one to doubt his sense of responsibility, and suggests a
more austere interpretation of the use he makes of the old customs of
courtesy and ceremony.

The second most famous speech of the final play helps us understand why the early Hal presents himself as a breaker of customs. On the
eve of Agincourt the mature Henry V compares the lot of a king with the
estate of a commoner and concludes that the commoner should be happier than the king. His reasons amount to a preference for otiose safety
over stately perturbation. The commoner feeds and sleeps more tran-
quilly than the king. The royal mind is vexed by responsibilities, while
the man of low estate enjoys the rest of an existence unencumbered by
the duties of high office. Henry thus rehearses to himself several of the
arguments addressed against tyranny by authors dating from antiquity,
most notably, perhaps, those recorded by Xenophon in his dialogue *Hiero*.[1]
The difference between Henry's soliloquy and the classical anti-tyranni-

cal writings is that Henry considers his case applicable indifferently to tyrants and just kings alike. His expansion of the case suggests a deliberate and significant transformation of the classical argument. Whatever its claims to truth, the belief that the lot of the tyrant suffers by comparison with the commoner is politically beneficial. The tyrant desires that which the plain man desires, only more, and will practice injustice to secure more pleasure, more freedom, more wealth. Therefore, it would be salutary to induce the tyrant to believe that by seeking more, he enjoys less. But applied to kings the same argument has an obvious answer. Decent kings, unlike tyrants, may willingly accept their polished perturbation because they identify their end with justice. The good king loves justice and willingly works to promote the public good. This, however, is not Harry's answer, nor does it ever occur to him that justice may be a sufficient recompense for the burdens of statecraft. Harry's idea of royal perquisites turns on the word *ceremony*. To balance his debit of broken feasts and intermittent sleep, the king, he says, has only ceremony; and ceremony, in his opinion, affords inadequate compensation. He complains that the formalities of royal office produce no rent or other income and that they cannot mend broken bones. Moreover, the formalities associated with royalty prevent friendship. The awesome customs that surround monarchs make men fear rather than love their kings, and the ruler is less happy being feared than the men who fear him. Finally, ceremony extorts a formal homage which Hal equates with "poisoned flattery."[2]

Although in the soliloquy Henry fails to say what considerations make it worthwhile to wear the hollow crown, his most famous speech seems to provide an answer with its celebration of honor. The St. Crispian's Day oration succinctly defines the love which moves the king. Only honor can make good the defects of ceremony. Wars fought for the sake of honor produce the income which ceremony cannot provide and, more important for the man who values the love of other men, devotion to honor can restore the amity which formalities undermine. Unlike cold ceremony, honor strengthens friendship. Men who unite against a common enemy in a mutual pursuit of distinction become thereby a warm "band of brothers." They forget the fear of the king bred by stiff rituals of court while they come to share in the most intimate lifeblood of the kingly person. Loving what the king loves and venturing their lives for that for which the king risks his life, they become one with him in a way that no servile subject can know. To the bonds of comradeship based on mutual usefulness Hal adds the self-forgetting ardor that comes from the desire to possess a useless but surprisingly beautiful thing. The most decisive respect in which honor surpasses ceremony has to do with the purity of the praise which singular actions can excite. The homage men render the kingly office Henry calls mere flattery, a form of praise which he finds insipid. Yet he does not traduce himself when he says in the St. Crispian's speech that "if it be a sin to covet honor" he is "the most offending soul alive" (IV.iii.28-39). Henry desires praise for his deeds rather than the tributes rendered Caesar merely because his image appears on the coin. Deeds resist that adulteration of praise concomitant with office and routine accolades. One can commend the official king for qualities he does not possess, but one cannot deny him the deeds he has established in the public eye—provided, that is, that the deeds be spectacular and therefore memorable. Spectacle is the indispensable ingredient in the production of the kind of deed for which Henry desires to be honored. Spectacle ventilates the stale air of ceremony. By means of carefully prepared spectacles, Henry brings to public sight the distinction between what he is as merely hereditary king and what he is as Henry Monmouth. His career is devoted to making this distinction as sharp as it can possibly be drawn. He succeeds because he knows that the most arresting spectacles are those which dramatically overturn expectations. While he wastes time in the Boar's Head tavern or at Gad's Hill, he is constantly arranging little shows. These pastimes are a trivial version of grander spectacles enacted at Shrewsbury, on the parade route of the coronation, and in France. What all his spectacles have in common is an effect of self-display and surprise. Hal knows how to arouse wonder by springing surprises, and he also knows that to sustain a constant wonder one must overcome the diminishing return on surprises. Each successive spectacle must demonstrably surpass its antecedent on a scale of wondrousness which ranges from the interest provoked by breaking customs, to the astonishment called forth by a sudden conversion of character, to the stupefaction earned by a miracle. Henry's career ascends this scale.

By wearing a whore's glove to a tournament, Henry makes a statement and offers a proof. His statement is a repudiation of the conventional and ceremonial basis of feudal kingship and thus comports with one part of the drift of the action in *Richard II*. The play itself breaks images from the beginning since it opens with a ceremony that fails. The formal joust, like the kingship itself and the entire social order it supports, depends upon a willing suspension of disbelief which makes possible the acceptance of two useful but fragile conventions. The first of these conventions holds that the king shall be the unquestioned umpire

of the combat. The second presumes upon divine justice. Jousting becomes a sacred ordeal when all consent to the proposition that God decides the conflict in favor of the just cause. Bolingbroke and Mowbray
pronounce elaborate oaths attesting to their acceptance of these opinions. The medieval conventions manifestly derive their sustenance from
lovely words and superabundant speeches. By his iconoclastic bravado in
degrading his father's coronation tournament Hal announces his understanding that the old ceremony has lost credit. With his whore's favor he
proclaims his intentions to act on that knowledge. He will assert a new
standard of decorum by demonstrating that it is not the token which
counts, but rather the man who gives worth to the sign by lending it his
own worth. His strategy resembles calculated quixotism. Don Quixote
forces men to acknowledge the drudge he mistakes for a noble lady; Hal
will force men to bow before a word he knows to be false. He will state
his view of the arbitrariness of tokens, then prove it on the body of anyone who thinks otherwise. The gesture gives notice to the world that the
next king will be a maker of custom rather than its creature. His claim
upon men's allegiance will owe less to his being the son of Henry IV than
to his having proved the apt pupil of that courteous usurper, who has
demonstrated that power resides in strong arms rather than in the ceremony of legitimacy. Hal's first public act is thus at once a spectacular
repudiation of Richard's dependence upon words as well as a demonstration that whatever words *he* may pronounce, he possesses the power to
make them good.

To promote the next spectacle of his career Harry enlarges his audience, refines this method by learning the use of foils, and coordinates his
efforts by reference to a guiding political purpose. Like Julius Caesar,
and by means not altogether different from the means of Caesar, Hal
bypasses the great men to found his power first on the affections of the
people.[3] He professes to the vulgar sort that the king-apparent is a man
like them in all things, including sin.

In the first soliloquy of *1 Henry IV* Hal explains to himself and to the
audience his reasons for associating with Falstaff and his crew of robbers
and wine-bibers. He says he will in this way imitate the sun, which allows
its light to be obscured by clouds only to shine forth more resplendently
when it finally breaks cover. The unclouded sun bores and satiates by
dispensing too much of a good thing. Its predictable splendor allows it to
be taken for granted, and what can be taken for granted, no matter how
splendid in its own right, can be contemned. As Hal remarks of holidays,
"Nothing pleaseth but rare accidents" (I.ii.195), a fitting corollary to his

father's condemnation of Richard's constant clear day accessibility, of which Bolingbroke says "more than a little is by much too much" (III.ii.73). Hal will use his present life to prepare for a pleasing rare accident. His greatness will be more spectacular if his keeps its origins obscure, then lets it blaze forth suddenly when it is most despaired of.

Ceremony depends on the unvarying repetition of acts and words, acts which follow a time-worn rubric, instance the formal joust, words which adhere to a time honored rhetorical code, instance the royal analogy of king to sun. Richard dotes on the solar analogy; Bolingbroke applies it to Richard on at least one notable occasion;[4] and both Richard and Bolingbroke employ the figure conventionally. Their conventional rhetoric is classically pure and forthright, allowing the sun, and hence the king, only the one activity of proudly shining forth. Hal's simile is manneristic: it plays off against classical expectations by introducing tortured and fanciful variations upon a well-known figure. His sun is cunningly coy, busies itself with stage effects, and makes use of the darkness which had been for Richard and Bolingbroke the natural enemy of light. Hal's sun needs a touch of the night for a proper foil.

Various explanations of Hal's Eastcheap vagaries have sought documentation in this first soliloquy. Critics have found reassurance in it: we should not fear for England because the soliloquy tells us early on that England's prince is no thief.[5] Or it has been suggested that Hal's evident distaste for his present companions compels us to postulate for his benefit some worthy reasons of state. Hal wants to learn firsthand the ways of his people so that he may rule them better when he enters upon his office;[6] or he uses the Eastcheap holiday to give scope to a healthy warmth which contrasts him favorably with the cold Bolingbroke, the too hot Hotspur, and the falsely warm Falstaff.[7] Whatever plausible appeal there may be in such explanations, Hal cites none of them. When he takes counsel with himself he offers a different reason which he states with tolerable clarity when he says, first, that he wants to be "more wondered at" (189) and when, twelve lines later, he sums up the result he desires from his impersonation of a prodigal rake:

> My reformation, glitt'ring o'er my fault,
> Shall show more goodly and attract more eyes
> Than that which hath no foil to set it off. (201-203)

Hal pretends to be dissolute so that he may attract eyes bedazzled with wonder. He desires acclaim, more precisely spectacular acclaim, and he will contrive a reputation for ignoble dissipation so that when he shows his true nobility it will make a better show. He does not move from ambition for glory to the practice of virtue, since he believes he already possesses virtue, but rather he chooses to put virtue in the service of glory. He will exercise his virtue only when to do so will most redound to his glory.[8]

Political teachers from Xenophon to Machiavelli and Elyot recommend for the king or potential king useful pastimes among which hunting rates particularly high as a sport that prepares rulers for their serious duties. Since hunting parks may become battlefields, it behooves the prince to learn in his idle times the ground he may some day defend. Tricksterism is Hal's improvement upon the traditional royal sport. His various acts of deception make light of his ceremonial position as Prince of Wales and undermine the official respect which hedges the king himself. Through his jests Hal portrays himself lord of the gallows, tyrant of barboys, arbiter of thieves, and chief justice of the brothels. His self-irony shows how much prestige of a merely ceremonial sort he believes he can afford to give up. Having established a reputation for dissipation—his equivalent of the earlier whore's glove—Hal takes his unlikely favors to Shrewsbury. There the self-revelation he produces to manifest his reformation brings to light his extraordinary dramatic talents and indicates that when he must he can extemporize as effectively as he plots.

Hal's second use of a chivalric token when compared with the first of the whore's glove evidences a refinement of taste. He delivers a gracious farewell speech to his fallen rival wherein he expresses the hope that Hotspur's honors may mount to heaven while his shame sleeps in the grave. To honor him and to cover his shame Hal places his official plumes upon the mangled face of the dead rebel. The gesture is touching and delicate in contrast with the contemptuous obsequy he proceeds to make for Falstaff, who lies beside Percy pretending to be dead. Harry's true friend is not Falstaff but Hotspur. Living or dead, the young Percy elicits from Hal the same reverence and love which a Coriolanus feels for an Aufidius, the warm esteem any man of honor feels for another. Hotspur was almost Hal's equal, and he *was* equal in the intensity of his devotion to honor.

Hotspur falls short of the prince not in the purity of his attachment to honor but in the mindlessness of his pursuit. His kinsmen know that his mind is filled with high-colored figures which cause him to neglect, as Worcester says, "the form of what he should attend" (I.iii.210). He has just lost his own life and the lives of his followers because he could not bear momentary shame for the sake of a greater future honor. In other words, Hotspur cannot do what Hal has done throughout the play. Hal does not lose his head for anything, not even for honor. That he can keep several ends simultaneously in view is most evident in the moment of his conquest, for just as Hal's desire for honor proves compatible with magnanimous courtesy toward his rival, so his genuine admiration for Hotspur accords with his earlier boasted aim (III.ii.147-151) of using the rival as an agent to bring himself greater glory. One can see a further meaning in the bestowal of the plumes besides the indisputable courtesy. By marking his corpse with the official insignia unique to the crown prince, Hal makes Hotspur his own and thereby claims his proper honor while he continues to pursue other rebels. On this occasion the trappings of ceremony enable Harry to extemporize a signature attesting his singular deed.

The handsome lie in favor of Falstaff provides another example of quick and effective invention. Falstaff, self-resurrected, carries on his back Hotspur's corpse, and threatens, therefore, to bear away a large part of the reason for which Hal has furthered his career of carefully planned notoriety. Hal must now choose either silently to accept Falstaff's lie (forfeiting public honors while contenting himself with a private knowledge of the truth) or to expose Falstaff's deception and thereby retrieve his threatened fame. He manages to do both. In the presence of his brother John of Lancaster, the best possible witness, he first corrects Falstaff and proclaims himself the vanquisher of Hotspur (V.iv.141). Then, still in John's hearing, Hal says to Falstaff:

> For my part, if a lie may do thee grace,
> I'll gild it with the happiest terms I have. (153-154)

Hal turns the dilemma to his advantage and matches, or surpasses, the skill of his father in constructing spectacles extemporaneously. He insures that he will crop a garland of honors from Percy's head as he had earlier vowed to do (71-72), while at the same time seeding the ground for an even more glorious reputation. He can count on John Falstaff to keep Shrewsbury in the public eye by claiming credit for killing Hotspur, and he can count upon John of Lancaster to correct Falstaff for Hal's doubt benefit. Hal will be known not only as the vanquisher of Hotspur but as the man who could afford to treat casually so great a victory. Greater glory has no man than to appear to lay down his glory for his friend.

The day of self-revelation at Shrewsbury thus concludes with a display of two estimable Italian virtues. By conquering Percy, Harry demonstrates his *virtu*, the manly vigor Machiavelli will praise as the enabling power behind all deeds which earn worldly beatitude. By promising to lie for Falstaff he exhibits *sprezzatura*, the quality of magnanimous casualness which Castiglione's Ludovico will recommend as the finishing accomplishment of the public man.[9] These are the sort of virtues which can be credited to Henry Monmouth only in his uniqueness as an individual personality. They are decidedly not qualities kings possess by mere prerogative—they do not come with the position and cannot be acquired through inheritance. Martial prowess and a noble carelessness are Henry's proofs against ceremony, qualities for the better display of which he has undermined his own and his father's official position.

One may feel that Henry's ambition causes him to ignore the importance of official usages to the general good. Ceremony, like hypocrisy, pays tribute to virtue. Even when they mask weakness, insincerity, and injustice, ceremonious observances oblige men to acknowledge publicly standards of conduct that promote public decency, however often these standards may be violated. The warrior who proves his prowess under the aegis of the whore's glove proves it indeed, but at the expense of conventions which his countrymen may ill afford to lose. Hal's country has just witnessed a change of rule which many of its citizens interpret as a palpable demonstration that legal right has given way to force. Such lessons can be salutary if they promote a resolve to strengthen right. But obviously they can also teach a disheartening cynicism and servile acquiescence to demonstrable might. England stands to lose the cutting edge of its devotion to moral right. The official rhetoric mocked by Hal hones that devotion by encouraging public acknowledgment of a conviction that power is only as honorable as the cause it serves. According to Yeats, ceremony can protect a healthy innocence. It can also foster sensitivity to justice. Especially in a monarchy, where the conduct of one man offers a pattern for every subject, the strict observance of the rituals of office can mitigate the ruler's unhappy personal defects and contribute to the strengthening of national character. If the king be a ceremonious scoundrel he damns himself but not the standards taught by the usages he has abused. England's chivalrous, religious, and monarchical conventions exist for the sake of regulating rather than liberating the will of the sovereign. They exist for the sake of the realm and benefit the country rather than the king personally. Hal depreciates ceremony because he rightly doubts its personal benefit, yet therein, we may suspect, he fails to grasp the point of the relation of these conventions to justice.

Many readers of the Henry plays appear to share Hal's opinion that his irregularities cannot be damaging because they are not real.[10] Everyone remarks the diseased state of the kingdom in the two plays, but, to my knowledge, no critic has seen the extent to which England's heir contributes to her troubles. His truancy in Eastcheap encourages a general lawlessness among men who miss his discrimination between robbing in play and robbing in earnest. From its center at the Boar's Head the thieving spirit extends out to Robin Ostler's tavern in the suburbs where Gadshill assures some carriers he robs by royal patent, protected, as he says, by nobility who "prey" on the commonwealth. Falstaff carries the disease to the countryside where he picks up recruits on the way to Shrewsbury and Gaultree Forest. Besides the open thievery, England suffers from a diminished sense of public spiritedness. Judging from the timidity expressed by the recruits, the common people can no longer be aroused to patriotism. Of all the commoners who appear in the plays, only the tailor Feeble speaks his willingness to serve in the king's wars (III.ii.220-225). The populace follows most of the nobility in looking out for itself at the expense of the commonwealth. Like Gadshill the commoners can claim a sanction for their pettiness in the example of the prince. The first cause of the decline of public spirit is Bolingbroke, whose usurpation of the crown can be cited (as it is by Falstaff) as a warrant for self-seeking on every hand. The second cause is Hal, who refuses to shore up law and ceremony to stay the confusion, but instead spreads unease by allowing, or even promoting, expectation of an indefinitely protracted period of self-seeking from the throne. Whatever their diverse private motives, the rebels agree that rebellion is both feasible and necessary. Hal's apparent dissoluteness encourages these dangerous opinions. The appearance of a rift in the royal household heartens the rebels, whereas the reality of the division distracts the king's mind from his duties and further weakens the center. Hal's plan to attract more eyes gives aid and comfort to the enemy. He suffers no immediate harm thereby, but the country does, for, although he can cast off the look of a thief and libertine whenever he chooses to do so, he does not acknowledge the extent to which his false appearance of viciousness promotes real vice in the realm. Nor does he consider whether the habits of self-indulgence he now countenances can be similarly cast off by his countrymen once he has chosen to reveal his true self.

We may also come to doubt the reliability of that true self upon which Harry sets his confidence. In preference to the traditional preparation for kingship, he educates himself in the art of evoking wonder and in the process acquires a certain craving for the delights of self-display, an inclination which appears to harden into a dependency. This habit cannot be set aside as easily as the false habits of dissoluteness. It threatens to usurp his character, crowding out more politically salutary concerns. Most especially, it threatens to breed in the prince a coarse and dangerously shallow misconception of justice. Hal's attack on ceremony appears to proceed from an understanding of justice which is personal or individualistic rather than properly political. For him justice is a matter of a personal, or even an hermetic, rectitude before the law. He does not conceive a standard of conduct which would subordinate all his actions, public or private, to the good of England. Indeed, the very distinction of public or private is in this case questionable. Whatever the young prince does must have an effect upon the present or future welfare of his country. Hal appears so to expand a true distinction between ceremony and natural right that it becomes a false distinction of public from private.

At the conclusion of 2 *Henry IV*, Hal opens a subject he has not touched before. He now acknowledges the king's debt to a divine overseer. Hal has scarcely mentioned the name of God before, but from this moment on he will not fail to invoke the Deity in his public speeches. He will call upon God to witness the justice of his rebuke to Falstaff and thereafter will invoke divine supervision upon every important occasion during his reign. Hal speaks God's name more frequently that any other Shakespearean character. He replaces the counsel of the Lord Chief Justice with that of two archbishops partly because he desires the highest authority to sanction his intents. His introduction of God at this point signals the beginning of the final phase of his career, a phase guided and characterized by his transformation of traditional beliefs into a new kind of political theology.[11]

Richard II thinks he can wager temporal contingencies against God's supervening government. The providence he trusts lies somewhere between the two forms of divine ordinance which theologians distinguish as the "general" and the "special." By His general providence God is believed to uphold natural cosmic processes regulating the rhythms of the heavens and the sublunary elements. Particular interventions in human affairs are attributed to a *special* divine providence. Richard looks to a God who should make His will apparent in highly particular human events—Richard's contest with Bolingbroke, for instance—yet a God who should intervene with the dependable regularity of general cosmic laws. Richard's expectations have a certain reasonableness inasmuch as the king's position requires a combination of the particular with the general. The monarch exists somewhere between the highly contingent particular human being and the enduring and universal sun. Richard trusts God will provide not for Richard Plantagenet but for the king who happens to be Richard Plantagenet. God's care for kings should imitate His governance of the planetary bodies, since His interest in safeguarding the order of society should at least equal His concern to preserve the heavens. Richard thus connects divine favor with the royal office, making it a part of the general ceremony to which he refers everything.

Henry Monmouth lays claim to a different kind of providence which has a more particular object. Consistent with the personalism he displays in the earlier phases of his career, he now makes the issue one of personal favor. The question of divine support is no longer resolved by appeal to the office but by appeal to the man who holds the office. God will favor Henry not because he is king but because he is Henry. God will uphold his good conscience and his just cause in the war against France. We may say that while depreciating the older emphasis upon a general, cosmic providence, Henry puts forward the claim to be privy to God's special providence. He constantly reminds the world that he has challenged God to prove him correct, and he constantly adduces compelling evidence that God has signaled His approval. The most Richard could have demonstrated would have been that he was a legitimate king, whereas Henry seeks to establish that, like the biblical David, he enjoys God's personal friendship. Henry does something other than create a civil religion. England already has something rather close to a civil religion in *Richard II*. It could be argued that by making war against another Christian state in the name of their common God he forces a discrimination between Christendom and English Christianity and thereby makes England's civil religion more emphatically civil. It is more certain that Henry transforms a ceremonial creed to his own personal use. The gain in power is doubtful since Henry, like Richard, can demonstrate only so much divine favor as he can translate into force of arms. But the gain in strictly personal credit is considerable.

Henry arranges the test of his claim upon divine approval by making another raid on ceremony. With his exchange of taunts with the Dauphin, his formal statement of the indictment at law, his challenge to combat, oath of innocence, and final appeal to God, he resurrects in a novel form the medieval joust. Ordeal by combat, as we have seen, is Henry Monmouth's touchstone of personal worth. It affords him the occasion for his first entry into the public eye, the setting for his demonstration of military virtue in his victory over Hotspur, and, now, the means by which he can display his sovereignty, his participation in divine grace, and his ability to raise men to his own vigorous pitch of soul. His escalation of the joust to the status of an instrument for adjudicating national differences, while in itself perhaps not without precedent, is at any rate consistent with the novel course he has charted for the English monarch. He will now reveal to the courts of the world a king who owes his sovereignty not to the untrustworthy sanctions of wordy customs but to the indubitable authority of his personal deeds.[12]

In one way Henry makes peace with ceremony. He conforms to the usage of jousting under a colorable cause. He refuses to brandish the whore's glove or its equivalent during his expedition to France, since the war requires at least the appearance of legality, and Henry works diligently to bolster that appearance. At the same time he shows himself aware of the expediency of the war, apart from considerations of its legality. He acts upon Bolingbroke's deathbed advice "to busy giddy minds/ With foreign quarrels" (2 Henry IV, IV.v.213-214). Bolingbroke's unexecuted plan of a crusade to the Holy Land gives way to his son's holy war against France. Henry has a better grasp upon expediency than his own guilt-bedeviled father. He will leave the matter of the crusade to his own son (V.ii.200-203) while he himself pursues a more practicable end. The offensive against France accomplishes the diversion that Bolingbroke intended without the inconveniences of a long pilgrimage to the Holy Land and with more tangible gains. The superior practicability of the French war is more than a logistical calculation. Given the present condition of the English character we doubt that England could be moved to embark on a crusade. Henry's subjects have become used to consulting their immediate self-interests. They respond to an appeal to their avidity for the near-at-hand profit when they follow their king to France.

Henry accomplishes what no other Shakespearean monarch can when he temporarily unites four races and three orders. Englishmen, Scots, Irish, and Welsh fight on the same side in a cause that has won the approval of clergy, nobility, and commoners. We see at the outset what the clergy stands to gain from the war—it keeps its lands by sanctifying the appropriation of foreign soil. From the chorus we learn why English aristocrats make common cause with Henry. Expectation sits in the air, the chorus says,

> And hides a sword, from hilts unto the point
> With crowns imperial, crowns, and coronets
> Promised to Harry and his followers. (II.9-11)

The chorus does not discriminate between this universal expectation of profitable venture and the thought of honor which it claims "Reigns solely in the breast of every man" (4). There follows immediately a scene, involving Hal's old acquaintances of Eastcheap, which seems designed to deny any discrimination between aristocratic craving for new lands and the sharp look-out of London's petty thieves. Bardolf composes Nym and Pistol's quarrel over Hostess Quickly by suggesting that the rivals cut French throats rather than each others' (II.ii.86-88). In their next scene Pistol makes Bardolph's policy his own: "Let us to France, like horse-leeches my boys,/ To suck, to suck, the very blood to suck!" (II.iii.50-51). Bardolph stands in for Hal among the London dregs uniting natural adversaries in the speculative venture of plundering a common enemy. Harry can move the nobility by the twin engines of honor and avarice, and he can mobilize that part of the populace he knows best by the single lever of its greed.

There remains the other part of the populace represented by men like Court, Bates, and Williams. They fight from motives of patriotism and duty, and, since they have less to gain from the war, are more demanding in searching its justification. Henry binds these men to his purpose by his selfless courage and vigorous rhetoric. Regrettably, even the law-abiding commoners can become lawless in the midst of lawful war. Harry's threatening speech to the citizens of Harfleur reminds them that bloody soldiers are conscienceless. Even solid yeomanry can turn to theft, murder, infanticide, and rape when loosed upon a captured town (III.iii.24-41). The king exercises what care he can, executing his old companion Bardolph for stealing a pax (what Harry thought Bardolph should do with himself in France is anybody's guess), but it is difficult to restrain soldiers from taking what they can when the king seems to be taking what *he* can.

The particular word for aggressive avarice in *Henry V* is *scambling*. Canterbury speaks at the beginning of the "scambling and unquiet time" of the late king's reign when Bolingbroke was preoccupied with quelling the divisive greed of his nobles (I.i.1-5). The word which editors gloss as "snatching," "predatory," or "scrambling for possessions" seems closely allied to the "commodity" which Falconbridge in *King John* offers as the designation for politic self-seeking and which Falstaff adopts as the catchword for his systematic profiteering from the wars.[13] Scambling is commodity in its bolder and less clandestine aspects. At the end of the play Henry can joke with Kate on the word. He thinks that she should breed good soldiers since he has obtained her by scambling (V.ii.199). As in the matter of his jest about coveting honor, Hal has a way of hitting simple truth when he means to exaggerate. At the moment he charms Kate we are reminded of the uncharming passions he generates in his subjects.

One responds to Henry's ingenuous amorality with something of the mixture of sympathy and alarm with which Conrad's Marlowe reviews the career of the imperialist adventurer Kurtz. The scale counts for something: if Henry's war is larger than theft, his disregard of the moral costs is so complete and carried so buoyantly that one cannot call it cheek. Whatever we call it, his moral oblivion does not appear to be shared by Shakespeare. The counterpoint of irony sustained by the comic scenes in which Pistol and Bardolph travesty the policies developed in the court serves to measure Harry's statesmanship and rein in mindless patriotism.[14]

A more precise critique emerges from placing the action of *Henry V* within the context provided by the other plays of the first and second tetralogies. Canterbury brings in the foreground of *Richard II* through *2 Henry IV* by his reference to the scambling times, whereas the Epilogue looks to the future wars of succession when it ends the play with a mention of the bad times "which oft our stage hath shown" (V.13), referring to the first tetralogy. Foreground and sequel cast doubt on Harry's war.

We have already noted the prevailing reckless acquisitiveness upon which England surfeits in the other three plays of the Lancastrian tetralogy. Without this climate the war would not be as popular as it is. We must wonder at a policy that augments the nation's most notable disease. The effects generated by Henry's war of acquisition are, in this respect at least, continuous with the effects of his earlier countenancing of thieves. These encouragements of avarice are the immediate by-products of the adventure in France. The later consequences are predictable. Shakespeare's earlier-written tetralogy portrays the ineffectual attempts of Harry's son to rule a country which has been taught the profits of scambling by his father. Harry may be capable of controlling a pilfering Bardolph or a noisy opportunist like Pistol, but Henry VI lacks the vigor necessary for even such small coercive efforts, not to speak of the resources that would be required to govern the grasping Yorkists. Harry fails to produce the virile son he expects from a conception in scambling. But even if he had, the son's chances would not have been good. Any successor to the fifth Henry would receive for his double legacy a nobility trained in plunder and a most tenuous hold upon still-hostile conquered territories. England's War of the Roses begins in France in the rivalries of the nobles who think less of fighting the French than of undermining their fellow lords. England cannot rule France, but its attempt to hold the territory conquered by Henry V is disastrous for its own peace. The ultimate result of Henry's emancipation of the acquisitive passions is Richard III, who carries appetite to its logical conclusion and lives for nothing but egocentric assertiveness. Parallels to the story run back to antiquity and Thucydides' account of the fortunes of Athens after the Sicilian expedition. Imperial aggrandizement breeds the yearning for individual self-aggrandizement which can be directed against other citizens as well as foreigners. The same kind of fever that produced in Athens the autarchic Alcibiades produces after Henry's death Richard Crookback with his motto "I am myself alone" (3 *Henry VI*, V.vi.83). Another generation pays the full cost of Harry's inspiring his followers with dreams of crowns and coronets dangling from swordhilts.

In a more subtle fashion than his chorus, Shakespeare, at the end of *Henry V*, reminds the audience of another earlier play. Prior to the French king's signing a treaty of submission, Burgundy urges peace in a long speech (V.ii.23-67) which stresses the devastation of civil arts caused by the war and which takes for its governing figure the image of France as a disordered garden. Burgundy complains that the "best garden of the world" languishes without husbandry, that from lack of cultivation weeds overrun the good land, and that from a similar absence of social culture, the people and their children fail to learn the sciences. Instead they

> grow like savages, as soldiers will,
> That nothing do but meditate on blood,
> To swearing and stern looks, diffused attire,
> And everything that seems unnatural.

We are reminded of the similar lament of the royal gardeners in *Richard II* (III.iv.29-66). There, England had been the uncultivated garden grown wild under Richard's neglect. The burden of both speeches is the responsibility of the king to provide a government that nurtures the good gifts of nature.

The point of the artistic echo spanning four plays seems to be Shakespeare's raising the question whether the just monarch must not acknowledge in his dealings with other countries the same responsibility which directs him in governing his own people. France's devastation owes to Henry because he has conducted a war of aggression. In view of the bad consequences which befall England now, and in the immediate aftermath of the war, it does not seem that Henry can find an excuse for making foreign turmoil by appeal to the interests of his own country. By the end of his play when all the debits have been totaled, including those one can know from acquaintance with the other plays of the sequence, Harry's cause, which had been first introduced with a great show of probity, begins to resemble the whore's glove after all. Hal does conform with the legal forms of ceremony, but continues to corrode the principles of justice and good order which the ceremonial forms were intended to serve.

Critics have noted the obvious ironies that cast doubt upon the council of war convened in the first scenes of *Henry V*. They have called attention to the self-serving policy of Canterbury and Ely who lend the moral authority of the Church to support the war in exchange for Henry's lifting his threat of a substantial tax upon ecclesiastical property, have remarked the anomaly of the king's making war in the name of his lineal rights to the French throne while executing Cambridge who seeks to further what seems to be a better inherited right to the English throne, and have observed the continuity of this policy of belligerence with Henry IV's shrewd advice to "busy giddy minds with foreign quarrels." By introducing the witch's kitchen of *Realpolitik* in his opening scene, Shakespeare seems rather abruptly to deflate the expectations of high epic decorum voiced by the Chorus. However, when they take these ironies as definitive indications of Shakespeare's disapproval, Henry's critics may tell us more about their own political tenderness than about the tough-minded understanding of politics which characterizes the histories generally and the present play in particular. The ironies raise rather than settle questions, and to the extent that he is at all conscious of these obliquities, Henry might feel that they are exonerated by his situation. It could be argued that the war with France and all the questionable means employed to open hostilities are justified because necessary as a desperate remedy for a desperate illness. Henry inherits a regime undermined by endemic unrest and disaffection with royal authority. The three earlier plays of the tetralogy have presented a series of plots against a king who lacks that essential support to authority which time bestows. If Hal is not a new prince in an old regime, as his father was, he is in any case new enough that he must find means to shore up his position. The war answers this need, serving to unite the English factions against a common enemy and to divert nice inquiries into the illegitimate source of the power bequeathed to Hal. The fact that foreign wars have been the doubtful resort of insecure tyrants does not mean that the expedience is practiced only by tyrants. We can imagine Shakespeare portraying Henry's aggression in such a way as to acknowledge one of the harsh necessities of politics. Injustice against a foreign enemy may be required to secure order at home. Such a case might be made for Henry V.[15]

In the present instance the apology from necessity is, I think, unconvincing for two reasons, the first having to do with the domestic circumstances of England, the second pertaining to Henry's motives. Moreover, Shakespeare seems to suggest a possible alternative, a way of bringing order to England without bringing war to France.

Whereas Henry IV had to deal with many nobles bent on deposing him in the same manner he had deposed Richard, his son must dispose of merely one. To be sure, not only for his own interest but for sake of the good order of the realm Henry must eliminate the threat posed by Cambridge. He does so early in Act II of the play, making use of his exposure of Cambridge's conspiracy with the French to obscure the dynastic issue. Although the heady patriotism aroused among Englishmen by the mobilization presumably helps to make the condemnation of Cambridge more palatable than it would otherwise be, one doubts that anyone, including Henry, could think the war a prelude without which the conspirator could not be prevented. And once Cambridge has been executed Henry seems to enjoy about as much safety as any king could reasonably expect.

In contrast to the previous plays in which rebellion had fed on the blood spilled from kinsmen, no one rises up to avenge Cambridge's death. In fact we have good cause to wonder whether there still survives any faction of sufficient power to attempt vengeance. It is crucial to grasp an elementary fact of the sequence that has never, I think, received critical recognition. The opposition of Yorkists to Lancastrians has a continuous ground but is not continuously enacted. The Percies acknowledge that Mortimer has a claim to the throne, but, as their plan for dividing the kingdom (*1 Henry IV*, III.i) makes clear, they revolt to further their own interests, not on behalf of Mortimer. The descendants of Cambridge suffer a general attaint in consequence of Cambridge's execution, but in *1* and *2 Henry VI* these very descendants are ignorant of Mortimer's claim and must be informed of it. Richard, the son of Cambridge, first learns of the claim from the dying Mortimer himself (*1 Henry VI*, II.v). After he becomes Duke of York, Richard traces his title ultimately to the third son of Edward III through his mother, who was the heir of Edmund Mortimer. Thus the claims of York are linked to the claims of Mortimer, yet apparently the only person who understands this is Mortimer himself.

Aside from Cambridge, Mortimer does not appear to have supporters, and Cambridge's heir would not have found his lineal grounds for opposing the Lancastrian Henry VI had he not been disposed to look for them out of the grievance he feels over the attaint imposed by Henry V upon his family. Henry's execution of Cambridge is necessary to protect the throne, but his attainder against the descendants (York claims it was not even a legal bill of attainder but a tyrannical attachment [*1 Henry VI*, II.iv.96]) creates the Yorkist opposition.

In any case, Henry IV had more to fear from the men who assisted in deposing Richard II than from the family of Mortimer, for it is these king-makers who pose the greatest threat to the internal order of England. If this opposition were still virulent, Henry V might indeed adduce a compelling reason of state for his foreign war. However, at the beginning of Henry's reign these men are all either dead outright or moribund. Without Worcester, Douglas, and Hotspur, Northumberland cannot stand up against the mere sheriff of Yorkshire (*2 Henry IV*, IV.iv.99). Mowbray, Scroop, and Hastings have been captured at Gaultree Forest; and Glendower, whose promises had always been better than his performance, is reported to have died (III.i.103). Hence, Harry enjoys a respite from the factionary strife that wore down his father and will overcome his son. With Yorkist opposition not yet vigorous and the older rebels extinct, the threat of civil war is not nearly so grave as it is in the plays that precede and follow *Henry V*.

This is not to say that Shakespeare portrays a tranquil England. The politically traumatic deposition of a legitimate king leaves a rent in the social fabric which must be patched with cloth of any color. Something must be done to restore the power of the monarchy since its moral authority has suffered perhaps irreparable harm. Bolingbroke appears to have given more thought to this problem than has been generally credited him. He leaves to his son a piece of legislation which, if properly administered, promises a means to domestic order without war. Bolingbroke's tax bill upon ecclesiastical property could provide an added strength to the throne far in excess of a simple increase in revenues. In view of his other bequest—to make war as a diversion of domestic unrest—Bolingbroke appears not to have fully grasped the possibilities afforded by his own policy. However, Shakespeare dwells upon details that bring these possibilities to our attention.

Canterbury knows not only the amount of the levy Harry hangs over his head but its intended use. He explains to Ely that the tax "would maintain, to the king's honor,/ Full fifteen earls and fifteen hundred knights,/ Six thousand and two hundred good esquires" (I.i.12-14). Critics could benefit by recognizing the importance or the consequences which Canterbury fears. Bolingbroke's intended expropriation of the

Church's lands aims at a social rather than merely a fiscal end: he plans to create a new nobility. The trouble with the old nobility was that Henry IV was as much, if not more, its creature than it was his. Men like Worcester and Northumberland could not stand in awe of a king whom their own hands had "holp to make so portly" (1 Henry IV, I.iii.13). The country at large could not revere a king whose unkingly origins were known to everyone. To restore the ceremonial awe once accorded the throne, something must be done which might show the king to be an independent source of power. Nothing attests power so manifestly as creation. By making a new nobility the king would demonstrate his power and by the same act provide for its continuation. Instead of putting himself under the obligation of making known his gratitude to others he could expect the new lords to be mindful of their indebtedness to him and of their dependence upon him for further advancement. The risk of alienating worldly churchmen could be more than balanced by the gain of depriving prelates like Scroop of the means for sustaining revolts, and, in any event, new lords living off former church lands could be expected to side with the king against any troublesome bishops. Shakespeare knew of just such a social revolution from the successful policy of Henry VIII.

The greatest flaw in the English constitution is the disparity between the king's authority and his actual power. Every monarch from Richard II to Richard III finds himself the recipient of heavy honors and light arms. The glaring disability of the English monarchy is its lack of a standing army. Without troops subsisting on the king's pay, and therefore answerable to the king alone, the British monarch enjoys little actual independence. His nobles assure him of his supremacy while they know he is impotent. His real ability to coerce extends little farther than his throne room, and to control even his capital city he must win the favor of the Lord Mayor (as evidenced in Richard III). For all military purposes he is dependent upon his friends who, if they are so disposed, may raise a makeshift force from their personal retainers. He cannot make war unless he can persuade the nobles to lend money and troops. As we see in the scenes given over to Falstaff's recruiting, the king depends on his nobles even to draft common footsoldiers. A standing army is the indispensable condition for making real the nominal sovereignty attributed to the throne and for moderating England's chronic factionalism. Yet the crown can hardly expect the present nobility to give him his army. The best the king can do is just what Bolingbroke proposes: make use of the nobles' and commoners' resentment against a wealthy Church for the sake of accumulating the money and lands he will need to create a new gentry and, hence, the foundation for a standing military force. When Henry V relents on his father's ecclesiastical tax, he rejects a prudent measure consistent with the old constitution of ceremony in favor of a more personal strategy which may enhance his own prestige but will not strengthen the monarchy as institution.

Although a king in Harry's position might conceivably view the war as another means of accomplishing what the tax would make possible, there is no indication that Harry entertains that view. Instead there is fairly abundant evidence that he makes war from the same motives which have shaped his career since the Oxford tournament. That is, *Henry V* emphasizes the continuity of Henry's career by stressing the continuity of his motives.

One does not believe that Harry promotes his war from zealous dedication to the principle of legal inheritance. Nor can we believe that his end is simply to emancipate the acquisitive instincts of his people. Harry's spirit is sufficiently capacious to despise the legal quiddities of Canterbury and the casual avarice of a Bardolph or a Pistol. Legality and avarice are only the means by which he solicits lesser men to follow his private and grander quest, somewhat as an Ahab binds his crew with maritime law and promises of doubloons. For Henry the end of the war lies in the war itself, or more precisely, in the spectacle which the war affords. We can see this spectacle taking shape for Henry in the first scenes of the play.

After Canterbury's disposal of the legal question, the deliberation upon the war continues with the consideration of the theme of fame. First Canterbury, then his fellow prelate Ely, then the nobles Exeter and Westmoreland, urge the king to secure his glory. Canterbury incites Henry with the precedent of his ancestors Edward III and Edward the Black Prince who defeated the French at Crecy. The manner of their victory comports with Henry's distinctive style: the Black Prince fought the French with half the army while his father kept back the other half to give the enemy the odds. Canterbury points the moral:

> O noble English, that could entertain
> With half their forces the full pride of France
> And let another half stand laughing by,
> All out of work and cold for action! (I.ii.111-114)

Exeter and Canterbury directly challenge Henry to equal the fame of his glorious ancestors. The archbishop then hints how the present war may be made equivalent to Edward's one-handed conquest. Henry should

take only a quarter of his forces to France, leaving the bulk of his army to
defend against the Scots (I.ii.215-217). Hal has long planned the expedition, but the present rehearsal of ancestral deeds gives him a proper dramatic build-up and a handle upon his anticipated great scene. Canterbury has just spoken of Edward's chronicle "rich with praise." Shortly
thereafter the king takes an oath upon his own expectation of a high
place in the annals. He swears that he will bend France to his will or
"break it all to pieces" (226) and concludes

> Either our history shall with full mouth
> Speak freely of our acts, or else our grave,
> Like Turkish mute, shall have a tongueless mouth,
> Not worshipped with a waxen epitaph. (231-234)

We notice that Henry begins to speak with enthusiasm only after he has
gotten past the legal issues and come to his usual theme of glory. He will
earn a chronicle richer than his great-grandfather's by surpassing the military prowess of both Edward III and the Black Prince. He sets out to
conquer France with only a fourth of his total power, and by the time of
Agincourt his troops fight against far greater odds than had the army of
Edward III. We cannot say whether Henry actually welcomes the five-
to-one advantage the French enjoy at Agincourt, but we do know that he
encourages an enemy attack by carefully detailing his army's weakness to
the French herald, after alerting the herald to the imprudence of his
irrepressible honesty.[16]

One of the most careful judges of honor among Shakespeare's contemporaries listed three conditions for enhancing one's distinctions:

> If a man perform that...[which] hath been achieved but not
> with so good circumstance; he shall purchase more honour,
> than by effecting a matter of greater difficulty or virtue, wherein
> he is but a follower. If a man so temper his actions, as in some
> one of them he doth content every faction or combination of
> people, the music will be the fuller.... Honour that is gained
> and broken upon another hath the quickest reflexion, like dia-
> monds cut with fascets. And therefore let a man contend to
> excel any competitors of his honour, in outshooting them, if he
> can, in their own bow.[17]

Harry knows how to eclipse Edward's victory by stretching the circumstances, and he ensures a "fuller music" by enlisting the passions of all
factions in support of his war. He achieves the "quickest reflexion" of

fame by gaining it at the expense of the glory-enamored French, competing with them in the art they claim is their special excellence.

In the previous plays we have noted that Hal prefers to work with foils. The dark background gives a high lustre to his sudden brilliance. Now his foil becomes the vainglorious French in general and the superabundantly boastful Dauphin in particular. The Dauphin is a severely diminished version of Hal's earlier factor, Hotspur. By displaying his prowess at the expense of the French heir, Harry shows the superiority of quietly competent valor to noisy braggadocio. After hearing the French prince strain the praises of his horse, we are grateful for the fresh air of the modestly noble Crispian's Day speeches. Henry can count on the Dauphin to provide the fustian against which his own noble simplicity will stand out most resplendently. Indeed, the French nobility on the whole appear in such a bad light that it seems the English take on a liability in seeking to rule them. But Harry's intention is less to rule than to conquer, and for this purpose the Dauphin's insulting gift of tennis balls proves a helpful prop.

Harry takes the jibe with a good grace, promising to turn the tennis balls into cannon balls and to play a match for possession of France. He chides the Dauphin for reminding him of his "wilder days" while "not measuring what use we made of them" (I.ii.268-269). The Dauphin's knowledge of the cultivation of glory extends no further than crude boasting. He has not appreciated the subtlety with which Hal carefully demeaned himself in preparation for a great windfall of renown. At this moment the Dauphin has already unwittingly become Henry's factor by reviving the old reputation just when the king is preparing a further exhibition of his reform. What Hal could hardly bring up himself his rival has said for him, and Henry proceeds to capitalize on the slight to his former days by elaborating a new conceit. He now jokes that he gave his youth to "barbarous license" because he did not value the English crown, desiring only his proper throne in France. Now he will rouse himself to take possession of his rightful legacy. The image through which Henry proclaims his latest self-revelation establishes the continuity of his present enterprise with the strategy he announced at the beginning of *1 Henry IV*. He will "show his sail of greatness" only when he has taken France:

> For that I have laid by my majesty
> And plodded like a man for working days,
> But I will rise there with so full a glory
> That I will dazzle all the eyes of France,
> Yea, strike the Dauphin blind to look on us. (277-281)

To inaugurate the last phase of his career as the master of the spectacular, Harry resurrects once more the ancient hub of ceremony, the image of the sun-king. The earlier phases of the sunrise—Shrewsbury, reconciliation with the Lord Chief Justice, renunciation of Falstaff—had only cleared away a portion of the clouds which the young prince had interposed between his full splendor and the general eye. Henry's present use of the image shows that he still holds to the purpose he first conceived: to arouse wonder and attract more eyes. Now, however, he will dazzle and strike blind. The stakes have been raised to a new level.

In the earlier plays we may fail to appreciate the degree of the wonder which Henry seeks to arouse and the scope of the audience he seeks to play before. In both respects his requirements seem now to be total. He solicits a wonder that approaches awe and appears to justify the Chorus's initial evocation of the horsemen of Revelation (*Pro.* 7-8). Like the Chorus, he expects an audience wider than his English subjects, "monarchs to behold the swelling scene." The war completes the spectacle begun in the last act of *Richard II* and reveals the full potency of Henry's love for honor—war establishes the natural *telos* towards which he has been moving all along.

When we view the conflict in the light of Henry's precedent career, we may understand why with the coronation his first thoughts turn to France and why any other sequel to that career would be anticlimactical. Established routines of bland government offer few prospects for the dramatic self-affirmations that Henry has learned to live for. The example of Bolingbroke has already taught him that there is no glory in painstaking administration. Harry's temperament would chafe under the confinements of careful administration as it had earlier chafed under the self-imposed restrictions of pretended vice. To a man who tolerates life only for the sake of its marvels, the respect laboriously won by a king who devotes himself to domestic welfare cannot compare with the swift acclaim that follows the successes of the maker of empires. Hal prefers foreign adventures to domestic rule for the same reason that Machiavelli prefers to speak of foreign policy rather than domestic affairs. Consequently, it is not surprising that when Henry looks to the past for models he finds his exemplars in the pagan emperors Caesar and Alexander.

Henry's one great competitor in his quest for glory is God. His present design aims at surpassing his revelation of hidden powers at Shrewsbury and his pretended moral reformation at the coronation by presenting something close to a miracle. But Harry accomplishes his miracle with his incredible victory at Agincourt only to find himself embarrassed by the wrong kind of success. On the one hand, he has frequently alluded to his divine support, and immediately after the victory has been certified he makes a point of stressing its supernatural character. He instructs his soldiers to sing *Te Deum, Non Nobis*, states three times that the credit belongs to God only, then decrees death for anyone who boasts of the victory (IV.viii.108-111). Henry wants to be known as a latter day David who achieves wondrous triumphs with preposterously slender forces because he enjoys the favor of God. On the other hand, if the miracle is taken too literally, the king's personal glory will be diminished. The price of David's grace was self-effacement before the all-sufficing power of the Lord.[18] Henry finds himself back in the old dilemma of ceremonial kingship. Although he has succeeded in attaching divine favor to the person of the king rather than the office, he still faces the problem of distinguishing his own virtue from the grace of God. Henry's favorite captain, Fluellen, has earlier compared him to Alexander. But Alexander is known for his own prowess, not for his borrowed honor as the poor instrument of a divine will.[19] Henry can choose either to be known as an Alexander or Caesar, or, yielding all claims to a personal glory, to follow the example in humility provided by the youthful David.

We can see his solution through the account of his staunchest admirer. The Chorus at the beginning of Act V recounts a solemn parade to London wherein Henry's followers advise him to wear his dented helmet and carry his battle-worn sword.

> He forbids it,
> Being free from vainness and self-glorious pride;
> Giving full trophy, signal, and ostent
> Quite from himself to God. (19-22)

Despite his efforts to yield his praises to God, the Londoners pour forth to view the man who conquered France; so that the Chorus, after just commending Henry's Christian humility, equates the triumphal entry with a Roman victory procession, the mayor and aldermen playing the part of "Roman senators" and Henry "their conqu'ring Caesar" (24-28). The Chorus and the people refuse to accord the honor of the conquest to God alone, and, in fact, no one gives any part of the credit to God. Henry V, not God, is known as the victor of Agincourt. But by his repeated disclaimers Henry does earn the credit of magnanimously declining his great honor in obeisance before God. Shakespeare makes a doublet of Agincourt and Shrewsbury, inviting us to recall that we have seen something like the present display earlier in the career. When he adds the final measure to glory by giving away honor at the very moment it descends upon him most spectacularly, Harry makes the sequel to his conquest of France a repeat performance of the finale to his conquest of Hotspur. Only now God takes the place of Falstaff. Hal treats God as he had treated Falstaff! We are left to ponder whether Harry, for all his wit and courage, possesses the boldness to make this gesture knowingly or whether (and more likely) the boldness owes to Shakespeare's own audacious playfulness.

Shakespeare does not appear to question the sincerity of Henry's professed piety. Besides his many public references to God, Harry prays in private. Prior to Agincourt he asks God to inspire his soldiers and delay divine retribution for his father's sin of usurpation. The question is not the sincerity of the king's piety but its depth. Harry's religion apparently allows him to enjoy an easy conscience (his qualms attach only to his father's sins) while he perpetrates the sizeable injustice of an unprovoked, aggressive war. We wonder if it is Henry's imperfect piety which prompts him to care for his individual soul but not for justice, or whether Shakespeare means to point up an anomaly within Christianity itself.

The question just posed leads to what may be the most decisive issue of the history plays, Shakespeare's conception of the connection between Christianity and politics. The plays present kings who profess Christianity, but nowhere do we discern a clear answer to the question of what a Christian ruler ought to be.[20] It is not even clear whether Christianity puts greater rather than less exacting demands upon kingship than does the requirement of natural justice. These ambiguities surface in Henry's exchange with the commoner Williams on the night before Agincourt. By attending to the implications of this conversation and their relationship to the view of kingship that underlies the conversation, we may gather something about the direction of Shakespeare's inquiry.

Henry's reply to Williams's challenge that the king should be morally responsible for the condition of his soldiers' souls is remarkable for its sophistry. However, it is less Henry's sophistry than his theory which raises the crucial issue of the exchange. For the conclusion of his argument is a statement of the general principle that "every subject's duty is the king's, but every subjects's soul is his own" (166-168). Henry thus endorses Williams's belief that "to disobey [the king] were against all proportion of subjection" (138) while rejecting the weighty moral responsibilities that Williams thinks should accompany royal sovereignty.[21] The subject owes absolute obedience to the king. What the king owes is unclear.

In the soliloquy on ceremony which immediately follows the conversation with Williams, Henry depicts the king as a laborer for peace
(IV.i.267-270). The fact that he makes the speech while standing on foreign soil indicates that the peace-providing vocation admits qualification. Besides the task of promoting peace, Henry ascribes no other duty
to the king. Henry apparently conceives monarchy in rather narrowly
limited terms, denying it the function of nurturing the moral well-being
of subjects. It appears we are to take his reply to Williams in the full force
of its restrictiveness: caring for their own souls is the business of individual men; the king's business lies elsewhere. We have been prepared
for such an extreme statement of limited government by the three previous plays of the tetralogy which have indicated the prince's indifference
to the effects of his pretended viciousness upon the character of his people.
A theory of monarchy that would charge it merely with the task of preserving the realm, allowing the king to remain indifferent to the cultivation of virtue in his subjects, fits what we know of the earlier Henry and
squares with what he is saying and doing at the present moment. At first
sight Henry's teaching appears impious; yet there is something in Christianity that may be taken to suggest that political authority ought to restrict itself to concerns of the body while leaving to God, or to God's
faithful, the concerns of the soul. Among Christian theologians the question of the province of government in the spiritual weal is always a matter
of controversy. We have no record of where Shakespeare stood in the
controversy other than the indirect and problematic testimony of his
poetry. The Chorus's seemingly indiscriminate praise of Henry as the
"mirror" of Christian kings and as a "conqu'ring Caesar" might be justified on the assumption that the exemplary Christian king would make
himself a certain kind of Caesar—a Caesar who views himself in the way
that Christ is thought to have viewed the Emperor in his remark about
rendering unto Caesar. On this assumption the model Christian monarch might properly confine himself to keeping the peace and abstain
from the care of souls. Does Shakespeare endorse the Christian-Cae-
sarian praise voiced by the Chorus?

My impression is that the testimony of the history plays inclines
against the assumption that would approve the Chorus and Henry. The
general attitude of Shakespeare's characters seems to be that the king
ought to promote the moral well-being of his realm and not merely attend to its bodily needs. Put more accurately, the general run of
Shakespeare's characters do not discriminate between an authority which
ordains the goods of the soul and an authority which governs affairs of

the body. The king takes on the role of educator and moral spokesman under the forms of the old monarchy of ceremony. This view of the exemplary and nurturing role of the monarchy seems taken for granted by most of the personages depicted in the history plays. It informs the apodictic rhetoric of Canterbury, the patriotism of the Chorus, and, of course, the moral indignation displayed by Williams. Harry is the first king to state his opposition to the view on the level of principle, although it seems fairly clear that none of Shakespeare's kings succeeds in living up to the orthodox belief. Henry's doctrine, as doctrine, is novel and may be the necessary complement to his general depreciation of ceremony.

The two Richards and Bolingbroke fail to fulfill a role of moral stewardship, yet pay for their failure with troubled consciences. Henry protects his clear conscience by denying the very duty of moral stewardship. The novelty of his denial hardly suffices to condemn it, but the contrast between his conception of rule and what appears the accepted traditional standard makes us look carefully at the alternatives Shakespeare envisions. The issue could be fairly stated as the choice between a perspective upon political things essentially ancient and a view that is characteristically modern. Modern politics—thought and practice—breaks from the ancients by repudiating the ancient teaching that the end of politics is character formation. The modern political regime owes its founding to a revolution in thought which elevates peace and self-preservation to the status of the sufficient ends of political life, a place once reserved for moral and intellectual virtue. In the character and statecraft of Henry of Monmouth, Shakespeare presents an early version of this revolution. Henry seems to be the first—possibly the only—Shakespearean ruler who embraces the modern political premise. The English alternative to a regime devoted to peace and self-preservation is not the educative ancient polis but rather the Christian monarchy of court and moral ceremony wherein the goal of character formation is jointly pursued by Church and secular government. The Church promotes moral training through its laws, worship, and preaching; the crown through its laws, customs, and conspicuous example.

It is hard to decide whether Shakespeare's plays, as distinguished from his characters, identify such an arrangement with the best practicable regime. We could be more certain about Shakespeare's assessment of the educative monarchy if we ever saw it at its best in act. We see it only in theory, so to speak, and neither Richard II nor King John are adequate representatives of the practical products of the theory. But the plays do indicate one great obstacle to Henry's alternative of a monarchy indifferent to moral education. Shakespeare's portrayal of the Church throughout the histories militates against the notion that its efforts could be sufficient to care for the moral virtue of the population. In the first place, from what we see of the spiritual arm though Shakespeare's portrayals of its ecclesiastical representatives, the Church does not seem disposed to make great efforts to that end. Moreover, the plays suggest that even were the clergy better motivated, its moral guidance could not effectively shape the British character if it were not supported by the coercive powers of the temporal government. Falstaff and his acquaintances in town and country have heard sermons yet cannot be counted upon to submit to order without being coerced.

The alternative to a regime in which the power of the crown promotes character formation seems not to be an arrangement in which the Church alone fulfills that end, but a regime which simply fails to provide for moral virtue at all. In place of the ceremonial monarchy with its interest in cultivating the soul, Henry promotes a monarchy which offers a plurality of ends accommodating different sorts of men. Henry's version of kingship affords the delights of glory to the king and to anyone who should risk his life in the king's enterprise. To the timid it offers the vicarious satisfactions of national prestige and the more immediate pleasures of sharing in the acquisitions which accompany the king's quest for fame. For the unenterprising it promises some protection for their enjoyment of whatever they may already possess. At the price of absolute obedience to the monarch ("every subject's duty"), men are left free to care for their own souls. Their freedom is subject only to the limitation that it must not hamper the king's policy on behalf of personal and national glorification. The freedom of the king to pursue his glory and the liberty of the subject to care for his own soul necessitates a certain relaxation of the old regime's moral demands and a certain casualness in weighing the justice of foreign wars. Henry never does confront Williams's doubt about the cause that underlies the war. That Shakespeare accepts these expenses as a fair exchange for the glory, wealth, and freedom Henry provides is doubtful in view of the cumulative testimony offered by his art. The plays and poems portray human beauty under the aspect of moral and intellectual excellence. We assume, therefore, that Shakespeare's dramatic art provides the standard by which to judge his portrayals of political art. A political arrangement that aims to promote moral and intellectual virtue would appear more consistent with this standard of beauty than one which does not.

Henry V winds down with some modest reflections concerning the doubtful beauty of the king's conduct. Shakespeare's pendant to the Williams debate offers a dutiful commoner's comment on Henry and ceremony. So that Williams may later recall their conversation, Harry formally challenges him to combat and gives him a glove to be worn as a challenge. When they had first met, the disguised king had said of himself, "His ceremonies laid by, in his nakedness he appears but a man" (IV.i.101-102). Harry wants Williams to love him for his human qualities rather than simply render him ceremonial respect. He will prove his common touch by subsequently revealing to Williams that the man who talked with him the night before Agincourt was the troubled king himself. Between bestowing the glove and revealing himself, Henry decides to enlarge the matter by making it a public show. He indulges his playfulness by telling Fluellen that the favor Williams wears betrays his allegiance to the French Duke Alencon, then sends Warwick and Gloucester to keep Williams from harm. Thus, when Henry arrives with Exeter, he has assembled a crowd of nobles sufficient to observe his display of noblesse. For once, however, a Monmouth spectacle fails to come off. After Harry has set things straight, Williams, instead of exhibiting the requisite gratitude, remains indignant. He tells the king that, having put by his ceremonies, he deserved whatever treatment he received in disguise (IV.viii.46-52), and he seems to deliver a subtle insult when he says his offense did not "come from the heart" (43). In a curious turn of Henry's thoughts on ceremony, Williams is saying that what he told against the king should not count, since he did not know he addressed the king. Only ceremonial speech is "from the heart"! Williams resents the trickery and may understand something of what is at stake in Harry's breach of ceremony. He does not care for Henry's exhibitions of personality but expects the king to conform to the regularities prescribed by his station. Williams may perceive more of the essence of ceremony than Henry. When the king and Fluellen seek to salve his resentment with gifts of money, Williams maintains outward courtesy yet comes as close as he dares to an outright reproof by rejecting Fluellen's gift. Only in this his final play upon the old convention of the formal challenge does Henry's indifference to established decorum result in his personal embarrassment. For a moment Williams makes Henry appear low.

The courting scene with Katherine shows the extension of Henry's politics to his private life. He captures the girl's heart in the same way he captures French towns, with boldness of address and frank manners. His lovemaking, like his politics, is iconoclastic. Henry makes a point of ridiculing the conventions of courtship—he will not die for love, he will not swear his devotion, he will not exaggerate the lady's charms. He wants to seal the betrothal with a kiss, and when Kate demurs, pleading the custom of her country, Henry wins the kiss with a motto that applies equally to his political career, "nice customs curtsy to great kings" (V.ii.260).[22] Henry is once more the boyish Hal who can say he would prefer to take a wife as a horseman would vault into his saddle. He works close to the borders of flippancy.

Kate seems to find his manner refreshing, perhaps by contrast to the fulsome insincerity of conventional court play, and she is not much disturbed by the overstated unconventionality that seems as insincere as the bombast it ridicules, nor does she express misgivings over a bluffness that skirts contempt. We may find Katherine's intelligence charmingly pert rather than fine; her confidence in the solidity of Henry's affections seems naive. Henry finally tells her that her charms have swayed him more than the French Council (269). But he consents to the marriage only when he is assured that with his espousal all his claims to France will be assented to (312-313). Kate should perceive from his conversation that the better parts of her attractions are the political advantages she can confer. Harry as much as tells her so when he informs her she is his "capital demand" (96) in the list of treaty articles, and when he tells Kate she "should love the friend of France, for I love France so well that I will not part with a village of it—I will have it all mine" (169-171).

During the conversation itself Henry manages to convey a forthright sense of the narrow possibilities of love between a conqueror and the token of his conquest. His directness wavers between a kindly humorous appreciation of his and Kate's mutual predicament and a presumptuous indifference to the woman's situation. In the end, however, he seems to treat the ceremony of marriage with as little weight as he has treated all ceremonies. The scene loses whatever delicacy there was in its beginnings when Burgundy engages Henry in an exchange of tasteless innuendoes at Katherine's expense. After some thirty lines of conventional indecencies in which he joins a stranger in making light of the woman he has just betrothed, the play concludes with Henry's bargaining on a point of protocol. The final scene of Harry's play suggests that an unanticipated liability in his career is the impairment of his sense of taste.

Henry understands that the conventions of the political religion surrounding the monarchy—*ceremony* in its broadest sense—do not suffice to protect the king from the weakness of his personal character. Henry's limitations may derive from his rejecting a necessary condition for rule because it is not sufficient. By showing the defects of Henry's solution,

Shakespeare suggests a more perfect resolution of the tension between the royal office and the royal person. A king who could maintain respect for ceremony but who could understand its prescriptions as imposing upon himself ethical obligations rather than as conferring providential assurances of his personal privileges might protect himself from the presumptuousness of a Richard while binding himself to the task of rule. A monarch who could see in royal usages a public trust necessary to right order would not be tempted to equate ceremony with personal revenue. Such a monarch might discover in promoting justice the recompense which Henry demands and fails to find in the perquisites of office. Shakespeare's portrayals of rulers capable of this distinction may suggest an answer to Henry's indictment of the "idol, Ceremony." It seems clear that such rulers fail to appear in the histories. To appreciate Shakespeare's inquiry into a more complete statesmanship, we should have to compare his reflections on the unmoved mover of Sonnet 94 with his portrayals of statesmen on the order of Theseus, Duke Vincentio, and Prospero.[23]

Notes

1. See the translation of the *Hiero* by Marvin Kendrick in Leo Strauss, *On Tyranny* (New York: Free Press, 1963), especially pp. 2-6.
2. *Henry V*, IV.i.237. My text throughout is the Penguin *Complete Shakespeare*, general editor Alfred Harbage (Baltimore: Penguin, 1969).
3. Shakespeare read Plutarch's account of Caesar's rise by popular arts. Considering that *Julius Caesar* was probably his next play after *Henry V* Shakespeare may well have know this aspect of Caesar's career while he was writing his version of Hal's populism.
4. Bolingbroke describes Richard's appearance on the walls of Flint Castle in the standard solar terms (III.iii.62-67) which include the sun's rebuking "envious clouds." The imagery is precisely parallel to that which Hal employs in his soliloquy, but opposite in meaning.
5. See E.M.W. Tillyard, *Shakespeare's History Plays* (London: Chatto and Windus, 1944), p. 271.
6. M.M. Reese accepts Warwick's unfounded hypothesis that the prince "puts on a kind of moral disguise, in order to know his people better." *The Cease of Majesty: A Study of Shakespeare's History Plays* (New York: St. Martin's Press, 1961). p. 297.
7. See C.L. Barber, *Shakespeare's Festive Comedy* (Princeton: Princeton University Press, 1959), pp. 195-213.
8. Neither Holinshed, Hall, Fabyan, nor *The Famous Victories of Henry V* suggests that Henry's early wildness was anything but genuine. Shakespeare thus departed from every known source in making the prodigality an elaborate pretense on Henry's part.

9. *The Book of the Courtier*, trans. George Bull (Baltimore: Penguin Books, 1967), especially pp. 59-60, 67-70. The whole of Machiavelli's *Discourses* could be understood as a celebration of Roman *virtù* qualified by Machiavelli's assertion of a further excellence identified with his own new ways and orders.

10. Reese's view is typical: "In practice he does not abuse his easy familiarity with the London underworld—the crimes he commits are trivial, if they are crimes at all" (*Cease of Majesty*, p. 297).

11. The most recent trend in critical approaches to *Henry V* is indicated by Norman Rabkin, "Rabbits, Ducks and *Henry V*," *Shakespeare Quarterly* 28 (Summer 1977), 279-296. Given the present emphasis upon dialectical oppositions it seems inevitable that someone should suggest that the play be taken as an unresolvable antinomy—Rabkin's rabbits and ducks refer to the gestaltist's illusionist silhouette. Criticism of *Henry V* has followed the same phases one notes with regard to any Shakespearean play (*Antony and Cleopatra, Julius Caesar*) which features a striking opposition. Early critics stage out clear positions for or against the play and protagonist, a later group attempts to mediate by proposing a judiciously mixed view, and finally the work is assigned to the ever-growing roster of "problem" plays which tease us out of thought while assuring us that Shakespeare was as adept as suspending judgment as we are. Rabkin and Karl P. Wentersdorf, "The Conspiracy of Silence in *Henry V*," *Shakespearean Quarterly* 27 (Summer 1976), 264-287, provide a run-down of the critical fortunes of the play. My contention is that one can better grasp Shakespeare's portrayal of the fifth Henry by understanding more precisely what moves Henry throughout his career, beginning with his earliest deeds in *Richard II*. The ambiguities of the last play of the tetralogy can be resolved only by attending to the continuity established between Henry's actions in that play and his earlier projects.

The most thoughtful study of *Henry V* with which I am acquainted is Michael Platt's *The English Prince*, as yet unpublished. Platt argues that Henry is Shakespeare's answer to the Machiavellian prince, combining genuine Christian piety with clear-sighted political virtue while creating a political religion which enables him to engraft ancient martial and political virtues upon the Christianity of his subjects. I agree that Henry is personally pious but doubt that his statesmanship could be called Christian. More fundamentally, I find myself disagreeing with Platt's conviction that Henry is a just king bent upon re-educating England.

12. Exeter and Westmoreland (I.ii.122-129) stress the necessity of Henry's making an impression upon his "brother kings and monarchs of the earth" (122). The French war can be understood as Henry's re-enactment on the international stage of the spectacle he has just concluded in the domestic realm.

13. Compare *King John* (II.i.561-598) with Falstaff's speech in *2 Henry IV* (I.ii.232-234).

14. H.C. Goddard, *The Meaning of Shakespeare* (Chicago: University of Chicago Press, 1951), Vol. I, pp. 226-239 and R.W. Battenhouse, "Henry V as Heroic Comedy," in *Essays on Shakespeare in Honor of Hardin Craig*, ed. R. Hosley (Columbia: University of Missouri Press, 1962), pp. 169-180, have commented upon the comic scenes as ironic reflections upon the main action of Henry's statecraft.

15. As it has been made quite forcefully by Marlo Lewis, "On War and Legitimacy in Shakespeare's *Henry V*," in Harry V. Jaffa, ed., *Statesmanship: Essays in Honor of Sir Winston Spencer Churchill* (Durham: Carolina Academic Press, 1981), pp. 41-61. I am grateful to Mr. Lewis for allowing me to read the manuscript version of his essay.

16. Consider the skillful provocation conveyed by Henry's confessions to Mountjoy (III.vi.133-146), which virtually ensures an immediate attack from the overconfident French.

17. Sir Francis Bacon, "Of Honour and Reputation," *The Complete Essays of Francis Bacon*, ed. H.L. Finch (New York: Washington Square Press, 1963), pp. 137-138.

18. Platt notes the parallel between Agincourt and Gideon's triumph. However, he does not see a problem for Henry in Gideon's example of yielding the glory to God.

19. Actually, Alexander was also known for his rapaciousness in the pursuit of empire, as we are reminded by the result of Fluellen's lisping malapropism, "Alexander the Pig."

20. For an account of Henry's conformities with the qualities attributed to Christian kings in handbooks of Erasmus and Chelidonius see J.H. Walter's introduction to his New Arden edition of *Henry V* (London: Methuen, 1954). Two difficulties militate against Walter's argument: first, he gratuitously assumes that Shakespeare identifies good monarchs and Christian monarchs; second, he fails to establish that Henry is a just king, although justice is the crucial excellence of the Christian king according to Erasmus and Chelidonius.

21. Another possible interpretation of the line is that Henry acknowledges he has the same duty as any subject; that is, of saving his soul: "every subject's duty is the king's [duty]." I think this reading is not as likely as the one I suggest, but in any case such a rendering would not alter the argument here developed.

22. The motif of chivalric favors also receives a final rendition in Hal's assurance to Kate: "My comfort is that old age, that ill layer-up of beauty, can do no more spoil upon my face.... Thou shalt wear me, if thou wear me, better and better" (V.ii.222-226).

23. That Shakespeare's best rulers appear exclusively in the comedies, works which withdraw a certain distance from the intractabilities of the more real-

istic histories and tragedies, suggests that Shakespeare's expectations of an historical monarch possessed of the virtues of a Prospero or Vincentio were decidedly modest.

THE TWO TRUTHS
OF *TROILUS AND CRESSIDA*

Thomas G. West

Troilus and Cressida portrays the war between Greece and Troy as the earliest instance of an enduring rivalry between two understandings of truth. What may be called the Eastern and Western views of truth find their expression in the conduct of the play's characters, in the parallel plots of the Trojan War and the love story. The drama allows us to see how the distinctive casts of human souls answer to their formation by or espousal of one or the other of these contestant alternatives.

We may tentatively call these two truths *faith* and *reason*. Faith is at home in Troy, in the East. Reason is found with the Greeks, in the West.

Embattled Troy is the most ancient of Shakespeare's settings, and because it is also the setting for Homer's *Iliad*, the first epic poem of the West, Shakespeare adopts it as an appropriate starting point for his own multi-play epic of Western civilization. *Troilus and Cressida* announces a theme that will recur through the entire range of the dramas. The tension between the Oriental and Hellenic principles runs like a bright thread through the succession of political regimes, whether Roman, Italian, French, or English, that follow the Greek and Trojan beginnings. The history of Western civilization is informed by a melding, not always coherent, of the Trojan (Eastern) and Greek (Western) understandings of truth.

The Greeks, at their most distinctive, discover truth in the knowledge of the natures of things, especially of the nature of man. Keen discernment of the arrangement of the cosmos and a grasp of the human passions through accurate observation of others and of oneself offer them a foundation for the conduct of life. The Trojans, at their most distinctive, identify truth with faith in something whose value is established by an act of the will. This faith becomes their foundation for living.

This duality surfaces in *Troilus and Cressida* through the contrast between the Greek Ulysses and the Trojan Troilus. It is worked out in the main love plot, which tells the story of Troilus's love for Cressida, its consummation, its dissolution, and Troilus's subsequent destructive fury. We see the same themes at work in the war plot. Ulysses schemes to draw Achilles back into the battle by appealing to his self-interest. The Trojans justify fighting to keep Helen as a willful fidelity to a cause that cannot be defended by reason.

The action of the play roughly follows the Homeric plot of Achilles' proud withdrawal from the Greek army, his eventual return to combat, and his final slaying of Hector. Shakespeare adds to Homer a love story portraying the affection of Troilus and Cressida, whose tale had already been famously told by Chaucer in his *Troilus and Criseyde*. In contrast to his two models, Homer and Chaucer, Shakespeare's play is suffused with an air of relentless mortality. No hope for an afterlife comforts the reader in his pity for Troilus, as in Chaucer. No immortal gods dignify the war with their interest and favor, as in Homer. Through Zeus's oversight and direction of the action of the *Iliad*, the human, all-too-human motives and conduct of the principals are molded into a plot that secures justice by granting glory and sufferings to the warriors in some proportion to their merits and faults. The obtrusive absence of gods in Shakespeare's play robs the war of its splendor and even of its sense. No divine government checks or redeems hot blood and meanly calculating self-interest. Shakespeare strips away benign eternity and allows his Trojans and Greeks to be overwhelmed by the manifest sway of transience. The characters find themselves distressed, in one way or another, by the merciless power of "envious and calumniating time" (III.iii.173). From their various understandings of truth spring the variety of their responses to the oblivion threatened by time's destructive flux.[1]

I. Trojan Truth

The question of the truth about love is unfolded in the story of the two lovers. In the opening scene of the play Troilus impatiently urges Pandarus to solicit for him the affection of his beloved Cressida. He sees Cressida as a valuable object indeed, but one whose value he reckons, without noticing it, in the language of commerce and consumption. Pandarus, he says, will be the ship that will carry Troilus the merchant to Cressida the pearl of India. Pandarus's gross likeness comparing Troilus's suit to the baking and eating of a cake confirms Troilus's admission that his passion is aroused when Pandarus speaks of "her eyes, her hair, her cheek, her gait, her voice"—in short, her body (I.i.51). In fact, Pandarus had spoken not of her voice but her wit (43-44), but Troilus falsely exchanges in his memory a quality of sense for one of intellect. Shakespeare exposes the sensual ground of Troilus's love from the start, although Troilus conceals that ground from himself. The pearl's durability appears to distinguish it from the fleeting satisfaction supplied by a cake consumed at one sitting, but a merchant computes the worth of a pearl by what the market will bear. A fall in demand yields a corresponding decline in price. A love grounded on the appetite of the lover is exposed to a like risk. Satiation breeds indifference. We will see how Troilus later attempts to exalt his love for Cressida above the vulgar transience of a market commodity or sensual delectation.

Cressida knows or guesses the inner truth of Troilus's affection for her. So although she loves him from the heart, she hides her sentiments: "women are angels, wooing," she tells herself, but "Things won are done, joy's soul lies in the doing" (I.ii.272-273). She believes that she (like all women) is like a commodity which, once obtained, loses its value: "Men prize the thing ungained more than it is" (275). She seems to mean that the lover's imagination, stirred by appetite, attributes exaggerated virtues to its object, as does Troilus in the scene just discussed. But her strategy is futile, for only if she were a heavenly being, an immaterial substance, could her secret love be content forever basking in the incorporeal glow of Troilus's devotion. Mere spirituality will not do. She must consider not only that Troilus's patience will not endure indefinite postponements, but that she too is an earthly creature and must finally come together with her lover if their love is to find completion, though by doing so she risks losing him as soon as, in Troilus's phrase, his "wat'ry palate" tastes "Love's thrice-repured nectar" (III.ii.19-20). Her vacillation in the scene that opens the lovers' night of consummation reflects this predicament. She wishes to confess her love for Troilus, but she hesitates, fearing that her surrender may encourage him to "play the tyrant" (III.ii.112). She finds herself in contradiction with herself: to be herself, the admitted lover of Troilus, she must be untrue to herself, the inaccessible angel (110-119, 140-142).

Troilus also believes that human deficiency mars perfect love, but he attributes the defect to the body's limited strength, not to the glutting of the senses: "This is the monstrosity in love, lady, that the will is infinite and the execution confined" (III.ii.74-76). He believes, however, that the lover's pledge of truth to his beloved can transfigure and eternalize the merely sensual appetites that first aroused his passion. He hopes to exempt their love from worldly decay. Troilus affirms that his truthful simplicity, his faithfulness to Cressida, will become a standard for future ages. His very person will become the sacred, eternal principle of truth:

> True swains in love shall in the world to come
> Approve their truth by Troilus. When their rhymes,
> Full of protest, of oath, and big compare,
> Wants similes,
> ....
> As truth's authentic author to be cited,
> "As true as Troilus" shall crown up the verse
> And sanctify the numbers. (165-168, 173-175)

Caught up in Troilus's enthusiasm, Cressida imitates her lover by calling eternal infamy down upon herself if she should ever prove false to him.

The next morning, Troilus behaves just as Cressida feared: now satisfied, he is eager to depart, and he speaks to her prosaically and abruptly.

> *Tro.*   I prithee now, to bed.
> *Cres.*   Are you aweary of me?
> ....
> *Tro.*   You will catch cold and curse me.
> *Cres.*   Prithee tarry;
> You men will never tarry.
> O foolish Cressid! I might have still held off,
> And then you would have tarried. (IV.ii.7,15-18)

When Cressida urges him to come back into her bedroom so that he will not be seen by a visitor, Troilus responds with a conspiratorial smile and a coarse laugh, "as if [Cressida] meant naughtily" (IV.ii.37). Later, when he is informed that Cressida must be taken from him to be sent to the Greek camp in exchange for a Trojan prisoner of war, at first he has nothing more to say than, "Is it concluded so?... How my achievements mock me!" (IV.ii.66, 69).

For Troilus, the real, embodied Cressida standing before him has lost her worth, insofar as that worth consisted in her sensual desirability. But the Cressida of his poetic imagination, as it were, the perfect soul of beauty implicitly posited in his oath of eternal fidelity to her, endures. What had begun in sensual desire has been transformed through the enthusiasm of Troilus's passions and fancy into a quasi-religious devotion to an ideal construct. In the following scene, when the two lovers are about to separate, Troilus repeats his fervent pledges, now expressed in ornate Latinate diction replete with elaborate similes (IV.iii). Cressida may well sense the willful artfulness of Troilus's protestations, especially in light of his frequent expressions of doubt about her ability to be faithful. Troilus believes himself to be still in love with Cressida, but he is now increasingly beguiled by a product of his own making.

As soon as Cressida arrives at the Greek camp, she is wooed by Diomedes, an intelligent, spirited, but blunt soldier free of illusions. At the conclusion of the day's combat, Hector and Troilus are invited to dine with the Greek captains, and the visit provides Troilus with a lucky opportunity to spy on Diomedes' seduction of Cressida. With astonishment and despair, Troilus watches Cressida's abrupt repudiation of her earlier promised fidelity as she now consents to become Diomedes' mistress. Confronted with the contradiction between the "true" (faithful) Cressida to whom he is bound by sacred vows "strong as heaven itself" and the "true" (real) Cressida whose "mind is now turned whore" (as Thersites remarks), Troilus nearly goes mad (V.ii.110, 151). Her "truth" has proved false, yet if truth is true, as it must be, it cannot be false: "This is, and is not, Cressid" (142). His speech expresses the shattering of his world:

> Within my soul there doth conduce a fight
> Of this strange nature, that a thing inseparate [namely Cressida]
> Divides more wider than the sky and earth;
> And yet the spacious breadth of this division
> Admits no orifice.... (143-147)

What has happened, of course, is that the truth supposedly secured by the lover's oaths has not overcome the previously hidden but now unconcealed truth of changeable human passions. Cressida sums up her apostasy:

> The error of our eye directs our mind.
> What error leads must err. O then conclude,
> Minds swayed by eyes are full of turpitude. (106-108)

Her heart must love whomever she finds attractive because she is a slave to her "eye," her senses, and so to time and transiency.

However, her consciousness of having betrayed her beloved may cause her to exaggerate her fault. Troilus is gone, and she must go on living. Changed circumstance may call for new allegiance. When Cressida

first enters the Greek camp, she is kissed by the Greek captains in succession, being passed from man to man like common currency, and she
may see in the manly, relatively courteous Diomedes a haven from the
predatory lust of the other soldiers. Fidelity to the lost Troilus seems to
make sense no longer, though she regrets her abandonment of faith, knowing that she has no other standard of truth, no firm purchase, within the
endless flux of appetite and of calculations of safety.[2] We may add, in our
modest defense of Cressida, that Troilus, who had professed his faithfulness to her again and again, had never managed to ask her to marry him!
(Troilus speaks explicitly and favorably of marriage in II.ii, quoted below.)

For his part, Troilus cannot grasp the truth he has seen with his
eyes—Cressida's unfaithfulness—because he will not give up the truth
certified by his will's commitment:

> Never did young man fancy
> With so eternal and so fixed a soul. (161-162)

Incapable of intentionally duplicitous conduct himself (as Ulysses points
out in IV.v.100-101), he cannot understand such waywardness in his sanctified beloved. His first recourse is to seek revenge on Diomedes,
Cressida's lover, as though he, not she, were the source of her infidelity.
But as the final chaotic battle of the play unfolds in the last act, Troilus's
anger becomes increasingly generalized, and when Hector is slain, Achilles
replaces Diomedes as the prime object of his wrath. Finally, Troilus calls
on the gods to

> effect your rage with speed;
> ....
> I say at once, let your brief plagues be mercy,
> And linger not our sure destructions on. (V.x.6-9)

"Hope of revenge," he says, will comfort Troy in its loss, although he is
quite aware that "sure destructions" will follow the pursuit of that hope.

What has happened to Troilus? The corruption of Cressida has deprived him of his "truth." Instead of learning from her example that faith
in flesh is no way to eternity, he curses life altogether and is finally content to see Troy fall in order to avenge himself on life. Honorable fidelity
to the will's sworn purpose, now shown to be absurd, is succeeded by
irrational fury. Once the world is exposed as false, its annihilation is the
only course for one whose will still craves consistency. Nietzsche's claim

that "man would rather will nothingness than not will"[3] aptly glosses Troilus's rage at the play's end.

Troilus's principle of truth may be seen at work in a martial setting in the deliberations of the Trojan war council (II.ii). Offered the opportunity by the Greeks to end the war by returning Helen, the Trojans meet to deliberate. In their discussion Hector argues in favor of giving her back, setting forth reasons of rational fear as well as of justice in accord with the law of nature and nations. He is supported by the priest Helenus, whom Troilus denounces in terms that resemble a Nietzschean attack on reason and priestly morality:

> Nay, if we talk of reason,
> Let's shut our gates and sleep.
> ....
> [R]eason and respect
> Make livers pale and lustihood deject. (II.ii.46-50)

Reason is a fit standard for cowardly priests because it reckons nothing more than means to security: its aim is rest and escape from life's sufferings.[4] Against reason Troilus poses the standard of will:

> I take today a wife, and my election
> Is led on in the conduct of my will.
> ....
> How may I avoid,
> Although my will distaste what it elected,
> The wife I chose? There can be no evasion
> To blench from this and to stand firm by honor. (61-69)

This "mad idolatry," which "makes the service greater than the god" (as Hector quite reasonably calls it, 56-57), excludes all considerations of the goodness or usefulness of an action or purpose. Once a choice is made, honor requires a commitment to its execution even to death. This dedication is both honorable and yields honor. Whatever Helen's intrinsic worth may be, says Troilus,

> She is a theme of honor and renown,
> A spur to valiant and magnanimous deeds,
> Whose present courage may beat down our foes
> And fame in time to come canonize us. (199-202)

Even if the outcome of the war should prove disastrous, it "hath our several honors all engaged/ To make it gracious" (124-125). The grace that flows from faith redeems earthly suffering. Hector seals the decision by explicitly abandoning his reasonable opinion "in way of truth" for the sake of a willful "resolution to keep Helen still" (188-191).

One of the play's many striking anachronisms is Hector's mention in II.ii of Aristotle and the "law of nature." He seems to champion, and then precipitously abandon, what sounds like the medieval natural law doctrine. Hector also seems "medieval" in his chivalric notion of combat as witness to one's lady's virtue (I.iii.260-283) and in his scrupulous attention to what he calls "fair play" on the battlefield (V.iii.37-49). His "scholasticism" has no roots in reason. Instead, he bows to authority, whether he is quoting Aristotle or appealing to the "moral laws...of nations" (II.ii.166, 184-5). He attributes to convention—for example, to the convention of marital fidelity (175-77)—the truth of nature. To accept authority for its own sake is to accept a merely willed standard, so when Troilus exhibits a more vigorous and persistent present will, appealing to the passion for glory, Hector yields to it. Hector's change of mind could be taken as an illustration in miniature of the shift from late scholastic Christianity, where "natural law" had become for many an almost empty phrase synonymous with Church dogma, to early Protestantism, where God's will and man's faith became the exclusive standards and nature was explicitly jettisoned, to modernity, where one's own will does away with all external authority, whether divine or natural.

Troilus explains in this scene the principle that grounds his conduct in both love and war, and Hector shows by his resolution against his own reasonable words that he accepts that principle. Here we see that, on the Trojan side, the unity of the love plot and war plot springs from Troilus's and Troy's fidelity to the will's election, whether it be Cressida or Helen, love or war.

II. Greek Truth

The Greeks exemplify a different approach to truth which depends on knowledge rather than will. As the play opens, the war against Troy has been dragging on for years without result. Achilles, reputedly the Greeks' most skillful warrior, is refusing to fight. When the Greek leaders beg him from time to time to return to the war, they succeed only in heightening Achilles' already gigantic vanity.

A war council is called to discuss this predicament (I.iii). Agamemnon, the head of the Greek expedition, and old Nestor open the discussion with platitudinous speeches excusing the absence of results, blaming the war's failure on the vagaries of chance. They also assert, with self-satisfied complacency, that a protracted conflict elicits virtue by testing men's mettle with worthy obstacles. Ulysses responds with his famous speech on degree, in which he implicitly corrects the elder statesmen by alluding to dangerous errors in their rule of the Greek camp. The orderly movement of the heavenly bodies around the sun provides men with a fit model of political rule. Human life, Ulysses implies, should imitate that eternal and necessary order, as far as it lies within the capacity of human choice acting upon mortal beings subject to the depredations of temporality. He vividly details the consequences that follow when rulers are unable to provide a conventional order in the human sphere corresponding to the natural order in the heavens:

> Then everything include itself in power,
> Power into will, will into appetite,
> And appetite, an universal wolf,
> So doubly seconded with will and power,
> Must make perforce an universal prey
> And last eat up himself.   (I.iii.119-124)

Ulysses appears to blame Achilles for this "neglection of degree," but the argument of his speech, as opposed to its explicit conclusion, suggests that the fault is rather Agamemnon's. When the planets "in evil mixture to disorder wander," then the sun, with his "med'cinable eye,"

> Corrects the ill aspects of planets evil,
> And posts like the commandment of a king,
> Sans check, to good and bad. (92-94)

Ulysses attributes the Greek failure, then, not to the recalcitrance of earthly stuff to men's high designs, as Agamemnon said, but to a defective execution of the design in question. Not bad luck, but bad statesmanship blocks the war's progress. Agamemnon has failed to prescribe appropriate medicine for the errant warrior.

Ulysses follows his speech on degree with an apparent denunciation of the factious Achilles. In fact, however, the burden of his speech describes how Achilles amuses himself by staging in his tent satirical mimes mocking Agamemnon's pretentious pomposity and Nestor's aged foibles. Ulysses seems to inflame the very infection he has diagnosed, for he further discredits the elders' authority by broadcasting these all-too-plau-

sible portraits. But he has a sensible purpose. Agamemnon's loss is
Ulysses', and the Greeks', gain. Ulysses lays the foundation for his own
quiet assumption of political power for himself, so that he can administer
the remedy that the titular leaders are unable to provide. They are soon
ready to follow Ulysses' advice.

He proposes to deflate Achilles' pride by having all the Greek captains pretend to honor the warrior Ajax above Achilles. The aim is to
attract Achilles back to battle in order to recoup his lost reputation. Nestor,
delighted with the suggestion, comments:

> Two curs shall tame each other; pride alone
> Must tar the mastiffs on, as 'twere their bone. (I.iii.389-390)

In Madison's phrase from the fifty-first *Federalist*, calculated employment
of opposite and rival interests will supply the defect of better motives.

Ulysses exercises kingly authority and applies his useful but ignoble
medicine covertly. He never disturbs the dignified appearance of
Agamemnon,

> the glorious planet Sol
> In noble eminence enthroned and sphered
> Amidst the others. (I.iii.89-91)

Ulysses understands that a public fiction of beauty and "degree" is a necessary part of the political imitation of nature. Just as nature enlists our
admiration by its manifest ordered beauty and not by the hidden mecha-
nisms and principles that sustain that beauty, so too man's political regime cannot dispense with its outward look of *kosmos*, although the ugly
designs of prudence may uphold the fabric.

The Greek term *kosmos* conveys at once the notions of order and
ornament. Its later application to what we call the "cosmos" followed
from observation of the regular motions of the sun, moon, and stars. The
thought behind the Greek philosopher Heraclitus's Fragment 124—"The
most beautiful *kosmos* is like a heap of rubble thrown together at random"—may be the same as the understanding that Shakespeare attributes
to Ulysses.[5]

Paul Valery's comparison of Western and Eastern art (which he may
have learned from Hegel) describes in the realm of the aesthetic the
outstanding feature of Greek truth: "What differentiates Greek art and
Oriental art is that the latter is concerned only with giving pleasure, Greek

art with attaining *beauty*, that is, giving to things a form which will make us think of universal order, divine wisdom, the domination of mind, things that do not exist in close, tangible, existing nature, all made up of *accidents*."[6] Valery's remark reminds us of Pandarus's song for Helen in Act III, Scene i, and the Servant's remark in the same scene on the pleasure of music (III.i.107-116, 23).

This difficulty blemishes Ulysses' solution: he offers no account of the ends of human life. Indeed, conspicuously absent from all the Greek martial deliberations is any consideration of what the war is being fought for and whether it should be continued. All participants in the argument assume the desirability of victory, but no one explains why. The omission obtrudes particularly because in the parallel Trojan war council in II.ii, the only subject of discussion is the purpose of the war and whether it is worth fighting to keep Helen. The Greeks talk of nothing but means, the Trojans of nothing but ends. It appears that although knowledge of natural necessity, especially of the operation of the human passions, can be profitably enlisted in the execution of goals once chosen, it affords no knowledge of the worth of those goals.

Are the Greek ends, then, merely arbitrary, posited by random fiat, passionate intensity, or fraud? Surely Ulysses' cosmic analogy provides nothing like a detailed ethical code of conduct. But in a broader sense the solar system can indeed be a guide for the formation and preservation of political community. Taken as a similitude for political life, it suggests that the citizens be formed into a hierarchy of rulers and ruled according to manifest principles of distinction, whether of birth or accomplishments, by means of laws applicable to all. With the quarrelsome tumult of domestic faction checked by habits and institutions preserving due degree, the most gifted citizens would be in a position to undertake those "high designs" of which Ulysses speaks (I.iii.102), which the chaos of uncontrolled strife wrecks. A space is cleared for the exercise of the rational faculty, otherwise thwarted by the predominance of rude body and passion.

Ulysses' dealings with Achilles thus instance a more general political problem: how can physical strength and the body's passions be brought under the governance of wit and intelligence? Not only does Ulysses have to circumvent Achilles, the palpable rebel, but also Agamemnon himself, nominally capable but in fact inept at statecraft. In the Greek camp, as in life, prudence and power rarely coincide. Yet Ulysses aims to yoke together "the still and mental parts" with "the ram that batters down the wall" (I.iii.200, 206).

Plato's *Apology of Socrates* dramatizes the disjunction of intelligence and strength in the contest between wise Socrates and powerful Athens.[7] Shakespeare renews the theme here on a more laughable plane through his presentation of smart but ugly Thersites. We first see him being beaten by "beef-witted" Ajax who refuses to countenance Thersites' claims to intellectual superiority (II.i). The spectacle of Ajax thrashing Thersites, who throughout his cudgeling stubbornly persists in asserting his right not to be ruled by the dull but vigorous warrior (II.i.89-94), offers a comic tableau of this deepest of political problems.

Thersites' otherwise outstanding intelligence is marred by his ignorance of the need for calculating intellect to dress itself in robes of cosmic or divine justice. He lacks Ulysses' rhetorical capacity to order and adorn. He scatters about publicly the truths that Ulysses keeps to himself. Thersites' ugly appearance—he is a bastard by birth, deformed in body, cowardly in battle, and incautiously blunt of speech—matches the ugly truths of his understanding. In his person, just as in Troilus's, every separation between seeming and being collapses. Thersites discerns the low passions that govern human conduct, but he does not know how to arrange those passions into a binding, visible unity of beautiful form. By despairing over the power of reason to rule—he says he can cure folly only if "too much brain" causes it (V.i.48)—he condemns himself to the peevish envy of the leading men whom he considers undeserving of their honors. His mind discerns no fulcrum by which he might apply the lever of his wit to lift the lecherous and proud above their blind pursuits.

Thersites believes that reason ought to rule, but all around him he sees weaknesses of mind and body, stupidity and disease. His angry railing against these favorite evils of his betrays his attachment to the thoughtless opinion that thought should be able to overcome necessity. He calls himself a "knower" who is "a fool to serve such a fool" as Agamemnon, and the others who rule him (II.iii.40-61). Thersites' truth, then, is the mirror opposite of Troilus's. While Troilus believes the will's attachment enables man to hold fast to a truth that escapes necessity, Thersites sees everywhere the repellent sway of necessity. Neither Troilus nor Thersites comprehends the blending of attention to the passions and willful teaching of goals that enables Ulysses to imitate the heavens while trafficking in low motives.

In the third act, after Achilles' pride has been shaken by the calculated snub inflicted upon him by the Greek princes, he is ripe for Ulysses' counsel. Ulysses purports to quote from a book maintaining that one cannot claim to own what is one's own except by reflection from others.

Achilles confirms the point with an analogy. The eye sees itself only by reflection in another's eye (III.iii.92-123). The language and image used by the two men recall the *First Alcibiades* of Plato, but a moment's reflection reveals that Shakespeare has Ulysses distort Socrates' words.[8] Socrates had maintained that self-knowledge and self-possession come only through knowledge of the intellectual part of another's soul, but Ulysses asserts that they are bestowed by the applause of others. The example he cites to prove his case—"the lubber Ajax" who has suddenly come into eminent repute (123-141)—undermines his argument, for Ajax in his pride is utterly ignorant of himself.[9] But the honor-infatuated Achilles does not take up the hint. Since love of honor has usurped the place of love of knowledge in him, he depends wholly upon the whims of public opinion for his self-estimation and so is blind to himself. Ulysses provides him with an appropriate mirror of himself: Achilles is time's slave; he must stay in perpetual motion if he is to retain the crowd's short-lived adulation. "Perseverance, dear my Lord,/ Keeps honor bright" (III.iii. 150-151). Nothing human endures beyond the transiency of the moment.

> For beauty, wit,
> High birth, vigor of bone, desert in service,
> Love, friendship, charity, are subjects all
> To envious and calumniating time. (169-173)[10]

Ulysses is elaborating for Achilles' sake what it means to embrace honor as life's standard. Achilles grasps perfectly the correctness of Ulysses' argument and its practical consequence that he should return to battle, and he is persuaded by it.

But another passion, his love for a Trojan girl, holds Achilles back. This revelation comes as an abrupt surprise to the reader, as we now learn that Achilles dotes on love even more than on ambition. The unruly bias of his passions thwarts Ulysses' careful effort to harness them by threatening Achilles with fameless oblivion. The scheme is overturned by the hot blood whose irrationality Ulysses understands so well.

Thersites' pessimism over the weakness of rational policy seems vindicated, and he concludes from Ulysses' failure that the Greeks have lost their claim to distinction from the Trojans: "whereupon the Grecians begin to proclaim barbarism, and policy grows into an ill opinion" (V.iv.15-16). (The Greeks called all non-Greeks "barbarians." For Thersites, what makes barbarians barbarous is their failure to follow reason or "policy.") But Achilles has been moved. His mind, he says, is "like a fountain stirred" (III.iii.303), and he wavers back and forth between "to fight" and "not to fight." In Act IV, Achilles says he will meet Hector in the field tomorrow (IV.v.268). Then a letter from the mother of his Trojan beloved insists that he keep his vow to hold back from the fight, and he says he will (V.i.36-44). Finally, enraged by Patroclus's death, he vows vengeance on the enemy (V.v.30-35). In the end we cannot know whether this loss would have been sufficient by itself to recall Achilles to his station. That is, we do not know whether Ulysses has had any effect on the action or not. We do see that Achilles' pursuit of honor, in contrast to the Trojans', is not honorable in the least. He cares only for the repute of deeds and not for the deeds themselves. When he chances upon Hector momentarily disarmed, he does not hesitate to order his men to slay him in cold blood. Afterward, he boasts shamelessly of his supposed heroism.

If our judgment is not bewildered by the *Iliad's* prettified presentation of these actions, Shakespeare's account does not look so different from Homer's. The goddess Athena tricks Hector into fighting Achilles against his better judgment (*Iliad*, XXII.226-247). During the fight, she retrieves Achilles' spear for him when he casts it at Hector and misses (276-277). Achilles' shield, which saves him from Hector's well-aimed spear, was crafted by a divine artisan. Athena rightly takes partial credit for the slaying (218), and Achilles admits it too (270-271). Her active participation in the combat gives Achilles a preponderant advantage that could be counted as great as that of chancing upon Hector unarmed (cf. 446). The notable difference between the two accounts (other than the absence of the gods in Shakespeare's) lies in the role of Achilles' Greek comrades. In the *Iliad*, Achilles prevents them from aiding his attack on Hector, reserving the actual killing for himself. This difference permits Shakespeare to make explicit Achilles' preoccupation with mere reputation.

These differences between Greeks and Trojans are more properly described as tendencies than as sharp distinctions, for we see Greek lovers in Achilles and Diomedes, and Trojan concern for present opinion in Paris's speech in the war council (II.ii.130-131). As for the two women who leave their countrymen, sensuous Helen and calculating Cressida, they find their ultimate repose where the soul of each is most at home. The Greek-Trojan difference, then, is only in part a consequence of the manner of life in each society; natural differences in individual character incline human beings toward the alternative ways of life embodied in the two warring sides.

III. Trojan and Greek Truth: Difficulties
Although Shakespeare attributes to the Greeks and Trojans the two no-

tions of truth that we have discussed, neither side is able to live up to its own ideal.

The typical Trojan deviation from truth is sensuality. We have mentioned the imaginative effort Troilus must expend to make himself see in Cressida more than a lily bed to wallow in (III.ii.11) and then to abandon once his appetite is sated. The lascivious scene preceding the lovers' union, which depicts Helen and Paris, whetted by Pandarus, idly indulging in erotic banter (III.i), anticipates the stale bawdry into which Troilus and Cressida's purer love might easily decline. And Hector's vulnerability to murder by Achilles is caused by his greedy pursuit of some nameless Greek soldier's glittering armor (V.vi.27-31, V.viii.1-4). The cloying facilitations of Pandarus minister to the pleasures of his favorites: the inane, obscene ditty he sings at Helen's behest (III.i.107-116) is probably no different, in his mind, from his service as go-between for the lovers. Sensuality's debauch threatens to dissipate the honorable firmness to which both Troilus and Hector subscribe.

Similarly, the typical excess in the Greek camp is pride, living for the sake of praise and the good opinion of others. The proud and the prudent both look to a standard outside themselves, but living in light of opinion confuses nature, the eternal order, with convention, what holds fashion here and now. Ajax suffers from a woefully self-ignorant pride that foolishly mistakes transparent flattery for confirmation of his worth. In Achilles' more complicated case, the warrior knowingly feeds on praise, whether merited or not, like Helen and Paris on their sensual delights. The vanity of Agamemnon and Nestor makes them complacent in the face of Greek failure; it hard for them to see what needs to be done to achieve victory.

While the Greeks tend to look beyond mere willfulness for guidance, the Trojans look toward their own willful constructs or commitments. This gives to the Trojans an aspect of self-preoccupation. They pay more regard to their poetic fancies, chivalric manners, and dreams of future glory than to the tumultuous present in which they are embroiled. Both sides speak of honor, but for the Greeks that term refers to present praise, whereas the Trojans conceive honor as fidelity to one's sworn purpose or the imagined canonization of future ages.[11] Although the Greeks sometimes swear oaths, they keep them only as long as calculation or passion inclines. Achilles breaks his oath to the mother of his Trojan beloved (that he would refrain from fighting the Trojans—V.i.36-43, V.v.30-35). He also breaks his agreement with Hector to meet him in combat (IV.v.267-269).

Both sensuality and mere reputation are exposed to the oblivion of "calumniating time." Honorable faith and knowledgeable conduct are the respective Trojan and Greek redemptive paths. They alone lift men out of the flood and ebb of the bodily desires and fickle opinion. It is noteworthy that the two most insightful Greeks—Ulysses and Thersites— seem to be indifferent to the attractions of sex or honor.

The Greek truth, however, is exposed to serious doubt as to its efficacy. Ulysses appears to fail utterly. There seem to be limits to human reason's ability to discover the way things are, as we see in Ulysses' failure to reckon on Achilles' being in love. The ambiguous issue of Ulysses' scheme shows how circumstance resists government by prudence. Greek truth is also not so clearly able to rank human ends, although it seems able to discover means to whatever ends men might choose. Even if knowledge of ends as well as means is attainable, its elusiveness bars access to all but a very few. Others will necessarily disparage it or despair of gaining it.

Trojan truth, on the other hand, although more generally accessible, cannot satisfy. Its delusion is to forget that the earthly objects dignified by honorable fidelity (Helen or Cressida) must inevitably reveal themselves as corruptible and hence unworthy of that fidelity. By cutting themselves off from rational calculations of relative worth, they find themselves attributing infinite value to things of finite merit. In his fleeting mood of rationality, Hector tells Troilus: "'Tis *mad* idolatry/ To make the service greater than the god" (II.ii.56-57, emphasis added). When the truth of the body and the truth of faith collide, madness threatens, for the simplicity of faith is revealed to be untrue to the duplicity of human nature. "Rule in unity" (V.ii.137) is not a metaphysical truth, as Troilus would like, but, in human affairs at least, a useful fiction, as Ulysses shows through his speeches and deeds.

One solution to the Trojan difficulty is granted by Christianity, which the manners and vocabulary of the Trojans frequently foreshadow. Particularly striking is Paris's servant, who says "I do depend upon the Lord," speaks of "the state of grace," and exclaims "the Lord be praised!" (III.i.5, 8, 14). The earthly body is sanctified and eternalized through Christ's resurrection and the promised Last Judgment. Christ's human body thereby becomes a uniquely worthy earthly object of the will's commitment, for through it one finds eternal salvation from the endless and pointless motions of the sensual world.[12]

The other solution is the one adopted by modern philosophy, whose principles sometimes appear in Troilus's speeches. "What's aught but as 'tis valued?" is an apt summation of the modern idea that value is a construct of the will. This notion identifies the source of value with the individual "I" which willfully attempts to dissolve whatever natural limits stand in its way. Modern science, with its ultimate aim, the absolute subjugation of nature to human control (and that means the abolition of the death of the body), is the contemporary substitute for the Christian God's will, whose grace endows bodies with transcendent incorruptibility. The Marxist faith in mankind's apocalyptic transformation through revolutionary political action is a further variation on the modern theme, promising quicker results than science through well-employed violence serving the final and self-abolishing stage of the class struggle.[13]

IV. Shakespeare's Truth

What about the truth of Shakespeare? In this play at least, it is Greek, and could even be called Thersitean, were it not for the poet's dispassionate stance toward the low truths he unveils. He seems to be free from Thersites' bitter cynicism. By adopting the debunking posture of Thersites, Shakespeare reveals the truth of Ulysses without practicing it. The play is full of intentional disproportions in its action and language, beginning with the Prologue's promise of warlike "high blood chafed," followed directly by Troilus's indifferent "I'll unarm again." One scholar argues that these discontinuities reflect Shakespeare's intention to make the audience participate in disorientation.[14] I maintain, on the contrary, that these unsettling difficulties are meant to dispel any comfort one might be tempted to take in familiar appearances, so that one's comprehension of the play may be a product of thought.

In the case of *Troilus and Cressida* ugliness is a concomitant of truthfulness. We are granted a glimpse into the uncouth engine room of Western civilization. What is revealed here in all frankness is concealed again, for instance, in *A Midsummer Night's Dream*, whose plot shows poetic semblance covering over the harshness of political and erotic passions. There Shakespeare practices the truth of Ulysses without revealing it. Self-knowledge calls for clear-headed insight into the heart of things, but the good life also relies on a public order whose appearance belies its inner truth. Shakespeare points to this double truth by allowing us only a single look, in this play about the origins, into the inward motions within the souls of Western men; elsewhere he devotes his art to the making and maintaining of beautiful surfaces, which he permits to remain comparatively undisturbed.

Troilus and Cressida might seem to be peculiarly modern in its ruthless debunking of martial nobility and romantic love.[15] But it would be more accurate to call it philosophic than modern, for its intention is not so much to dethrone the high as to show its inner workings. The overtly philosophical language and manner of many of the play's speeches have been noticed by critics.[16] They have generally not noticed the connection between its philosophicality and its deliberate repulsiveness. The play was rarely produced on stage before 1900, and since then only with mixed success.[17] It is unpopular because truth, when fully exposed, is unpopular. The letter to the reader preceding the play in the Quarto edition boasts of the distance between the play and the common understanding: "you have here a new play, never staled with the stage, never clapper-clawed with the palms of the vulgar." It also boasts of the play's "wit"—its intelligence. These two features go together. The play is Shakespeare's wittiest comedy, as the letter promises, because it is his most truthful, and being so, it must be remote from the crowd. Here poetry is strained about as far as it can go in the direction of philosophy without bursting its self-prescribed limits. If Shakespeare's poetic immortality had depended on this play alone, he might well have been long since forgotten—with some justice, for such is the truth taught by *Troilus and Cressida*.[18]

Notes

1. The best account of this theme in the play that I have found is David Kaula's "Will and Reason in *Troilus and Cressida*," *Shakespeare Quarterly* 12 (Summer 1961), pp. 271-283. Other helpful treatments are Winifred M.T. Nowottny, "'Opinion' and 'Value' in *Troilus and Cressida*," *Essays in Criticism* 4 (1954), pp. 282-296, and L.C. Knights, "The Theme of Appearance and Reality in *Troilus and Cressida*," in his *Some Shakespearean Themes and An Approach to Hamlet* (Stanford: Stanford University Press, 1966), pp. 55-73. John Bayley, "Time and the Trojans," *Essays in Criticism* 25 (January 1975), pp. 55-73, focuses on the imagery of transience in the play. See also R.A. Yoder, "'Sons and Daughters of the Game': An Essay on Shakespeare's *Troilus and Cressida*," *Shakespeare Survey* 25 (Cambridge: Cambridge University Press, 1972), pp. 16, 21. Citations from Shakespeare's text are taken from the *Complete Works*, Pelican Text Revised, ed. Alfred Harbage (New York: Viking, 1977). The quotations have sometimes been corrected from the New Variorum Edition of *Troilus*, ed. Harold N. Hillebrand (Philadelphia: Lippincott, 1953).

2. On Cressida's character, see Carolyn Asp, "In Defense of Cressida," *Studies in Philology* 74 (October 1977), pp. 406-417; Joseph Papp, in *The Festival Shakespeare: Troilus and Cressida*, ed. Bernard Beckerman and Papp (New York: Macmillan, 1967), pp. 50-52.

3. Nietzsche, *Genealogy of Morals*, Third Essay ("What Is the Meaning of Ascetic Ideals?"), no. 1.

4. Nietzsche, *Genealogy of Morals*, First Essay, nos. 7, 10; Third Essay, no. 13; *Thus Spoke Zarathustra*, "On the Teachers of Virtue," "On the Afterworldly."

5. Fragment 124, quoted by Martin Heidegger, *An Introduction to Metaphysics* (New Haven: Yale University Press, 1959), p. 133 (my translation).

6. Valery, *Selected Writings* (New York: New Directions Paperbacks, 1964), p. 150.

7. Thomas G. West, *Plato's Apology of Socrates* (Ithaca: Cornell University Press, 1979). For a briefer account, see West's Introduction to *Four Texts on Socrates: Plato's Euthyphro, Apology, and Crito, and Aristophanes' Clouds* (rev. ed.; Ithaca: Cornell University Press, 1998).

8. *First Alcibiades*, 132c-133e. L.C. Knights comments intelligently on the matter in "The Theme of Appearance and Reality," pp. 60-62.

9. See II.i.63 ("that fool knows not himself"); II.iii.154-156, 199-250 (Ajax proudly chides Achilles for his pride).

10. Cf. Knights, "The Theme of Appearance and Reality," p. 64.

11. Nowottny's "'Opinion' and 'Value' in *Troilus and Cressida*," pp. 282-288, intelligently explicates these differences.

12. Augustine, *City of God*, IX. 15, 17.

13. See Marx's "Contribution to the Critique of Hegel's *Philosophy of Right*: Introduction," in *The Marx-Engels Reader*, ed. Robert C. Tucker (2d ed.; New York: Norton, 1978), pp. 53-65.

14. Richard D. Fly, "'Suited in Like Condition as Our Argument': Imitative Form in Shakespeare's *Troilus and Cressida*," *Studies in English Literature* 15 (1975), pp. 273-292.

15. Jan Kott calls the play "amazing and modern," quoted by Bernard Beckerman, *The Festival Shakespeare*, p. 18. Virgil K. Whitaker, in his Introduction to the Pelican Shakespeare edition of the plays, p. 979, says "*Troilus and Cressida* is certainly not his greatest play, but it is in some respects his most modern."

16. Whitaker complains in his Introduction of "large, unassimilated chunks of philosophy" (p. 978), but he then admits, "In the tragedies Shakespeare presents in action what he explains here in theoretical terms" (p. 979). Cf. also Knights, "The Theme of Appearance and Reality," p. 56; G. Wilson Knight, *The Wheel of Fire* (4th ed.; London: Methuen, 1949), pp. 47-72.

17. Beckerman's essay in *The Festival Shakespeare* outlines the production history of the play. See also David Bevington, ed., *Troilus and Cressida*, Arden Shakespeare, Third Series (Walton-on-Thames, UK: Thomas Nelson and Sons, 1998), p. 90.

18. Thanks to Leo Paul de Alvarez, through whose 1976 seminar on

Shakespeare's Greek and Roman plays I learned much about *Troilus and Cressida*. The essay has received some welcome improvements through exchanges with Barbara Tovey, Sanderson Schaub, and John Alvis.

TROILUS AND CRESSIDA:
POETRY OR PHILOSOPHY?

Christopher Flannery

An old article in the Chinese Communist Party newspaper, the *People's Daily*, helps to understand the relationship between poetry and politics with particular reference to Shakespeare.[1] In the article, which, of course, expresses the authoritative views of the party leadership, the music of Beethoven and Schubert was blacklisted because of their "bourgeois and capitalist mentality," and because their music did not reflect the correct "class spirit." Beethoven's Sonata No. 17 was compared to one of Shakespeare's plays which, the article proclaimed, "only serves to disseminate the filthy nature of the bourgeoisie." Acceptable music or poetry, the piece continued, would glorify "the Red sun of Chairman Mao Tse-Tung and the Chinese Communist Party in the heart of the Chinese People." Every form of art "must be an instrument of the class struggle."

The Chinese leadership is right in deeming Shakespeare's poetry a deadly enemy of the Chinese regime and of communist tyranny generally. The political order maintained in China depends for its very existence upon the inculcation, "in the heart of the Chinese people," of a certain understanding of man, a comprehensive understanding of his internal make-up and his external relations, with other men and the world around him. This understanding must govern the lives of Chinese citizens, telling them what is good and what is bad, what is noble and what is despicable. And it must speak to their hearts, to govern their actions. But Shakespeare's poetry also reflects a comprehensive view of the soul of man and man's place in the universe. And in Shakespeare's universe there is no proper place for the class struggle. He is, indeed, the poet of "nature," not the poet of "history." Let the poetry of nature spring up "in the heart of the Chinese people," and the march of history must come to a dramatic halt.

Every political regime corresponds in some way with a certain view of man's place in the universe; and all great poetry reflects a view of the whole of man's life. Both universes, or views of the whole, are conjured up "in the heart" of their audience, an audience that is naturally made up of citizens. It is here, in their respective views of the whole, conjured up in the hearts of citizens, that poetry and politics meet.

That Shakespeare had considered this relationship between poetry and politics, and in much the same terms, I will try to show in my discussion of Act I, Scene 3 of *Troilus and Cressida*. I will then speculate briefly on the relationship that exists between the poetry of *Troilus and Cressida* and the human or political realm to which it is addressed.

Act I, Scene 3 is our introduction to the warring Greeks, who are holding council. When we first meet the "princes orgillous," encamped upon the Dardan plain, they no longer have a stomach for the war. They have lost the courage and resolution which carried them to Troy in their famous cause. The first utterance of the Great Agamemnon seeks the cause of this malaise: "Princes,/ What grief hath set the jaundice on your cheeks?" (I.iii.1-2).[2]

It is fittingly the wise Ulysses who addresses Agamemnon's concern, discovering and expounding the nature and causes of that fever whereof all the Grecian power is sick. The nature and substance of this sickness is the famed "neglection of degree," degree "which is the ladder to all high designs" (127, 102). Ulysses' great speech on degree has rightly been a favorite subject of critical interpretation over the centuries. Its political philosophy, imagery, and metaphysics have been traced by respected scholars, with varying degrees of success, not only to the obvious Chaucer and Homer, but, persuasively, to the *Ecclesiastical Polity* of Richard Hooker, Sir Thomas Elyot's *The Governour*, to Boethius, and, perhaps more hopefully than convincingly, to Plato himself.

To prove that Shakespeare drew on many or all of these sources in writing this passage does not tell us anything conclusive about the *substance* of Shakespeare's thought, any more than Thomas Jefferson should be considered a strict Lockean because he drew on the *Treatises of Government* in writing the Declaration of Independence. We should always be hesitant to take any single speech as fully representative of Shakespeare's final considered opinion on a matter. But that the substance of this passage should in depth and comprehension be comparable to such ostensibly serious works by such ostensibly serious men should be an added reason to take the passage seriously, certainly a reason *not* to consider the passage mere "rant," as at least one worthy critic has done, or as a mere "epitome of contemporary commonplaces" as another critic views it.

I leave aside the speech proper for the moment to consider the immediately succeeding passages. In these, having already expounded the nature of the profound malady afflicting the Grecian warriors, Ulysses turns to the *causes* of this sickness. These passages are less often honored with the close scrutiny of the critic, as they are obviously of less universal significance than the famous speech on Degree. But they tell us a great deal about the meaning of the preceding speech and, at the same time, about Shakespeare's understanding of the relation of poetry to politics.

We learn in these passages that the source of the political sickness that had undermined the great endeavor of the Greeks, the cause of that neglection of degree that "by a pace goes backward in a purpose/ It hath to climb" (128-129), is nothing other than poetry itself, specifically, dramatic poetry. As Ulysses tells us, Patroclus, "with ridiculous and awkward action/ (Which, slanderer, he imitation calls)" (149-150), pageants the Greek chieftains for the amusement of the Great Achilles. And further, "like a strutting player whose conceit/ Lies in his hamstring" (153-154), Patroclus acts out the greatness of Agamemnon and the old age of venerable Nestor, with such ridicule as to make Achilles burst in pleasure of his spleen. And Patroclus's imitations, or slanders, are not limited to the greatness of Agamemnon or the old age of Nestor. He presents a comprehensive imitation of the individual souls and collective purposes of the Greek camp. Again, to quote Ulysses,

> All our abilities, gifts, natures, shapes,
> Severals and generals of grace exact,
> Achievements, plots, orders, preventions,
> Excitements to the field, or speech for truce,
> Success or loss, what is or is not, serves
> As stuff for these two to make paradoxes. (179-184)

Shakespeare's Patroclus, momentarily assuming the classic role of the dramatic poet, imitates the whole Greek universe for the pleasure of Achilles. The paradoxes of Patroclus, paradoxically, find great favor in the "opinion" of the Greek camp. In the words of the venerable Nestor, "...in the imitation of these twain,/ Who,...opinion crowns/ With an imperial voice, many are infect" (185-187). The sickness of the whole Greek camp can thus be said to derive directly from an imitation of Patroclus's scandalous imitation. There is an epidemic of scurrilous poetry in the Greek camp, poetry in the service of the imperial voice of opinion, that so reflects on the natures, virtues, and stations of the Greek chieftains that the political order that depends on reverence for them is falling into factions.

What is the nature of that poetry that, in Ulysses' mind, makes it so destructive of the "high designs" of the Greeks? He tells us in lines 197-210, where his disquisition on degree properly comes to an end. The contagious flaw inherent in the poetry that infects the Greek camp is that it esteems the virtues of Achilles as the highest of all virtues. Falling prey to the communicable charm of this poetry, the whole camp places the virtues of the warrior above all others. Specifically, the Greeks

> Count wisdom as no member of the war,
> ...and esteem no act
> But that of hand.
> ....
> So that, the ram that batters down the wall,
> For the great swing and rudeness of his poise,
> They place before his hand that made the engine,
> Or those that with the fineness of their souls
> By reason guide his execution.

It is because *this* degree is neglected, the degree placing the "still and mental parts"—reason—above mere physical power—"the ram that batters down the wall"—that the Grecian "enterprise is sick" or literally suffering a political disorder.

Every political community, like the Greek camp, establishes some "degree" by which men are distinguished from one another for the purposes of rule; when this degree is shaken, chaos or disorder threatens. But in this scene Shakespeare clearly has in mind the question: "What is it that makes any such degree 'stand in authentic place'?" The answer given by Ulysses is the recognition of the pre-eminence of "the still and mental parts" of man to all others, particularly to "the great swing and rudeness" of an Achilles. If this measure of distinction among men—this "degree"—is neglected, the argument runs, man is reduced to the level of beasts, for there is no sure ground to distinguish him from them. But this is precisely what the poetry infecting the Grecian camp *does* deny, leading unconsciously but inevitably to the conclusion, so aptly put by old Nestor, that "Achilles' horse/ Makes many Thetis' sons" (211-212). It is when *this* degree is suffocate, that that universal chaos ensues, wherein,

> everything includes itself in power,
> Power into will, will into appetite

And appetite, an universal wolf,
So doubly seconded with will and power,
Must make perforce an universal prey
And last eat up himself. (119-124)

The particular sickness of the Greek camp is the failure of the Greek warriors to recognize the "degree" which is the ordering principle of the Greek polity. Recognition ultimately must mean viewing the ordering principle of that particular polity as reflecting the order of the cosmos itself, or the will of the gods. The scurrilous poetry of Patroclus and his imitators undermines that view by making "paradoxes" of all that "is or is not" for the Greeks. So much Ulysses tells us. But Ulysses' analysis of the causes of this sickness does not provide the political "remedy" sought by Agamemnon. According to Ulysses, as I have said, the decisive distinction among men, the distinction according to which one man rightly may rule another, is founded on the degree of wisdom possessed, a distinction in "the still and mental parts" of men, in the "fineness of their souls." This is hardly less revolutionary than the scurril jests of Patroclus to a political order in which the basis of "degrees" among men is the authority of the gods. But this is the final formal argument made by Ulysses to defend such an order against the self-consuming poetry which threatens chaos in the Greek camp and would reduce Achilles, and all the other Greeks, to the level of Achilles' horse, or worse.

Having allowed Ulysses to make this argument, Shakespeare immediately shows us, not by argument but by action, that the conclusion arrived at is somehow not politically applicable. Consider: Ulysses' famous argument has just been concluded pithily by old Nestor when the stage is interrupted by a trumpet blast. Enter Aeneas from Troy. Aeneas has a message for the Great Agamemnon and, after some courtly formalities, which are not without a point, he asks—speaking of course to Agamemnon himself—"How may/ A stranger to those most imperial looks/ Know them from eyes of other mortals?"

> *Aga.* How?
> *Aen.* Ay.
> I ask that I might waken reverence,
> And on the cheek be ready with a blush
> Modest as morning when she coldly eyes
> The Youthful Phoebus.
> Which is that god in office, guiding men?
> Which is the high and mighty Agamemnon? (I.iii.223-232)

The mocking tone of this address is not lost on Agamemnon, who turns to his fellow chieftains saying, "This Troyan scorns us, or the men of Troy/ Are ceremonious courtiers" (233-234). Nor should the irony of Aeneas's query be lost on the audience. Imagine Aeneas on stage staring the high and mighty Agamemnon square in the face, speaking directly to him and asking "Where is the divine Agamemnon, how am I to distinguish him from other mere mortals?" And all the divine Agamemnon, for all his glory, can reply is a lame—if imperious—"How?" It is a good question, one which he never answers. Of course, there is *no recognizable mark* of nature or divinity to distinguish Agamemnon from the other mere mortals over whom his sceptre holds sway. There is no *apparent* natural or divine ground to justify a blush of reverence on Aeneas's cheek. In fact, it would seem that the most obvious, if not the most satisfactory, mark of distinction among men, especially in a warring camp of Greeks, is precisely the one recognized by the factious elements in the camp— the "act of hand," the great swing and rudeness of an Achilles. The implication of Aeneas's puzzlement, in light of the discourse which precedes it, is that Agamemnon's position as ruler over the Greeks, the degree that sets him apart from those over whom he rules, and before which men should by nature blush with reverence, though it claims the authority of the gods, is, in fact, purely a product of convention. This convention has been called into question by the infectious poetry which raises the natural, if insufficient, claim of Achilles or of physical power in general.

But more to the point: Suppose that Agamemnon possessed that "fineness of soul" proclaimed by Ulysses to be the only natural basis of rule. Would this be any more apparent to Aeneas, or to any Greek or Trojan, than the supposed touch of divinity in Agamemnon, which is not visible at all? No. The fineness of their souls may be Ulysses' and nature's final measure of degrees among men; this final degree, standing in authentic place, may be the ladder to all high designs; neglection of this degree may by a pace go backward in any purpose it has to climb; perhaps Ulysses would go so far as to say that this degree may somehow be the soul of the political community; but this degree is no more acceptable than the divinity of Agamemnon as the actual ordering principle of the Greek camp, or of any other body politic.

To return then to the relation of poetry to politics. An imitation of a slanderous imitation of the political universe of the Greeks has undermined both the actual ordering principle or degree of the Grecian camp, which is the divine authority of Agamemnon, and the true or natural ordering principle among men, consisting in the degrees of fineness of their souls. The nexus in the relation of poetry to politics, as it is reflected in this scene, is the view of the political universe, of the degrees within individual souls and the corresponding degrees in the external relations among the citizens, implicit in both politics and poetry. Poetry infects the body politic when it introduces into it an alien and hostile substance, a view of the political universe which is incompatible with that view which breathes life into the civil authority and reverence into the citizens. The disease is introduced into the body politic through the over-indulgence of the "spleen" of the citizens and the natural susceptibility of the imperial voice of opinion. Perhaps Ulysses would say that it becomes mortal when it cuts the body politic off altogether from its soul.

It is impossible to think that Shakespeare could have been unconscious of the parallel between the "imitation" of the political universe of the Greek camp by Patroclus and his imitators, and that which he himself was preparing for his own audience. In fact, quite the opposite must be the case. Shakespeare could not but have been acutely conscious that his imitation of the Greek and Trojan universes bore an inherent relation to the individual souls and collective lives of his audience and to whatever "high designs" his audience might affect. Just as the scurrilous poetry of Patroclus played upon the spleen and opinion of the Greek camp, Shakespeare plays upon the passions and sentiments of his audience.

The best efforts of earnest scholars leave us still unsure of the more immediate "political" purposes of Shakespeare's *Troilus and Cressida*, that is, of those idiosyncrasies peculiar to Shakespeare's contemporary audience, to which some specific passages of the play might, in whole or part, be addressed. And we are not much the worse for that. We do, however, know with certainty that *Troilus and Cressida* contains some immortal verse, poetry with a significance not just for Shakespeare's time or some transient purpose of that time, but for all time and for the highest purposes. It seems best, then, to understand the play as it is addressed to men of all times, particularly as it bears upon any high design affected by them. This is the Grecian camp to which the best of Shakespeare's poetry is ultimately addressed.

How then does *Troilus and Cressida* affect the high designs of this universal camp of Greeks? For there can be no doubt that opinion has crowned its author with an "imperial voice," and that with imitation of him, of one sort or another, many are infect. Do all our abilities, gifts, natures, shapes, achievements, plots, orders, and preventions merely serve as stuff for the great poet to make paradoxes? And if so, what does this mean for our Helens and our wars?

The effect of a given work of drama on its audience is inseparably linked with its form. To oversimplify, tragedy incites admiration and tears; comedy incites ridicule and laughter. From the first, however, publishers and critics have been hard pressed to say what form of drama *Troilus and Cressida* is. The textual history of the play foreshadows the centuries of critical confusion that have followed its first publication.

In the Quarto edition of 1609 the title page refers to "The Historie" of Troilus and Cressida. But there was a second issue of this Quarto text to which was added an epistle describing the play as a comedy. In the Folio of 1623, the play is titled "The Tragedie" of Troilus and Cressida. Yet it is not placed properly with the tragedies, but in a nameless position between the tragedies and the histories. Later critics have tried, with limited success, to resolve this dilemma by placing the play in a new category altogether, naming it a "problem play" or a "comical satire." Clearly, the play does not fit comfortably into any traditional dramatic mold.

It has been possible for this confusion over the form of the play to persist through the centuries because of the confusing dramatic effect the play has consistently had on each generation of its viewers and readers. It is the common, if not universal, reaction to *Troilus and Cressida*, to feel that it is dramatically fragmented, that it lacks dramatic unity and completeness, and that as a result it is somehow dissatisfying or perplexing, even unpleasant. We must give due attention to this common effect of the play on the sentiments of its audience. It is an injustice not infrequently inflicted upon poetry to reduce it prosaically to its supposed elements or philosophic implications, and to call this "understanding" it. When one ceases to be sensible of the laughter and tears and the whole range of subtler human passions brought to life in good poetry, one ceases to be capable of understanding it. It may be as impossible to understand poetry by "transcending" its pathos as to understand moderation and courage while being a glutton and a coward.

The confusion of the sentiments which is the common reaction to this play occurs in part, I think, because the play arouses in the audience passions and sentiments the *grounds* for which are contradictory. Everyone has tasted the bitter ridicule of Thersites which flavors virtually every character and every action of the play. Where Thersites is not at work, there is Pandarus, or Shakespeare himself, directly casting upon Homer's heroes and their heroic endeavor a shadow of ridicule and disgust. From the midst of all this ridicule, however, rise numerous instances of apparently unsullied nobility for which the audience is irresistibly moved to admiration. Yet neither admiration nor ridicule is dramatically resolved into the other. To be sure, the play is in part a debunking of the Homeric heroes; but it also debunks the debunkers. Dramatically, at least, a certain portion of heroism is left intact, if in doubt, at the end. The minute textual support demanded of such an argument is impossible to give here. But I will offer one example of what I think to be the contradictory sentiments aroused and left in contradiction by the play. In Act IV, Scene 5, Ulysses identifies Troilus for Agamemnon. Drawing on a private account given him by Aeneas, Ulysses describes Troilus as

> a true knight,
> Not yet mature, yet matchless, firm of word,
> Speaking in deeds and deedless in his tongue;
> Not soon provok'd, nor being provok'd, soon calm'd,
> His heart and hand both open and both free;
> For what he has, he gives; what thinks, he shews;
> Yet gives he not till judgment guide his bounty,
> Nor dignifies an impair thought with breath;
> Manly as Hector, but more dangerous. (96-104)

The description is not without its ironies, but in the main the audience is here made to sense—to believe—the integrity, magnanimity, courage, judgment, and self-control attributed to Troilus by Ulysses. We feel that this is generally an authoritative account of the true Troilus, and we admire his virtues. But the play began by showing us the changeable nature of Troilus, who at one moment could not fight upon the argument of Helen, and at the next was off to the wars with Aeneas. And it ends showing him rapt in revenge, which we know to be at once characteristic of him and one of the primary destructive forces in the play, inasmuch as it is "deaf as an adder" to the voice of reason. Ulysses' attributions are partly untrue and partly overshadowed by the tragic flaws of Troilus. In addition they are diluted by the railings of Thersites for whom Troilus is a doting young Trojan ass who is willing to risk his arm for a sleeve. Still, this expression of Troilus's virtues does not completely lose its force over the sentiments of the audience. Our admiration is not dispelled, it is only unsettled. There are many passages in the play which convey a similar sense of self-sufficient nobility or virtue. This sense is not destroyed, even by all the railings of Thersites. It lingers, even to the end, but with a sense of doubt as to the grounds on which it stands. The audience is made to harbor simultaneously in its breast the mockery of the empty heroism of the play, and the distaste for that mockery because it seems to destroy the grounds for the true heroism that the play allows us to believe is possible. Troilus himself senses a like dichotomy of soul and desperately wishes to resolve it in favor of all that is beautiful and noble:

> ...there is a credence in my heart,
> An esperance so obstinately strong
> That doth invert that test of eyes and ears,
> As if those organs had deceptious functions,
> Created only to calumniate. (V.ii.128-132)

It is doubtful whether he succeeds. It is also doubtful that the play would endorse his success even if he were to achieve it. The play offers little comfort for the innocently noble. But it offers *no* comfort for the mockers of that nobility, and in this view cannot be better summed up than in the words of a great modern poet:

> Come let us mock at the great...
> Come let us mock at the wise...
> Come let us mock at the good...
>
> Mock mockers after that
> That would not lift a hand maybe
> To help good, wise or great
> To bar that foul storm out, for we
> Traffic in mockery.

One only wonders whether the author of *Troilus and Cressida*, when speaking about the mockers of the good, great, and wise, would have spoken in the first person.

This explanation of the nature of the dramatic confusion or perplexity of *Troilus and Cressida* does not depart much from common opinion on the matter. However, many have been inspired by their dramatic confusion to seek the *causes* of the incoherence or fragmentation experienced in the play. And here common opinion is on less sure ground. Some argue that the "incompleteness" or lack of conclusion that one senses in the play results from Shakespeare's having "lost interest" in the play before he finished it; others argue that he did not finish it at all, but left it to some less skilled hand. Some blame the dramatic incoherence of the play on the supposed fact that Shakespeare was rewriting a play already in existence; still others claim that the "material" on which Shakespeare drew (meaning the diverse accounts of the Troy legend) was impossible to weave together into a dramatic unity. All of these explanations are alike in seeking the cause of the apparent incoherence of the play elsewhere than in the art of the author. It is as impossible to disprove as to prove them. But there is another more interesting and more fruitful explanation suggested also by common opinion.

It is almost as frequently said that *Troilus and Cressida* is "intellectual," "analytic," or "philosophic," as it is said that it lacks dramatic unity or coherence. And surely there is something to this, if we recall the Greek council scene and Ulysses' degree speech, its Trojan counterpart in Act II, Scene 2, and the great dialogue between Ulysses and Achilles in Act III, Scene 3. I am not concerned with whether, as some have maintained, Ulysses' speech on degree is drawn from Plato's *Republic*, or whether the Achilles-Ulysses dialogue is taken directly or indirectly from *First Alcibiades,* or with Hector's anomalous reference to Aristotle. The point is that all these passages, while they play a part in the drama, also evince a concern for the truth of their respective arguments, independent of the effect of that truth on the action of the play. Indeed, it is worth noting that in each case the effect of the argument on the action of the play is emphatically nothing.

We have seen in the case of Ulysses that the conclusion of his argument on degree does not solve the political problem facing the Greeks. In the Trojan Council, Hector no sooner concludes his exposition on political morality than he dismisses his apparently true conclusions, with an abruptness that cannot but give pause, and follows the dictates of an empty honor. Achilles is temporarily moved by the arguments of Ulysses in their dialogue (though it is well to remember that it is not the profundity of those arguments that moves Achilles, but their success in eliciting his envy of Ajax). But in the end the arguments come to nothing when challenged by Achilles' previous engagement with Polyxena. If the arguments of these passages do not contribute to the action of the play, they nonetheless affect our understanding of it. And by their very detachment from the action they encourage us to consider their truth for its own sake. In this sense, they seem to be more philosophic than poetic, at least if we can say that philosophy aims more at discovering the truth, poetry at moving the passions.

It does seem to be the special province of the poet to have a deep sense of the human passions and sentiments and of the reigning opinions of his times. He plays upon them deftly, with utmost precision, instinctively sensing what image, word or phrase, what nuance of character or juxtaposition of scene, will stir elation, hope, anger, dread, or sorrow in the breast of his fellows. When he takes his eye off this anticipated reaction of his audience, his poetry may be expected to suffer. Though he may hit upon a phrase truer in itself, it will not strike home as truly as it might. Though he follows a flawless train of logic, he may *seem* to discourse inconsequentially—not, to be sure, to that god among men, the philosopher, but poetry, in its nature, is not written for an audience of philosophers. Indeed, deception, which, in being opposed to truth, must be presumed to be anathema to a philosopher, is the very "bark" and "convoy" of the poet, carrying him unerringly to his intended effect. One might say, then, that by keeping his eye on the truth of his arguments, Shakespeare took his eye off the anticipated reaction of his audience; by seeking consistency of thought, he sacrificed the *appearance* of consistency in the drama. Or, perhaps, in seeking to inform our understandings, he failed to direct our passions and sentiments. It seems to be a prerequisite of good poetry that the poet himself should *feel* the passions he imitates, as Shakespeare surely does in some of the passages of *Troilus and Cressida*. But overall the play manifests the detachment of its author from the passions portrayed in it, a detachment similar to that of the philosophic passages cited above from the drama of the play.

From this point of view the dramatic confusion of the play comes to light as an *accident* of Shakespeare's preoccupation with the truth of his arguments as opposed to the appearance of truth. But one might say instead that the dramatic inconsistencies of the play are consistent with the truths sought in it, and that the discordant passions portrayed in the play and excited by it in the audience are harmonized, if not dramatically, then intellectually or philosophically. Such a reading of the play as a whole is suggested in both the council scenes, where reason and truth respectively put the unruly passions of Greeks and Trojans in their proper perspective. But just as in these scenes reason and truth prove incapable of actually governing the unruly, destructive passions guiding the political fortunes of both Greeks and Trojans, so in the play as a whole these passions prevail over the drama.

Philosophy puts the passions in perspective, but reason and truth are also put in perspective by the drama. They cannot be depended upon to govern the political life of men. That life will continue to be governed by such passions and sentiments as we see still ruling at the end of the play, passions swayed perhaps by poetry, through the spleen and the susceptible opinion of men, but not, as the play repeatedly shows us, by the truths of the intellect addressed to the understanding. The fineness of men's souls, to the extent that this consists in that reason which apprehends the truths of the intellect, does not govern the fates of political communities.

Also from the point of view of reason, both laughter and tears, ridicule and admiration, may seem insufficient, incomplete responses to the political or human universe, each reflecting perhaps a part of the truth about it, but in that very fact necessarily being blind to the rest of the truth. From this point of view, poetry itself, whatever form it might take, whatever passions it may elicit, might be incapable of representing the human or political world in its fullness. Each attempt of poetry to do so must end in the arousal of one passion or another, the implicit grounds of which reflect at best a partial truth, and therefore a partial falsehood, about the soul of man and his place in the universe.

Troilus and Cressida displays the contradictory or chaotic tendencies—the insufficiencies—of the passions governing the political life of man, and of the passions associated with poetry of any form. It suggests a resolution of this chaos, but it appears to be a resolution that is neither political nor poetic.

Notes

1. Quoted in the *Los Angeles Times*, January 15, 1974.
2. All quotations are from *The Tragedy of Troilus and Cressida* (New Haven: Yale University Press, 1965).

NATURE AND THE CITY:
TIMON OF ATHENS

Leo Paul S. de Alvarez

*T*imon of Athens, according to Howard B. White, is perhaps "the most complete political tragedy in Shakespeare."[1] Such a statement might be justified by the lack of any other focus in the play but that of the city. No question of love, for example, diverts us from the story of Athens. We have very little in the way of anything pleasant—there seems to be no delight in the play. The banquet and the masque, for all their brilliance, are somehow unpleasant. The three principal characters, Timon, Apemantus, and Alcibiades, act in terms of the city. No beautiful speeches charm us; the poetry is a scolding, harsh, vituperative poetry. Despite the outward glitter, the play reproduces the unpleasantness and harshness of the political itself.

We first hear of Timon as a wealthy patron of the arts. We also hear of his beneficence and how this virtue brings to him a great flood of visitors who profess their love for him and honor him as they would a god. We first see him as a benefactor, paying the debt of Ventidius and providing a young man in his service with sufficient money to marry above his station. Timon explains his act of generosity to Ventidius in terms of friendship. Ventidius is a friend and a gentleman, and it is the duty of friends and gentlemen to give freely one to another. Giving, he ways, when he provides Lucilius with the money whereby the latter might wed, is a "bond in men." Giving is the highest expression of friendship, and Timon has a vision of community as a loving brotherhood:

> We are born to do benefits; and what better or properer can
> we call our own than the riches of our friends? O what a pre-

> cious comfort 'tis to have so many like brothers commanding
> one another's fortunes! O joy, e'en made away ere't can be born!
> Mine eyes cannot hold out water, methinks....[2]   (I.ii.95-101)

So deeply moved is he by his vision of friendship that to think of it is a joy which dissolves into tears.

In the lines preceding the ones we have just quoted, Timon presents his fullest explanation of why he gives. His giving is made possible by the gods so that he, Timon, might be able "to have much help" from his friends. Every benefit Timon confers means that there is another who then becomes more greatly capable of giving in return. When Ventidius, newly released from debtor's prison, comes to thank Timon, Timon speaks of his love and how he freely gives requiring nothing in return. It becomes clear, however, in the second act, that Timon expects the gentlemen of Athens to reciprocate his love and generosity. He cannot believe that they will refuse him in his need, and his anger assumes terrible dimensions when he learns of the ingratitude of his supposed friends.

Timon's actions have been sanctioned by the gods themselves. As they have provided wealth for Timon, so he provides for others, and we can assume that such bountiful provision may then continue throughout the city, friend providing for friend. Giving permits others to be helpful; it seems as if the gods wish for everyone to be like them and they have therefore made men "born to do benefits."

Timon goes on to say that his giving is a selection out of thousands of those whom he chiefly cherishes and entitles with the charitable name of "friends." He declares that he knows each of those whom he benefits, and can speak more to himself about each one than each, out of modesty, could speak on his own behalf. Timon thus claims that his giving is not indiscriminate; he knows well to whom he gives. He learns his mistake, but he insists that, although unwise, he has not been ignoble in his giving (II.ii.171). Can one give nobly if he does not know what he is doing? His giving is in fact indiscriminate, but Timon believes that he knows to whom he gives. On what basis does he found that belief? Is he simply boasting, that is, deluding himself?

Before we attempt to answer this question, however, we need to continue with that argument. We note that Timon's ardor leads him to exclaim, with an oath, that friends are to be used when one is needy. Otherwise, friends would be "needless," that is, there would be no reason for them to be. The gods have apparently made certain that there are inequalities among human beings so that friends must be called upon and used. Without need, there would be no possibility of exercising the highest and therefore god-like virtue of beneficence. Timon wishes himself poorer, so that he might be nearer to those to whom he gives. The implicit argument appears to be that since the exercise of beneficence is the highest human good, the greatest benefit one could bestow upon one's friends would be to permit them to exercise the highest virtue. Giving is the true bond between men, for the rich and the poor, the high and the low, are brought closer together and are each made nobler through giving.

Let us return to the question previously asked: why does Timon suppose that he knows to whom he gives? The answer, I believe, is that Timon looks upon citizenship as linking men together in a special bond of love—all citizens cannot but be friends. The private bond of friendship is made one with the public bond of citizenship. As he says to Apemantus, "Thou'rt an Athenian, therefore welcome." He who is an Athenian is a friend, and Timon's door is open to all Athenians. The fine words said to him by those who are parasites and flatterers are taken by him at their face value, for they are said by fellow citizens. The selection of friends has been made for Timon through the city, and he believes therefore that he knows to whom he gives, for he gives to fellow citizens.

Timon's principal characteristic is that he gives money generously. He gives, as we have said, for two reasons—he gives to his fellow citizens who claim to be in need, and he gives to those who make beautiful things. We have spoken briefly of why he gives to his fellow citizens; we must now look at his patronage of the arts.

The play begins by introducing us to a Poet, a Painter, a Jeweller, and a Merchant, who are all waiting in attendance upon Timon. The three craftsmen have brought gifts, and the Poet and the Painter exchange comments, while waiting, upon how art imitates nature. According to the Poet, the picture brought by the Painter not only imitates natures but tutors her. The artifact is "livelier than life." When Timon is presented with the picture, he confirm the Poet's judgment. It is, Timon says at first, "almost the natural man." He then seems to say that the painting is better than the man—man's nature cannot be truly seen for it traffics with dishonor—while the painting clearly reveals what the man is. Human beings may conceal that which art reveals; art shows more than nature can.

The play thus opens with a contrast between the natural and the artificial, a theme which is to culminate in Timon's abandonment of the city and all human company for the woods where he eats roots. When we first see Timon, however, he clearly prefers the artificial to the natural, so much so that Apemantus suggests that he seems wholly to have for-gotten the natural. Timon is a patron of the arts because the arts remove the stain of dishonor from the human being. That is, the harsh and ne-cessitous are removed by the arts, leaving only the pleasurable and the beautiful. The city is to be the place of ease, refined pleasures, love and beauty.

The darker side of Athens, however, is revealed by Apemantus and Alcibiades. Apemantus is presented as an angry, scolding man, who seems always to be giving what he calls his counsel at the most inopportune times and in the most inappropriate ways. The consequence is that he is ignored by everyone, and only the great civility and humanity of Timon permit his being tolerated (I.i.175-177). Apemantus sees all too clearly the filthiness, depravity, and hypocrisy, which is concealed by the glory, courtesy, and graciousness of Athens. The Athenians, indeed all men, act entirely in terms of their self-interest, and they would as soon kill as they would pledge faith. His one concern is to make others, and especially Timon, see how foolish are all the feasts and pomps which Athens so much enjoys. He points to the natural man, saying in effect that he is a dangerous, ungrateful beast. Apemantus seems intensely to desire that Timon see this natural man. So concerned is he with Timon that he seems to spend a good part of his time observing Timon and his ways. One wonders why Apemantus should be so concerned. One wonders also why he addresses himself to his fellow citizens in such a self-defeating way. His angry denunciations only evoke the equally angry response that he is opposite to humanity. Is it proper for a philosopher to denounce? Can Apemantus, whose name means one free from misery,[3] be properly called a philosopher? We shall leave these questions for later consideration. It suffices for the moment to note Apemantus's vision of Athens.

Alcibiades, the great captain, finds himself banished from the city when he attempts to persuade the Senate to pardon one of his soldiers who killed in anger. The Senate refuses to do so on the ground that it would encourage a misbegotten valor in the city which would result in factions and sects and more quarrellings and killings. The senators fear spiritedness, and they prefer an Athens free of it. The warrior does not represent Athens and is not honored by the city. The city, as Alcibiades bitterly remarks upon his banishment, is an usurious one. What is hon-ored is the misbegotten breeding of money by money. Apemantus shares in this judgment—Athens is a city based upon unnatural and unlimited acquisition. For Apemantus and Alcibiades alike, usury leads to the for-getfulness of natural necessity. The implicit argument is that usury, by replacing man's natural productive relationship to nature, leads to a for-getfulness of nature. For Alcibiades, the senators forget the need to de-fend the city; for Apemantus, Timon forgets that it is only by a prudent self-interest that one is able to get and maintain wealth. Both Apemantus and Alcibiades point to usury as the ignoble basis of Athens, and, as Timon discovers, it is the true governor of the relations among Athenians.

We are reminded of Pericles' Funeral Speech. Pericles describes Athens as a city of decent enjoyment of delights. It is a city which loves the beautiful, but does so with thrift and without softness. Thus the love of the beautiful is also connected by Pericles with the question of the getting of wealth—if there is to be the beautiful there must be acquisi-tion. I believe that the Athens which Shakespeare sees in *Timon of Ath-ens* is described in the following passage from the Funeral Speech:

> We have also found out many ways to give our minds rec-reation from labour, by public institution of games and sacri-fices for all the days of year, with a decent pomp and furniture of the same by private men; by the delight whereof we expel sadness. We have this farther by the greatness of our city, that all things from all parts of the earth are imported hither; whereby we no less familiarly enjoy the commodities of all other nations than our own.[4]

Athens is an empire and a commercial city. It is thus the usurious city of which Apemantus and Alcibiades speak. Athens, however, also loves the beautiful and depends upon her private men, her Timons, to give delight with decent pomp. The Athens of Pericles and the Athens we are shown by Shakespeare seem fundamentally to be the same city. Athens' pecu-liar claim is thus that she, of all the cities, is best able to use her wealth liberally and magnificently. Timon fully dedicates himself to realizing this claim of Athens. He wishes therefore to be the complete Athenian.

However, the society Timon wishes to bring into existence is not political. The political is much too harsh for him. He remarks that Alcibiades prefers a feast of enemies to a banquet, and he himself shows no interest in honors and glory, although he is offered the captainship, i.e., to be commander-in-chief, of Athenian arms with absolute power. The senators seem fully to expect that he will be a match and more than a match for Alcibiades in the field of battle. Certainly, Alcibiades shows considerable respect for Timon, and he speaks of Timon's great deeds with his sword and fortune, when neighboring states trod upon Athens (IV.iii.93-96). One is reminded of Cimon, the great general who was re-sponsible for Athenian expansion after the Persian Wars, and one is indeed tempted to think that Shakespeare's Timon is modelled upon Plutarch's Cimon. Here, for example is Plutarch's description of the generosity of Cimon:

> And since he was already wealthy, Cimon lavished the revenue from his campaign, which he was thought to have won with honour from the enemy, to his still greater honour, on his fellow-citizens. He took away the fences from his fields, that strangers and needy citizens might have it in their power to take fearlessly of the fruits of the land; and every day he gave a dinner at his house—simple, it is true, but sufficient for many, to which any poor man who wished came in, and received a maintenance which cost him no effort and left him free to devote himself solely to public affairs....

Cimon, it is true, is not as sumptuous as Timon in his dinners; above all, Cimon never forgets the connection between acquisition and liberality. He is liberal and magnificent, one might say, with the goods of others. The Athens Cimon intends to bring into existence seems to be the Athens that Shakespeare's Timon also intends:

> but the generosity of Cimon surpassed even the hospitality and philanthropy of the Athenians of olden time...[for] he made his home in the city a general public residence for his fellow-citizens, and on his estates in the country allowed even the stranger to take and use the choicest of the ripened fruits, with all the fair things which the seasons bring. Thus, in a certain fashion, he restored to human life the fabled communism of the age of Cronus—the golden age....[5]

Is it not that golden age which Timon desires? It seems to be a desire shared by the greatest of Athenian statesmen, who think of Athens in terms of the beautiful—where harsh necessity is banished, anger set aside, and the appetites given over to a refined and decent enjoyment of pleasures.

We turn now to the second half of the play, where Timon abandons and curses Athens, declaring that:

> Timon will to the woods, where he shall find
> Th'unkindest beast more kinder than mankind. (IV.i.35-36)

He not only curses Athens and her citizens, he also curses all of humanity. He will have nothing to do with man, and where he formerly believed the human artifact to be superior to nature, he now finds all human things to be detestable. He looks for a nature which is without man.

Timon, alone in the woods, reflects upon man's relationship to nature:

> O blessed breeding sun, draw from the earth
> Rotten humidity; below thy sister's orb
> Infect the air! Twinned brothers of one womb—
> Whose procreation, residence, and birth
> Scarce is dividant—touch them with several fortunes,
> The greater scorns the lesser. (IV.iii.1-6)

The sun draws forth from the earth that which is contrary to the fire of the sun, rotten humidity. This contrariety in nature curses and infects mankind, such that twin brothers can become subject to differing fortunes. And these differing fortunes lead the one who has the greater fortune to have contempt for his poorer brother. It would seem that nature herself, being contrary, cannot serve as a basis for the human good. Thus the passage continues:

> Not nature,
> To whom all sores lay siege, can bear great fortune
> But by contempt of nature.   (6-8)

Nature herself would turn against nature should it escape the sores to which nature is always subject. No one and nothing escapes natural necessity, and there is nothing noble in human nature or in nature as such. Instead, self-preservation is the ruling principle. Men will do anything to escape necessity, and all subject themselves to fortune or wealth which alone seems to provide escape. In so doing, men reveal their fundamental bestiality:

> Raise me this beggar and deny't that lord;
> The senator shall bear contempt hereditary,
> The beggar native honor.
> It is the pasture lards the wether's sides,
> The want that makes him lean.... (9-13)

Man's nobility is entirely a question of fortune or money. The distinction between the senator and the beggar is "pasture," that is, what they feed upon. So strongly are men governed by necessity or self-preservation that none can show "purity of manhood":

> Who dares, who dares
> In purity of manhood stand upright
> And say, "This man's a flatterer?" If one be,
> So are they all; for every grise of fortune
> Is smoothed by that below. The learnèd pate
> Ducks to the golden fool. All's obloquy;
> There's nothing level in our cursèd natures
> But direct villainy. (13-20)

The villainy is the result of man's inability to be in direct and happy relationship to nature. Instead, man's happiness comes from having to become unnatural. Timon makes this clear in a subsequent passage where he speaks of the earth as a common mother:

> Whose womb unmeasurable and infinite breast
> Teems and feeds all; whose self-same mettle
> Whereof thy proud child, arrogant man, is puffed
> Engenders the black toad and adder blue,
> The gilded newt and eyeless venomed worm,
> With all the abhorrèd births below crisp heaven.... (IV.iii.178-183)

Man is not the especial child of earth. Man's pride in himself does not take into account the indiscriminateness of the earth in her relationship to all her children, who are in the main dangerous to man. Man, moreover, is an ungrateful child; unlike the black toad and the blue adder he is capable of contempt for his mother. Man is ungrateful, we surmise, because he can do more with nature; he can plant and plough, and thus, by "liquorish drafts/ And morsels unctuous," he "greases his mind" in such a way "That from it all consideration slips."

The conclusion of Timon's analysis is the complete rejection of society:

> Therefore be abhorred
> All feasts, societies, and throngs of men.
> His semblable, yea himself, Timon disdains.
> Destruction fang mankind! (IV.iii.20-23)

Timon has discovered what Marx is later to call the alienation of man. Man's work to make for himself a more comfortable state, his building of the city, is a criminal act against nature. Man must be unnatural and therefore ungrateful to his mother, and this ingratitude makes the seem-

ingly beautiful, the humane, and the free possible. The price man pays,
however, is that he is in truth ungrateful in all his relationships.[6]

Timon's discovery of gold during the speech in which he calls for the
destruction of mankind points up what we have just said. Gold is the
means whereby nature is dissolved and transformed into any shape one
pleases. Timon promises to use the gold, but not as a blessing for men
but rather as a curse:

> Come, damnèd earth,
> Thou common whore of mankind, that puts odds
> Among the rout of nations, I will make thee
> Do thy right nature. (IV.iii.42-45)

Upon Timon's speaking these lines, a drum beats and Alcibiades enters.
In the ensuing scene, Timon gives the gold to Alcibiades and the courtesans, declaring that it will be a plague and curse to Athens. In Alcibiades'
hands, however, the gold becomes the means for the salvation of the city.
The paradox of the relationship between nature and man could not be
more emphatically stated.

The encounter with the bandits makes the point even clearer. The
bandits declare themselves not to be thieves, "but men that much do
want." Timon makes the obvious reply that they do not so much want as
they want much:

> Why should you want? Behold the earth hath roots;
> Within this mile break forth a hundred springs;
> The oaks bear mast, the briars scarlet hips;
> The bounteous housewife Nature on each bush
> Lays her full mess before you. Want? Why want? (IV.iii.413-417)

The reply of the First Bandit to this query may be regarded as mankind's
general answer to all such questions:

> We cannot live on grass, on berries, water,
> As beasts and birds and fishes.

Timon had declared that the greatest want of the bandits is meat, hence
their insatiability. But it is not simply the meat of beasts, birds, or fishes
that they want—"You must eat men." Civilization is based on the eating
of men. That is what usuriousness, man's unlimited acquisitiveness, finally signifies, and this is something which Timon, who loved the beauti-

ful, cannot accept. The price of liberality and magnificence is indeed finally too high, for there must be acquisition if there is to be spending, and Timon sees to his horror that such acquisition is Alcibiades' banquet of enemies. Whatever artifices the city makes to hide this fact, it still remains. Thus Timon will have nothing to do with man and his works.

Timon now tells the thieves that they imitate nature and the city in being thieves:

> I'll example you with thievery:
> The sun's a thief, and with his great attraction
> Robs the vast sea; the moon's an arrant thief,
> And her pale fire she snatches from the sun;
> The sea's a thief, whose liquid surge resolves
> The moon into salty tears; the earth's a thief,
> That feeds and breeds by a composture stol'n
> From gen'ral excrement. Each thing's a thief.
> ....
> All that you meet are thieves. To Athens go;
> Break open shops; nothing can you steal
> But thieves do lose it. (IV.iii.431-444)

Paradoxically, then, usury is imitative of nature. Usury imitates nature in that man, like everything in nature, wants and therefore gets. Man cannot be kind because nature is not kind, despite Timon's initial reference to that "bounteous housewife." Timon's discontents, as the First Senator notes, are "unremovably coupled to nature." They are coupled to his nature; they are also coupled to nature simply, and, of course, to the nature of the city and of Athens. He who was the epitome of Athens' love of the beautiful cannot accept the worse than beastly cannibalism which has been laid bare. Timon is a man of extremes; he desires a humanity purged of all the beastly and will have none of a humanity that must be beastly and perhaps worse than beastly.

Besides man and nature, there are the gods, and Timon asks them to help confound the Athenians and increase his hate "to the whole race of mankind, high and low." Do the gods then intervene in human affairs? Will they help punish the ungrateful city? Flavius, Timon's faithful steward, speaks of the gods, however, not as those who curse but as those who are made by bounty and yet not marred (IV.ii.41). That is, the gods are the gods because they can be bountiful without harm either to themselves or to others. They can, in other words, act as Timon had acted without the consequences he brought upon himself. Only the gods, then, in Flavius's view, can do what apparently neither nature nor man can do—be bountiful without harm. The lesson Flavius draws from his understanding of the gods is that men ought not seek glory or pomp. Only the gods can do so without harm, whereas man must necessarily do harm. Flavius sees what Timon's strange fault is:

> Poor honest lord, brought low by his own heart,
> Undone by goodness! Strange, unusual blood,
> When man's worst sin is he does too much good!
> Who then dares to be half so kind again? (IV.ii.37-40)

It would seem that only the gods may be so loving or so kind. Men cannot do so without marring themselves and others.

The gods are mentioned again when Flavius, visiting Timon in the woods, begs to stay with him. Timon asks the gods to forgive him for condemning all of mankind when one man, Flavius, is honest. Timon refers to the gods as the "perpetual-sober" who do not, as he does, act rashly. It is possible to understand Timon as saying that the gods, unlike him, are sober because they know when to give and when to curse.

Timon, we recall, attributed his fortune to the gods, who had given it to him that he might make his friends more able also to give or to help. Beneficence and bounteousness would seem then to be an imitation of the gods. According to Flavius, however, man cannot imitate the gods. Timon admits that he does not have the soberness of the gods. Do men in general lack this sobriety and is man therefore foredoomed to failure if he tries to be like the gods? One wonders, therefore, if the divine is so distant from man and nature alike, that what the gods do or do not do becomes irrelevant to the question of what men and nature do. Certainly, there is no divine intervention in the play. If the gods act in human affairs, they act through human and perhaps natural intermediaries. It is Timon who discovers the gold which he then says was meant, at least in part, for Flavius; and Athens is saved by Alcibiades' medicine. The gods do nothing about the fundamental human dilemma we have described above—that man in the attempt to be more than the beasts becomes worse than the beasts. The gods in *Timon of Athens* seem to act as chance acts. The argument seems inescapable. If the gods are the only ones who are unaffected by what they do, then that very fact makes it impossible that they be models for man or nature, who are alike affected by what they do. What the gods do may have consequences for man and nature, but neither man nor nature can ever act as the gods do.

Athens' own understanding of the gods, however, is different from that of Flavius. The Merchant, who appears in the very first scene together with the Poet, the Painter, and the Jeweller, tells Apemantus that, "If traffic do it, the gods do it...." To which Apemantus responds, "Traffic's thy god" (I.i.236-237). What does it mean to say that what traffic does, the gods do also? Does it signify that traffic or commerce is as necessary to gods as it is to man? Can one think of the gods as having to depend upon trade, as having to engage in trade? Now the most obvious traffic in which the gods engage is that with men. Can the intercourse between gods and men properly be called a traffic? What is it then that the gods would need in such a traffic, since commerce is understood to be an exchange of goods? It is well understood, of course, what men need from the gods, for men are weak and poor. But do the gods need men? One wonders if the gods need men's attentions as men need the gods. Do the gods become rich, powerful, and beautiful through the attentions of men? Magnificence is, after all, that virtue of spending money rightly upon the most beautiful things, and the most beautiful of things are the divine things. Timon's magnificent Athens, we have seen, is dependent upon the Merchant. Is not the Merchant then saying to Apemantus that the gods are equally dependent upon him?[7]

It is, I believe, intelligible that these two views of the gods should be present in the play. On the one hand, the gods appear simply as the culminating expression of the Athenian love of beauty. On the other hand, the gods appear as independent of man and nature alike. In either case, the gods are irrelevant to human action. They are either reflections of the city, or they cannot be imitated by the city. They never therefore intervene directly in human affairs, although human beings may attribute what happens in the world to the gods.

One further suggestion about the gods is made by Apemantus in his Grace (I.ii.60ff.). Apemantus prefaces his Grace by saying that, "Feasts are too proud to give thanks to the gods." In the prayer proper, however, he tells the immortal gods that he craves for nothing, prays for no one but himself, and trusts no oaths, no harlot's tears, no sleeping dogs, no keeper with his freedom, nor any friends if he be in need. He does not, that is to say, expect anyone or anything to act outside of what might reasonably be expected from their natures. Apemantus's Grace, in Christian terms, is surely most lacking in grace. His prayer is not a prayer to the gods; instead, the prayer is a statement of his self-sufficiency. Such self-sufficiency would seem to be an imitation of the gods. Can the life of the gods be imitated after all, and has Apemantus succeeded in doing so? His name, we have noted, means "free from misery," and again this is one of the principal attributes of the gods. Timon, unlike the gods, is full of discontents—what of Apemantus? We turn next then to Apemantus, to try to see what he is.

Apemantus claims that he visits Timon's feasts for two reasons. He wishes to observe the folly of human beings, and he wants to chide Timon to prevent him from sinning the faster. Apemantus also claims to be able to open or close heaven to Timon; that is, he claims to be able to show the way to happiness.

He appears, however, to be only an angry man whose railing spares no one and must be borne because Timon would have it so. He is called proud by Timon, for he obviously believes himself to be greatly superior to other human beings. What he does above all is tell the truth in a most unpleasant and discourteous way. He is therefore called "opposite to humanity."[8] Yet nowhere in these early scenes does he express a general hatred of humanity. What he desires is that human vanity be seen for what it is, and that Timon especially see that the Athenians have no love for him or for one another but are only feeders upon him and upon one another. Apemantus does not disdain all human beings; he invites a Fool to come with him, for the Fool understands his own foolishness and that of others.

Apemantus visits Timon in the woods because he has heard that Timon imitates his manners (IV.iii.198-199). According to Apemantus, Timon ought not do so, because he does so "enforcèdly," and not therefore by understanding. Apemantus thus still comes to vex Timon, as he did when Timon was more prosperous, for Timon has not learned whatever lesson it is that Apemantus has to teach. Apemantus does, however, admit that he loves Timon more in the woods than in the city, and it would seem then that Timon has learned more and become better by going to the woods.

Timon replies that Apemantus's manners are equally enforced. It is by necessity and not by virtue that Apemantus has kept himself free of the sweets and flatteries of this world. Apemantus has not only a nature inclined to bear hardship, but fortune has given him nothing. He has never been tempted, never had the occasion, as Timon has had, to taste the delights of wealth and philanthropy. Apemantus has no cause to complain, for he has had nothing and has given nothing.

Apemantus does not answer Timon's accusation; instead, he still seeks to persuade Timon to eat and think of Athens. He points out that there is no use in the woods for the gold which Timon has found; he seems to imply that there might be in Athens. Apemantus seems to want Timon to return to Athens. He says that Timon needs to learn "the middle of humanity." If Timon learned the middle of humanity, he could return to the city for he would then not be mocked. Timon was mocked by flatterers in the city; he is now mocked as a madman in the woods. Timon needs to return to the city and not be mocked, and that also means that in Apemantus's view Timon can neither be a beast nor a god. We know that Apemantus is mocked and that he is an extreme. Does not this mean that Apemantus is saying that he himself is not a model to be followed by Timon, and probably therefore not by most men?

That Timon does not understand is shown, it seems to me, in the subsequent exchange of questions. Apemantus asks Timon, "What man didst thou ever know unthrift that was beloved after his means?" (IV.iii.308-310). And Timon, in reply, asks, "Who, without those means thou talk'st of, didst thou ever know beloved?" Timon here indicates that he had thought that love between human beings was always dependent upon means. But if that were true, he would have seen to it that he continued to possess those means and therefore continued being loved. He in fact concedes Apemantus's point. But Apemantus goes further; he has known one man who has been loved for himself alone, and that is himself. Timon retorts that he must then have had the means to keep a dog. If Timon knew what he was saying, he would have heeded the counsels of Apemantus and Flavius; for if men and dogs love only those who feed them, why then did not Timon see to it that he always had the means to feed? Timon is saying, of course, that there is no other way to gain the love of men than to do them benefits. He holds tenaciously to his old beliefs.

Since Timon has responded that only a dog could love Apemantus because he has only the means for keeping a dog, Apemantus wonders what Timon calls his former flatterers. Women, declares Timon, or rather men. His first answer, therefore, is that they are unmanly men. He immediately qualifies his answer by saying, in effect, that all men are unmanly. Again, one wonders why there is then no acceptance on the part of Timon of the fact that if men cannot be expected to behave differently, then one should not be angry with them. Why should one expect more of beings who cannot be other than they are? Timon, however, wants to know what Apemantus would do with the world if it were in his power. The answer is surprising, for heretofore Apemantus has apparently been trying to persuade Timon to return to Athens. Apemantus, for the first time, shows a misanthropy exactly like that of Timon—he answers that he would return the world to the beasts to be rid of men. Why, then, one has to ask, had he concerned himself thus far with Timon?

In the context of the argument, I suggest that Apemantus's answer is ambiguous. Timon, in the previous exchange of answers, admitted in effect that beasts and men are alike incapable of gratitude, for they go to whoever can feed them. Timon's great error is in supposing that he could forget or transcend this fact. Apemantus's answer therefore may say only that we must return to that beastly nature of man. That his answer is ironic and meant to provoke thought is suggested by what he subsequently tells Timon:

> If thou couldst please me with speaking to me, thou mightst have hit upon it here. The commonwealth of Athens is become a forest of beasts. (IV.iii.344-346)

We do not know, we need parenthetically to note, if "here" refers to the place in the argument or the woods. Apemantus wants to return the world to be beasts because Athens has become a commonwealth of beasts. But it has become beastly without knowing that it has. The acknowledgment of beastliness would be the beginning of Athenian self-knowledge. I do not believe, therefore, that Apemantus can be called a misanthrope, even a philosophical misanthrope. As he himself says, his effort throughout has been to bring Timon to know the middle. Despite Timon's supposed disillusionment, he still expects more of mankind than can properly be asked. Timon is still prodigal in his demands, still a man of extremes. He does not, in sum, accept the beastliness of man, while Apemantus does.

Timon, in truth, has an irredeemable prejudice against Apemantus. He will not accept Apemantus's counsel because he continues to believe himself superior to Apemantus. Thus Apemantus puts his finger upon the difficulty when he asks Timon, "Art thou proud yet?" Timon, we have seen, believes himself to be superior because he has been given great wealth and has yet acted nobly. When told by Apemantus that he would give the world back to the beasts, Timon wonders if Apemantus is willing to fall "in the confusion of men, and remain a beast with the beasts." Apemantus replies affirmatively, whereupon Timon makes clear the basis of his contempt for Apemantus—Apemantus is ineffectual; in a kingdom of the beasts he would always be the helpless victim and subjugated. Apemantus has no power in him—his defense is absence; his safety is always in escape. As Timon, asks, "What beast couldst thou be that were not subject to a beast?" Timon at least was a sovereign; he ruled men as Apemantus never can. He had the eyes and hearts of men, and they stuck upon him numberless (IV.iii.261-263).

The difficulty with Apemantus is that he seems to be only a scold. He tells people that what they do is foolish, but he does not show them what it is that they then must do.[9] Whatever the philosophical life is, we do not see it in the play. We do not understand the life Apemantus finds superior to the city. Timon understands Apemantus's life to be the result of accident, a combination of fortune and nature. Some natures are meant to be opposite, and they are especially so if fortune keeps them poor and humble and unable to do anything else except to pretend to superiority by railing against everyone.

The exchange between Timon and Apemantus ends in stones being thrown by Timon and name-calling on both sides. It is a most undignified brawl, and it underscores the complete failure of Apemantus to teach Timon.

Apemantus promises that he will send throngs to Timon. He makes us aware that Timon in the woods is as wealthy and as sought after as he ever was in the city. He is very seldom alone in the woods. We are also made aware that he gives his gold to more worthy beneficiaries and with better effect in the woods. He gives gold to Alcibiades, Flavius, and the Bandits, and each puts the gold to good use. We know what Alcibiades does, and the Bandits apparently become soldiers once again. Flavius, of course, is the only justly deserving recipient. Thus, when Timon gave out of love, he believed he gave nobly for the sake of the city, and the consequence was misery for himself and the corruption of those to whom he gave. When he gives out of hated to Alcibiades and the Bandits, he intends that the gold should be a destroyer of men and the city, and instead it becomes a means of salvation for both. Timon never understands what he is doing when he gives.

Apemantus had tried to remind Timon that man cannot live naturally. If Timon will not return to the city, he can only die. Timon seems to accept this alternative, for he now says that he must prepare his grave, "where the light foam of the sea may beat" his gravestone daily. Timon's death will not simply be a return to the elements; he wants his epitaph to teach men. His death is to be a rebellion against gold, the basis of human civilization. He wants to use the gold he found to encourage faction and set men at odds one with another. Apemantus agrees with Timon's wish that men may descend into faction, but says that it will not happen until he, Apemantus, is dead. It is difficult to know what Apemantus is saying, except that the gold Timon gives will not have the desired effect. But why must the fall of man into beastliness wait until Apemantus is dead? Is he in some sense the last obstacle against such a fall? That would mean that it is Apemantus, not Timon, who will be last upholder of the city. It would indeed be strange if Apemantus is somehow the last representative of Athenian principle, in the sense that only without him would Athens finally fall.

Apemantus's self-sufficiency is of course an imitation of the gods. And his way of life remains as hidden to men as the life of the gods. The philosophic life appears to be a vauntingly ambitious claim to a superiority which cannot be seen or understood. It is a claim, moreover, which appears to hide a contemptible weakness which arises from a lack of being favored either by nature or by fortune. Timon rejects Apemantus, in the city and in the woods, because Apemantus does not and cannot rule human beings. Timon still loves the noble, the beautiful, and still desires that man in some way transcend nature. As we shall see, he finally succeeds. But before we come to Timon's ending, we need to consider one more Athenian, the one man who, without question, is effective, able to rule.

The first thing we note about Alcibiades is that the image of eating men is especially connected with him. Eating is an image which generally informs the play. Apemantus refuses to eat with Timon, for he prefers to be self-sufficient and feed on root. Alcibiades' first words are that he feeds "most hungerly" upon the sight of Timon. It is soon said of him that he loves to feed upon enemies—to which Alcibiades replies that there is no better meat nor a better feast for one's friend. If Apemantus does not eat, or eats but little, and others feed upon Timon, then Alcibiades is the hungry feeder upon men. When Alcibiades approaches Athens with his Powers, as the stage instructions say, the Second Senator offers a tenth of the city as a "tithèd death" to Alcibiades, if he desires "that food/ Which nature loathes" (V.iv.31-35). Unnatural tastes are attributed to Alcibiades, and that is perhaps why it is through him that Athens is saved.

Apemantus seems to recognize the usefulness of Alcibiades from the beginning. He is the only one whom Apemantus does not scold; instead, he wants to turn Alcibiades against the flatterers in Athens that they might be made meat for a feast (I.ii.75-77). That is of course exactly what happens at the end of the play.

When next we see Alcibiades, he is pleading for the life of his own men, and he speaks to the Senate as a captain (III.v.1ff). He cares for his own, and it is perhaps an especial mark of a captain that he have this care of his own. The Senate lacks this care, which they show by banishing Alcibiades. Alcibiades' banishment turns him into an enemy of Athens, as Timon and Apemantus are also enemies of Athens.

The third scene in which we see Alcibiades is his meeting with Timon in the woods (IV.iii.48ff). The scene begins with Alcibiades not at first recognizing Timon. He asks what Timon is and for his name. When Timon says that he is Misanthropos, Alcibiades acknowledges that he knows him well, but declares that he does not know of Timon's fortunes. Subsequently, Alcibiades adds that he has heard "in some sort" of what has happened. The inconsistencies are soon revealed to be deliberate, for Alcibiades finally confesses that he has heard of everything that has happened to Timon. It would seem, then, that Alcibiades has deliberately sought out Timon and is carefully testing his temper. Alcibiades then declares that although he is penurious, he still has a little gold to offer Timon. Timon refuses the gold and, upon hearing that Alcibiades is at war with Athens, gives him the gold which he has just unearthed. One is tempted to say that Alcibiades has sought out Timon for his gold, but since the gold has been just been freshly discovered Alcibiades could not possibly have known of it. Nevertheless, it seems to me evident that Alcibiades has come on purpose to find Timon. What brings him to Timon could be the memory of past benefits. Alcibiades, after all, takes care of his own. One might also speculate, however, that Alcibiades seeks out Timon to enlist the latter in his cause. As the senators say later, only Timon can defend Athens against Alcibiades. Is Alcibiades' visit meant to offset this possibility? Whatever the cause of Alcibiades' visit, however, it redounds to his great benefit.

Alcibiades welcomes Timon's gold, but refuses his counsel as to how it should be used. He does not need advice on what needs to be done. Of all the Athenians, he alone is able to prescribe a remedy for the disease which afflicts Athens. The remedy is to be a leeching or a purging of blood. He is a shepherd culling an infected flock, and we have already heard of the tithe which is to be offered him. Alcibiades knows what to do with beasts, and he shows no hesitation in applying that knowledge to men. He is the one man in the entire play who is able to act in accordance with the beastly nature of man.

We cannot at this point avoid commenting upon the presence of strangers in Athens who remark upon the ingratitude shown to Timon (III.ii.62-86). They have no other role in the play than to make this observation. Their names are Roman, and we must ask the question, were

not the Romans, like Alcibiades, great eaters of men, perhaps the greatest eaters of men? We are told that the Romans visited Periclean Athens,
and it is certainly tempting to speculate that this is the embassy sent by
the Senate.[10] If so, then the shadow of Rome is shown to be falling over
Athens; the future belongs not to the city which loves the beautiful, but
to the one which knows how to rule the man and the beast and, like
Alcibiades, uses each to prescribe to the other.

The salvation of Athens, however, belongs also to Timon. Timon is so
much present in the last scene that we cannot but conclude that he shares
in Alcibiades' refounding of Athens. The punishment of the enemies of
Timon is first among the conditions which Alcibiades lays down for the
surrender of Athens. Moreover, when the Soldier arrives with the news
of Timon's death, Alcibiades reads the epitaph and promises that Timon
will be remembered. Timon's death is to be a lesson for Athens and for
all men, as Timon himself had said he intended it to be. What then is that
lesson? What is the meaning of Timon's death?

Timon intends his epitaph to be an oracle to Athens (V.i.217). An
oracle is, of course, always obscure. The epitaph thus cannot be read by
the Soldier who finds it; it seems to be written in characters different
from those used for a sign near the grave. But Alcibiades sees that it is
not the epitaph which is of significance but the grave. Timon's rejection
of human griefs, he says, is redeemed by the "conceit" of the grave. It is
placed at the extreme of the earth's edge, on the mere of the sea, as close
to formless chaos as it can possibly be. The "conceit" is that "niggard
nature" is thus made to weep eternally upon his grave. The impersonal
forces of nature now appear to be the eternal mourners of human mortality.

The epitaph, however, seems to be at odds with the meaning given
by Alcibiades to the grave. The epitaph commands that no one seek the
name of the dead, and yet gives Timon's name. It speaks of hatred for
those who live and declares the expectation that those who pass will curse
the grave. Timon seems to wish to be remembered, for the sign and the
epitaph both bear his name, but he appears not to understand what it is
that will make him be remembered. He seems to believe that the epitaph contains his oracle or his teaching to mankind, which is one of hatred. Yet, according to Alcibiades' interpretation, the grave is a source of
grace and redemption. It is the grave, not the epitaph, which permits
that Timon be remembered as noble and that faults be forgiven.

The way in which Timon's death is presented makes us wonder if

Timon is not in the end a poet. Now the Poet and the Painter are included among the enemies of Timon, and when they come to him in the woods they are stoned and driven away, as Apemantus is also stoned and cursed. No others are so treated—the Senators are treated far better than are Apemantus, the Poet, and the Painter. Curiously, Apemantus makes a reference to the coming visit to the woods of the Poet and the Painter, a reference which appears to be out of place. All other visitors to the woods are given gold, but not these three. Nevertheless, the ending of the play forces us to reconsider the Poet and the Painter, for it would seem that the greatest thing Timon does is to make an image of his own life and death. The title of play is *The Life of Timon of Athens*. But, according to Alcibiades, it is the grave which redeems the life.

The significance of Timon's grave is that he has somehow buried himself and provided his own gravestone. Surely this is the greatest conceit of all, in both meanings of that term. It is an overweening act, a mark of his attainment of complete self-sufficiency. The burial of the dead is where the human being is shown to be most dependent on others; Timon makes it an image or conceit of his self-sufficiency. Is it not a conceit in the sense of an act of the imagination? Is such self-sufficiency only possible as a fancy?

We return now to the beginning to consider further the Poet and the Painter, for the reasons given above. We begin with the Poet, for he is the first to speak.

The Poet is a man who is "rapt," and he speaks of his poesy as something which spontaneously "oozes" out of him, as a tree oozes gum. As the image suggests, there is something unconscious about this exudation. One suspects that the description we are given here of the Poet is one which repeats common opinion. This suspicion is deepened by the Painter's judgment of the Poet's work. It is, the Painter says, common, and one has to agree that the poem's subject, Fortune casting her favorites down, is a commonplace. The Painter claims that there a "thousand moral paintings" which demonstrate the subject more "pregnantly than words." The rivalry between the two turns on the question of who imitates nature better, and who, in the imitation, may be able even to surpass nature.

In this respect, painting appears to be superior to poetry. The painting in its direct representation of nature is superior to speech. The Poet himself speaks of the Painter's picture as tutoring nature and being livelier than life. One notices that the Poet's account of his own poem is more like the description of a painting than it is the argument of a poem. When the Poet and the Painter present their works to Timon, the latter receives the poem in a perfunctory manner and reserves his ardent praise for the picture. The painting, he says, is superior to nature. Since Timon also receives the Jeweller's gift with a stronger show of interest than he gave to the poem, it would also seem that jewels are superior to poetry. Timon thus reveals a preference for that which may be immediately seen and touched, for that which is immediately available. A book, after all, cannot be immediately seen for what it is, and, of course, it lacks showiness.

When Timon sees the ugliness which is concealed by the beautiful surface of the city, he also turns against the Poet and the Painter (V.i.1-113). He drives them away because they are not honest men. He turns, of course, especially against the Painter, for it is the deceitful surface of things which he curses. The Painter, he says, draws a "counterfeit/ Best in all Athens." As for the Poet, he is not a counterfeiter but an alchemist. Timon will have none of either, for he has ceased to believe either in the possibility of the beautiful imitation correcting and replacing nature, or in the possibility of transforming a rough and ugly nature into the noble.

We have raised the question: Is the play saying that Timon is in some sense a poet? How are we to understand his turning away from the city and the arts, on the one hand, and his desire, on the other hand, to make a "rich conceit" which will cause him to be remembered? We have seen that Timon is ambivalent on how it is he is to be remembered. Is he to be nameless or is his name to be remembered? Does he intend a curse or does he wish to make his life and death a kind of blessing?

We remind ourselves that Alcibiades looks beyond the epitaph which curses mankind to the grave itself. Timon, however, speaks of his epitaph and not his grave as that which is to teach Athens and all mankind of his rebellion against gold. It is the epitaph which he wishes to be the oracle for Athens. He seems unaware of the significance of his making

> his everlasting mansion
> Upon the beachèd verge of the salt flood,
> Who once a day with his embossèd froth
> The turbulent surge shall cover.... (V.i.213-216)

He goes on to say that he wants that "Graves only be men's works." That remark, as we shall see, takes on a special meaning.

In his unconsciousness of what he does, he is like the Poet. And what he has done is not to imitate nature, but rather like an alchemist to transform his grave into an everlasting image. But he does what neither Poet nor Painter was able to do, and that is to transform the fact itself, here the fact of death, into a "rich conceit." Timon dissolves the distinction between the image and that which is imitated—the two become one in his grave. What Timon always wished for, the dissolving of the distinction between the beautiful images and nature, he finally achieves. We are led to reflect upon the possibility that what Timon wishes for is what the poet wishes for. Does the poet wish for his images to be one with what is? Does the poet desire to be an alchemist, transforming nature in and through his images? One is reminded of Herodotus's discussion of why the Egyptians make mummies. The reason is that they desire to make the natural body and the everlasting artifact one. Such a desire is a consequence of their being a people whose lives are governed in every aspect by the sacred. Perhaps Timon, then, is more like an Egyptian priest than he is a poet. And like the Egyptians he cannot make the living natural body into an artifact, but he can turn the grave into one.[11]

We are left thinking about what Alcibiades can mean when he says that Timon's grave is a forgiving of human griefs and faults. It would seem that what is being said is that the terrible conditions of human existence, which Timon would not accept, and which drove him into the woods, are forgiven; that there is, in other words, a remission or setting aside of these conditions. Thus Timon, through his grave, shows us the way in which there may be a transformation of the beastliness of human existence.

What Timon is may now be summed up. Timon, in his extreme love of the beautiful, is led into an extreme awareness of the polarities of human existence. Unlike Apemantus and Alcibiades, he has a nature which cannot accept these polarities. Apemantus has a hard nature, as Timon himself says—are we to conclude that Alcibiades has a cruel nature? At any rate, both are able to accept what necessity imposes. Timon begins by thinking too highly of human beings and, when he is disappointed, refuses to accept them as they are and instead curses mankind, calling upon the gods to extinguish the human race. But what redeems the folly of Timon's life is that he shows that the extreme love of the beautiful may be fulfilled by transforming the grave, which is to say the decay and dissolution of the beast, into an imperishable image. It would seem that only upon this possibility would Timon's life gain the nobility which Alcibiades attributes to it. In terms of the play we know only of the grave, we know of nothing beyond the grave, and Shakespeare seems to be saying that Timon's grave as an image of self-sufficiency will indeed be enough to justify such an extreme love of the beautiful. Only if it is possible for someone to bury himself will such an extreme love of the beautiful be justified—there is no further need for some kind of knowledge of what is beyond the grave.

Finally, we must remember that Athens produces not one but a multiplicity and variety of character. The ruling principle of Athens is the love of the beautiful. That is, Athens is the city which pushes that love to an extreme. Such an extreme love makes the polarities of human existence sharply apparent and choices can then be made by men as where they are to place themselves with respect to these polarities. Timon is Athens at one extreme, and we surmise that Apemantus is the other extreme. Is Alcibiades then the "middle of humanity?"

Shakespeare ends his play with an Athens which is to be reordered by Alcibiades. This Athens will not be the one wished for by Timon, and it will not be the one which was finally brought down by Sparta. An Athens refounded by Alcibiades, as the play indicates, would have been saved, and that means saved from the disaster of defeat in the Peloponnesian War. By permitting Alcibiades to rescue Athens, Shakespeare permits Athens to win the Peloponnesian War—he thus rewrites the history of Western civilization. That Alcibiades should rule Athens as he pleases is the advice, of course, which Aeschylus gives in the *Frogs* to Dionysus.[12]

We are reminded that *the* history of the Peloponnesian War, that is, the one written by Thucydides also ends with an Athens which is ruled by Alcibiades. We are told by Thucydides about this Athens reordered according to Alcibiades' instructions:

> And now first (at least in my time) the Athenians seem to have ordered their state aright; which consisted now of a moderate temper, both of *the few* and of *the many*. And this was the first thing, that after so many misfortunes past made the city again to raise her head.[13]

Only an Athens ruled by Alcibiades would have won the Peloponnesian War. Upon this point Shakespeare agrees with such as Aristophanes and Thucydides, two of the greatest observers of that war. But would not a victorious Athens have then become supreme over the Greek world? And would not Athens then have been free at last to do what Alcibiades desired: "to subdue the Sicilians; after them the Italians; after them to assay the dominions of Carthage and Carthage itself"? Would Alcibiades, at the head of a victorious Athens, have given up his hopes of conquering all of Greece and the western Mediterranean? Moreover, Xenophon, in the *Anabasis* and the *Agesilaos*, indicates the weakness of the Persian Empire and how easily it might have been conquered. A new possibility occurs to one—could Athens have done what Alexander later did, i.e., conquer Persia? An Alcibiadean Athens could then have become mistress not only of the Mediterranean but also of Asia.

Shakespeare's answer to these questions is indicated, it seems to me, in the lines spoken by Alcibiades at the very end of the play:

> Make war breed peace, make peace stint war, make each
> Prescribe to each other, as each other's leech. (V.iv.83-84)

Peace, of course, is the end for which a statesman works, and Alcibiades appears to be speaking a commonplace. What every decent man would say is said—war and expansion will be moderated by the end of peace. But the next line leaves one wondering. War is equally to prescribe to peace, as peace prescribes to war. The city cannot remain simply at peace. We have seen at the beginning of the play how peace corrupts the city and how the soldier is forgotten. The variability of human affairs forbids that the city remain in a condition of rest. Not in rest but in the fluctuation between peace and war is moderation to be found. Alcibiadean Athens would not remain at rest, for she would understand the harshness of political life and the necessity of acquisition. Such an Athens would, as we have indicated before, prefigure Rome and her deeds.

But we must not forget that Timon's death is to be remembered. The memory of Timon is somehow important to Alcibiades' new orders. Perhaps Timon and his grave are the last reminders of the beautiful Athens, of that Athens of the golden age, the vision of which seems to have possessed the souls not only of Timon but also of Cimon and Pericles. Is the new Athens of Alcibiades still somehow linked to the extreme love of the beautiful? It would seem then that the new Athens is to be kept reminded of the beautiful through the image of a self-sufficient grave. That self-sufficient grave, we have said, is the revelation of the complete independence of Timon from necessity. Such self-sufficiency is not possible in political life but is made seemingly possible through the conceit of Timon's grave. We end, necessarily it seems to me, with a question: does the new Athens, which would appear to have to be an imperial Athens, require an image of the self-sufficient life in order to be ennobled?

Notes

1. *Copp'd Hills Towards Heaven: Shakespeare and the Classical Polity* (The Hague: Martinus Nijhoff, 1970), p. 36.

2. Line citations follow the Penguin edition of Shakespeare's *Complete Works* (Baltimore: Penguin, 1969), Alfred Harbage, general editor.

3. Dain Trafton has pointed out to me that the Shakespearean audience would have understood the name as the "ape-man." The "ape-man" who is free from misery is a good summation of Rousseau's understanding of what man is like in the state of nature.

4. *Peloponnesian War* II.38 (Hobbes's translation).

5. *Lives, Cimon*, X.1-3, 6-7.

6. Marx quotes Timon's speech here on gold in *Capital: A Critique of Political Economy* (New York: Modern Library, 1936), p. 148, n. 2.

7. See Aristophanes, *Birds*, ll. 187-193, 1515. Line 1549 speaks of Timon as the hater of the gods.

8. Thomas West has called my attention to the fact that the description of Apemantus's way of life reminds one of what has been said of the way of life of the young Socrates. See Leo Strauss, *Socrates and Aristophanes* (New York: Basic Books, 1966), pp. 311-314.

9. It is the same accusation made against Socrates by Cleitophon in the *Cleitophon* 410b-e. In *The Roots of Political Philosophy: Ten Forgotten Socratic Dialogues*, Thomas Pangle, editor (Ithaca: Cornell University Press, 1987), pp. 111-116.

10. Livy, III.33.

11. See Seth Benardete, *Herodotean Inquiries* (The Hague: Martinus Nijhoff, 1969), pp. 57-58.

12. Aristophanes, *Frogs*, ll. 1431-1433.

13. *Peloponnesian War* VIII.97. On Alcibiades' instructions see VIII.86. See also Leo Strauss, *The City and Man* (Chicago: Rand McNally, 1964), p. 227, n. 89.

CHASTITY AS A POLITICAL PRINCIPLE: AN INTERPRETATION OF SHAKESPEARE'S *MEASURE FOR MEASURE*

Harry V. Jaffa

The city of Vienna is in bad shape. It has been misruled—or allowed to go without being ruled—for no less than fourteen years. The nominal ruler is a philosopher. However good philosophic rule may be in theory, in practice it seems to be nearly the worst. This is confirmed by the *Tempest* no less than by *Measure for Measure*. Prospero's negligent government of Milan, from which he is roughly expelled by his usurping brother, is as unprosperous as Vincentio's has been. Vincentio loves the life removed (I.iii.7) and his study has been to know himself (III.ii.245), instead of practicing "his judgment with the disposition of natures" (III.i.165).[1] Similarly, Prospero, in Milan, was preoccupied with the liberal arts (I.ii.73), instead of spying out the plots of malefactors (something he almost forgets to do even on the island). And so it has come to pass in Vienna, that "liberty plucks justice by the nose, / The baby beats the nurse, and quite athwart / Goes all decorum" (I.iii.29-31). But decorum is too decorous a word for what goes athwart. Lechery and fornication are rampant. In scene ii, which precedes the conversation between Friar Thomas and the Duke, we observe the young bucks of the city engaged in witty repartee and badinage concerning their venereal sports and diseases. Their humor is keen but their characters are dissolute. They are not the stuff of which public spirit and citizenship are compounded. We learn from Aristotle's *Politics* that a city must be a collection of families in order to be a collection of citizens. These young gentlemen are such as ought to form the officer class. But they are poor matter for the making of soldiers. And we learn that war with Hungary may threaten. The opinion as to the Duke's strange absence—which he himself has encouraged—suggests that he is on a diplomatic mission abroad. But the

Duke knows that he must put the city into better order at home, before it can meet a challenge from abroad. None of the young men appears to be married or contemplating marriage. Not even Claudio, whose fiancée is approaching her confinement, seems to think of it. Later, when Angelo declares his love for Isabella, it seems never to occur to him to court her, or to ask her to marry him. Celibacy and fornication seem to be the only alternatives. Vienna is a city—or perhaps we should write "city"—of monasteries, nunneries, whorehouses, and prisons. But we do not see any families. Sexual desire may be sublimated or indulged. But we do not see sexual desire as an extension of self-preservation, and self-preservation extended to include the family, whence it is transformed into patriotism. There is no evidence of sexual desire becoming conjugal love, producing domesticity. Angelo, we learn, has broken off his engagement to Mariana when her dowry was shipwrecked. But it was also for the sake of a dowry that Claudio and Juliet postponed their nuptial ceremonies, but not their nuptial relations. The only "family man" we see is Elbow the Constable, who is also the only one to display a public spiritedness—however malaprop. He is also the only one to refer to Christianity by name (II.i.57). The action of *Measure for Measure* seems to constitute a kind of Hegelian dialectic, in which the thesis is celibacy and sexual abstinence, the antithesis unbridled lechery and fornication, and the synthesis an eroticism in harmony with the family and the virtue of the citizen.

In the Vienna which the Duke sets out to reform we see no such virtuous and lawful love of husband and wife, or of parents and children, as dominates *Coriolanus*. Citizen soldiers do not spring from the illicit intercourse of playboys and prostitutes, as of course they do not from the non-intercourse of monks and nuns. The ambition to conquer or to die for the city is an extension of the natural willingness to fight without regard to one's individual self-preservation, that we see in birds and creatures other than man, which form families in the course of perpetuating their kind. But the human family, unlike other families in nature, does not become fully a family, except in that association with other families that we call the political community. The dynastic impulse, rooted in the family, remains the root of the political impulse. In fighting for the city, the citizen soldier sees himself as fighting for his family, or his family's city.

Chastity is a political principle because it is the principle of the integrity of the family, and the city is a collection of families. In its rudimentary but not in its completed sense, the family is pre-political, and may be said to exist by reason of natural necessities. But the family, as the element of which the city is compounded, exists by law as well as by natural necessity. And chastity is that virtue or principle by which a harmony is assured between the nature and the law of the family. In the meeting in III.i between Isabella and Claudio, when she tells him of Angelo's infamous offer, he first voices his repugnance to it, and says that if he must die he will "encounter darkness as a bride, and hug it in my arms." Isabella replies. "There spake my brother, there my father's grave did utter forth a voice." But when Claudio loses his courage (and when he no longer imagines death as a bride to be hugged, but as something cold and fearful), and begs Isabella to save him at any cost, she turns upon him in uncontrolled anger. She calls him a beast, a faithless coward, and a dishonest wretch. (The central charge connects infidelity with cowardice.) She accuses him of being willing to commit "a kind of incest, to take life/ From [his] own sister's shame." Then she adds, "Heaven shield my mother played my father fair! / For such a warped slip of wilderness/ Ne'er issued from his blood" (III.i.138, 141-143). Here we see Isabella as the very incarnation of the spirit of the family. She is as much her father's daughter as Coriolanus is his mother's son. The warrior spirit is strong within her, as it is within Volumnia. Her denunciation of Claudio's cowardice reminds one of Caius Marcius's—himself echoing his mother— as he reviles the plebeian soldiery for turning its backs upon the enemy before Corioli. (Volumnia, imagining her son addressing his troops, says "Come on you cowards! You were got in fear, though you were born in Rome." She thus anticipates Isabella in equating cowardice with a kind of bastardy; making the coward the offspring not of attraction, but of repulsion.) Incest and adultery are crimes (rather than sins) because they are evidently inconsistent with the integrity of the family, and hence of the city. The importance of chastity derives from no delicate feelings in regard to sex. As a prospective votary of St. Clare, and as a representative of Pauline Christianity, Isabella does indeed have such feelings. (She calls fornication the "vice that most I do abhor," in II.ii.29.) But her emotional distance from the very idea of sex is later swept away in a tide of family pride, by reason of which she had rather her "brother die by the law than [that her] son should be unlawfully born" (III.i.195). At this point we may be sure   however little she herself may be conscious of it—that she will never return to the nunnery. She will indeed put on her "destin'd livery" (III.i.138), not as Angelo intended, as a courtesan, but as a Roman matron. Virtue, politically understood, belongs of right not merely to individuals, but to men and women as representatives of families. Isabella, like the great Roman matrons, sees herself as the guardian of family reputation and of family pride. She had rather suspect her mother of playing her father false, than of admitting that her brother, when he showed himself a coward, could be a legitimate scion of her family. She shows us the origin and political meaning of illegitimacy. If a man misbehaves, he casts a reproach not only on himself but upon his progenitors. Isabella does not mean to sully her mother's reputation: she rather goads Claudio into saving the reputation of both her mother and her father. She reminds us of the origin of the Roman republic, in the death of Lucrece. An honorable death is better than a shameful life, because it involves the reputation of both one's ancestors and one's posterity. Isabella does say, in II.iv.106, that it were "cheaper" and "better" that a brother "died at once, than that a sister, by redeeming him, should die forever." This economizing of morality (or, perhaps, de-politicizing of it) occurs however in a context in which Isabella is appealing to Christian doctrine in order to justify to Angelo her demand for a pardon for Claudio, a pardon in which she herself does not believe on secular or political grounds.

The connection between the family and the city or, more precisely, between the family and the aristocratic republic, has never been presented more powerfully than in *Coriolanus*. If Antony's speech over the dead body of Caesar is the quintessence of the rhetoric of a democratic republic, Volumnia's speech, in Act V, scene iii, of *Coriolanus* may be considered equally representative of the rhetoric of an aristocratic republic. It is the speech in which Volumnia pleads for mercy for Rome at the hands of the Volscian army commanded by her son, whom the democracy of Rome had banished. In this speech the identification of family and city is nearly complete. To see her Roman son commanding an alien army, bent on destroying Rome, causes

> Mother, wife, and child to see
> The son, the husband, and the father tearing
> His country's bowels out. (V.iii.101-103)

She calls the country, Rome, "our dear nurse," but the son, husband, and father is "Our comfort in the country." Neither Volumnia nor Coriolanus have conceded any truth to the democratic thesis, that the plebeians— "Rome's mechanics"—are the city. For them the Senate, or the senatorial families, the patricians ("fathers"), are the city. But Coriolanus cannot seek vengeance against Rome for the misdeeds (as he sees them) of the plebs without in effect conceding that they are, after all, and in the decisive sense, the city. Only as Volumnia saves the city—and the plebeians—from Coriolanus's wrath, will the plebeians be forced to concede that Coriolanus was right all along, that they owe their safety to the Senate, which in the end turns out to be Volumnia (not a father, but a mother!) herself. Both the genius and the power of Rome—its power to conquer and its power to make peace—lie in its matrons. Volumnia displays a strength of character, an ability to conquer (through her son), and to rule (by conquering the conqueror), which represents a higher degree of political capacity than is displayed by any other character in the Roman plays—and perhaps by any other character in Shakespearian tragedy. One can understand Isabella, in *Measure for Measure,* only in the light of what it means to be a Roman matron. Roman matriotism is presented to us primarily, although not exclusively, in the character of Volumnia. It is presented comprehensively in the characters of the three Roman women who surround Coriolanus: Volumnia, Virgilia, and Valeria. Isabella has the *eros* and the *telos* of a Roman matron. Her nature can be fulfilled only in such a matriarchal family as rules in such a city as Volumnia's Rome.

We return to the last act of *Coriolanus.* As the victorious general at the head of the alien army sees mother, wife, and son approaching the camp, to make Rome's last plea for mercy, he braces himself for the coming trial.

> But out, affection!
> All bond and privilege of nature, break!
> Let it be virtuous to be obstinate.
> What is that curtsy worth? Or those doves' eyes,
> Which can make gods forsworn? I melt, and am not
> Of stronger earth than others. My mother bows,
> As if Olympus to a molehill should
> In supplication nod. And my young boy
> Hath an aspect of intercession which
> Great Nature cries "Deny not." (V.iii.24-33)

The outcome is perhaps even more clearly anticipated in the words which follow, in which Coriolanus continues the struggle to deny the claims of nature.

> Let the Volsces
> Plow Rome and harrow Italy. I'll never
> Be such a gosling to obey instinct, but stand
> As if a man were author of himself
> And knew no other kin. (33-37)

Coriolanus says he will not be such a "gosling" as to obey instinct. But instinct has also been called—by him—"Great Nature." Coriolanus has already said that the only ground upon which nature might be denied would be if a man might be author of himself. Julius Caesar was struck down at the very moment he proclaimed himself "unshak'd of motion" (*Julius Caesar*, III.i.70). Coriolanus understands himself better than Caesar in that he knows that a man cannot remain unmoved unless he is also unmade, or *causa sui*. But his mother and his wife will remind him that he is nothing, if not a link between their wombs, the one that gave him life, and the one that would keep his name "living to time."

From this perspective, to obey instinct is not to be a gosling. In the battle before Corioli, Marcius calls the fleeing plebs geese. But Coriolanus's attachment to his family, so far from being cowardly, is the very foundation of his courage. "Great Nature" represents authority, authority in accordance with instinct, but infinitely higher than mere instinct. The families of the lower animals dissolve with the season that brought them forth. The members of such families do not recognize each other beyond their seasons. They are, we might say, as regularly divorced by nature, as they are united by nature. Mere instinct does not produce families, in the properly human and political sense. The latter requires that law complete and fulfill nature. Geese do not differ as Roman geese and Volscian geese. Coriolanus is no more self-sufficient than he is self-made. What made him Volumnia's son made him a Roman. For Rome is a compound of Roman families. He cannot divorce himself from Rome, because he cannot divorce himself from his mother or his wife.

When his family comes into his view Coriolanus first notices his wife. And what he notices, after her curtsy, are "those doves' eyes,/ Which can make gods forsworn." Virgilia's modesty and beauty, like Isabella's before Angelo, inflame Coriolanus's desire. Yet the desire in this case is virtuous. It will cause Coriolanus to melt; it will cause him to become forsworn to the Volscians; but it will ensure his fidelity to Virgilia, and to Rome. A few lines later, he addresses Virgilia thus:

> Best of my flesh,
> Forgive my tyranny, but do not say,
> For that "Forgive our Romans." Oh, a kiss
> Long as my exile, sweet as my revenge!
> Now, by the jealous Queen of Heaven, that kiss
> I carried from thee, dear, and my true lip
> Hath virgined it e'er since. (V.iii.42-48)

She is his "flesh" in a sense recognizable by us—and by Shakespeare's audience—as Biblical. Her kiss has been as long as his exile, because the kiss that he carried with him into exile has "virgined it e'er since." The kiss was "sweet as his revenge." Revenge is indeed sweet. And kisses are sweet. Coriolanus was compelled by the folly of the plebs to seek revenge among the Volscians. But nothing could compel him to seek kisses among the Volscians. In the end, it is this fidelity to his wife which saves Rome. Volumnia's great speech ends, not with an argument, but with a taunt. And it is this taunt which breaks Coriolanus's obstinacy.

> Come, let us go.
> This fellow had a Volscian to his mother.
> His wife is in Corioli, and his child
> Like him by chance. (V.iii.177-180)

Coriolanus could have had a wife and child in Corioli. There was no natural necessity to prevent it. "Great Nature" might then have spoken differently. This is prevented by his erotic attachment to his wife. Mars can be both armed and disarmed by Venus. That for Coriolanus, the field of Venus is the bed of matrimony, arms him to fight for Rome, but disarms him to war against Rome.

In Act II, scene i of *Measure for Measure,* Pompey the bawd protests to Escalus the measures being put into effect against prostitution. "Does your Worship mean to geld and splay all the youth of the city?" Pompey asks. "No, Pompey," replies the old gentleman. "Truly, sir," Pompey rejoins, "in my poor opinion, they will to't, then. If your Worship will take order for the drabs and the knaves, you need not fear the bawds" (II.i.241-246). Escalus says that there are orders for "heading and hanging" of offenders. To which Pompey replies that if they head and hang all that offend that way for ten years, the fairest house in Vienna will rent for practically nothing. It does not occur to Pompey—as it has apparently not occurred to his customers—that there is an alternative (besides gelding and splaying) to fornication and prostitution. Angelo's discovery that a virtuous maid could stir him more than ever "could the strumpet, with all her double vigor, art and nature," is a discovery that needs to be made by all the young men of the city. It is instructive in the highest degree that Angelo, when he makes this discovery, assumes as a matter of course that he too must find satisfaction in fornication. After telling Isabella that he loves her, he makes an indecent proposal, as if that was the only kind that he could make. "Ever till now, when men were fond, I smiled, and wondered how." Now he knows, but knows no other outlet for his "fondness," than to join the ranks of the lechers. If Vienna is to have a citizen army, Venus must once again—as in Coriolanus's time—become the ally, and not the enemy of Mars. To endow chastity with the charms of *eros*, the field of Venus must once again be found upon the bed of matrimony. This is the manifest purport of the reforms of the "Duke of dark corners."

Measure for Measure begins with the Duke, Vincentio, delegating his authority to one Angelo, with the learned Escalus as his second-in-command. The Duke's leave-taking is done quickly. Neither Angelo nor Escalus is given any definite information as to where the Duke will go, or why he is going. In the third scene we learn that Vincentio has "strewed it in the common ear" that his travels are to Poland; and he knows of course that Angelo and Escalus will hear this. In fact, the Duke travels a very short distance, to a monastery not far from the city. There he asks to be fitted with a monk's habit and for instructions

> How I may formally in person bear me
> Like a true friar. (I.iii.47-48)

From the monastery he will return to Vienna, to go undetected among the people and their rulers.

In the monastery he tells Friar Thomas that his purpose in pretending to go away is to leave the government in the hands of those who will enforce the laws that he himself has long neglected to enforce. This is his principal, or only clearly stated, reason for "going." However, near the end of his speech to Friar Thomas he says that there are more reasons for his action, which "at our leisure shall I render." Yet he goes on to tell "Only this one," namely that

> Lord Angelo is precise
> Stands at a guard with envy, scarce confesses
> That his blood flows or that his appetite
> Is more to bread than a stone. Hence shall we see,
> If power change purpose, what our seemers be. (I.iii.50-54)

The Duke then will make an "assay" of Angelo's virtue, by practicing upon him that "judgment with the disposition of natures" that he is later ironically to impute to Angelo himself. It is important to remember however that the testing of Angelo is only *one* of those additional reasons that he has promised to tell Friar Thomas. His strange reserve is expressed in similar fashion in the very last line of the play. As Duke Vicentio prepares to lead the court party back to his palace, he tells them that there "we'll show/ What's yet behind, that's meet you all should know" (V.i.544-545). Despite the apocalyptic ending of the play, we are told that not everything has been revealed. Nor will everything be revealed, except those further things that are "meet" to be known. *Measure for Measure* is a play in which, until the Duke is finally "uncovered," the audience participates in a secret concealed from all the actors but one. Yet at the very end, the audience is told that there are additional secrets that will be revealed to the actors but not to the audience. At the same time, we become aware of still further secrets that will be withheld from both!

Concerning the long neglected laws, Friar Thomas remarks to the Duke that it rested with himself to "unloose this tied-up justice." (The tying-up of justice refers to birch rods whose office is to chastise children, but which when long disused lose their terror.) This unloosing of justice, says the Friar, would have seemed "more dreadful" in himself than in Lord Angelo. The Duke replies that it would have seemed "too dreadful" in him. For he who had been too permissive to be thus severe would have seemed tyrannical. This would bring his government into disrepute. It is his intention to have Angelo, in his stead, strike "in the ambush of [his] name," yet leaving that name untarnished by the striking.

It is Vincentio's plan to have a necessary harshness imposed upon the city, but to make someone else the instrument of that harshness. He means thus to hide his own agency and avoid the reputation which such harshness would bring upon him. This recalls irresistibly a lesson celebrated by Machiavelli in *The Prince*. In the seventh chapter in that famed (and once "justly decried") work, we learn how Cesare Borgia brought order and peace to turbulent Romagna. Cesare, we learn, was called Duke Valentino by the people, a name closely resembling that of Duke Vincentio. Cesare, says Machiavelli, put in charge one Remirro de Orco, "a man cruel and ready, to whom he gave the most complete authority." This man promptly put an end to all theft, brawls, and other excesses, rendering the country peaceful and united. When Cesare decided that such boundless power as Remirro was exercising was no longer necessary, he reintroduced civil authority and the rule of law. "And because he knew that past severities had made some men hate him," wrote Machiavelli, "he determined to purge such men's minds and win them over entirely by showing that any cruelty which had gone on did not originate with himself but with the harsh nature of his agent." Remirro was then executed and his mutilated body displayed in a public square. "The ferocity of this spectacle," Machiavelli concluded, left the people at once "gratified and awestruck."[2]

The resemblance of the plan or plot outlined by Machiavelli to that outlined by Duke Vincentio to Friar Thomas in the third scene of *Measure for Measure* cannot be coincidental. Still, this key, by itself, does not unlock the interpretation of the play. Another key, to be used in conjunction with it, is necessary. This is provided by the title. As the one key comes from the seventh chapter of *The Prince*, the other comes from the seventh chapter of the Gospel according to St. Matthew. The first two verses read: "Judge not, that ye be not judged. For with what judgment ye judge, ye shall be judged: and with what measure ye mete, it shall be measured to you again." *Measure for Measure* appears to begin with a Machiavellian scheme to bring good government to a bad city, by employing bad means that will be justified by their good results. It ends with a scene of reconciliation and harmony, of charity and forgiveness. No innocent—or even guilty—blood has been shed. All the apparent evil-doing has been in the service of a catharsis by which the bad and unruly passions have been purged. It is almost as if an earthly city had been transformed into a heavenly one. The returned Duke, like a returned Christ, has brought good out of evil, in the process of revealing himself.

Measure for Measure is one of Shakespeare's "dark" or "problem" comedies, perhaps the darkest and most problematic of them all. The central conflict, between Isabella and Angelo, seems to offer no possibility of a non-tragic solution. The "happy" ending that does come about, seems to be superimposed upon the conflict almost as much as one of the hypothetical happy endings proposed in the eighteenth century for *King Lear.* The disguised Duke moves like an invisible providence, intervening to prevent the passions and actions of the protagonists from having their necessary consequences. The crux of the play, the infamous "bed-trick," whereby one woman keeps the assignation accepted by another, is the improbable device by which we can smile grimly—although certainly not laugh—as death and defilement are averted. The central tendencies generated by the plot seem to be a commentary on a text supplied by Sonnet 129:

> The expense of spirit in a waste of shame
> Is lust in action, and till action, lust

Is perjured, murderous, bloody, full of blame,
Savage, extreme, rude, cruel, not to trust,
Enjoyed no sooner but despised straight,
Past reason hunted, and no sooner had,
Past reason hated, as a swallowed bait,
On purpose laid to make the taker mad.

The enforcement of the laws, which the Duke has set in motion by his "departure," begins as soon as he "leaves." The houses of prostitution are "plucked down," bawds and pimps are arrested and imprisoned, there are "pretty orders" for "heading and hanging." The brunt of the new regime, however, falls upon a young gentleman named Claudio, who is imprisoned, and sentenced to death, for getting with child the young woman, Juliet, to whom he is betrothed but not married. Claudio's sister, Isabella, who is about to enter the nunnery of the Order of St. Clare as a novice, is summoned from the gates of the nunnery, to plead for her brother's life with the deputy, Angelo, who has sentenced him. Her petition is rejected but, unknown to her, she makes a deep impression upon the apparently unrelenting judge, who in a second interview offers a pardon, on the condition that she yield to Angelo's lust. When Isabella reveals the proposition to her brother in prison, he first spiritedly denounces Angelo and says he would not think of having her purchase his life at such a price. But soon the fear of death seizes him and he begs her to save him at any cost. Isabella denounces his cowardice in terms far harsher than had been used against him even by Angelo, in his highest moralistic judicial vein, and at this point the disguised Duke, who has overheard what has passed between Isabella and Claudio, intervenes. He tells Claudio that Angelo never meant his infamous bargain, that it was only a device to test Isabella herself. He even goes so far as to commit the lie direct, in telling Claudio that he knows this to be true, because he is Angelo's confessor. After Claudio leaves the stage, the Duke proposes to Isabella the infamous bed-trick. She will accept Angelo's proposition, but someone else will keep the assignation. He will substitute one Mariana, a lady who was betrothed to Angelo, but whom Angelo had jilted when her dowry had been lost at sea. The unfortunate maiden, says the Duke, still retains a passion for her cold lover, a passion apparently all the more keen for being unrequited.

The immorality of the Duke's plot is all the more astonishing for the facility with which it is accepted by the two women. On the one hand, there is the promotion of the corrupt bargain with Angelo, involving the sale of justice. On the other hand, there is the deception of Angelo, with the intention of compelling him to marry someone against his will. The Duke justifies the stratagem on the grounds that "the doubleness of the benefit defends the deceit from reproof." But the deceit is perhaps the lesser of the evils, which include both fornication and the subornation of officials. Later, the Duke compounds the deception, by causing the Provost to fail to do his office, and to substitute the head of Ragozine for that of Claudio. The argument of the double benefit is, moreover, a clear instance of permitting the end to justify the means, and making the magnitude of the illicit gain the extenuation of what would otherwise be prohibited means.

The plot promoted by the Duke is moreover implausible even as means to supposed ends. It was unreasonable to expect that Angelo would keep the corrupt bargain with Isabella. The execution of Claudio would become all the more necessary to conceal the misuse of his official position. Even had Angelo been filled with remorse at Isabella's defilement (as he is in the end, in IV.iv.22-36), the remorse might equally well have operated to carry out the execution as to stop it.

The second benefit proposed by the Duke to Isabella, is that, if Mariana's encounter should "acknowledge itself hereafter," Angelo could be compelled to marry her. But this too is wholly improbable: first, because of the unlikelihood that such a single encounter would "acknowledge itself"; and second, because Angelo himself would not know it was Mariana with whom the encounter took place. There would be no witnesses who could credibly inform him of the actual fact, nor compel him to admit what he had done. The only certain result would be Mariana's deflowering, with the chance of another bastard for the ranks.

What makes the bed-trick and its sequel plausible is the double perspective in which it is viewed: first by the audience, and second by the characters in the play. We know that it is the Duke, and not the mysterious Friar, who is behind it all. The Duke, in his disguise, plays the role of Providence, and thereby makes the otherwise implausible become plausible. God may permit evil, because God can bring good out of evil. Men may not do evil that good may come, in part because there is no assurance that the good they intend will actually come to pass. Where the evil is certain and the good uncertain, to have the ends justify the means is unreasonable and impermissible. We accept the bed-trick because we know that the Duke can prevent its miscarriage. The Duke knows that it is Mariana and not Isabella who is keeping the assignation. The testimony of the Friar against Angelo would mean nothing to official Vienna. In the last scene the Friar is in fact about to be carried off to prison for just such testimony, when Lucio pulls off his hood, and the Duke stands revealed. Then all is well and safe. We accept the legitimacy of the illicit means embodied in the bed-trick, because the Duke's presence ensures success. The Duke here presents a practical example of what Machiavelli in *The Prince* meant by the conquest of fortune or chance. The tyrannical reputation the Duke has determined to avoid will be avoided, but his actual means are not for that reason less outside the bounds of morality. Because of his indirect and invisible government, however, they *seem* to be moral. Mariana and Isabella accept the bed-trick, not because of the doubleness of the benefit, but because each passionately desires the good it promises to each, and because they have the assurance of someone they think to be a holy man. Isabella, in her dialectical and dramatic confrontation with Angelo, had sought vainly for theological sanction for her demand for mercy for Claudio. But, as we shall see, she has been out-argued at every turn. She has no passion—and hence no reason—to dispute with a man of God concerning the morality of a plot that offers her a way out of her dilemma.

We may still wonder at the judgment of the Duke in asking the woman he apparently intends to make his wife, to countenance, and even pretend to commit, fornication. In the last scene she is even induced to make a false confession of this. Perhaps this is part of the process of education, whereby an apparent lust for Pauline sanctity, with its depreciation of marriage as preferable to incontinence (but not to continence), is transformed into the pride of a Roman matron. We think however that the Duke's reasoning is derived in part from what the Duke attributes to his own authority as a prince. And this authority he will share eventually with Isabella herself, when he makes her his consort. In short, this will become part of her political, even more than it will become part of her moral, education. The reasoning we have in mind is perhaps better expressed in *Othello,* in the dialogue between Emilia and Desdemona (just before Desdemona's murder), than anywhere else in Shakespeare. In her innocence, Desdemona cannot believe that there are wives who would commit adultery. She asks Emilia, "Wouldst thou do such a deed for all the world?" Emilia replies, "The world's a huge thing. It is a great price for a small vice," which reminds us of the Duke's double benefit. Desdemona still doubts, and Emilia adds that, although she would not commit adultery for any petty benefit, "who would not make her husband a cuckold to make him a monarch?" (IV.iii.64-69, 75-77). This certainly comes close to Isabella's case, who consents to a kind of inverted cuckoldry, by taking on (however temporarily) an evil reputation, to make her future husband's policy succeed. This will make him, if not a king, at least a true prince. Emilia explains her casuistry to Desdemona thus:

> Why, the wrong is but a wrong i' the world, and having the world for your labor, 'tis a wrong in your own world and you might quickly make it right.
> (80-83)

The "world" in question is the political world, governed by the laws coming from the sovereign. In this world, it is the voice of the sovereign which is the voice of God. Apparent vices, done under the authority of a prince, or, as in Emilia's example, to make a man into a prince, are indeed deeds done to make or preserve a world. As such, they cannot be censured by the world they have made. That is why slandering a prince is casting an aspersion upon the foundation of all morality in the state, and is unforgivable. The Duke's (and Isabella's) sanction to Mariana's fornication and his punishment of Lucio at the end are linked by this underlying argument.

The necessity, and even the reasonableness of the bed-trick, so implausible on the surface, must be seen finally in the light of the confrontation that precedes it. The dialogue between Isabella and Angelo has about it many elements of a *Questio Disputata* in the medieval academic tradition. But there is nothing academic about the drama. We never forget that a beautiful and austere young woman is trying desperately to save her brother's life, and then her own chastity. Nor is there lacking a certain prurient interest to sustain the drama, as we are compelled to balance in our minds the prospective execution and the prospective debauchment. Why and how the tragic conflict is resolved into comedy, we may now consider, not in its denouement, but in the issues that actually develop in the clash of the two great protagonists.

Should Claudio have been condemned to death for fornication? We must examine this question seriously, and not merely as an exercise in the willing suspension of disbelief. What we might call "our" point of view is represented within the play, when Lucio exclaims, "Why, what a ruthless thing is this...for the rebellion of a codpiece to take away the life of a man!" And he seems to speak in the spirit equally of Christianity and of liberal democracy, when he asks,

> Would the Duke that is absent have done this? Ere he would
> have hanged a man for getting a hundred bastards, he would
> have paid for the nursing a thousand. He had some feeling of
> the sport, he knew the service, and that instructed him to mercy.
> (II.ii.123-128)

Lucio's point of view seems however to be out of favor with the Duke, and Lucio is treated with a harshness that distinguishes him from the other sinners at the end of the play. He is sentenced to marry the woman whom he has reportedly got with child, after which he is to be whipped and hanged. At the last, however, his other "forfeits" are remitted, and only the sentence of marriage remains. Since marriage is the same sentence imposed by the Duke on Angelo (not to mention Claudio, and, finally, himself), it would not seem to be disproportionately severe. Nonetheless, Lucio protests,

Marrying a punk, my lord, is pressing to death, whipping, and hanging.

To which the Duke retorts,

Slandering a prince deserves it. (V.i.528-530)

We cannot help thinking, however, that the slander that the Duke was putting down, in sentencing Lucio to marriage, was not merely personal to himself. As a ruler, the Duke will no longer countenance, or allow the opinion to spread that he countenances, bastardy, or the getting of bastards, as a gentlemanly sport.

Lucio, however, did not think that he was slandering the Duke when he declared him to be one instructed in mercy. In a Christian society, no praise of a ruler is more potent than that of being merciful. Consider Isabella's testimony.

No ceremony that to great ones 'longs—
Not the king's crown, nor the deputed sword,
The marshal's truncheon, nor the judge's robe—
Become them with one half so good a grace
As mercy does. (II.ii.59-63)

Lucio's explanation of the Duke's mercifulness, although in itself hardly complimentary, is nonetheless consistent with a view of human nature as fallen, that runs throughout the play. For with the exception of the Duke, all the leading characters see themselves as St. Paul sees himself, when he declared himself "captive to the law of sin which dwells in my members" (Romans 7:23). This is even true of Isabella, who, at the gate of the nunnery of St. Clare, complains to Sister Francisca that she wishes "a more strict restraint" than that provided by the rules of that exceptionally strict order. This lust for restraint is the obverse of her Pauline belief in captivity to the law of sin. Certainly none of the other characters seems to have any conception of a "complete bosom." As we shall see shortly, even the most respectable Escalus thinks that only chance and circumstance separate the apparently strictest virtue from mere incontinence. But the Duke means something different by a bosom proof against temptation: he means a character so habituated in right action, that it is incapable of being tempted. He puts us in mind of Aristotle's gentleman, who does not even have a sense of shame, so far removed is he from the possibility of shameful things. And this reminds us of that strangest of all the revelations that accompanies the apocalyptic ending of the play: the discovery (in IV.v) of a circle of the Duke's friends, of whose existence we have had no previous inkling. They are Flavius, Valentius, Rowland, Crassus, and Varrius. Only Varrius appears on stage, although he does not speak. He is sent to the others, "to bid them bring the trumpets to the gate," for the Duke's entrance into the city in his proper person. "Valentius" reminds us of "Valentino," the name borne by Cesare Borgia in the Romagna.

These names—except for Rowland—have an ancient Roman sound, and remind us of ancient virtue. They—and the Duke's "complete bosom"—remind us in particular of magnanimity, or greatness of soul, as celebrated in the fourth book of the *Nicomachean Ethics*. The greatsouled man, according to Aristotle, is one to whom "nothing is great." That is, nothing is great in comparison with himself, and his own virtue. The contemplation, and admiration, of that virtue is so pleasant to him, that he cannot be tempted to do anything inconsistent with it. Of course, to a Christian, nothing is as great as the *megalopsychos* is to himself, except God. Greatness of soul is but another name for that pride which is the opposite of Christian humility. Christian humility is however consistent with that opinion—notably as expressed by Escalus (but also by Isabella)—by which the greatest human virtue is still susceptible to temptation. The Christian, conscious of his own weakness, needs the grace of God to safeguard his virtue; the Aristotelian gentleman anticipates the need for such grace by the satisfaction he takes in the sense of his own impregnable superiority.

Nothing is more indicative of the Duke's classicism—which sets him apart from all the other characters (all, that is, except the silent Romans)—than the manner in which he performs his "priestly" functions. He visits the condemned Claudio in prison, ostensibly to bring him Christian comfort, on the eve of his execution. But in the speech in which he exhorts him to prepare for death, there is not a word, not a hint, of Christian doctrine. There is no suggestion of personal salvation in a Christian sense. He is merely taught how to reason well about the vanity of human desires. He is taught that nothing is either good or bad, except as thinking makes it so. The art of living well is then the art of thinking well, since thought can make one's fate desirable, whatever that fate turns out to be. Claudio is indeed taught "learning to die," and learning to die becomes identical with learning to live. It is Socratic sophistry at its best; the kind, no doubt, that Socrates himself went to school with the sophists to learn, in the *Euthydemus*. "To sue to live," Claudio declares at end of the Duke's speech, "I find I seek to die/ And, seeking death, find life" (III.i.42-44). But this life that he finds, by seeking death, has nothing to do with personal immortality. The reasoning to which the Duke subjects Claudio is moreover eminently materialistic. He tells him, "Thou art not thyself,/ For thou exist'st on many a thousand grains of dust" (III.i.19-21). However, the conclusion is not only Socratic but in the form of one of the most familiar of Socratic paradoxes. At the same time we should notice that the Duke's appeal to a materialist metaphysics is also Biblical: man is formed from dust, and to dust returns. By extracting this Socratic conclusion from a Biblical premise, the Duke gives a demonstration that is all the more impressive of the power of unassisted human reason.

The argument against Claudio's execution is first made by Escalus, in conversation with Angelo.

> Let but your Honor know,
> Whom I believe to be most strait in virtue,
> That in the working of your own affections,
> Had time cohered with place or place with wishing,
> Or that the resolute acting of your blood
> Could have attained the effect of your own purpose,
> Whether you had not sometime in your life
> Erred in this point which now you censure him,
> And pulled the law upon you. (II.i.8-16)

Later, Isabella briefly repeats the substance of this argument to Angelo.

> If he had been as you, and you as he,
> You would have slipped like him, but he, like you,
> Would not have been so stern. (II.ii.64-66)

Because of universal moral weakness, those in authority are no better than those they are called upon to judge. The thesis of Matthew 7, "Judge not, that ye be not judged," becomes then an argument against all political punishment, and hence against all government. Angelo quickly and sensibly points this out.

> You may not so extenuate his offense
> For I have had such faults, but rather tell me
> When I that censure him do so offend,
> Let mine own judgment pattern out my death.
> And nothing come in partial. (II.i.27-31)

The idea of law implies the idea of law enforcement. For the law to go unenforced, because those who enforce it might at some time also be law-violators, is absurd. Here however we are confronted with something that seems on its face to be an absurd law: a law making illicit sexual intercourse a capital offense.

In his interview in the monastery with Friar Thomas, the Duke says that

> We have strict statutes and most biting laws,
> The needful bits and curbs of headstrong steeds,
> Which for this fourteen years we have let slip.... (I.iii.19-21)

This law would seem to be the representative *par excellence* of such "needful bits and curbs." The conception of such a law—which seems absurd to us in its severity—compels us to remember what lies at the root of the idea of law, which requires the domestication of *eros* by *nomos*. As we have noted, Aristotle, in the first book of the *Politics*, characterizes the political community as a collection of families. Except as it is a collection of families, it does not become a collection of citizens. A citizen is not an "individual," an abstract entity imbued with "rights" which inhere in him as a "person." (We may observe parenthetically that "individual" and "person" both abstract from the distinction between male and female.) He is the representative of a family, if not the head of a family. And all members of families have genders. It is this that makes the polity a complex, and not a homogeneous, entity. Although a political community is composed of a number of citizens and families, it cannot be identified by the numbers of those citizens or families: they are distinguished by their qualities. They constitute something more than, and different from, an aggregate. One of the reasons that Aristotle gives for the necessity of the political community is that the power of the family is insufficient for the government of the family. The needs of the family transcend the resources

of the family. Hence the polity or regime comes to sight, in its foundation, as an exercise of collective familial authority. This is why Lincoln at
Gettysburg spoke of "our fathers" bringing forth a new nation. We thus
see a supreme political action characterized as a supreme act of paternal
power. Sexual promiscuity can thus be seen as striking at the very root of
the idea of paternal power—of patriotism—and hence at the ground of
authority. To derive authority from paternity, paternity itself must not be
unlawful.

It is given to Angelo, more than to any other character in *Measure
for Measure*, to express the foregoing view of fornication. Ironically, he
does so at the very moment when his own soul has succumbed. The evil
he does not want is what he does—or at least attempts. In this he appears
almost to impersonate St. Paul, in Romans 7:19.

> Ha! Fie, these filthy vices! It were as good
> To pardon him that hath from nature stolen
> A man already made, as to remit
> Their saucy sweetness that do coin Heaven's image
> In stamps that are forbid. 'Tis all as easy
> Falsely to take away a life true made
> As to put metal in restrained means
> To make a false one. (II.iv.42-49)

Fornication and murder are here equated: the unlawful getting, and the
unlawful taking, of life are looked upon as virtually two aspects of a single
crime. This is achieved by a figure of speech drawn from the idea of
coinage. God's creation of man in his own image makes those who generate children "coiners" of "Heaven's image." And those who do so outside
the law become false coiners. We are reminded that the coining of money
has always been regarded as one of the chief prerogatives of sovereignty.
(In the United States Constitution of 1787, to coin money and regulate
its value, is one of the powers of the United States; and it is a power
specifically prohibited to the individual states. This is one of the principal indications of where sovereignty lay in the more perfect union.) Traditionally, money was stamped with the image of the sovereign. To make
this stamp without authority was more than forgery or theft. It was usurpation, and hence treason, and for this reason was always a capital offense. Fornication, as a kind of false coinage of citizens, becomes more
than a private action. Lucio thinks that the Duke would sooner pay for
the nursing of a thousand bastards, than hang a man for getting a hundred. But no ruler can be indifferent to whether his subjects are or are

not born under the laws by which he rules. It is by no accident or perverse whim that "bastard" is such a term of opprobrium, however unfair
it may seem that the sins of the parents should be visited upon the heads
of the children. Bastards, not being proper members of families, do not
properly inherit. They do not share in those rights of property generated
by the family, the protection of which may be called the first object of
government. The full dimension of bastardy, as an alien and enemy thing,
is revealed to us by Edmund, in *King Lear.* The bastard, like the slave,
has an inherent interest in overthrowing the regime which excludes him
from its rights and privileges. We should mention, however, that in *King
John* Shakespeare reveals another, and more attractive, possibility of bastardy. In this case, however, the hero deliberately renounces legitimacy,
to be known as the king's bastard, which is, to say the least, a very special
kind of bastardy. Isabella, however, shares Angelo's—and the Duke's—
view, when, in a passage already noted, she says that she had rather that
her brother died by the law, than that her son should be unlawfully born.

With the exception of Lucio (and Pompey) no one seriously questions that fornication ought to be an offense, or even that it ought to be a
capital offense. Lucio himself calls it "transgression" and "vice," but thinks
that one cannot "extirp it quite...till eating and drinking be put down"
(III.ii.9-10). Pompey, of course, merely thinks that he is "a poor fellow
that would live." As a supplier of the necessities (as he thinks of them) of
young gentlemen, he does not see why he is more to blame than purvey-
ors of food and drink. He does not see why he should be held responsible
for venery more than the others are for gluttony or drunkenness. In his
failure to comprehend the distinction between the "mean" of virtue and
the "extreme" or "excess" of vice, he is a reflection—in more ways than
one—of his "betters." He knows that his occupation is unlawful, but does
not understand why.

The commission that the Duke gives Angelo in the opening scene is
not nominally one to establish or institute the puritanical and tyrannical
regime that in fact follows. Angelo is given the discretion.

> So to enforce or qualify the laws
> As to your soul seems good. (I.i.66-67)

This means that the soul of the judge, rather than the soul of the laws,
will be revealed by the manner in which the law is enforced. This is how
the Duke will "practice his judgment with the disposition of natures."
The severity of the law is merely hypothetical. It need not be as severe as

Angelo would make it, nor as lax as it has been under the Duke. Escalus has this in mind when he says to Angelo,

> Let us be keen, and rather cut a little,
> Than fall, and bruise to death. (II.i.5-6)

(The figure of speech refers to the manner of execution in ancient Rome, when the condemned man was hurled from the Tarpeian Rock. See *Coriolanus* III.iii.103.) One of the strange features of the play is that the debate over Claudio's fate turns entirely—with the exception of this one suggestion by Escalus—upon whether he should be executed or pardoned. No middle ground is given serious consideration. We divine from the Duke's speeches in his private conversation with Friar Thomas, that he anticipates what will happen. The laws will be enforced in a manner both tyrannical and necessary for their authority. The force or vigor of this tyranny will come from an asceticism which is but suppressed lust. The city will however be cured of the secret tyranny within it at the same time that it will be cured of dissoluteness. The extremes will cure each other, "measure for measure," to re-establish the mean. In so doing, the city will be re-founded.

The foregoing helps to explain why, although in theory mercy and justice may be distinct, in practice they may become indistinguishable. Escalus, although a pleader for Claudio's pardon, can find no good or sufficient argument to support that plea. Yet Isabella, out of love for her brother, pleads for his life.

> Good, good my lord, bethink you,
> Who is it that hath died for this offense?
> There's many have committed it. (II.ii.87-89)

But the reply, given the premises, seems irrefutable.

> The law hath not been dead, though it hath slept.
> Those many had not dared to do that evil
> If the first that did the edict infringe
> Had answered for his deed. (II.ii.90-93)

But Isabella—prompted by Lucio (that man of mercy)—pursues her demand. Pity and mercy now assume a form that stands in opposition to justice. "Yet show some pity," she pleads (II.ii.99). But Angelo will not—yet—be moved from his ground. Pity and justice, he declares, cannot be dissevered. He says that he most shows pity when he shows justice:

> For then I pity those I do not know
> Which a dismissed offense would after gall,
> And do him right that, answering one foul wrong,
> Lives not to act another. (II.ii.101-104)

However, when, a few moments before, Angelo had declared that Claudio was "a forfeit of the law," Isabella had replied with the following speech, perhaps the most memorable of the play:

> Alas, alas!
> Why, all the souls that were were forfeit once,
> And He that might the vantage best have took
> Found out the remedy. How would you be
> If He, which is the top of judgment, should
> But judge you as you are? Oh, think on that,
> And mercy then will breathe within your lips,
> Like man new-made. (II.ii.72-79)

We must not allow the breath-taking beauty of these lines to overcome our own "top of judgment," and permit their reasoning to go unexamined. It is not Claudio's soul which the law is claiming as forfeit. Isabella elsewhere declares that the death of the body is nothing fearful. Rather than give her body up to shame, she says, she would "strip [herself] to death, as to a bed/ That longing have been sick for" (II.iv.102-103). And she will tell Claudio himself that

> The sense of death is most in apprehension,
> And the poor beetle that we tread upon
> In corporal sufferance finds a pang as great
> As when a giant dies. (III.i.78-81)

The death of the body is then but a momentary pang, but the soul lives, or dies, forever. Claudio's execution, so far from forfeiting his soul, may consist better with its eternal welfare than—in Isabella's own words later in the play—"a feverous life" of "six or seven winters" more. By Isabella's theology, the condemned criminal himself is then better off who, in Angelo's words, "answering one foul wrong,/ Lives not to act another."

Isabella's speech is one of the most notable invocations of Pauline theology in the literature of the West. This is, we might say, born-again Christianity with a vengeance, notwithstanding the relentless refusal of the poet actually to name the non-vindictive "top of judgment," nor to describe the actual "remedy" that "He" found out. We cannot therefore pretend not to notice that, within the play, the Duke himself, in disguise, will be the top of judgment, of Angelo, of Claudio, and of Isabella herself. The entire play is an instrument for practicing that discovery of "the disposition of natures" which will enable a more than merely human justice to prevail. Isabella appeals to the principle of divine revelation, presumably to correct and perfect the imperfect human administration of justice. In fact, her appeal is such as would render any administration of justice impossible. Let us, for the moment, take Isabella's exhortation at face value. She is saying, in effect, that every judge, before every judgment, should first examine the purity of his own soul. Since, however, every soul is presumed to be tainted with original sin, every soul is defective. Recognizing this, and recognizing that he himself needs God's pardon, every judge should pardon every criminal! As Angelo had pointed out to Escalus, and as he again points out to Isabella—at the outset of their first interview—this would make the judge's "the very cipher of a function" (II.ii.39). Every judge would pardon every criminal, because there would not be any judge sufficiently pure in soul to exercise judgment.

Isabella's plea to Angelo, to spare her brother's life, because God had spared a guilty world, makes no sense in terms of the logic of political life. Hitherto, Angelo has represented a kind of Aristotelian reasonableness, however extreme the action he finds necessary. Lechery is too general a vice, precisely because no one has believed that the laws against it would be enforced. The time has passed when cutting a little, instead of bruising to death, will serve. The Duke tells this to Friar Thomas in their interview; and Isabella concedes the point when she says that there is one vice which she most wishes to meet the blow of justice. Isabella's argument—apart from its theological reference—is then a plea for favor for Claudio, simply because he is her brother and she loves him. At the outset of the interview with Angelo, she confesses that she is "At war 'twixt will and will not." She wills that the law against fornication be enforced, but she wills that it not be enforced against Claudio! Finally, she is driven to declare that to enforce it is tyrannical. "So," she says to Angelo,

> you must be the first that gives his sentence,
> And he, that suffers. Oh, it is excellent
> To have a giant's strength, but it is tyrannous

To use it like a giant. (II.ii.106-109)

But is not Isabella being unfair to Angelo? Angelo has been given a task of cleaning out Augean stables. Certainly this takes a Herculean, a giant's strength. Yet we know—from no less an authority than the Duke—that the beginning of the reform of the city will necessarily appear tyrannical. Indeed, there will be no external or visible difference between a tyrannical and a non-tyrannical beginning of reform. The first falling of the "blow of justice" will appear to be, *and indeed will be,* arbitrary. It will be arbitrary, because there is no *reason* why that first blow should fall on one rather than another of those "many" that have committed this offense. Yet, if there is to be a rule of law, one where crime and punishment are justly and reasonably and surely proportioned to each other, the blow must fall somewhere upon someone. For cities to be a formed—or founded—arbitrariness must, so to speak, take the lead. Arbitrariness therefore underlies non-arbitrariness.

Isabella says that it is excellent to have a giant's strength, but tyrannous to use it like a giant. But what does it mean to be a giant, and who can have such strength? The answer of course is that the power that transforms man into citizen brings the "giant" city—or political community—into existence. It is the political community which enormously enhances the power of man. If the political community becomes what it is by nature intended to become—a partnership in virtue—then it is indeed good. If it becomes tyrannical—if it is separated from that virtue which it is intended to enhance and perfect—then it becomes something terrible. The tyrannical giant is then the lawless city: for anarchy and tyranny are twins. Aristotle says that the man who first united men into the political community—the first founder of a city—was the greatest of benefactors. (Literally, "the greatest cause of good things": *Politics,* 1253a21.) We cannot help noticing that, according to the Bible, the man who first founded a city was Cain. That both Cain and Romulus slew their brothers is, more or less, the fundamental perception underlying the Machiavellian teaching. And it is, we might say, a rebellion against this Machiavellianism which underlies Isabella's revolt against the necessity that her brother be killed in order that Vienna be reformed.

Having told Angelo that it is excellent to have a giant's strength, but tyrannous to use it like a giant, Isabella pursues the theme of the absurdity of political authority.

Could great men thunder

As Jove himself does, Jove would ne'er be quiet,
For every pelting, petty officer
Would use his Heaven for thunder.
Nothing but thunder! Merciful Heaven,
Thou rather with thy sharp and sulphurous bolt
Split'st the unwedgeable and gnarled oak
Than the soft myrtle. But man, proud man,
Dressed in a little brief authority,
Most ignorant of what he's most assured,
His glassy essence, like an angry ape,
Plays such fantastic tricks before high Heaven
As make the angels weep—who, with our spleens,
Would all themselves laugh mortal. (II.ii.110-123)

Certainly this speech is one of the great exposures of the pretensions of men in authority. One is reminded of Gogol's *Overcoat,* and the mixture of crude despotism (to those beneath them in the hierarchy of authority) and crude obsequiousness (to those above them) exhibited by nineteenth-century Russian bureaucrats. But there is an eternal bureaucracy, transcending boundaries of time or space, which is inherent in the idea of political authority. When Angelo declared to Isabella that

It is the law, not I, condemn your brother,
Were he my kinsman, brother, or my son,
It should be thus with him.... (II.ii.80-82)

he was appealing to that principle which is mankind's chief defense against the false pretensions arising from political authority. That defense is the rule of law, which Angelo—up to this point—is attempting to re-establish.

After Angelo has fallen, after he has become that rebel against the authority he has hitherto represented, he looks upon the law in a different light, as is evident from the speech wherein he writes good angel on the Devil's horn:

When I would pray and think, I think and pray
To several subjects. Heaven hath my empty words,
Whilst my invention, hearing not my tongue,
Anchors on Isabel. Heaven in my mouth,
As if I did but only chew His name,
And in my heart the strong and swelling evil
Of my conception. The state, whereon I studied,

Is like a good thing, being often read,
Grown sere and tedious. Yes, my gravity
Wherein—let no man hear me—I take pride,
Could I with boot change for an idle plume
Which the air beats for vain. O place, O form,
How often dost thou with thy case, thy habit,
Wrench awe from fools, and tie the wiser souls
To thy false seeming! Blood, thou art blood. (II.iv.1-15)

We here see that Angelo—after the fall—accepts Isabella's thesis concerning the absurdity of human political authority. Angelo had studied the state and had taken himself and his duties with utmost seriousness—something now impossible, since his passions now run in a different channel. In the opening scene we heard the Duke commending Escalus as the gravest student of "the nature of our people," and of the "city's institutions, and the terms of common justice." Yet Escalus, who is moreover possessed of the "science" of government, commends Angelo as being worthiest to undergo the "ample grace and honor" of bearing the Duke's authority in his absence. Until Angelo's virtue and honor fall before Isabella's assault, we do not know anything genuinely discreditable about him, whatever the suspicions of others (notably the Duke). It is true that the Duke's suspicions prove to be wise ones. But in his stringent devotion to the execution of the law Angelo is just, and not a hypocrite. When, at the end of the third act, Escalus tells how he had labored to the utmost extremity for Claudio's life, and labored in vain, he concludes wryly that

my brother Justice have I found so severe that he hath forced
me to tell him he is indeed Justice. (III.ii.265)

Remembering Escalus's qualifications, we can see that this is at least as much a tribute as a reproach. The element of compulsion indicated in "he hath forced me" suggests also that Escalus could never have restored the authority of the law, as Angelo is doing. He is indeed doing the Duke's dirty work, like Remirro de Orco. Angelo, moreover, shows his integrity at the very end of the play. He had said at the outset that there must not be any partiality in justice. When Mariana and Isabella plead for his life, he himself declares that he craves death "more willingly than mercy./ 'Tis my deserving, and I do entreat it" (V.i.481-482). He does not whine, but considers himself exactly as he had hitherto considered Claudio. Left alone he would (like Lucio!) have been executed rather than married! In the scene in which the Duke arranges the bed-trick, we learn that Angelo had been betrothed to Mariana and had jilted her when her brother perished with her dowry. This behavior, which is held up to our scorn, was not, however, unjust. The proposed marriage, although respectable and conventional, was not (at least on his part) a love match. When Mariana was unable to perform her part of the contract, it was broken off. Law, according to Aristotle, is reason unaffected by desire. And Angelo—before this great speech of Isabella, is precisely a man of reason unaffected by desire. His non-erotic character evokes our contempt. But that may be because we moderns instinctively prefer love to law, and nature to convention. In any event, Isabella awakens something in him that he had not hitherto suspected was there. Before, he says, when men were "fond" he smiled, and wondered how. Isabella, as we shall see, transforms him from a man of reason and law, into one of passion and nature.

Let us now return to Isabella's speech against authority. In it she strangely conflates Christian and pagan theology. Although—perhaps out of puritanical fastidiousness—she will not speak directly of the Biblical God, or of His Son, she does speak of "Jove" by name. He is the chief of the Olympian Gods, called "Zeus," in Greek. The "Z" becomes "D" when Zeus is declined, and hence the name is cognate with the Latin "Deus." "Jove" is a contraction of "Jupiter," itself the result of the contraction of "Deus Pater." "Jove" is then the Father of gods and men, known above all for his philoprogenitiveness. Isabella says that it is good that men in authority cannot thunder, since if they could they would do so constantly. As a result, Jove would have to thunder constantly, in order to be heard. She means by this that the administration of justice is properly a divine, not a human, function. Jove (or Heaven) is merciful, she says, because it splits "the unwedgeable and gnarled oak" and not "the soft myrtle." By this she means it strikes down the hardened and incorrigible wrongdoers while sparing the innocent and thus is merciful, because infallibly just. This, we note, is an argument remarkably different from the one she had made in behalf of Claudio, since there is no question of Claudio's guilt under the human law by which he is condemned. (An example of an unwedgeable and gnarled oak in the play would be Barnardine, the man who cannot be executed, because he will not be. One wonders why the lightning has never struck him!)

Isabella's attack on the possibility of human justice is absolute and uncompromising. We must, however, examine the reasoning of this attack on reason and law. We are obliged to notice what Isabella has apparently forgotten, that Jove (or Zeus) was famed for nothing more than for his fornications. Indeed, thunder and lightning were supposed to be manifestations of his sexual activity. According to legend, Semele, being prompted by the jealous Hera (in disguise), who revealed to Semele the identity of her lover, demanded to be loved by him *in propria persona*. As a consequence, she was struck by Jove's lightning-bolt and turned into a cinder. However, the embryo was snatched from her womb and carried to term in his father's thigh, eventually to join the ranks of the gods. But Isabella also forgets that the oak was supposed to be sacred to Jove, and not an object of his thunderbolts. She is correct, however, in supposing that lightning does strike oak trees. In Aristophanes' *Clouds*, Socrates subverts the piety of Strepsiades by pointing this out to him. Isabella does then revert to a kind of prephilosophic paganism, in believing that the lightning discriminates among its targets, and as such is the just instrument of divine justice. This she contrasts with human authority which, she says, is most ignorant of that of which it is most assured. We hear in this assertion an echo of Socrates' examination, in Plato's *Apology of Socrates,* of the politicians and the poets. Yet her piety is more akin to that of the politicians and poets than is Socrates'. Still, her antinomianism has something in common with the regime of philosopher-kings in the *Republic.* She, like Socrates, finds no genuine authority in any rule other than the perfect rule. Her notion of perfect rule would appear to be that dispensed by the gods, whereas his would appear to be that of philosophers. The practical result in both cases is to undermine any reasonable—but imperfect—human government.

In denying that man can know what he needs to know in order to be a minister and executor of justice, Isabella caricatures not only Platonism, but the tradition of the Bible. According to that tradition, man is made in the image of God. Alone among the creatures, he is governed not by instinct or natural necessity, but by his own will. It is man's duty to conform his will to that of God, but God has given him understanding for this end. It remains God's will that man's obedience be voluntary. Of course, man will be rewarded and punished according to his deserts by God. But this will be done according to that judgment which is denominated "last." Such a judgment does not obviate the necessity or propriety of human officers and human judges to enforce human law. "Judge not, that ye be not judged" refers to the Last Judgment. It still leaves us the duty, in Lincoln's words, to be firm in the right, as God gives us to see the right. This has reference of course to the execution of the human law. Isabella's doctrine would leave the Last Judgment as the First Judgment. Government would be impossible. Anarchy would ensue.

According to the same biblical tradition, man's being made in the image of God leads properly to the *imitatio Dei,* as a legitimate human endeavor. Again, we turn to the authority of Abraham Lincoln, who often cited the verse, "Be ye perfect, as your Father in Heaven is perfect." This did not mean, Lincoln said, that any human being could be as perfect as God. It meant that in striving towards the divine perfection, human life was improved, and human beings were made better and happier than they otherwise might be. But it is precisely this point of view that Isabella rejects. She compares man imitating God to a monkey imitating man. In aspiring towards God, she implies, he becomes a beast. Man, "dressed in a little brief authority," conjures a grotesque figure moping and mowing before a mirror, admiring his "glassy essence." According to Isabella's metaphysical physiology (now leaving the world of Jove behind her, a world of laughter and fornication), angels, lacking spleens *inter alia,* cannot laugh. They weep, she says, at this human imposture, even as she will weep for Claudio. But the angry ape, seen in his true absurdity, is properly an object of scorn, contempt, and laughter. With this, as we shall see, she will have fatally undermined Angelo's self-respect, along with his belief in his duty to the law. We are reminded, finally, that apes—or monkeys— were, like Jove, notable for their lecherousness.

Isabella's speech is the dialectical turning point of play. It is here that Angelo begins his transformation. That shrewd observer, Lucio, perceives this.

> Oh, to him, to him, wench! He will relent
> He's coming, I perceive't. (II.ii.123-124)

Lucio's words prove bawdier than even he intends them to be. Under his encouragement, Isabella returns to the attack: her next two speeches, although punctuated by Lucio's and the Provost's asides, are dramatically uninterrupted and are therefore essentially continuations of the previous speech. Here is the first:

> We cannot weigh our brothers with ourself.
> Great men may jest with saints, 'tis wit in them,
> But in the less foul profanation. (126-128)

And again:

> That in the captain's but a choleric word
> Which in the soldier is flat blasphemy. (130-131)

At this point, Angelo responds, asking,

> Why do you put these sayings on me? (133)

Until this point, all of Angelo's speeches to Isabella have been simply repetitions of the death sentence, or re-statements of the reasons for the death sentence, followed by the repetition of that sentence. Now he asks a question. He no longer knows his own mind; or, perhaps we should say, he discovers a different mind within himself. Isabella, now sensing the change already sensed by Lucio, drives home her argument.

> Because authority, though it err like others,
> Hath yet a kind of medicine in itself
> That skins the vice o' the top. Go to your bosom,
> Knock there, and ask your heart what it doth know
> That's like my brother's fault. If it confess
> A natural guiltiness such as is his,
> Let it not sound a thought upon your tongue
> Against my brother's life. (134-141)

Angelo then speaks—but only aside, and to himself (and us):

> She speaks, and 'tis
> Such sense that my sense breeds with it. Fare you well. (141-142)

This is indeed a "farewell" to the Angelo who has hitherto occupied the stage. It is not however a farewell to Isabella, but rather the beginning of a "come hither," not for well but for ill. The "sense" that his breeds from hers will be a new birth, but one that will be diabolic rather than angelic. Angelo will in fact concede that he has no further right to execute Claudio. He will say to himself, in the soliloquy which follows,

> Oh, let her brother live.
> Thieves for their robbery have authority
> When judges steal themselves. (175-177)

Lashed by Isabella's antinomianism, Angelo looks within his heart, and does indeed find there—and not only there—"the strong and swelling evil" of his "conception." Now he embraces the principle of the argument that originally Escalus, and then Isabella, had brought against his legal rationalism. Before he had argued that if judge or jury prove corrupt, let them be tried and punished too. From the argument that all the guilty should be punished, he now goes over to the other side, with the conclusion that none should be! Now, from the premise (which was also Escalus's and Isabella's) that thieves have authority from judges he will proceed to the further inference, that judges have authority from thieves. Or, to put it more bluntly, that judges of fornication have authority from fornicators! If he ought not to condemn Claudio, because there is guilt in his heart, then why should he not act the guilt of which he is already convicted? If the corruption of "natural guiltiness" levels mankind, then the distinction between the will and the deed disappears. Earlier, he had replied to Escalus,

> 'Tis one thing to be tempted, Escalus,
> Another thing to fall. (II.i.17-18)

But that distinction itself has fallen before Isabella's onslaught. The result is however different from the one she intended or expected.

Isabella has, unknown to herself, seduced Angelo. The seduction has been begun by convincing him that he has no right to execute Claudio. He now believes that neither he nor Claudio should, or indeed can, be lawfully punished for fornication. However, that is because he no longer believes in the idea of law, or the rule of law. He thinks that it is indeed "excellent to have a giant's strength." But he also thinks that it is excellent to use it like a giant. It may be tyrannous to do so, but it is foolish not to do so! We can recognize in Angelo's new position, the attack by Glaucon, in the second book of the *Republic,* on justice as something conventional but not natural. Glaucon's thesis is not merely that justice is conventional, but that it is the good of the weaker. The stronger—the giants— are entitled by nature to the objects of their desire. It is against nature to share "equally." The logical result of Isabella's antinomianism is that justice—and the rule of law—have no basis in nature or reason. There can be no just punishment, and hence there can be no unjust action. This would have been the conclusion of Isabella's argument, but for one thing: she believes in final rewards and punishments. Isabella is a kind of Augustinian. There may be a city of the revealed God, but to that there corresponds no earthly city to be ruled by "the laws of nature and of nature's God."

Isabella is now perceived as a saint by Angelo who, as we shall see, accepts her theological premises. Before examining Angelo's consciousness of Isabella's sainthood, we must notice, however, that it was antici-

pated by Lucio. When Lucio first greets her at the nunnery gate, he calls
her

> a thing enskied and sainted,
> By your renouncement, an immortal spirit,
> And to be talked with in sincerity,
> As with a saint. (I.iv. 34-37)

But Isabella's saintliness is based upon "renouncement." Her chastity is
that of the vestal, not that of the matron. In her conversation with Sister
Francisca about the rules of the order of St. Clare—which was famous
for its austerity—she complains about their rules, as one

> rather wishing a more strict restraint
> Upon the sisterhood.... (I.iv.4-5)

These rules, as we learn, make virtually all intercourse between the nuns
and men impossible. Isabella, before she is snatched from this vocation,
was a refugee from the discipline of virtue no less than from the city.
Virtue belongs to the city, the good earthly city. But she does not believe
in the possibility of either virtue or the city. For her, as for Augustine, the
former is at best but splendid vice.

Angelo, we repeat, now sees her as a saint. For the first time in his
life, his lust is aroused, and he finds it overpowering. At first, he cannot
understand why. Above all, he cannot understand why her purity should
attract him rather than the earthier attractions of other women.

> Can it be
> That modesty may more betray our sense
> Than woman's lightness? Having waste ground enough,
> Shall we desire to raze the sanctuary,
> And pitch our evils there?
> ....
> What is't I dream on?
> O cunning enemy, that to catch a saint
> With saints dost bait thy hook! Most dangerous
> Is that temptation that doth goad us on
> To sin in loving virtue. Never could the strumpet,
> With all her double vigor, art and nature,
> Once stir my temper, but this virtuous maid
> Subdues me quite. (II.ii.168-172, 179-186)

Angelo speaks of the strumpet's "double vigor." But the strumpet's paint does not add vigor to nature: rather is it a substitute for nature's defect. The aim of the "cosmetic" art is to produce the illusion of nature in place of nature. Angelo had in fact been repelled by the spuriousness of the strumpet's attractions. Unable to share the coarser taste of a Lucio, he did not patronize Mistress Overdone, or Pompey, or Kate Keepdown. In his own way, Angelo had retreated into the law, and the state, whereon he had studied, as Isabella had retreated to (or toward) the nunnery. The art of the strumpet has in fact repelled his more fastidious taste. Believing that strumpets or strumpetry are the proper objects of sexual desire, he has been deluded into believing that he lacked such desire, or that to suppress such desire was an easy thing. This, we might add, was Lucio's opinion of Angelo as well. Both Angelo and Lucio thought that "study and fast" played a larger role in the formation of his character than they actually did.

Isabella's antinomianism has for the time being, at least, destroyed Angelo's moral sense. She has persuaded him that he is naturally guilty, and his passion now turns—naturally—toward forbidden fruit. Angelo wonders at himself. Why is he attracted to Isabella? Why must he "raze the sanctuary" of her virginity and chastity, having, as he says, "waste ground enough" elsewhere? He sees himself the object of a "cunning enemy." Of course, Angelo refers here to the Devil, the same that Macbeth called "the common enemy of man" (III.i.69). Macbeth, we know, sells his "eternal jewel," meaning his immortal soul, to this gentleman, for the crown. He does so because, as he speculates,

> If the assassination
> Could trammel up the consequence, and catch,
> With his surcease, success...
> We'd jump the life to come. (I.vii.2-4, 7)

That is to say, Macbeth considered that if he was assured of success in his enterprise of murdering Duncan and usurping the kingship, he would be willing to say, in effect, "to Hell with Hell." That close student of *Macbeth*, Abraham Lincoln, in his *Temperance Address*, observed that "Pleasure to be enjoyed, or pains to be endured, *after* we shall be dead and gone, are but little regarded...." Lincoln was reflecting here precisely upon the terrors of "the day of judgment." And most students of criminal jurisprudence have concluded that incontinence and incorrigibility in human conduct are best met by punishment that is swift and sure. Great punishments that are far off, and uncertain, are little counted; certainly they are much less counted than punishments that are relatively mild, but thought to be very near and inescapable.

There is however particular irony in Angelo's discovery of a "cunning enemy." The plot, we know, is from the outset arranged by the Duke. Angelo, in the bed-trick, falls into the Duke's trap. The Duke suborns the Provost to postpone Claudio's execution because, as he tells the Provost, now "Claudio...is no greater forfeit to the law than Angelo who hath sentenced him" (IV.ii.166-168). The Duke, referring to "his judgment with the disposition of natures," flatters the Provost, saying,

> my ancient skill beguiles me, but in the boldness of my cunning
> I will lay myself in hazard. (IV.ii.164-166)

The diabolic cunning is the Duke's "ancient skill" in judging human character. The Devil turns out, then, to be the Duke playing God. Angelo has fallen in love with a saint, because his pride in his own virtue has kept him aloof from any lesser attachment. It is nevertheless Isabella's antinomianism which underlies, and indeed drives Angelo to, the paradox of "sin in loving virtue." For surely, if there is a sin in loving virtue, there must also be a sin in not loving it. Had he not loved virtue, he might have loved the strumpet. Love of the strumpet means love of the low, of the meretricious as well as the illicit. But love of virtue, or at least that virtue represented by saintliness, is too high for the law, since it is too high for the flesh, or for nature. Angelo's saintly love of the high should have been consummated on the level of the spirit, transcending the body and transcending the law. Saints, like harlots, are united with their lovers outside the bounds of marriage or the law. But Angelo is a man of the law. It is the state, not the soul, that he has studied. He says that the strumpet, with all her double vigor, art and nature, never stirred him. But he mistakes strumpetry and himself. He is clearly mistaken in thinking that health, youthful beauty, and chastity are less vigorous in their attractions than the unchastity and cosmetic art of the prostitute. Comparing himself to those who were "fond," he smiles and wonders how. That is to say, believing that prostitutes are much more attractive than good girls, he thinks that his own weak appetite for strumpets constitutes an immunity to the temptations of sex. And he has preened himself in this belief. So it is not surprising that, in being exposed to a chaste beauty, he is attacked on his blind side. He has no defense precisely because he no longer believes in the authority of the law, which represents that middle ground between the prostitute and the saint. In a sense, Angelo is taking a proper revenge upon Isabella: she has destroyed his dignity as a judge; he will do the same to her saintliness. She has put him on a level with fornicators; he will treat her as a prostitute. Here too we find a measure for measure.

Should she or shouldn't she? We have concluded that, upon the basis of reason and law, Claudio's execution was certainly justified, paradoxical as that conclusion may seem to our moral taste. It is of course the Duke's judgment as well, as is shown by the fact that, rather than sparing Claudio, he causes him to be "executed," and then resurrects him from the dead.

In the scene in which Angelo demands Isabella's virginity and chastity, in exchange for her brother's pardon, he presents himself, over and over again, as the representative of the law. Of course, he now does this ironically, taunting her with her own thesis, which had denied any moral authority to the law or its representative. "Answer to this," he demands:

> I, now the voice of the recorded law,
> Pronounce a sentence on your brother's life.
> Might there not be a charity in sin
> To save this brother's life?

Isabella replies:

> Please you to do't,
> I'll take it as a peril to my soul,
> It is no sin at all, but charity. (II.iv.61-66)

But if she is confident that her demand is not sinful, she must be confident that it carries no peril to her soul. She risks nothing. But his risk is great: as a judge he will be forsworn, since by his own casuistry—which remains uncontradicted—Claudio's execution is required by justice, pity, and mercy (and therefore by the recorded law). Hence Angelo rejoins:

> Please you to do't at peril of your soul,
> Were equal poise of sin and charity. (67-68)

That is to say, unless Isabella does something that imperils her soul, as much as the violation of Angelo's judicial oath risks his, there is no "equal poise" between his sin and charity on the one hand, and her sin and charity on the other. Isabella however remains obtuse through several exchanges, apparently not catching the drift of Angelo's argument. At last he becomes exasperated.

> Nay, but hear me.
> Your sense pursues not mine. Either you are ignorant,
> Or seem so, craftily, and that's not good. (73-75)

Swiftly, he proceeds to the blunt question. If she could fetch her brother "from the manacles of the all-binding law" by no other means, but to "lay down the treasures of [her] body," what would she do? Here now is the sinful charity he demands of her, in exchange for the sinful charity she has demanded of him. Her answer is that she would do as much for her brother as for herself. She would lay down her life for him, but would not yield up her body "to shame." But, asks Angelo,

> Were not you, then, as cruel as the sentence
> That you have slandered so?

Her reply is:

> Ignomy in ransom and free pardon
> Are of two houses. Lawful mercy
> Is nothing kin to foul redemption. (109-113)

But here she is attempting to stand on ground that no longer exists. She knows that lawful mercy required Claudio's execution, not his pardon. The mercy that she asks cannot then be lawful. To continue to demand mercy, knowing that it is lawless, is to ask for lawless mercy, and hence sinful charity. If then there cannot be charity in sin, neither can there be charity in mercy. She rejects this conclusion, but is trapped in contradiction, as Angelo points out.

> You seemed of late to make the law a tyrant,
> And rather proved the sliding of your brother
> A merriment than a vice. (114-116)

She did not actually say that her brother's sliding was a merriment; but calling the law a tyrant—which she did by calling its execution a giant's tyranny—implied the innocence of the action for which Claudio stood condemned. Here Isabella, who is anything but fair-minded (although she has certainly been single-minded), is compelled to concede Angelo's logic.

> Oh, pardon me, my lord. It oft falls out,
> To have what we would have, we speak not what we mean.
> I something do excuse the thing I hate
> For his advantage that I dearly love. (117-120)

Here Isabella abandons her antinomian argument. She attempts to reclaim the ground upon which she has been defeated. She abandons the quest for Claudio's pardon, as she now asks for her own. She has abandoned the struggle to save his life and now begins the far profounder struggle to save her own chastity. To let her brother die is, as we have already noted, to her "cheaper" and "better." After Angelo has confronted her with the blunt and brutal alternative, she concludes, without hesitation, "more than our brother is our chastity." Her defiance is spirited. But the cause of spirited womanliness, like that of spirited manliness, lies in that conjunction of the two called the family, whence comes patriotism. However, it should be understood—as we have learned from Volumnia in *Coriolanus*—that this phenomenon arises from mothers no less—perhaps more—than from fathers. In the defense of her chastity, Isabella is driven back to law, the honor of her family, and the city. But the connection between honor and family makes chastity the concern of the matron rather than of the vestal.

Angelo had been the appointed guardian of the law. His legal rationalism proves to be dialectically impregnable. But his dry-souled asceticism is an insufficient foundation for his reason. The passion in his soul, which had been hidden even from himself, is not on the side of his argument. And so his defense of the law crumbles before Isabella's passionate attack. Isabella's defense of Claudio, which fails on the ground of reason, triumphs by reason of its passion. In awakening Angelo's lust, she overcomes his attachment to the law. But her victory is also a defeat. She must retreat to the law at the moment Angelo deserts it. Both together have prepared the way for the Duke's refounding of the city. Angelo and Claudio both stand forfeits of the law. But the Duke will rescue them both. Lechery and asceticism will have corrected each other. *Eros* and *nomos* will be harmonized. Isabella, in the defense of her chastity, will have been turned away permanently from the Order of St. Clare. She will now prove the foundation, as well as the instrument, of the Duke's policy.

Notes

1. Shakespearean quotations and citations are from *The Complete Works,* ed. G.B. Harrison (New York: Harcourt, Brace, & World, 1948).
2. Quoted from the translation by Allan Gilbert of Machiavelli, *The Chief Works and Others* (Durham, N.C.: Duke University Press, 1965), vol. I.

PROSPERO'S REPUBLIC:
THE POLITICS OF SHAKESPEARE'S
THE TEMPEST

Paul A. Cantor

"Unless," I said, "the philosophers rule as kings or those now called kings and chiefs genuinely and adequately philosophize,and political power and philosophy coincide in the same place, while the many natures now making their way to either apart from the other are by necessity excluded, there is no rest from ills for the cities, my dear Glaucon, nor I think for human kind, nor will the regime we have described in speech ever come forth from nature, insofar as possible, and see the light of the sun." —Plato, *Republic*[1]

To talk about the politics of Shakespeare's *The Tempest* may seem like a boorish intrusion upon the visionary and dreamlike mood of the play. And yet just such an intrusion is dramatized within the play, if we consider the way in which Prospero's masque is interrupted in Act IV. Prospero is absorbed in the beautiful visions he has created, when he suddenly remembers the "foul conspiracy" that has been organized against him.[2] Cutting his entertainment short, he is forced to turn to the very practical concern of dealing with the rebels against his rule. In short, *The Tempest* contains a play-within-a-play, and dramatizes how politics intrudes upon that seemingly self-contained play world. The way in which Caliban and his confederates disrupt the world of Prospero's imagination is a good reminder that *The Tempest* takes up the story of a man whose original failure to be concerned about politics led to a disaster from which it took nothing less than a miracle to rescue him. Perhaps, then, *The Tempest* is not as remote from down-to-earth political concerns as its light and airy poetic texture might at first lead us to suppose.

Paying attention to the political aspects of *The Tempest* can help us to define the place of the play in Shakespeare's career as a dramatist. *The Tempest* is filled with verbal echoes and motifs from the whole range of Shakespeare's works, with the emphasis on his tragedies. It seems as if Shakespeare is taking a retrospective glance at his own career, perhaps to sum it up, perhaps to place his earlier works in some kind of final—or at least larger—perspective. Viewed in the abstract, the dramatic material out of which *The Tempest* is built is not far removed from the familiar ground of Shakespearean tragedy. We have the story of a man who wants to murder his brother to gain his throne, a situation reminiscent of *Hamlet*. We have the story of a father thrust from power who escapes to a kind of pastoral retreat with his loving daughter, a situation which calls to mind what King Lear comes to long for at the end of his story. We have the story of a handsome young man who falls in love with the daughter of a man his father hates, suggesting the situation in *Romeo and Juliet*. Somehow *The Tempest* works to perform a sea-change upon this tragic material, transmuting it into "something rich and strange," and ultimately comic. And yet despite this magical transformation, the play does not lose touch with the fundamental problems dramatized in the tragedies; indeed, through a process of abstraction or distillation, it seems to reveal their pattern with a new clarity.

The recurrent political tragedy portrayed in Shakespeare's plays (including the histories) is that somehow the evil characters push their way to the top of the political order, while the morally good and humane characters either fail to achieve rule or, if they do, cannot maintain it properly. This pattern is only a rough description of what happens in the histories and tragedies, where the moral issues often become extremely complex and the line between good and evil becomes difficult to draw sharply, but it does describe quite accurately the situation in *The Tempest*, which seems to pose this political dilemma in the starkest possible terms. On the one hand, we find the corrupt court party, who have attained power through morally questionable means, and who presumably rule with their own interest foremost in mind. On the other hand, we find Prospero, a wise and virtuous man who, through neglect of his public responsibilities, fell from power. This division of the cast of characters suggests a more basic disjunction of wisdom and power in the world: those who have power are for a variety of reasons cut off from the wisdom they need to rule,[3] while those who are wise find their wisdom undermines their ability to act with the force and decisiveness political life requires.[4]

In the situation of the storm-tossed ship, threatened with destruction, the opening scene of *The Tempest* provides a symbolic statement of this disjunction of wisdom and power. At least since Plato's *Republic*, the ship has served as a metaphor for the political community[5] and the vessel in *The Tempest*, with its clearly divided groups of courtiers and mariners, seems to symbolize the ordering of society into nobles and commons. The question which sets the keynote of this opening scene is: "Where's the master?" (I.i.9-10). Who does have authority in the face of a true crisis, and, more importantly, who *should* have authority? The courtiers, the professional politicians, try to take command, asserting the power that is theirs by convention. But the boatswain questions their authority according to the standard of nature: "What cares these roarers for the name of king?" (I.i.16-17). The power the community confers upon its rulers loses its force in the face of a hostile nature, to which titles are merely names, with no substance behind them. As King Lear learned when the thunder would not peace at his bidding (IV.vi.102-103), nature does not always support human convention by obeying the commands of kings. Thus the first scene of *The Tempest* subtly opens up the question of whether the court party, rulers by convention, are in fact rulers by nature.

The fact that there is more to ruling than having the authority in name is revealed clearly by the situation of the ship on the brink of destruction. Those who know best how to save it must be given free rein. In this crisis, every man's basic self-interest, his will to survive, dictates that he surrender his pretensions to rule if he does not have the wisdom needed to avoid disaster. The courtiers can only "mar" the "labor" or "assist the storm" (I.i.13-14), and, however willing the mariners might be under ordinary circumstances to defer to their political superiors, they are not prepared to throw away their lives in blind obedience to authority. That is why the tempest dissolves the structure of the political community, the order of rank and chain of command. The prospect of imminent death brings out man's fundamental egoism, his interest in his self-preservation. When Gonzalo tells the boatswain: "remember whom thou hast aboard," the mariner pointedly replies: "None that I more love than myself" (I.i.19-20). Under the threat of death, men act according to necessity, and thus conventional distinctions of rank, having become a luxury, are stripped away. The storm of the opening scene, like the storm in *King Lear*, is a trial of men. It shows the so-called rulers to be weak, confused, cowardly, and ineffectual, while the mariners, their inferiors by convention, are as much in control of the situation as men could be.[6]

The opening scene of *The Tempest* thus confirms and in a sense sums up the impression of political life we get from Shakespeare's histories and tragedies: those who have the knowledge to rule are not always those who have the authority to rule. The scene subtly introduces what one might call the natural standard of rule. In these extreme circumstances we see that only wisdom ultimately confers the right to rule. The opening scene thereby prepares us for what the play will examine in the case of Prospero, the problem of the wise man and political power, or, as Plato would express it, the problem of the philosopher-king. Having previously looked at this problem from the angle of how those in power might be led to wisdom, Shakespeare considers in *The Tempest* how a wise man might be led to power. To put the point somewhat schematically to highlight the relation of *The Tempest* to the tragedies: if Lear, the most kingly of men, must be thrust out of power to be led to his confrontation with the noble philosopher on the heath (III.iv), then Prospero, the man with a philosophical nature to begin with, the man whose library was at first "dukedom large enough" (I.ii.110), must be taught what Lear refers to as "noble anger" (II.iv.276) so that he can develop something of the commanding nature of a ruler.

In order to understand fully the Prospero of *The Tempest*, we must look back at the original Prospero of Milan. In his account of his past to his daughter, Prospero confesses that he was truant to his public responsibilities as Duke of Milan for the sake of his "secret studies" (I.ii.77). At first this does sound like the story of the wise man, more concerned with the pursuit of knowledge than of power. Yet on second thought, the original Prospero was in one decisive respect not wise, or at least his original wisdom was not complete. We do not know exactly what his great knowledge consisted of, though presumably it was some form of "natural philosophy," related to his practice of magic. But one thing we can say with certainty: the Prospero of the past did not know men. By his own admission, he had grown a "stranger" to his "state" (I.ii.76), and was even unaware of the traitorous nature of someone as close to him as his brother. The kind of knowledge of human nature Prospero lacked was exactly what allowed his brother to supplant him:

> Thy false uncle—
> ....
> Being once perfected how to grant suits,
> How to deny them, who t'advance, and who
> To trash for overtopping, new created
> The creatures that were mine, I say, or chang'd 'em,
> Or else new form'd them. (I.ii.77-83)

Antonio reveals his mastery of the political art in knowing the right man for the right job, which enables him to shape men in accord with his plans for rule. Antonio is the last in a long line of Shakespearean villains, like Richard III, Iago, and Edmund, who frighten us by the insights into human nature they display in the course of their villainy. Though dangerous in the hands of a villain, this knowledge is surely a part of human wisdom, perhaps the fundamental part. The way Prospero leaves the study of human nature to his brother suggests a basic defect in his original form of wisdom. Like the young Socrates, the "pre-Socratic" Socrates,[7] the Milanese Prospero seems to have sought knowledge of the heavenly things at the expense of the human things. *The Tempest* shows us the redirection of his enquiries. Far from interfering with his quest for wisdom, his involvement in ruling proves to be the agent of his education, his gaining knowledge of the nature of the human soul, or of human souls.

Beyond learning how to rule, Prospero even more fundamentally learns the need to rule. The experience of being deposed in Milan taught him that men beneath him in intelligence could nevertheless force him out of power and even threaten his life. His brother's treachery shattered Prospero's illusion of his philosophical self-sufficiency. The experience may well have been powerful enough to change his nature, or at least to awaken something in Prospero that had long lain dormant. After all, the Prospero we see in the course of the play does not strike us as the sort of man who would let his dukedom slip through his fingers. He is too alert to what is going on around him and too conscious of his own dignity, ready to take affront at any questioning of his authority, whether it comes from Caliban, Ariel, Miranda, or a newly-arrived Ferdinand. The Prospero of the play is an irascible man, although sometimes we get the impression that the irascibility is forced, an appearance he feels he must maintain (see, for example, I.ii.450-452). But that only confirms the point: Prospero has developed something of Lear's noble anger, or at least he has learned that a ruler must display noble anger in public. As Lear's case shows, the capacity for indignation in public is essential to the moral force of a ruler.

The origin of Prospero's noble anger is most probably the original wound to his dignity caused by his brother's treachery. We seem to have a glimpse of this original anger during the one moment in *The Tempest* when Prospero relaxes his control over the events of the play. Absorbed in the masque he has created, Prospero momentarily forgets the conspiracy formed against him, re-enacting his original mistake in Milan of

being too "transported and rapt" in his own thoughts (I.ii.76-77) to notice what is going on in the world around him. Perhaps the comic conspiracy of Caliban recalls to Prospero the far more serious conspiracy
Antonio and Alonso formed against him. In any case, Prospero's unusually angry reaction may be a clue to how he felt about being deposed
back in Milan. Ferdinand and Miranda are struck by his reaction:

> Fer.   This is strange. Your father's in some passion
>   That works him strongly.
> Mir.   Never till this day
>   Saw I him touch'd with anger, so distemper'd. (IV.i.143-145)

What seems to be Prospero's overreaction to the essentially trivial machi-
nations of Caliban and company is actually the best measure of what he
has learned from his political experience: if he is to maintain his power
this time, he must be capable of feeling and expressing anger, even at
men who are normally beneath his contempt.

Our first clue that the Prospero of *The Tempest* is not the same as
the Prospero who let himself be turned out of Milan is the way he handles
Caliban and Ariel in the second scene. Almost from the beginning it
becomes evident that Prospero has learned how to be tough when he has
to. More specifically, Caliban and Ariel, due to their peculiar natures,
offer Prospero a singularly enlightening lesson in government, providing
an opportunity to observe in an ideal and controlled environment the
forces that make it difficult to rule real men in the real world. In some
sense, Caliban and Ariel are abstractions from human nature, developing one side of man to the exclusion of all others. To put it another way,
they are pure forms of forces that are ordinarily mixed in all men, which
is precisely why it is so difficult to rule them. Caliban, for example, is
characterized in terms of his desires, his appetites and lusts. He is only
concerned about his bodily needs, and satisfying his primitive hungers.[8]
As we soon learn, he would have raped Miranda if given the chance
(I.ii.347-348). Thus in ruling Caliban, Prospero must concentrate wholly
on keeping his desires in check, and this in turn requires making it physi-
cally more painful for Caliban to yield to his desires than to suppress
them. The basis of Prospero's rule over Caliban is the concrete threat of
bodily punishments (I.ii.369-371, II.ii.4-14). What makes Caliban different from a full human being is that he seems to lack any pride or sense of
shame about his desires, laughing off the charge of rape with animal
innocence:

O ho, O ho, would't had been done!
Thou didst prevent me; I had peopled else
The isle with Calibans. (I.ii.349-351)

Even when dealing with greedy or lustful men, normally one can appeal
to their pride, their sense of dignity as human beings, in trying to get
them to restrain their desires. Coriolanus, for example, finds in dealing
with the Roman plebeians that even with their well-developed appetites
for plunder he can shame them into acting like true soldiers by appealing
to their sense of honor on the battlefield.[9] But Prospero cannot take this
approach with Caliban; he cannot reproach him with the charge: "a human being does not act that way," because there is some doubt as to
whether Caliban is in fact a human being, and certainly the way people
treat him, appealing to his sense of dignity would be ridiculous. In Caliban,
Prospero sees how one would have to rule a being characterized solely by
his pure, physical desires. In that sense, the case of Caliban allows Prospero
to isolate one of the forces that makes human beings recalcitrant to the
rule of reason, namely their desires.

The character of Ariel is more difficult to analyze, and one naturally
hesitates to try to capture such an elusive creature in the net of an abstraction. Nevertheless it does seem that Ariel presents Prospero with
problems of rule which are directly opposite to those involved in ruling
Caliban. Perhaps the best way to understand Ariel is in negative terms:
by contrast with Caliban, he has no physical desires. One always thinks of
him as an airy spirit, raised above the limitations and urges of the body.
With all his thoughts of the future, he never thinks of asking Prospero for
a little Ariella to keep him company in Bermuda. We tend in fact to think
of him as sexless, and the role has been played by both male and female
actors. Curiously, Ariel's lack of desire presents a problem to anyone wishing to rule over him, simply because there are no material rewards that
will entice him into service. The one thing that evidently concerns Ariel
is his freedom. All he ever asks his master for is to be set free, as if his
only value were independence. Free of the limits of the body, perhaps he
wishes to be free of all limits. This is what makes Ariel a nobler creature
than Caliban, but it also is what makes him in his own way a difficult
subject to rule. Caliban is a slave to his desires, but at least his slavish
nature makes him susceptible to being ruled by others. Indeed the problem with Caliban is that he is too eager to serve a master, any master who
comes along, especially one like Stephano, who promises to help Caliban
indulge his desires:

> That's a brave god, and bears celestial liquor.
> I will kneel to him.   (II.ii.117-118)

For Caliban, freedom is merely the chance to serve a new master (II.ii.185-187). But Ariel has a nobler notion of freedom, and far from being enslaved to the power of desire, he is wholly free of it. Thus he presents the political problem of rule in its purest form: how do you get someone to obey your orders whose only real wish is to be independent of all orders?

Independence of spirit of course presents difficulties in ruling any man, but again the problem with Ariel is the purity of his nature, the fact that he embodies the will to be free and nothing else. Because of his lack of material desires, there is simply no way of bribing him. In ordinary circumstances, one can induce men to compromise the demands of their spirit of independence by appealing to their material interests. To refer to *Coriolanus* again, the Roman patricians are certainly a proud and independent lot, and yet they are willing to be flexible about their principles in their dealings with the plebeians if they feel their material well-being is at stake.[10] The exception to this rule is of course Coriolanus himself, who shows the problem in dealing with a man who puts his spirit of independence above all his material interests (though even Coriolanus is eventually softened by the power of love). In Ariel Prospero encounters in pure form this spiritedness that makes men chafe under the yoke of any form of rule. Since Ariel asks only to be released from servitude, the only way Prospero can rule him is to hold out the promise of that release, in the meantime appealing to Ariel's sense of loyalty by continually reminding him that it was Prospero who released him from the bondage in which Sycorax placed him (I.ii.261-263). The only threat Prospero can hold over Ariel is the threat of an even greater restriction of his freedom than he feels he is suffering under Prospero's command, namely a return to imprisonment in a tree:

> If thou murmur'st, I will rend an oak
> And peg thee in his knotty entrails till
> Thou hast howl'd away twelve winters.   (I.ii.294-296)

Prospero can get as tough with Ariel as he does with Caliban, only, in accord with Ariel's different nature, his threats take a different form. The threat of physical pain would not work with the virtually bodiless Ariel, but the threat of being permanently rooted in the base earth brings him back in line. On the whole, Prospero is far more cordial in his relations with Ariel than he is with Caliban, and it seems characteristic of *The Tempest* that the force Ariel is aligned with, spiritedness, is shown in a better light than the force Caliban is aligned with, desire. Perhaps this is so because spiritedness is portrayed as freer of the body and thus more closely allied to the force Prospero himself represents, namely reason. In the end, Prospero is dependent on the fact that the same spiritedness that makes Ariel want to be independent also makes him loyal to Prospero's cause. The one reward Prospero can offer Ariel is praise, and, in marked contrast to the way he treats Caliban, Prospero is liberal in complimenting his "tricksy spirit" (see I.i.206, 215, 237-238, IV.i.35-36, 184-185, V.i.225-226, 240-241). Fortunately, Ariel believes he has a "noble master" (I.ii.299), and because he wants to participate in the nobility of his master's cause, he is willing to do Prospero's bidding on the condition that he will someday be entirely free. In many respects, Prospero shows greater political wisdom in dealing with Ariel than with Caliban. He must have learned something about politics to show such a sympathetic understanding of the special needs of this being who at first sight seems to have no needs.

After seeing how Prospero handles Caliban and Ariel, we have some reason to be confident about the abilities as a ruler he has acquired on his island. If Prospero can control Caliban and Ariel, he should be able to rule ordinary human beings, because each in his own way presents an extreme case of what makes it difficult to keep men in line. Nevertheless, one should not underestimate the problems Prospero faces in trying to restore himself to power in Milan. *The Tempest* might at first glance appear undramatic, because everything of importance seems to have happened before the play begins and Prospero's restoration seems a foregone conclusion. In fact, Prospero has a great deal to accomplish in the course of the play. The way to appreciate how much he has to do is to ask oneself what would have happened if Prospero had simply hailed the ship ashore and announced: "I'm Prospero, the former Duke of Milan, the one you tried to murder. Would there be any objections if I returned to power?" There are several characters who have reason to hate and fear Prospero and others who may never even have heard of him, and certainly do not recognize his authority. Hence Prospero has to prepare his return to power very carefully. By good fortune, everyone he needs to deal with has been delivered into his hands, and, as we have seen, the storm has destroyed the structure of the society that expelled Prospero by undermining the authority of its rulers. Prospero thus has the opportunity to reconstitute the society as he sees fit, to refound its regime. He disperses its elements in order to work on each party separately in a fashion appropriate to its nature. The greed and ambition of these more or less representative human beings must be moderated so that the common good may prevail under Prospero's wise direction. The key to this process of moderation turns out to be the lessons Prospero learned from observing the unmixed natures of Caliban and Ariel, at least if we are to judge by the fact that in each case Prospero uses one side of human nature to moderate or balance another. This process can be observed in each of the three subplots which Prospero, with his dramatist's instincts, sets in motion: the story of Ferdinand and Miranda, the story of Stephano and Trinculo, and the story of the court party.

Ferdinand presents a potential challenge to Prospero's authority by the mere fact that he is a spirited young man, proud of his high lineage and unwilling to defer to the wisdom of his elders. We can imagine what would have happened if Prospero had introduced himself to Ferdinand with the words: "Your father helped to expel me from Milan." As it is, Ferdinand draws his sword on Prospero at the first opportunity and at the slightest provocation. If he hopes to return to power, Prospero must somehow make an ally out of Ferdinand and also moderate his spiritedness. Prospero accomplishes both purposes with one plan, taming Ferdinand with the one force guaranteed to overcome his youthful pride, romantic love. When we first see Ferdinand, he is quite conscious of his political position. He has in fact jumped ahead to imagine himself already king: "I am the best of them that speak this speech," "Myself am Naples," and, as he politely tells Miranda, "I'll make you/ The Queen of Naples" (I.ii.430, 435, 449-450). Prospero further ignites Ferdinand's spiritedness by challenging his right to call himself king and threatening him, like Ariel, with bondage (I.ii.462). The young prince replies with the noble anger we would expect from him, and tries to resist Prospero's power. But Ferdinand becomes reconciled to Prospero's authority for the sake of Miranda. His love turns out to be stronger than his pride:

> this man's threats
> To whom I am subdu'd, are but light to me,
> Might I but through my prison once a day
> Behold this maid. All corners else o' th' earth
> Let liberty make use of; space enough
> Have I in such a prison. (I.ii.489-494)

Like Ariel, Ferdinand prizes the ability to range freely over the world, but there evidently is something for the sake of which he will accept imprisonment. Prospero is able to play upon Ferdinand's desire for Miranda to neutralize his otherwise rebellious spiritedness.

Later in the play Ferdinand even accepts the role of a mere drudge to further his love-suit. What seems base from the viewpoint of a political man, a man of honor, seems noble to him now that he has become a lover:

> some kinds of baseness
> Are nobly undergone; and most poor matters
> Point to rich ends. This my mean task
> Would be as heavy to me as odious, but
> The mistress which I serve quickens what's dead,
> And makes labors pleasures. (III.i.2-7)

Ferdinand's revaluation of nobility might remind us of a similar moment in *Antony and Cleopatra*:

> Let Rome in Tiber melt, and the wide arch
> Of the rang'd empire fall! Here is my space,
> Kingdoms are clay; our dungy earth alike
> Feeds beast as man; the nobleness of life
> Is to do thus *(embracing)*. (I.i.33-37)

Faced with a conflict between his honor as ordinarily understood and his desires, Ferdinand, like Antony, reformulates his notion of nobility so that it becomes a matter of nobility in love.[11] Ferdinand's situation might become tragic like Antony's, if Ferdinand and Prospero remained enemies. As events turn out, however, Ferdinand's match with Miranda, far from being a Romeo and Juliet affair of star-crossed lovers, has all the trappings of a dynastic marriage. Yet it is a sign of Prospero's newly acquired insight into human nature that he conceals from the young lovers as long as possible the knowledge that he has designed their match. If they realized they were intended for each other, they might rebel against the intrusion of political motives into their love. Prospero lets them play at being Romeo and Juliet, or Antony and Cleopatra, by appearing to oppose their match, and thus adding spice to their passion. Only later do they find out that their love will reconcile Naples and Milan once Prospero is restored to the throne. Having begun as a potentially dangerous enemy for Prospero, Ferdinand, by the end of the play, is about to become his son-in-law and the chief reason for reconciling the King of Naples to Prospero's restoration.

Turning now to the subplot of Stephano and Trinculo, we see that, with the old order of authority dissolved, the way is open to all to grab for political power, even to the basest and most stupid. Now that the court party has proven inadequate in a moment of crisis, nothing remains to hold back the pure fools: they might as well try their hand at public life too. Even though Stephano and Trinculo do not pose a genuine threat to Prospero, he must do something about the ambition their momentary freedom from convention has awakened in them. Evidently Prospero decides to allow their ambition free rein for a while to show them the consequences of attempting to rule themselves. Stephano's story in particular illustrates the vanity of political power when pursued merely for the sake of personal glory and private ends. Stephano's political ambitions are awakened when Caliban mistakes him for a god. To the extent that Stephano's spirit is puffed up to heroic proportions by the worship of a lesser being, he re-enacts on a comic plane the tragedy of Julius Caesar. Shakespeare's Caesar is, as Cassius points out, a man "become a god" (I.ii.116) in the eyes of the Roman people.[12] Their total submission to the greatest of their rulers tempts him to forget his limitations as a man. All his fatal errors stem from his attempt to live up to the divine image the Romans have of him, an image he himself largely created. Having to be Caesar always, and as such to show no fear, he must go to the Capitol on the ides of March, despite the signs of danger (II.ii.41-48). He even dies identifying himself with the gods: "Hence! wilt thou lift up Olympus?" (III.i.74).

Stephano's situation parodies Julius Caesar's, as he is forced to live up to the inflated image Caliban has of him:

> *Cal.*   Hast thou not dropp'd from heaven?
> *Ste.*   Out o' th' moon, I do assure thee. I was the Man i' the Moon, when time was. (II.ii.137-139)

Having accepted this divine office, the role of a cosmic god, Stephano is soon proclaiming majestically: "we will inherit here" (II.ii.175). Even Trinculo is concerned about the absence of wisdom in this new regime:

> ...the folly of this island! They say there's but five upon the isle: we are three of them; if th' other two be brain'd like us, the state totters. (III.ii.4-7)

But having set up a provisional government, Stephano rises to the responsibilities of his new position. He sees himself as the defender of his loyal subject, Caliban, and will make sure that justice is done to him:

> Trinculo, keep a good tongue in your head. If you prove a mu-
> tineer—the next tree! The poor monster's my subject, and he
> shall not suffer indignity. (III.ii.35-37)

Stephano's heart seems to be in the right place, even if there is some
question as to the precise location of his brains. The dubious side to his
ambition begins to surface, however, when Caliban tempts Stephano to
displace Prospero. Entering upon the critical phase of his rise to power,
Stephano even begins to sound like Julius Caesar. His resolute statement: "He that dies pays all debts" (III.ii.131) echoes Caesar's famous
lines:

> Cowards die many times before their deaths,
> The valiant never taste of death but once. (II.ii.32-33)

Such verbal echoes do not show that Shakespeare was blind to the differences between a Stephano and a Julius Caesar. But from the perspective
of the highest standpoint, they are both prey to the same delusion, letting others flatter them into thinking that they are something greater
than they really are. Thus although Caesar, the great-souled man, may be
better able than Stephano to live up to a divine image, he is no less mistaken in pursuing a form of greatness that leaves him dependent on the
opinion of the many. In other words, once Shakespeare brings the truly
wise man onto the stage in the form of Prospero, we must take a fresh
look at the way we normally conceive the difference between the noble
and the base. What from the conventional perspective seems like a great
difference may pale into insignificance from the philosophical perspective of a Prospero. Alternatively phrased, in some ways what *The Tempest* accomplishes is to shift our attention from the difference between
the heroic and the unheroic in action to the difference between the wise
and the foolish in knowledge.

The conspiracy of fools in *The Tempest* must be brought to an appropriately comic resolution, but in the process they must be shown as
concretely as possible the vanity of their ambitions. Ariel makes the fools
run the gauntlet, leading them through "tooth'd briers, sharp furzes, prick-
ing goss, and thorns" (IV.i.180). Finally, by distracting them from their
rebellion with some fancy clothing, Prospero shows that they have been
merely reaching for the external trappings of kingship all along. Their
hopes of glory dashed, they end up losing what they began with, unable
to satisfy either their ambition or their original desires:

| Trin. | Ay, but to lose our bottles in the pool— |
| Ste. | There is not only disgrace and dishonor in that, monster, but an infinite loss. (IV.i.208-210) |

When we last see the fools, they seem to have learned a lesson from this brief flirtation with public life: they are not born to rule. We have seen that in dissolving the conventional hierarchy of society, the tempest let loose the basic egoism in man. This fact is most clearly evident in the story of Stephano and Trinculo. Freed from any authority over them, their desires and aspirations become unlimited, and they reach for all they can grab. But once they are brought face-to-face with their own stupidity, they are shamed into submitting once again to the rule of others. Stephano's drunken declaration is thus more cogent than it seems at first: "Every man shift for all the rest, and let no man take care of himself" (V.i.256-257). This statement is the effective counterweight in the play to the boatswain's original line: "None that I more love than myself." Having let loose the egoism in man, Prospero, if he hopes to restore and reorder society, must see to it that this egoism is once again submerged.[13] Stephano's drunken claim may sound crazy, but in a sense "let no man take care of himself" is the premise upon which all society rests. Men must give up their simple-minded attachment to their private interests for the sake of the common good. By whirling the fools around and confusing them, Prospero breaks them of their brief habit of thinking for themselves. Embarrassed by their own display of stupidity, they will drop their pretensions to rule and be disposed to obey Prospero's authority.[14]

With his display of trumpery, Prospero tames the ambitions of the comic conspirators by showing them the illusory character of their goals. A similar lesson is brought home to the court party, suggesting that, despite their higher social rank, when it comes to the baseness of their goals, they are on the same level as Stephano and Trinculo. Prospero provides Alonso, Antonio, and Sebastian with a vision that reduces their ambitions to its essentials: they have been ogling a banquet that disappears even as they reach for it. The speech Ariel delivers as a harpy reminds them that robbing Prospero of his dukedom was no better or more profitable than grabbing for the illusory banquet. Being more steeped in evil deeds, the court party requires stronger measures than Stephano and Trinculo, and Prospero does everything he can to awaken their guilty consciences. He allows Alonso, for example, to think that he has lost his son as punishment for deposing Prospero. With such men, the force of shame is evidently not enough to check their greed and ambition. They must feel that the powers of the universe are arrayed against them, that destiny will punish them for their crimes.

In the final scene, Prospero arranges matters so that he appears to be "some heavenly power" to the court party (V.i.105). As the man who leads them out of the maze in which they have been wandering, as the man who restores Ferdinand to his father, as the apparent possessor of magic powers, his right to return to Milan stands unquestioned. Even Antonio is for the moment struck dumb, although we may have our doubts about how long it will be before he starts plotting again once he gets back to Italy. Prospero handles the end like a master playwright, suddenly weaving together all the plotlines to bring about the denouement he desires. The key to his success is the speed with which the various characters who have been kept isolated from each other are thrown together again. Prospero does not allow them time to compare notes and try to comprehend rationally what has happened. Since each little group has thought all the others were dead, their simple reunion strikes all of them with the force of a resurrection, thus lending a supernatural aura to Prospero's power (perhaps the final clue to his new-found success as a ruler). Anyone who thinks that Prospero has no tasks to accomplish in the course of *The Tempest* should compare the impact he has on all the characters at the end with the impression he would have made if he had revealed himself to them at the beginning.

The Tempest seems to have taken us a long way from the world of Shakespeare's tragedies. By the end of the play, Prospero seems to have been successful in joining wisdom and power. Are we to say, then, that Shakespeare changed his view of the problem of wisdom and power between the writing of the tragedies and conceiving *The Tempest*? Having at first seen wisdom and power tragically disjoined in political life, did he come to see them in harmony as he grew older and mellowed? Shakespeare's last plays are often seen as reflecting a change in mood, a sort of autumnal phase of an old master. Much evidence can be found for some kind of ripening in Shakespeare's later works, but if this process involved his losing his sense of tragedy one might be tempted to see this phase as a decline rather than a growth. Perhaps we must take one last look at *The Tempest* to see how the story of Prospero is to be interpreted in relation to Shakespeare's tragedies. The central question we must consider is: what enables Prospero to reconcile wisdom and power? The answer must be: remarkable good fortune; one might even say, unbelievable good fortune. No one could have planned on being guided to Prospero's island, and no one could have planned on finding just the two beings there whom Prospero needed to develop his capacity for rule. We cannot, then, take Prospero's case as any kind of norm for real life. Moreover, the fact that Prospero must rely on magic power and the aid of fabulous beings to accomplish his purposes lends an aura of unreality to the wise man's achievement of rule. The characters in *The Tempest* feel that they have been passing through a dream world (see, for example, V.i.229-230, 239), and Prospero calls attention to the stage illusion (IV.i.148-156).

To bring up the unreality of the world of *The Tempest* is by no means a way of criticizing the play, but simply an important consideration in the question of how it is to be read in conjunction with Shakespeare's tragedies. The tragedies, especially *King Lear*, broach the problem of wisdom and power directly, by showing the two in open conflict. *The Tempest* reveals the problem only indirectly. It shows the ideal case in which power and wisdom are reconciled, but the case is only an ideal, a dream. The reconciliation depends on so many chance occurrences, on so many improbable events, that it is hardly to be expected in this world (though, it should be noted, there is nothing in principle impossible about a man like Prospero coming to power). Thus the portrait of Prospero only serves to sharpen our sense of the potential for tragedy in political life. Shakespeare for once brings the ideal ruler onto the stage, but he is an ideal by which we are to measure the deficiencies of reality, not a blueprint for imitation. Prospero is the standard according to which we see that all actual rulers are to some degree inferior to the natural ruler, the wise man. And in the course of analyzing Prospero's rule, we become aware of the irrational forces in man, such as desire and spiritedness, which can interfere with the wise man's regime. It is in this light that we can interpret the uneasiness with which most viewers and readers come away from *The Tempest*, an uneasiness rooted in our awareness of how many forces stand in the way of the wise man ruling, how improbable his success is, and how precarious his achievement threatens to be. We are worried about Prospero's future, once he abjures his magic. We are particularly suspicious of Antonio, and certainly skeptical that the next generation can maintain Prospero's wise rule. Our doubts are only deepened by Miranda's naive exclamation: "O brave new world," which Prospero can only answer with the almost cynical reply: "'Tis new to thee" (V.i.183-184), suggesting that Miranda, who may herself be called upon to rule someday, does not share in her father's knowledge of humanity. In the end, *The Tempest* does not leave the problem of wisdom and power any less problematic than it appears in the tragedies. We have seen for a brief moment a conjunction of the two, but it occurred on a magic island, which, we are told, may at any moment fade away, like a dream.

Indeed it is characteristic of Prospero that he has learned to view political life in light of the transitoriness of human achievement in general. Though his original error was to neglect political life entirely, he does not fall into the opposite error of becoming wholly absorbed in political life. Unlike the power-hungry usurpers who struggle against him, Prospero does not believe that political life is the "be-all and the end-all" of human existence. His original disposition to philosophy guarantees that he will remain aware of aspects of life beyond the political, and this larger perspective helps to moderate whatever ambition he develops. As is the case with Plato's philosopher-kings, Prospero's fitness for rule is shown precisely by his disinclination to rule.[15] In the end we learn that he is not looking forward to his return to power with the eagerness of a conventionally ambitious man. On the contrary, his declaration: "Every third thought shall be my grave" (V.i.312)[16] is an indication that at most only two-thirds of his mind will be devoted to politics and he is already looking beyond his responsibilities to the state. Examining the political aspects of *The Tempest* thus eventually takes us right up to the limits of politics, and perhaps gives us a glimpse of the world beyond.

The story of Prospero shows us that the wise man is able to view the ordinary concerns of political men in a larger context, to achieve a broader perspective on the goals men customarily set for themselves and pursue with full conviction. The perspective of the wise man in *The Tempest* ultimately turns out to be the perspective of eternity. The most famous lines in the play are an attempt to set human life in a larger framework:

> You do look, my son, in a mov'd sort,
> As if you were dismay'd; be cheerful, sir.
> Our revels now are ended. These our actors
> (As I foretold you) were all spirits, and
> Are melted into air, into thin air,
> And like the baseless fabric of this vision,
> The cloud-capp'd tow'rs, the gorgeous palaces,
> The solemn temples, the great globe itself,
> Yea, all which it inherit, shall dissolve,
> And like this insubstantial pageant faded
> Leave not a rack behind. We are such stuff
> As dreams are made on; and our little life
> Is rounded with a sleep. (IV.i.146-158)

As we see at the end of Chaucer's *Troilus and Criseyde*, the ultimate comic perspective is a cosmic perspective. Prospero is right to insist that his vision of the transiency of this world is a "cheerful" one, for it frees us from taking the ordinary concerns of human life too seriously by showing us how little they may matter in the grand scheme of things. *The Tempest* transforms the familiar material of Shakespearean tragedy into comedy by letting us share Prospero's detachment from human life as it is conventionally pursued. Because we see the action through Prospero's eyes, and are constantly aware that he is controlling the action for his own purposes, we keep our distance from the actors, always realizing the limited nature of their awareness. As Prospero's "revels" speech finally makes explicit, the aim of *The Tempest* is to make us aware that those who act in the play are merely actors. By momentarily opening up a perspective on the world beyond the borders of human life, *The Tempest* seems to take us beyond the borders of drama itself. No matter what its precise date may be, *The Tempest* is in the deepest sense Shakespeare's final play.

Notes

1. 473d-e. Quoted in the translation of Allan Bloom (New York: Basic Books, 1968).

2. IV.i.139. The text I am using is the *Riverside Shakespeare*, ed. G. Blakemore Evans (Boston: Houghton Mifflin, 1974). All subsequent line references will be incorporated into the body of the paper.

3. Among the tragedies, this theme is developed most fully in *King Lear*. See Harry V. Jaffa, "The Limits of Politics" in Allan Bloom, *Shakespeare's Politics* (New York: Basic Books, 1964), especially pp. 131-137.

4. Without committing oneself to the Coleridgean line of interpretation, one can see this theme as a strong element in *Hamlet*.

5. See, for example, *Republic*, 488a-489a.

6. See Northrop Frye, "Introduction to *The Tempest*," in the Pelican *Complete Shakespeare* (Baltimore: Penguin Books, 1969), p. 1369.

7. See Plato, *Phaedo*, 96b-100a. See also Aristotle, *Metaphysics*, 987b1-2, Xenophon, *Memorabilia*, I.ii.12-16, Cicero, *Tusculan Disputations*, V.iv.10-11, and Leo Strauss, *Socrates and Aristophanes* (New York: Basic Books, 1966), pp. 4, 313-314.

8. Even when Caliban shows awareness of what we could consider higher aspects of life, such as the beauty of music, his awareness is rooted in his desires. The "sweet airs" which charm Caliban are linked in his mind to his erotic dreams, and it is essential to him that they "give delight and hurt not," and also hold out the promise of riches dropping into his lap (III.ii.135-143).

9. See *Coriolanus*, I.vi.67-75. See Paul A. Cantor, *Shakespeare's Rome* (Ithaca: Cornell University Press, 1976), pp. 35-36.

10. For a detailed discussion of this point, see Cantor, pp. 64-71.

11. For an analysis of Antony's speech, see Cantor, pp. 185-187.

12. This point is developed at length by Allan Bloom in his essay "The Morality of the Pagan Hero" in *Shakespeare's Politics*, pp. 75-112.

13. The principle of Prospero's plan is enunciated in a different context, strangely by the villain Antonio: "The latter end of his commonwealth forgets the beginning" (II.i.158-159). The beginning of *The Tempest* shows us in some sense the beginning of society, when men are too concerned about their self-preservation to submit to authority. By the end of the play, this beginning must be obscured or forgotten in order to restore the regime. In the course of the play, Prospero has to cover over what he originally uncovered; in other words, in the deepest sense he refrains from sharing the truths he has learned about rule with other men, for these truths, if spread throughout society, would undermine his power to rule.

14. Even Caliban shows signs of developing a rudimentary sense of shame by the end of the play. He acknowledges that he has a "fine" master (V.i.262) and admits that he had been a "thrice-double ass" to take a "drunkard for a god" and "worship" a "dull fool" (V.i.296-298).

15. See *Republic*, 519d-520d.

16. Cf. the idea of philosophy as preparation for dying in Plato, *Phaedo*, 67e-68a.

THE GOLDEN CASKET:
AN INTERPRETATION OF
THE MERCHANT OF VENICE

Barbara Tovey

O, what may man within him hide,
Though angel on the outward side!
Measure for Measure, (III.ii.277-278)

The teaching that appearance often belies reality figures prominently
in many Shakespearean plays.[1] It seems fair to say, however, that there
is no play in which that teaching is given such frequent explicit utterance
as *The Merchant of Venice*. *Measure for Measure* is the only possible
rival. In that play there are at least two characters who concretely embody the appearance-reality antithesis. Angelo seems virtuous but is not.
The Duke, applying craft against vice, disguises himself as a friar. Contrary to what one might expect, in *The Merchant* there does not seem to
be any character who exemplifies the principle that "outward shows" are
least themselves. It is true that in the play's first enunciation of the appearance-reality antithesis Antonio says of Shylock:

> An evil soul producing holy witness
> Is like a villain with a smiling cheek,
> A goodly apple rotten at the heart.
> O what a goodly outside falsehood hath! (I.iii.94-97)

and this thought is echoed in Bassanio's words:

> I like not fair terms, and a villain's mind. (I.iii.175)

However, Shylock has no "goodly outside." He appears to be what he is.

The theme of appearance and reality is most fully developed in the story of the caskets, which turns on this antithesis. The alluring golden and silver caskets contain a death's head and a fool's head, respectively. Portia's portrait is to be found only in the "meagre lead"

> Which rather threaten'st than does promise aught. (III.ii.105)

The deceptiveness of appearances is the explicit theme of Bassanio's long speech which immediately precedes his correct choice of the lead casket. It begins with the lines:

> So may the outward shows be least themselves,—
> The world is still deceiv'd with ornament—

and continues with the statement:

> Thus ornament is but the guilded shore
> To a most dangerous sea: the beauteous scarf
> Veiling an Indian beauty; in a word,
> The seeming truth which cunning times put on
> To entrap the wisest. (III.ii.73-74, 96-101)

The scroll contained within the golden casket informs the unfortunate Morocco: "All that glisters is not gold" and "Gilded tombs do worms infold" (II.vii.65 and 69), while the scroll in the lead casket congratulates Bassanio as: "You that choose not by the view" (III.ii.131). Another warning against judging by the eye is to be found in the song depreciating Fancy (amorous inclination), which Portia arranges to have sung while Bassanio is deliberating upon his choice of the caskets. The song says of Fancy:

> It is engend'red in the eyes,
> With gazing fed, and Fancy dies
> In the cradle where it lies.[2] (III.ii.67-69)

It is interesting to note that the story of the caskets does not occur in the *Il Pecorone* tale[3] which is almost certainly Shakespeare's chief source for *The Merchant*. In that story the wooing test is of an entirely different nature. In most respects Shakespeare follows the plot of his source quite closely. The fact that he makes an alteration here is an indication that the casket story has an important function in the play. Some people think that the casket choice is a silly way to decide between the suitors. But the very fact that this is so shows that Shakespeare did not go to the trouble of inserting it into the play because of its excellence as a practical test of love or virtue or intelligence. Clearly he selected it only because of the ample opportunities it afforded for discourse on the subject of appearance and reality. Consequently, one would expect this theme to be of central importance in the play. Shakespeare apparently derived the idea of a choice between gold, silver, and lead caskets from a story in the *Gesta Romanorum*.[4] There it is a maiden who does the choosing. But whereas Bassanio is prompted to choose the lead casket because of his reflections on the appearance-reality antithesis, this is not what primarily motivates the maiden. She chooses the lead casket chiefly out of religious considerations, because that is the one which bears the superscription "Who so chooseth mee, shall finde that God hath disposed for him." Thus the notion of using the casket test as an illustration of the distinction between appearance and reality appears to have originated with Shakespeare.

In the story of the caskets, then, the theoretical teaching of the play receives an explicit statement. But this statement, if not accompanied by a convincing practical demonstration, has a tendency to strike us as platitudinous. That appearance often belies reality is the kind of principle which almost too readily wins our assent and which easily includes itself in our store of theoretical knowledge. To be able to apply it to particular cases, to be able to recognize actual instances of false "seeming," is, however, a far more difficult matter. Now it is interesting to note that a problem very much akin to that of putting theoretical knowledge into practice forms the opening subject of the first conversation between Portia and Nerissa.

> Portia: If to do were as easy as to know what were good to do,
> chapels had been churches, and poor men's cottages
> princes' palaces,—it is a good divine that follows his
> own instructions,—I can easier teach twenty what were
> good to be done, than be one of the twenty to follow
> mine own teaching.... (I.ii.12-17)

Portia tells the truth about herself when she says that it is easier for her to teach others what is good to be done than to follow her own teaching. She, of course, is fully aware of the correct principle to be employed in choosing between the caskets, and in saying to Bassanio: "If you do love me, you will find me out" (III.ii.41), she seems to assent to it. Furthermore, by the device of the song which she causes to have sung before Bassanio makes his choice, she successfully teaches this principle to him.

The song gives Bassanio a twofold hint. In the first place, it deprecates "judging by the view." Secondly, the end words in the first rhyming couplet both rhyme with "lead":[5]

> Tell me where is Fancy bred,
> Or in the heart, or in the head? (III.ii.63-64)

Nevertheless Portia rejects her dark-skinned suitor, the Prince of Morocco, on account of his outward appearance:

> if he have the condition of a saint, and the complexion of a
> devil, I had rather he should shrive me than wive me.
>   (I.ii.123-125)

When Morocco fails, she says:

> A gentle riddance,—draw the curtains, go,—
> Let all of his complexion choose me so. (II.vii.78-79)

I believe it is very important to notice that the cause of the downfall of the two unsuccessful suitors is their inability to apply theoretical knowledge of the appearance-reality antithesis to an actual situation. In his first speech to Portia, Morocco indicates his awareness that it is a mistake to judge a person by his looks:

> Mislike me not for my complexion,
> The shadowed livery of the burnish'd sun. (II.1.1-2)

But when he comes to choose, he commits the fatal error of assuming that what is inside the casket must be like its outer appearance:

> One of these three contains her heavenly picture.
> Is't like that lead contains her?—'twere damnation
> To think so base a thought, it were too gross
> To rib her cerecloth in the obscure grave,—
> Or shall I think in silver she's immur'd
> Being ten times undervalued to try'd gold?
> O sinful thought! never so rich a gem
> Was set in worse than gold. (II.vii.48-55)

This "forgetting" of theoretical knowledge is particularly evident in the case of Arragon, who in the very act of choosing states the correct theory. Unlike Morocco, he rightly rejects the gold because he refuses to be numbered among

> the fool multitude that choose by show,
> Not learning more than the fond eye doth teach,
> Which pries not to th'interior. (II.ix.26-28)

In his rather pompous discourse concerning the meaning of the inscription borne by the silver casket:

> "Who chooseth me shall get as much as he deserves,"

he again enunciates the correct principle in a slightly different form. Many men of high estate do not deserve the honors they enjoy which, rightfully bestowed, would belong to some who now are lowly peasants. Yet despite his tirade against "outward shows" Arragon never gives any serious consideration to the possibility that the "meagre lead" might be the casket containing Portia's portrait. He rejects it out of hand because of its ill-seeming appearance:

> You shall look fairer ere I give or hazard. (II.ix.22)

He behaves exactly like the "fool multitude" he condemns. In varying degrees, then, all three suitors display some theoretical understanding of the appearance-reality principle. Only Bassanio is able to apply it to a practical situation. In so doing he demonstrates that he alone truly grasps its significance.

I should like to suggest that Shakespeare places his audience in the position of the suitors. Portia coaches Bassanio concerning the principle which should guide his choice by means of hints. Shakespeare explicitly teaches his audience the theory that governs the play. At the same time, without comment, he confronts the audience with an instance of the theoretical teaching, a character who is the living counterpart of the golden casket. The audience is silently asked to recognize an actual case where appearance and reality are at odds. It is asked to apply the theory of the play to the play itself. It was mentioned earlier that in *Measure for Measure*, another play abounding in statements about the appearance-reality dichotomy, there are at least two characters who exemplify that antithesis. In *The Merchant*, on the other hand, exemplification of the theory seems to be lacking so far as the characters are concerned. Is it possible that Antonio constitutes just such an exemplification? May it be that the story of his relationship with Bassanio concretely embodies the teaching

that is explicitly asserted in the narrative of the caskets? I shall argue that
this is the case. If I am correct in this contention, the organic connection
between these two parts of the play, seemingly only superficially related,
will become clear.

On the surface Antonio is presented to us as an exceedingly noble
person and as the archetype of the devoted friend. He has bought golden
opinions. The characters of the play repeatedly hold him up as a supremely
good man. Both the Duke and Gratiano refer to him as: "royal merchant"
(III.ii.238 and IV.i.29). Salerio says of him: "A kinder gentleman treads
not the earth" (II.viii.35), and from Solanio we have:

> ...the good Antonio, the honest Antonio;—O that I had a title
> good enough to keep his name company!— (III.i.12-14)

It should be remembered, however, that Salerio and Solanio are the
Rosencrantz and Guildenstern of this play. Like the latter two, Salerio
and Solanio are exact duplicates of each other, and that, of course, is the
reason Shakespeare gives them such similar names. Philistines both, they
are clearly intended to serve as examples of the average Venetian. We
have to consider the possibility that they are also intended to be representatives of "the fool multitude that choose by show,/ Not learning more
than the fond eye doth teach." However that may be, nobler and more
intelligent characters also praise Antonio and his love for Bassanio in the
highest terms. Lorenzo refers to their friendship as "god-like amity" and
to Portia, who is about to set out to rescue Antonio, he says:

> But if you knew to whom you show this honour,
> How true a gentleman you send relief,
> How dear a lover of my lord your husband,
> I know you would be prouder of the work
> Than customary bounty can enforce you. (III.iv.5-9)

The greatest eulogy of Antonio is put in the mouth of Bassanio:

> The dearest friend to me, the kindest man,
> The best-condition'd and unwearied spirit
> In doing courtesies: and one in whom
> The ancient Roman honour more appears
> Than any that draws breath in Italy. (III.ii.291-295)

And certainly it seems that Antonio's devotion to Bassanio and his willingness to endanger his own life for his friend's sake well merit these praises.

Let us consider the relationship between Antonio and Bassanio more closely. In the *Il Pecorone* source story Antonio's counterpart, Ansaldo, is the godfather and guardian of Gianetto (Bassanio). Antonio and Bassanio are apparently not related in this way in *The Merchant*, although Bassanio is referred to as Antonio's "most noble kinsman" (I.i.57). The blood tie, however, does not seem to be a close one, for it appears that Bassanio's social rank is higher than Antonio's. The former is repeatedly called "Lord Bassanio," whereas Antonio is never referred to by such a title. Bassanio may be glancing at his high birth when he says "all the wealth I had/ Ran in my veins" (III.ii.253-254). We are not told Antonio's age, but as one of the leading merchants in Venice, it is obvious that he is substantially older than the youthful Bassanio. Now it is made clear to us that for a considerable period of time prior to the opening of the play, Antonio had been lending large sums of money to the impecunious Bassanio without making any effort to secure repayment. Bassanio speaks of:

> the great debts
> Wherein my time (something too prodigal)
> Hath left me gag'd: to you Antonio
> I owe the most in money and in love. (I.i.128-131)

Lending Bassanio a great deal of money would have been entirely appropriate, of course, if the latter had been using these sums to finance some worthwhile project, such as acquiring an education or establishing himself in business. But it is plain that Bassanio has been using the money for rather frivolous purposes.

> 'Tis not unknown to you Antonio
> How much I have disabled my estate,
> By something showing a more swelling port
> Than my faint means would grant continuance. (I.i.122-125)

There is no reason to think that he has been engaging in debauchery, but he has been self-indulgent. His manner of life is unnecessarily grand. He maintains numerous servants whom he decks out in fancy liveries (II.ii), and he feasts his many friends at sumptuous dinner parties where they are entertained by professional masquers—an extravagance which horrifies the sober and parsimonious Shylock! (II.v.28-36). When he goes to court Portia, he falsely believes it necessary to equip himself with an elaborate retinue; in fact, Portia would have gladly wed him even if he had come alone. At first glance it seems generous of Antonio to finance this expensive way of life, particularly since he had little reason to expect repayment, but thinking more carefully, we may well wonder whether he was acting in a way that was calculated to serve Bassanio's long-run interests. Antonio was spoiling Bassanio. He was encouraging a young person with slender financial means and expensive tastes to accustom himself to a manner of life that he could not possibly afford to maintain. This may lead us to question whether he had Bassanio's real welfare in mind. On the other hand, his policy was extremely well-calculated to make Bassanio dependent on him and to elicit from Bassanio feelings of love and indebtedness. Antonio buys Bassanio's love by lavishing money upon him. When the play begins Bassanio's affections are literally mortgaged to Antonio.

As the play opens we find Antonio in the midst of a conversation with Salerio and Salanio. Apparently the latter two have observed that Antonio is depressed, have complained that he is dull company, and have inquired into the cause of his melancholic mood. In the play's opening speech Antonio makes the following reply to them:

> In sooth I know not why I am so sad,
> It wearies me, you say it wearies you;
> But how I caught it, found it, or came by it,
> What stuff 'tis made of, whereof it is born,
> I am to learn:
> And such a want-wit sadness makes of me,
> That I have much ado to know myself. (I.i.1-7)

His companions propose several theories concerning the cause of his sadness. Salerio thinks that Antonio is worrying about the ships he has at sea and fearing that his merchandise may be lost. This is emphatically rejected by Antonio. Solanio suggests he is in love, to which Antonio replies "Fie, fie!" (I.i.46). And, indeed, throughout the course of the play there appears to be no woman whatsoever in Antonio's life. Solanio points out that some people suffer from a constitutional or endemic melancholy. But that Antonio is not numbered among them is made clear by Gratiano when, upon entering, he also notices Antonio's sadness, saying to him:

> You look not well Signior Antonio
> ....
> Believe me you are marvellously chang'd. (I.i.73, 76)

Normally Antonio does not look and behave as he does now. Gratiano theorizes that Antonio is feigning sadness in order to gain a reputation for wisdom and gravity, but this piece of silliness is ridiculed by both Antonio and Bassanio. So Shakespeare begins the play by setting the audience a problem to solve. Why is Antonio sad? The explanations offered by the characters are in each case rejected, and no correct explanation is ever explicitly put forward. This seemingly strange circumstance has caused some commentators to speculate that the episode of Antonio's melancholy is a relic of an earlier version of the play which Shakespeare forgot to delete.[6] Such speculation is misguided. Shakespeare has provided his audience with the resources to solve the problem. He has gone out of his way to let the reader know that shortly before the opening of the play Antonio had received a piece of news which might well account for his sadness. Bassanio had informed him of his intention to become a suitor for Portia's hand. Thus the conversation between Antonio and Bassanio which concludes scene one does not begin, as one might expect, with Bassanio's breaking news of his nuptial intentions to Antonio. That would appear to be the most straightforward way to start their dialogue as well as the most dramatic. But Shakespeare forgoes the drama and instead makes Antonio begin the conversation:

> Well, tell me now what lady is the same
> To whom you swore a secret pilgrimage—
> That you to-day promis'd to tell me of? (I.i.119-121)

Whether or not Antonio is consciously aware that the threatened loss of Bassanio is the cause of his sadness is difficult to say. He may be telling the truth when he concludes his opening speech with the statement that he has much ado to know himself. He may lack self-knowledge. On the other hand, even if he had clearly articulated to himself the nature of his feeling for Bassanio, he would certainly have a motive to conceal from his companions the real cause of his sorrow. John Russell Brown, who correctly identifies Bassanio's imminent departure as the reason for Antonio's sadness, also points out that when Solanio suggests to Antonio that he is in love, he may have gotten close to the real cause of the melancholy. This may be the reason why Antonio responds with the words "Fie, fie!"[7] Antonio's reproachful answer is, it seems to me, subject to two interpretations, not necessarily mutually exclusive. He may be angrily rejecting the suggestion that he is in love with a woman. It is the other possibility which I take it Brown has in mind, namely, that at some level of awareness Antonio feels his love for Bassanio is something to be ashamed of; hence his indignant reproach when it is suggested to him that he is in love. Shakespeare gives us an indication that the members of Antonio's circle were not unaware of the pleasure he took in being alone with Bassanio. When Bassanio comes on stage in the company of Lorenzo and Gratiano, Salerio and Solanio bid Antonio farewell, saying, "We leave you now with better company" (I.i.59). As soon as they depart, Lorenzo says: "My Lord Bassanio since you have found Antonio/ We two will leave you" (I.i.69-70).

Antonio recognizes, of course, that Bassanio's intention to sue for Portia's hand is inalterable. He knows that any attempt to prevent Bassanio from going to Belmont, or even a refusal wholeheartedly to assist him, would merely alienate him. The wisest course for Antonio at this point is to salvage what he can. This goal will be best accomplished by doing everything possible to intensify the love and the sense of indebtedness that Bassanio feels toward him. The most effective way to increase Bassanio's love and gratitude is to make a sacrifice for his sake. Borrowing money at interest constitutes for Antonio a moral sacrifice much more than a financial one. His belief that usury is a moral abomination provides the only justification for his extraordinarily harsh treatment of Shylock. Now, merely in order to outfit Bassanio with an elegant entourage, he is willing to pay Shylock interest, thereby lending support to the man and the institution he so bitterly condemns. Shylock clearly sees the inconsistency: "Me thoughts you said, you neither lend nor borrow/ Upon advantage." And Antonio, apparently failing to see it, replies "I do never use it" (I.iii.64-65).

When Shylock proposes to remit interest on condition that the penalty for forfeiture be a pound of Antonio's flesh, the latter's reaction is very revealing. One would expect a normal person at least initially to wince at such a horrible proposal, even although he might subsequently accept it on the grounds that there was no danger of forfeiture. Just such a reaction is displayed by Bassanio:

> You shall not seal to such a bond for me,
> I'll rather dwell in my necessity. (I.iii.150-151)

But Antonio instantly, joyfully, and even gratefully accepts Shylock's terms. He knows Shylock hates him and has cause to wish his death. But seemingly he never gives any consideration to the possibility that Shylock is angling for his life. Despite the fact that he himself has just referred to

Shylock as "An evil soul, producing holy witness," "a villain with a smiling cheek," he apparently takes at face value Shylock's assurance that the penalty would not be exacted even in case of forfeiture. His credulous acceptance of Shylock's false claim that the offer is being extended out of friendship is shown by his comment: "This Hebrew will turn Christian, he grows kind" (I.iii.174). Thus Antonio provides the play's first and most dramatic illustration of a person who has theoretical knowledge of the appearance-reality antithesis, but is unable to apply it in practice.

Antonio's behavior might well appear strange even if he had possessed absolute assurance that his ships would come safely in before the bond's expiration. But of course he had no such assurance. Mercantile shipping in the sixteenth and seventeenth centuries was an extremely hazardous business; it was for this reason that Venice required the venture capital provided by the Jewish community. The nature and variety of those hazards are eloquently described by Salerio at the beginning of the play's first scene (I.i.22-36). As an experienced merchant, Antonio should have realized that he had no complete certainty concerning the timely return of his ships. He is represented as being extraordinarily liberal with his money; surely he was not overcome by a niggardly desire to economize by avoiding payment of the interest. Why then is he so imprudent as to assent to Shylock's terrible terms? Why does he not insist upon a bond secured by monetary guarantees rather than his own flesh? I suggest it is because the proposal that his life be surety for the bond gratifies Antonio's desire to make Bassanio appreciate his willingness to sacrifice himself for Bassanio's sake. Antonio seems to think that Shylock is doing him a favor in offering him this opportunity. It may be that, unwittingly, Shylock is doing precisely this.

After the conclusion of the contract between Antonio and Shylock at the end of Act I, the audience does not again see Antonio and Bassanio in each other's presence until the courtroom scene in Act IV. However, Shakespeare employs Salerio to describe the scene of their parting on board the vessel that is about to carry Bassanio to Belmont. He says:

> I saw Bassanio and Antonio part,
> Bassanio told him he would make some speed
> Of his return: he answered, "Do not so,
> Slubber not business for my sake Bassanio,
> But stay the very riping of the time,
> And for the Jew's bond which he hath of me—
> Let it not enter in your mind of love:
> Be merry, and employ your chiefest thoughts

To courtship, and such fair ostents of love
As shall conveniently become you there."
And even there (his eye being big with tears),
Turning his face, he put his hand behind him,
And with affection wondrous sensible
He wrung Bassanio's hand, and so they parted. (II.viii.36-49)

Solanio appends the comment: "I think he only loves the world for him." This is an extraordinarily moving account. Antonio's love for Bassanio appears to be wholly selfless. Yet, as Allan Bloom points out, the scene "also reveals the pretense in Antonio's selflessness; Bassanio is reminded of the risks his friend is taking for him when Antonio tells him to forget them. The scene cuts in both directions."[8]

The element of pretense in Antonio's selflessness becomes fully apparent in the letter that he writes to Bassanio after the bond has become forfeit.[9]

> *Sweet Bassanio, my ships have all miscarried, my creditors grow cruel, my estate is very low, my bond to the Jew is forfeit, and (since in paying it, it is impossible I should live), all debts are clear'd between you and I, if I might but see you at my death: notwithstanding, use your pleasure,—if your love do not persuade you to come, let not my letter.* (III.ii.314-320)

Such a letter is calculated to make Bassanio spend the rest of his life in remorseful remembrance. That this is indeed Antonio's intention is borne out by his courtroom admonition:

You cannot better be employ'd, Bassanio,
Than to live still and write mine epitaph. (IV.i.117-118)

Hereafter Bassanio's function in life will be to serve as apostle to the "crucified" Antonio, who died for his sake.

The immediate effect of the letter upon Bassanio's self-esteem is revealed in what he says to Portia:

—when I told you
My state was nothing, I should then have told you
That I was worse than nothing; for indeed
I have engag'd myself to a dear friend,
Engag'd my friend to his mere enemy
To feed my means. Here is a letter lady,

The paper as the body of my friend,
And every word in it a gaping wound
Issuing life-blood. (III.ii.257-265)

Now, at last, Bassanio sees the terrible folly of Antonio's transaction with Shylock. He realizes his own selfishness and moral weakness in having assented to the arrangement, and he suffers the consequent pangs of remorse. What he does not see is that it was his friend who led him into wrongdoing.

The most appalling aspect of Antonio's letter is his stated wish that Bassanio be actually present to witness his sacrificial death:

all debts are clear'd between you and I, if I might but see you *at* my death. (Italics mine)

This wish is expressed even more forcibly in the next scene. Having failed to obtain a hearing from Shylock, Antonio resigns himself to death, saying:

—pray God Bassanio come
To *see* me pay his debt, and then I care not.
(III.iii.35-36; italics mine)

Bassanio is supposed to watch while Antonio dies in agony in order to discharge the debt incurred on Bassanio's behalf. Never does Antonio consider what effect such a sight will have upon Bassanio's future happiness. In the *Nicomachean Ethics* Aristotle points out:

to see [our friend] pained at our misfortunes is painful; for everyone shuns being a cause of pain to his friends. For this reason people of a manly nature guard against making their friends grieve with them, and, unless he be exceptionally insensible to pain, such a man cannot stand the pain that ensues for his friends.... (1171b5-8)

Had Antonio genuinely cared about Bassanio's welfare, he would have done everything in his power to keep Bassanio away from the scene of his death. More, he would have attempted to mitigate Bassanio's sense of guilt by reminding him of the truth, namely, that Bassanio had tried to prevent him from accepting Shylock's terms and had warned him concerning Shylock's intentions. Antonio would have emphasized that it was *he* who had misjudged Shylock's motives and that the responsibility for signing the bond was his and his alone. He does just the opposite. Bidding farewell to his friend in the courtroom, he twice points out that Bassanio has been the cause of his undoing:

> Give me your hand, Bassanio: fare you well,
> Grieve not that I am fall'n to this *for you*;
> ....
> Repent but you that you shall lose your friend
> And he repents not that he pays *your debt*.
> (IV.i.261-262, IV.i.274-275; italics mine)

What Antonio does here is similar to what he did in his shipboard parting from Bassanio. We have already seen that on that occasion he reminded Bassanio of his indebtedness to him in the very act of telling him to forget. In the courtroom he admonishes Bassanio not to grieve while showing him that he has, indeed, great cause for grief. Judged by classical standards, Antonio is not a true friend. It is ironical that immediately after he prays to God that Bassanio will come to see his death, Lorenzo refers to his friendship with Bassanio as "god-like amity." It is likewise ironical that Bassanio describes him as "one in whom/ The ancient Roman honour more appears/ Than any that draws breath in Italy." But the judgment on Antonio may be different if the standards employed are Christian rather than classical. Christians are constantly reminded that Christ died in order to atone for their sins; in Christian art and in Christian churches His death is figured everywhere. In return the faithful owe Him boundless love, gratitude, and repentance. Antonio's behavior is in some respects an imitation of Christ's. It would not have appeared noble to the ancients, but it is understandable that Christian audiences regard it as a manifestation of the highest love.

We have already remarked on Antonio's imprudence in initially assenting to Shylock's dangerous terms. After his ships have been (apparently) lost, he continues to display what seems to be a lack of good judgment. To Salerio and Salanio, Antonio has denied that his melancholy is caused by concern over the safety of his ships.

> My ventures are not in one bottom trusted, nor to one place;
> nor is my whole estate upon the fortune of this present year.
> Therefore my merchandise makes me not sad. (42-45)

So Antonio is presented to us as an excellent money manager who diversifies his investments and maintains a financial reserve. Why, then, doesn't he make use of this reserve to cover his indebtedness to Shylock? Even if these funds were insufficient for the purpose, they would have been adequate, it seems, to serve as a collateral on a new loan. This point is made by the eminent British barrister, George W. Keeton, who comments: "Now if Antonio had taken the precaution of borrowing the exact sum from his friends *before the day appointed in the bond,* instead of sending them messages couched in terms of martyrlike resignation afterwards, even Shylock would have been compelled to forego his revenge and accept the sum due."[10] After the bond falls due, Antonio's encounters with Shylock are marked by a strange passivity on the former's part. On the eve of the trial he is let out of prison in order that he may plead with Shylock for mercy (III.iii), but he makes no serious effort to get a hearing from his creditor. Twice he asks Shylock to listen to him; twice Shylock refuses. Without attempting any statement of his case Antonio then gives up, saying: "Let him alone,/ I'll follow him no more with bootless prayers" (III.iii.19-20). In the trial scene, prior to the entrance of the disguised Portia, he makes three speeches, each of them characterized by an attitude of passive resignation to his fate. Contrasting himself with Shylock, he says:

> I do oppose
> My patience to his fury, and am arm'd
> To suffer with a quietness of spirit,
> The very tyranny and rage of his. (IV.i.10-13)

To Bassanio:

> I am a tainted wether of the flock,
> Meetest for death,—the weakest kind of fruit
> Drops earliest to the ground, and so let me. (IV.i.114-116)

He asks the court to render judgment against him:

> Make no more offers, use no farther means,
> But with all brief and plain conveniency
> Let me have judgment, and the Jew his will! (IV.i.81-83)

Yet, as Keeton points out, Antonio has not exhausted his legal remedies. He has at least two possible defenses open to him. He could "urge that the bond was void as contrary to public policy" and, secondly, it was possible for him to plead "fraudulent misrepresentation," inasmuch as he had signed the bond on the strength of Shylock's assurances that it would never be enforced and had no legal signification.[11] But Antonio wants to die. As Bloom remarks, he seeks martyrdom.[12] In his farewell speech to Bassanio he says that Fortune has been kinder to him than to most men:

> it is still her use
> To let the wretched man outlive his wealth,
> To view with hollow eye and wrinkled brow
> An age of poverty: from which ling'ring penance
> Of such misery doth she cut me off. (IV.i.264-268)

The wealth Antonio has really outlived is not his lost shipping, but his close association with Bassanio. The age of poverty from which death cuts him off is a life without Bassanio's company. By dying for his friend, he wins a victory over his rival, Portia, and regains what he fears he has lost, Bassanio's love.

As soon as she hears of Antonio's predicament, Portia clearly recognizes the threat that his imminent martyrdom poses to her married life with Bassanio. She correctly diagnoses that Bassanio will be regarded by himself and others as the culprit in the affair (III.ii.297-301). She realizes that if Antonio is allowed to offer himself up as a sacrificial victim, Bassanio will never again enjoy tranquility of mind.[13] More specifically, he will not be able to look at her without thinking that it was on her account that he wrought the destruction of his devoted friend. Inevitably he will "lie by Portia's side/ With an unquiet soul" (III.ii.304-305). This outcome she is determined to prevent. Hence she sets out for Venice to save Antonio and, by saving him, her marriage with Bassanio.

The courtroom is the scene of two struggles. What is explicit and on the surface is the war between Jew and Christian, the Old Law and the New. Beneath the surface there is another conflict: the battle between Bassanio's male and female lovers. Portia has at her disposal the legal means that would enable her immediately to dismiss Shylock's claim. Part of her reason for not doing so is that she wishes to bring out in the open the conflict between Antonio and herself. She lets Antonio think he is on the verge of making the supreme sacrifice for his friend. It was only under these circumstances that he would permit himself the luxury of comparing his love for Bassanio with hers:

> Commend me to your honourable wife,
> Tell her the process of Antonio's end,
> Say how I lov'd you, speak me fair in death:
> And when the tale is told, bid her be judge
> Whether Bassanio had not once a love. (IV.i.269-273)

Subtly Antonio suggests that his love is superior to Portia's. It is he who is laying down his life for Bassanio. Greater love hath no man than this. She makes no comparable sacrifice. The irony is that Portia, who to the audience now appears to be rendering judgment against Antonio, in his mind will ultimately be compelled to render judgment against herself ("bid her be judge"). It is interesting to note that this episode has no counterpart whatsoever in the source story.

The implicit comparison between the two loves elicits from Bassanio the desired response. Whether consciously or unconsciously, he realizes that Antonio is asking him to state which of the pair he loves the best. He replies:

> Antonio, I am married to a wife
> Which is as dear to me as life itself,
> But life itself, my wife, and all the world,
> Are not with me esteem'd above thy life.
> I would lose all, ay sacrifice them all
> Here to this devil, to deliver you. (IV.i.278-283)

Portia is dear, but Antonio is nearer and dearer. In fact, Bassanio's preference for Antonio could hardly be stated in starker terms. If he were in a position to choose which one should be sacrificed and which one should be saved, it would be Portia, not Antonio, who would fall victim to Shylock's knife. If Bassanio could have his way, his voluntary redemption by Antonio would be replaced by a compulsory redemption of Antonio by Portia.[14] This is Antonio's moment of triumph. It is for this that he has been willing to lay down his life. Portia's ensuing comment shows that she recognizes Bassanio has been unfaithful to her:

> Your wife would give you little thanks for that
> If she were by to hear you make the offer. (IV.i.284-285)

Shylock also sees the infidelity. After Gratiano and Nerissa have echoed the statements of Bassanio and Portia, he exclaims in disgust: "These be the Christian husbands!" (IV.i.291).

Both prior to and during the trial Antonio has presented himself as the redeemer of Bassanio's debt. Twice he has said that he is dying in order to pay that debt. Portia herself has referred to the fact that Bassanio has been "dear bought" (III.ii.312). For the sake of retaining Bassanio's love, Antonio has bound himself to Shylock. In turn, Bassanio has become "infinitely bound" to Antonio (V.i.135). At the conclusion of the trial both bonds have been dissolved. The tables have been turned, not only on Shylock, but also on Antonio. He is no longer cast in the role of the redeemer. It is now Portia who is *his* savior and benefactor, and as the Duke says, he is "much bound" to her (IV.i.403). Bassanio, too, has been "acquitted of grievous penalties" and both men acknowledge that they "stand indebted" "in love and service" to her evermore (IV.i.405-406 and 409-410).

However, Portia's project is not yet complete. Antonio has threatened her marriage, and Bassanio, in preferring his friend to her, has been guilty of a form of conjugal infidelity. Bassanio must be chastised and Antonio chastened in order to ensure that this offense will never again be repeated. Portia accomplishes these ends through the device of obtaining from Bassanio the ring with which she had previously wed herself to him and from which he had been cautioned never to part. The erotic significance of the ring is made nearly explicit in the rhyming couplet which concludes the play. It is spoken by Gratiano whose greatest concern is that he will be cuckolded.

> Well, while I live, I'll fear no other thing
> So sore, as keeping safe Nerissa's ring.[15]   (V.i.306-307)

Portia's placing of her ring on Bassanio's finger on their wedding day symbolizes the fact that she gives herself to him sexually. When he removes the ring and returns it to her, he performs an act of sexual renunciation. The episode of the ring occurs in the source story, but in *The Merchant* version a significant alteration has been introduced. When the Lady of Belmonte in the *Il Pecorone* tale asks Gianetto for the ring, he reluctantly surrenders it to her. Ansaldo, Antonio's counterpart, plays no role. But in the play Bassanio initially refuses Portia's request for the ring. It is only after her departure that Antonio persuades him to yield it:

> My Lord Bassanio, let him have the ring,
> Let his deservings and my love withal
> Be valued 'gainst your wife's commandement. (IV.i.445-447)

In asking Bassanio to place a higher value on his love than on Portia's "commandement" Antonio again reveals the competitive situation that exists between them. And once more he wins the competition.

Act V, which is laid in Belmont, opens with a scene of great lyric loveliness in which Lorenzo and Jessica praise the beauty of the moonlit night. The theme of their opening conversation, however, is that of infidelity in love. They list four pairs of unhappy lovers: Troilus and Cressida, Pyramus and Thisbe, Aeneas and Dido, and Jason and Medea. In the case of three of these pairs the cause of the unhappiness was the faithlessness of one of the partners. Lorenzo then refers to Jessica's infidelity to her father, and she concludes the conversation by playfully accusing him of making false vows to her. The little exchange between these two is a prelude to the confrontation later in the act between Portia and Bassanio over the missing ring. Attempting to excuse himself, Bassanio says to her:

> If you did know to whom I gave the ring,
> If you did know *for whom* I gave the ring,
> ....
> You would abate the strength of your displeasure.
> (V.i.193-198; italics mine)

At this point Portia explicitly accuses him of sexual infidelity (208), and she proceeds to punish him by making him think that she, in her turn, has been unfaithful (259). John Russell Brown sees this episode as a comic statement of the appearance-reality theme, "for despite appearance Bassanio is really true to Portia."[16] The irony is that beneath his real truth there is yet another, deeper level of reality upon which he has been untrue. Antonio is more correct than he realizes when he says "I am the unhappy subject of these quarrels" (238). Antonio's courtroom triumph over Portia is now reversed. Bassanio swears by his wife by his soul: "I never more will break an oath with thee" (248). And Antonio for the second time becomes the surety for Bassanio's obligation; this time it is his soul, not his body, that is the forfeit. His yielding up of Bassanio is immediately rewarded by Portia. She partly recompenses him for his emotional loss by informing him that three of his argosies "Are richly come to harbour suddenly" (277). Antonio emerges from the whole affair far wealthier than he entered it. But he has lost that which he valued more than his ships.

It has been widely recognized that the quarrel between Shylock and Antonio is a depiction of the conflict between the principles of Judaism and Christianity, between the Old Law and the New. There can be no question that, just as Shylock stands for Judaism with its emphasis upon obedience to the law, so Antonio represents Christianity with its corresponding stress upon the virtues of love, charity, and self-sacrifice. Not only do Antonio's actions reflect Christian principles; at numerous points in the play he seems to be identified with the figure of Christ. His treatment of Shylock in the early part of the play echoes the driving of the money changers from the temple. There are many parallels between Christ's appearance before Pilate and the trial scene in Act III, where "both plot situation and language suggest a typical killing of Christ by the Jew."[17] These claims have been fully documented by Barbara Lewalski and Allan Bloom, among others, and I shall make no further attempt to substantiate them here. Antonio functions as a redeemer. Barbara Lewalski writes: "Antonio who assumes the debts of others (rescuing Bassanio, the self-confessed 'Prodigal,' from a debt due under the law) reflects on occasion the role of Christ satisfying the claim of Divine Justice by assuming the sins of mankind."[18] In fact, Antonio's very name suggests that he atones for the sins of others.[19]

Shakespeare's play is generally regarded as illustrating the superiority of the New Law to the Old. As Lewalski points out "it culminates in the final defeat of the Old Law and the symbolic conversion of the Jew."[20] It would be difficult to disagree with this estimate. But if I am substantially correct in my assessment of Antonio's behavior, the play also contains a veiled criticism of Christianity, a criticism which might be regarded as stemming either from the point of view of Machiavellian realism or from that of classical antiquity. The defectiveness of Antonio's love for Bassanio perhaps symbolizes what Shakespeare takes to be a corresponding flaw in the principles of Christianity. Now the defectiveness of Antonio's love does not consist primarily in the fact that it is the love of one male for another; the flaw in that love is rather its possessiveness. It is not wholly directed toward the well-being of the beloved one; it aims instead at securing from him the maximum return of love and gratitude. If Antonio had been allowed to sacrifice himself, Bassanio would have incurred an enormous indebtedness which could only have been repaid by a lifetime of remorseful gratitude. The payment of that debt would have poisoned for him and for Portia the earthly paradise symbolized by Belmont. Just so, Shakespeare may be suggesting, the Christian, who lives with the constant reminder of the enormity of the sacrifice made for him by Christ, is prevented from fully experiencing the joys of this world. The gratitude and repentance elicited by that sacrifice deflect him from the pursuit of his natural good on this earth.

I have argued that the courtroom scene, which appears to be exclusively a struggle between Shylock and Antonio, is in reality also a battle between Antonio and Portia, a battle that is waged for the soul of Bassanio. If Antonio stands for Christianity, as surely he does, we must now ask ourselves what it is that Portia represents. Bloom correctly says of

Belmont: "It is pagan; everyone there speaks in the terms of classical antiquity.... The themes of conversation and the ideas current have an ancient source." Most notably, the distinction between appearance and reality, which is of central importance in Belmont, has its roots in the philosophies of Parmenides and Plato. In Belmont, Lorenzo and Jessica gaze upon the beauties of the celestial bodies; for Plato such activity is a metaphor for philosophizing. Lorenzo's famous speech on the music of the spheres reflects the teaching of Pythagoras and Plato (V.i.58-65). In her first conversation with Portia, Nerissa echoes Aristotle's theory that virtue and happiness consist in following the mean (I.ii.3-9). In maintaining that the best kind of friends are similar to one another, Portia expounds one of the themes of the classical teaching about friendship (III.iv.11-18). Portia herself is named after the wife of the famous Roman, Marcus Brutus. It is reasonable to assume, then, that in her confrontation with the Christ-like figure of Antonio, Portia represents the spirit of classical antiquity. As Bloom points out, she also stands for Eros, seemingly in its manifestation as erotic love between man and woman. [22]

Can we say any more? Bloom thinks that Portia opposes "her lusty, gay, physical love" to "the gloomy spiritual love" of Antonio.[23] On one level that is certainly true. But is that all the confrontation between the two consists of? If so, Shakespeare's criticism of Christianity would be made entirely from the standpoint of a hedonistic philosophy. The censure of Christianity would be grounded on its interference with the pleasures of the flesh. This does not seem to me to be characteristic of Shakespeare's thinking. To do justice to Bloom, he apparently does think that Belmont represents something higher than a merely erotic paradise. On the one hand, he describes it as "a place where there are no laws, no conventions, no religions—just men and women in love."[24] But to that description he juxtaposes a very different account of Belmont. In the context of discussing Lorenzo's speech on the music of the spheres, he speaks of Belmont as the place where men transcend the level of their daily lives and become assimilated to the movement of the spheres. At Belmont they glimpse "the only true beauty, which lies somewhere beyond the heavens for the happy few."[25] Support for this last claim may be rendered by Jessica's statement:

> —it is very meet
> The Lord Bassanio live an upright life
> For having such a blessing in his lady,
> He finds the joys of heaven here on earth. (III.v.67-70)

To me, it seems necessary to choose between these two very different conceptions of Belmont. If Belmont is the place where men gaze with the eyes of the soul upon the intelligible forms that lie beyond the heavens, then it is only on the level of appearance that it is a paradise of sensual pleasure. And it is only on the level of appearance that Portia, its queen, is a representative of "lusty, gay, physical love." If Bloom's second account of Belmont is correct, then it would seem that Portia must stand for classical philosophy, particularly in its Platonic form. I believe there is evidence to suggest that this was, indeed, Shakespeare's intention.

Plutarch describes the Roman Portia as "being addicted to philosophy" and "full of an understanding courage."[26] Her father was Cato the Younger, a philosopher of the Stoic school, who committed suicide. According to Plutarch, he spent the last evening of his life discussing philosophy, warmly defending the Stoic thesis "that the good man only is free, and that all wicked men are slaves." Just prior to his death he is reported to have read three times over Plato's dialogue on the soul, the *Phaedo*. We have already mentioned that themes taken from classical philosophy figure prominently in the conversations which take place in Belmont. Remembering these things, let us consider the possible significance of the fact that Portia is an heiress "richly left" (I.i.161). Although I cannot here substantiate the claim, I believe that Boccaccio in *The Decameron* frequently uses monetary wealth as a symbol of the treasures of classical philosophy, and in this I think Chaucer follows him. It would be particularly appropriate if Portia's inherited wealth had the same significance in view of the fact that the Roman woman after whom she is named literally did inherit the riches of classical philosophy from her father. If this is what Portia's wealth is meant to represent, then what appears to be a somewhat mercenary desire on Bassanio's part to get his hands on her money would be explained and redeemed. The significance of his parting with Antonio would also be deepened. If Portia's riches stand for classical philosophy, Antonio's wealth may signify the teachings of Christianity. Bassanio's separation from Antonio and his union with Portia would then represent an abandonment of Christianity for the sake of classical philosophy.

Portia is presented to us as a person of the highest intelligence. She controls the action of the play. It is she who brings it about that Bassanio chooses the correct casket, she who breaks Shylock and saves Antonio, she who delivers Bassanio from his indebtedness to his friend. Without her intervention in the trial the play would have had a tragic ending. *The Merchant* is a comedy precisely because it exemplifies the rule of wis-

dom. There are certain analogies between Portia's behavior and that
of the philosopher-ruler as described by Plato in the *Republic*. Plato's
philosopher is compelled to cease gazing upon the heavenly bodies
and to descend into the cave where he must take upon himself the
burden of ruling. In Shakespeare's play Belmont is the place where
the heavenly order is an object of admiration. Portia is compelled to
make a descent from Belmont (literally, "beautiful mountain") and to
enter the city of Venice in order to rule it and to save it. In the *Republic* the rule of the philosopher-king has a double purpose. The first is
to bring about the well-being of the city. The second is to drag from
the cave those potential philosophers who are capable of being liberated from the shadowy realm of politically authoritative opinion. In
journeying to Venice, Portia also has two main purposes. She wants,
first of all, to save Antonio from Shylock. In other words, she defends
Christianity, the religion of the city, against its attacker. By stripping
Shylock of his wealth, his power, and his religion, she weakens, if not
annihilates, the power of Christianity's opponents. Although the means
are harsh, it can be said that she benefits Venice by unifying it. Her
second purpose is to free Bassanio from Antonio and in so doing to
emancipate the potential philosopher from the religion of his city. It
is this action that corresponds to the philosopher's dragging of the
prisoner from the cave. Having accomplished these goals, she departs
from the city, ascending again to Belmont, with Bassanio in her train.

As Bloom has pointed out, Portia is not characterized by undue reverence either for the law or for her father's will. She violates the spirit of
his will by giving Bassanio a double hint concerning the correct casket.
In order to entrap Shylock, she violates the canons of good legal proceeding; in the narrow sense of the term her dealings with him are unfair.

> No sensible judge, who wishes to bring about a compromise,
> will assure the party whom he wishes to persuade that he is
> certain of success if he persists in his legal claim; and no fair
> judge could give assurances of that kind knowing them to be
> false.[27]

But Portia is not aiming at a compromise. She wants to entice Shylock
into making a criminal attempt upon Antonio's life so that he will be
liable to the penalties for a felonious action. Had she wished, she could
have pointed out that the bond was illegal at the outset of the proceedings. She could have immediately threatened Shylock with the law that

punishes by forfeiture of life and property any alien making an attempt upon the life of a Venetian citizen.

> Here the skill of Portia becomes even more apparent. Had she raised her equitable defenses earlier...the Duke would have recollected the same law and stopped the trial. To bring an action on the bond is not a criminal attempt—the action is too remote from the final consequence—the removal of the pound of flesh. But Shylock, having obtained judgement, has been earnestly whetting his knife, and has actually been on the point of making an incision when Portia stopped him. This is clearly a criminal attempt, and, as such, a felony. At this date all felonies were punishable by death and forfeiture of the goods of the deceased. [28]

Portia's great speech exhorting Shylock to be merciful is not motivated by any hope that he will comply. Salerio has told her that:

> Twenty merchants,
> The duke himself, and the magnificoes
> Of greatest port have all persuaded with him,
> But none can drive him from the envious plea
> Of forfeiture, of justice, and his bond.

And Jessica, who must be accounted a very high authority in these matters, has said in Portia's hearing:

> When I was with him, I have heard him swear
> To Tubal and to Chus, his countrymen,
> That he would rather have Antonio's flesh
> Than twenty times the value of the sum
> That he did owe him: and I know my lord,
> If law, authority, and power deny not,
> It will go hard with poor Antonio. (III.ii.278-289)

Before she arrives in the courtroom, Portia has ample evidence that any attempt to move Shylock by persuasion will be futile. She makes the plea in order that he may reject it; he will then be debarred from pleading for mercy for himself. Portia manipulates the law. She is less than scrupulously fair. But her ultimate purposes are beneficent. Her exclusive concern is the achievement of what is good. She uses both law and religion to achieve her ends, but she stands above and outside of them. In this respect, also, she resembles the Platonic philosopher.

The conflict between Judaism and Christianity appears to be the dominant theme of *The Merchant of Venice*. Much less obvious, but of equal or greater importance, I would suggest, is the theme of the conflict between Christianity and classical philosophy, which is embodied in the silent struggle between Portia and Antonio for Bassanio. Shakespeare indicates what he conceives to be the proper solution of this conflict. Within the city, philosophy will be Christianity's ally and defender. In return, Christianity should release its hold over those gifted young persons who are capable of making an ascent from the cave.

Notes

1. Cf., for example, *2 Henry IV*, V.i.125-129; *Much Ado*, IV.i.33-37 and 101-105; *Twelfth Night*, III.iv.404; *Measure for Measure*, I.iii.54; II.iv.12-17 and 150; III.i.277-278; *Othello*, I.i.59-65.

2. In his introduction to the seventh Arden edition of the play (1955) John Russell Brown points out that the theme of appearance and reality is a "governing idea" of the play and he cites most of the passages which I have mentioned (p. lii). All quotations have been taken from this edition of *The Merchant*.

3. Ser Giovanni, *Il Pecorone*, First Story, Fourth Day. In this story the test that the wooer must pass is to stay awake until the lady he is courting joins him in bed. The lady makes this a difficult task to accomplish by giving the wooer a drugged drink.

4. History 32 of the *Gesta Romanorum*, translated and "now newly revised and corrected by R. Robinson" (1595).

5. Not all critics believe that the song is intended to tell Bassanio how to choose. Their refusal to believe this seems to be based primarily on the grounds that Portia says she will not teach him (III.ii.10-12) and that "it would belittle Bassanio and Portia and cheapen the themes of the play." (John Russell Brown, 1955 Arden edition of *The Merchant*, p. 80.) These objections will subsequently be dealt with.

6. John Russell Brown cites Schücking, *Character Problems* (1922), p. 171, as holding this view. Brown himself correctly sees that the cause of the sadness is Bassanio's imminent departure for Belmont. (Seventh Arden edition, p. 4.)

7. Ibid., p. 7.

8. Allan Bloom, "On Christian and Jew," in Allan Bloom with Harry V. Jaffa, *Shakespeare's Politics* (New York: Basic Books, 1964), pp. 32-33.

9. The letter is entirely Shakespeare's invention. No counterpart to it exists in the source story.

10. George W. Keeton, *Shakespeare and His Legal Problems* (London: A. & C. Black, 1930), p.11.

11. Keeton, pp. 11-12.

12. Bloom, pp. 27 and 33.

13. "She [Portia] is aware that the ties which bind Bassanio to Antonio are strong. If Antonio had died, those ties would have poisoned Bassanio's life." Bloom, p. 29.

14. Thus it is foreshadowed that Portia will, indeed, be Antonio's redeemer, not, of course, through a sacrifice of her life, but through the use of her intelligence to manipulate the law. Shakespeare suggests that redemption can be effected in different ways.

15. In his glossary of Shakespearean erotic terms Eric Partridge defines "ring" as "the pudend" and cites Gratiano's concluding lines as an illustration. *Shakespeare's Bawdy* (London: Routledge and Kegan Paul, 1955), p. 179. E.A.M. Colman says "jokes equating a ring with the female pudendum are fairly numerous in Renaissance literature." As an example, he cites Friar John's story of Hans Carvel in Rabelais, *Gargantua and Pantagruel*, trans. J.M. Cohen (1955), p. 368 (*The Dramatic Use of Bawdy in Shakespeare* [London: Longman Group, 1974], p. 77).

16. Seventh Arden edition, p, lii.

17. Barbara K. Lewalski, "Biblical Allegory and Allusion in *The Merchant of Venice*," *Shakespeare Quarterly* 13 (1962), 327-343. Reprinted in Sylvan Barnet, ed., *Twentieth Century Interpretations of the Merchant of Venice* (Englewood Cliffs, N.J.: Prentice-Hall, 1970), pp. 33-54, at p. 49. She cites a remarkable parallel between the actions of Antonio in this play and the behavior of Christ as described by Launcelot Andrews in a Christmas sermon on Gal. 3:4-5 delivered in 1609:

> If one be in debt and danger of the *Law*, to have a *Brother* of the same bloud...will little avail him, except he will also come *under the Law*, that is, become his Surety, and undertake for him. And such was our estate. As debtors we were, by vertue of...the *handwriting* that was against us. Which was our *Bond*, and we had forfeited it.... Therefore Hee became bound for us also, entred bond anew, took on Him, not only our *Nature*, but our *Debt*.... The debt of a Capitall Law is Death.

18. Lewalski, p. 42.

19. In *Twelfth Night* there is another Antonio, a sea captain, who bears much the same relation to the character Sebastian, as Antonio in *The Merchant* bears to Bassanio. The *Twelfth Night* Antonio claims to have rescued Sebastian from drowning:

> That most ingrateful boy there by your side,
> From the rude sea's enrag'd and foamy mouth

> *Did I redeem*; a wreck past hope he was;
> His life I gave him, and did thereto add
> My love, without retention or restraint,
> All his in dedication; *for his sake*
> Did I expose myself, pure for his love,
> Into the danger of this adverse town. (V.i.75-82; italics mine)

Like Antonio the merchant, Antonio the sea captain plies his young friend with money.

20. Lewalski, p. 47
21. Bloom, p. 24.
22. Bloom, pp. 24 and 30.
23. Bloom, p. 29.
24. Bloom, p. 30.
25. Bloom, p. 31.
26. Plutarch, "Life of Marcus Brutus," *The Lives of the Noble Grecians and Romans*, John Dryden, trans. (New York: Random House, Modern Library, n.d.), p. 1193.
27. Lord Normand, *University of Edinburgh Journal* 10 (1939), 44. Quoted by John Russell Brown, seventh Arden edition, p. li.
28. Keeton, pp. 20-21.

Shakespeare's *Hamlet* and Machiavelli: How Not To Kill A Despot

John E. Alvis

Why Hamlet delays killing his father's murderer, King Claudius, perplexes readers of the play as well as Hamlet himself. I propose to approach this familiar problem from a somewhat novel angle by asking whether Hamlet addresses in a politically responsible manner the task of killing Claudius. My view is that he does not, and my interest lies in seeking to understand the cause of Hamlet's failing to execute responsibly a just retribution for the king's crime. Why does Hamlet neglect his role as a prince entrusted with the duty of securing the welfare of his nation? In pursuing an answer to that problem one may understand something about Shakespeare's thoughts on tyrannicide as well as something about the way Shakespeare regards Christianity. Because it appears Hamlet's failure owes to his particular version of Christian belief.

We may begin by reminding ourselves of the teaching of Machiavelli, a thinker who faulted Christians for regarding it as morally reprehensible to assassinate even tyrannical rulers. On my reading of Shakespeare's play the dramatist agrees with Machiavelli that lacking a vigorous dedication to political liberty Christians prove weak opponents of tyrants. Shakespeare seems partly to agree with Machiavelli in the remedy he envisions. The problem of reconciling Christian morality with the necessity of tyrannicide comes to sight once we view the irresolute prince of Denmark in contrast to a responsible resistance to despotism Shakespeare had earlier depicted when he portrayed the expulsion of a bad king from ancient pagan Rome.

Shakespeare's plays concerned with the killing of kings encourage us to reflect upon the issue Machiavelli raises in a famous remark about the success of despotic rulers in Christian times. In his *Discourses on Livy*

Machiavelli draws a contrast between virile Roman paganism and effeminate contemporary religion.[1] Christianity, he maintains, elevates the life of passivity, humility, and contemplation of otherworldly rewards over the life of spirited activity, politics, and honor-seeking in this world. Christianity thus disposes men more to suffer than to perform deeds of strength. Machiavelli argues that Christianity makes men servile in two ways: First, by diverting hopes of happiness toward an afterlife, Christian piety weakens our devotion to the here-and-now; second, by extolling the nobility of patiently enduring one's lot in life, Christian teaching discourages men from undertaking a manly contest with fortune. Machiavelli warns that although the goddess Fortuna holds sway over about one half of human affairs, we ought not credit her with more. Yet Christianity, by equating the status quo with God's providence, in effect yields everything to fortune. The political consequence of this outlook is that contemporary Europe finds itself exposed to the mischief of wicked rulers who alone accept the invitation to enter upon a struggle with fortune. Christian threats of hell and promises of heaven have succeeded better in weakening resistance to tyrants than in preventing malefactors from grasping power. The remedy Machiavelli identifies is a revival of ancient Roman education with its focus on manliness and the acquisition of glory. Christians should learn to imitate the worldly Romans who beatified only captains of armies and leaders of republics, men like the military hero Camillus or Marcus Brutus, the slayer of Caesar, men distinguished by greatness of temper and strength of body.

Literary critics tend to believe that Shakespeare is an adversary of Machiavelli, an opinion which may be true in some final sorting out of the two authors' teachings. We should not suppose, however, that because Shakespeare's plays offer examples of generosity and justice correcting Machiavellian cynicism, he cannot agree with a portion of Machiavelli's diagnosis and program. Portrayals of the acquiescence of Christian realms to usurpers, tyrants, or corrupt rulers in the English history plays, Macbeth, and Hamlet suggest that Shakespeare intends to focus upon the same malady Machiavelli had claimed was afflicting Christendom. Hamlet depicts a murderer-usurper whose Christian conscience, however it may disturb him when he prays, does not deter his crime nor alter his resolve to continue to enjoy ill-acquired gains. The same play presents us with a prince who allows himself to be distracted from his duty by preoccupations with discontents arising from a Christian sense of universal sinfulness. Shakespeare wrote Hamlet not very long after he had composed the story of the Roman Republic's origin in response to the rape of a noble woman by a despot's son. In Shakespeare's Romans of that poem I propose we can perceive a solution to Prince Hamlet's problems.

Prior to staging *Hamlet*, Shakespeare had depicted two plots against reputed tyrants in a Roman setting. First was his early narrative poem *The Rape of Lucrece*. Later, probably just before writing *Hamlet*, he had dramatized Marcus Brutus's conspiracy against Julius Caesar. That the Lucrece poem affords the more revealing parallels I would argue on the following grounds. Lucrece's situation resembles Hamlet's in that she, like Hamlet, finds herself provoked to vengeance by a criminal act directed against her and her family. Like Hamlet, she confronts a ruler firmly established in his usurped position of authority. At a certain point in her sufferings, like Hamlet she blames fortune and, as Hamlet does, views suicide as her means of relief from her troubles. Like Hamlet, moreover, Lucrece must confront the moral challenge of avenging the tyrant's crime in a politically responsible manner, as opposed to taking revenge without thought of public consequences. The earlier poem offers a further illuminating parallel in the character who becomes Lucrece's partner in deposing the tyrant.[2] The Republican founder Junius Brutus resembles Hamlet in pretending insanity, but the Roman's effectiveness in taking purposeful action contrasts with Hamlet's ineffectuality and irresponsibility.

Lucrece suffers the ugliest crime Shakespeare attributes to any tyrant: violation by sexual humiliation of her right to her own body. Sextus Tarquinius, the son of the ruling despot Tarquinius Superbus, at sword point rapes this wife of his patrician rival, adding to his threat to murder her the vow that if she resists he will kill a slave, place the slave's corpse in the bed with her dead body, and testify that he discovered Lucrece in adultery. The narrative indicates that Lucrece submits partly out of fear of death but more from dread of the dishonor that would accompany her death if her assailant should make good his threat. In her first moments of distraction after young Tarquin departs Lucrece's thoughts resemble those of Hamlet when he thinks about Claudius's murdering his father. She impertinently seeks to place the blame for the crime upon remote impersonal causes, accusing Time, Opportunity, and Night for having made possible Sextus's violation of her bed. She gives way momentarily to the metaphysical disgust Hamlet voices whenever he considers the prevalence of strong evil over weak goodness.

Yet Lucrece soon realizes the impracticality of such complaints and gains an insight into her plight sufficient to produce purposeful action.

Her means of discovery is a work of art, a painting on the wall of her bedchamber depicting the burning of Troy. As she contemplates this portrayal of the destruction of a great city she draws two important conclusions: First, her personal ruin resembles the sack of Troy in that the offense she has suffered epitomizes the general wrong her city suffers from despotism—no person is secure in his rights if his very body is vulnerable to the tyrant's plunder. Second, Lucrece now perceives that since the crime standing behind the offense perpetrated upon her is the political crime of tyranny, to avenge it she must act politically, not privately. The despotic power of the king-father has licensed the son's lust much as the power of old Priam, autocratic ruler of Troy, had sanctioned the theft of Helen by his son Paris. When Lucrece exclaims that Troy would have survived had Priam checked Priam's son's criminal desire for another man's wife (1490),[3] we see that she has detected ultimate responsibility for the fall of the city not in the adulterer Paris, but in the despotic monarch who had not been accountable to the people he ruled. Similarly, she will not adequately avenge herself nor benefit her city unless she can manage to bring to justice the ultimate Roman criminal, the despotic king behind the criminal son.

Like Hamlet, Lucrece contemplates suicide, but the manner in which she eventually takes her life shows that she has advanced from initial desperation to resolute, politically beneficial conduct. In the course of deliberating her suicide Lucrece conceives a plan whereby she may make her self-destruction the means for her people's liberation. She resolves to take her life only after she has arranged for her husband and her father to be present to witness her death and has required their oath to avenge her. Her kinsmen arrive accompanied by friends whom Lucrece also charges to take an oath of vengeance. Lucrece thereby makes the private crime a public issue and thus ensures that her husband's vengeance will take the form of a political revolution. Although devout Lucrece believes in gods, she will not rely on divine punishment exacted from the Tarquins in the indefinite future or afterlife. She requires justice here and now by human means, and she relies on her own resources to get it.

Lucrece transforms herself from a private to a public person and from a subject to a citizen. She becomes as it were the first citizen of the new Roman Republic. The tyrant will be expelled and the Romans will pledge themselves never again to permit one man rule. Lucrece provides more than merely the occasion for founding a free government. Her intelligent public-spirited fashioning of her revenge has practically obliged her kinsmen and their friends to liberate the city if they are to avoid disgrace, and her example of valuing her honor more than her life has given Romans their first lesson in sustaining political liberty. Honor in Shakespeare's Rome will be tied to service to the commonweal. Her husband's companion, Junius Brutus, joins his resourcefulness to hers in founding the new regime. He earns his fame as co-founder when he makes a public speech citing the rape as proof that the tyranny is unendurable and charging the populace to join in avenging Lucrece, expelling Tarquin, and establishing free institutions in place of kings. By alluding at this point to Brutus's celebrated pretense of insanity, Shakespeare suggests his agreement with Machiavelli that the conspirator had long prepared for the tyrannicide and was awaiting just such a cause as Lucrece has provided.[4]

From these successful Roman tyrannicides we may extract three lessons on the responsible killing of bad kings. First, effective resistance to tyrants requires that one rely on human enterprise rather than on hope of some manifestation of divine providence. Both Lucrece and Brutus know that the gods do not intervene either to prevent or to punish crimes committed by despots. At least the gods do not punish in a timely manner in this life. Such a reflection causes one to view as weak-spirited the principle Shakespeare puts in the mouth of John of Gaunt who in response to an appeal that he avenge a murder ordered by a king says he must await judgment by "heaven" (*Richard II*, I.ii.6). The second lesson one might derive from the example of Lucrece is that the impetus for resistance to oppressive government arises from a sense of sharing a common political fate with one's countrymen. The deed of resistance must be regarded not personally, as the privilege of private revenge, but politically, as an obligation on behalf of the common good. Crimes committed in private that cannot be revenged without causing great damage to the civil community may have to go unavenged. On the other hand, crimes that strike at fundamental rights, which civil society exists in order to safeguard, subject the ruler to retribution carried to the point of killing if there are no institutions available for a public adjudication at law. The third principle one is entitled to gather from Lucrece's story is that a reliable guarantee of resistance to tyranny lies in a spirited sense of personal honor. Lucrece identifies her honor with earning the good opinion of her compatriots. She anticipates that her heroic suicide will win her fame among future Romans who will enjoy the liberty she has won for them. With the same concern, she states that she has taken her own life because if she consents to live on after her violation, she fears she would provide Roman wives with a damaging precedent for excusing infidelity

(1714-1715). A sense of one's honor as a citizen ensures against abject passivity under oppression. The understanding implied here may be that every person enjoys such honor as he possesses on condition of regarding that honor as held in public trust. In vindicating herself Lucrece vindicates her fellow Romans, as does Junius Brutus who explicitly states the principle at stake (1831-1833).

Having now before us Shakespeare's portrayal of an effective Roman resistance to tyranny, we may turn to the more complicated work and consider Hamlet's problems from a political vantage. What implications attach to Shakespeare's examination of a Christian prince confronting the task of exposing crime perpetrated by a ruler and called upon to provide relief for his nation? How do Hamlet's situation, thoughts, and deeds compare with the situation, thought, and deeds of the Roman tyrannicides, and what is it in Hamlet's character that accounts for the contrast one senses between the strength of the Romans and the weakness of the Dane? From the comparison I propose we may infer Shakespeare's purpose is to teach his predominantly Christian audience the wisdom of adjusting its religious beliefs to requirements of political justice.

Compared with those of Lucrece and Brutus, Hamlet's deeds appear ill considered and politically feeble. Although Hamlet belatedly manages to slay Claudius, he does so in a manner ruinous to Denmark. Instead of bringing Claudius to book Hamlet stabs his uncle in the midst of a confusion for which he is largely responsible. By choking off Claudius's last words, moreover, Hamlet prevents any dying confession, the only means of bringing to public knowledge Claudius's guilt for the original murder and usurpation. By his delay Hamlet has contributed to his mother's death, and by his own imprudent decisions he has made himself responsible for the murder of Polonius, the consequent madness and death of Ophelia, and the deaths of the (probably guiltless) Rosencrantz and Guildenstern. Most telling for his country's political fortunes Hamlet fails to preserve himself. The prince's death deals a serious wound to Denmark since, as the designated future king, Hamlet's obligation is to provide the realm with a transition from Claudius's despotism to decent government. Finally and most damaging to the political well-being of the state, Hamlet leaves his country defenseless against a foreign invader. In fact he ratifies Fortinbras's illegitimate acquisition of Denmark for Norway with his dying words. For Machiavelli, but not only for Machiavelli, losing the independence of one's fatherland is the gravest of political sins. Besides delivering the Danes into the hands of the man they have been preparing to defend themselves against, Hamlet leaves them dismayed with the spectacle of a bloodbath which, for all they can possibly know, appears to prove his own treason driven by ambition or madness.

Lucrece and Brutus address themselves to their duty more purposefully than Hamlet but not because they draw upon superior native endowments of courage. Although Hamlet once accuses himself of cowardice (II.ii.556-563), the play gives convincing evidence of his willingness to undertake dangers. Dismissing the cautions his friends advise, Hamlet insists upon confronting the Ghost on the battlements. He baits Claudius continually and insults the king's spies. He fights with pirates and accepts a challenge to duel with an enemy intent on lethal revenge. We have no reason ever to doubt his early declaration of indifference to preserving his life (I.iv.65). At another point Hamlet supposes too much thinking may account for his inaction. Yet it appears not too much thought but the wrong kind of thinking prevents decisive conduct. At several critical moments of the play we can perceive marked contrasts between Hamlet's character-revealing thoughts and those of Shakespeare's Romans. One constellation of Hamlet's thoughts revolves about the concept of fortune, another about the doctrine of human depravity. Both topics Hamlet finds disheartening, yet he does not realize that his dwelling upon them disables him for the task he must discharge.

Hamlet does realize some confusion of spirit deprives him of the footing he needs to undertake purposeful action. Early in the play he speaks of his mind as a "distracted globe" (I.v.97) and at the end of the scene in which he receives his commission from the Ghost to purify the throne of Denmark he says he feels the task to be a spiteful one and a curse (188-189). From the various meditations Hamlet displays over the course of the first three Acts one can infer that the distractedness he acknowledges but cannot account for owes to a particular recurrent idea. He is obsessed with the notion of human helplessness under a general despotism he attributes to the operation of fortune. The speech Hamlet commands the Visiting Player to recite in Act Two allows us to see how this sad theme has thrown him off balance. Although the verse is fustian, we have no reason to doubt Hamlet's own avowal when before the rehearsal he praises the lines as the part he chiefly loved of a play he highly esteems. The thirteen lines Hamlet thereupon recites to cue the Player establish his intimate familiarity with this set speech. The subject of the piece is the same as that of the tapestry Lucrece had contemplated, the fall of Troy. We have earlier noted the lesson Lucrece derived from her meditation, but the attraction of the Trojan disaster for Hamlet needs to be explained. Why does Hamlet admire these overwrought passages which seem so foreign to Shakespeare's own style?

Presumably Hamlet has chosen this particular material because the thoughts and emotions transmitted in the passage accord with his own thought and with the emotions he himself habitually feels. Obviously pathos attaching to King Priam's death agony accords with the sorrow Hamlet has felt over his own kingly father's death, and the indignation directed by the Player against the assassin, "hellish" Pyrrhus, matches Hamlet's outrage against his father's murderer. Beyond these immediate circumstantial connections, however, the speech echoes Hamlet's characteristic complaints against the malignancy of a personified "Fortune." I conjecture Hamlet has always enjoyed this particular diatribe because it satisfies his sense of indignation against a universal injustice that he imagines human beings suffer now and always. Hamlet hears in the Player's complaint confirmation of a philosophical conviction he expresses at beginning, middle, and toward the end of the play: a conviction that no caring deity overrules the wrongs imposed by blind happenstance.

Our supposition finds support in the observation that the Player's most notable addition to the narration of Troy's destruction comes with his lengthy indictment of Goddess Fortuna between lines 481 and 504. Even voluble Polonius complains against the length of the speech, but Hamlet irritably rebukes Polonius for breaking in and insists that the entire long-winded rant be heard. Hamlet evidently sympathizes with this plaintive Aeneas who interrupts his narration to Dido in order to call Fortune a "strumpet" and who proposes the other gods should expropriate Fortune's wheel and roll it down from heaven "As low as to the fiends." The Player has done no more than give expression to the same sort of protest a despondent Hamlet has uttered several times. We recall, for instance, Hamlet's having spoken of Fortune as a whore (II.ii.232) and having scolded her for her role in human disasters or misdeeds. Hamlet thinks of fortune as a capricious agent whose ordinary work is corruption and whose practice is inconstancy. To Horatio he has confided his disappointment in observing that otherwise perfect men are often ruined by some single defect, the effect of "fortune's star" (I.iv.32). In the best known of the seven soliloquies it will be the oppressiveness of "outrageous fortune" that will prompt Hamlet to question whether it be nobler to bear with injuries or escape them by self-destruction. Consequently one is not surprised to discover that the second theatrical performance Hamlet demands of the touring company features a couplet expressing the dismay Hamlet himself experiences when he puzzles over first causes: "'Tis a question left us yet to prove,/ Whether love lead fortune, or else fortune love" (III.ii.194-195). His mother's abrupt transfer of affections has provoked Hamlet's disgust by affording proof of woman's fickleness. Gertrude's weakness confirms his suspicion that "our loves...with our fortunes change" (193). Another item of Hamlet's charge against caprice seems to him provided in the recent popularity of Claudius, who now has people clamoring to purchase his miniature portrait although they had previously treated him with contempt (II.ii.355-358). From these several instances of Hamlet's disappointment over human instability one may infer that he now desires to hear again this account of Priam's woes because his own recent experience agrees with the tenor of the speech: ours is a world held hostage by degrading, undiscriminating chance. From *her* meditation on the fall of Troy, Lucrece draws a sense of her political responsibility. From *his* meditation on the same story, Hamlet extracts confirmation of his right to be disheartened by the instability of our lives under the buffetings of fortune.

Hamlet's conviction that fortune bears down every good thing trails a painful corollary in the thought that such divinities as may exist hold themselves aloof from human concerns. The gods would surely depose a capricious goddess of chance who allows Priam's slaughter and all the innocent deaths incident to the fall of this populous city. The pitiable spectacle would move their tears, says the Player, unless, he concedes, "things mortal move them not at all" (II.ii.504). Since, however, the gods obviously did not intervene to spare this calamity, the inference must be that indeed heaven is indifferent to mankind. Things mortal move them not at all. As far as suffering mortals can observe nothing is changed by replacing pagan divinities with the Christian God. To bring to cases, God has not intervened to preserve the good king or to prevent the criminal success of the wicked usurper. This attribution of indifference to heaven would deny the operation of God's benign providence in human affairs. Such a view of heaven's silence need not be discouraging as is evident from the example of Shakespeare's Romans. But for Hamlet the thought of an uncaring God seems to have produced despondency. Although Junius Brutus also puts no trust in heaven's care to right wrongs, neither does he exaggerate the powers of fortune. Like Hamlet he pretends he has lost his wits. But Brutus adopts the disguise only to permit seizing a favorable opportunity, understanding that for the bold and prudent man who holds himself ready for action fortune may also prove a benefactress. Brutus knew how so to dissimulate that he was not suspected of aiming to liberate his oppressed people. According to Machiavelli he made himself appear demented not only to protect his life and property but besides to gain freedom to plot a revolution. And in Shakespeare's poem the weapon he takes up turns out to be the very knife with which Lucrece has stabbed herself(1807,1843). Because Brutus exemplifies the soul who seizes upon a chance to take arms against fortune, Machiavelli advises those dissatisfied with their ruler to imitate his readiness. We note the contrasting outcome of Hamlet's subterfuge. Hamlet pretends insanity but fails to convey the inoffensive demeanor Brutus had. The reason his disguise fails is that constantly showing through is his truly felt and dangerous metaphysical revulsion. Consequently he alarms Claudius, provokes Polonius's spying upon him, and causes the king to send Rosencrantz and Guildenstern to keep an eye on this menacing malcontent. Hamlet's hatred so clearly evident throughout his pretense thus alerts his enemy, sets afoot Claudius's counterplot, and leads directly to his exposure when he kills the eavesdropping Polonius. Readers disagree over the question to what extent Hamlet's disjointed behavior should be ascribed to real mental derangement rather than to consciously fabricated dissimulation. It seems most likely that Shakespeare intends us to see Hamlet as sane but morally discreditable—discreditable because that animus which ruins his disguise is the product of his unjustifiable and debilitating cosmic resentments. Cynical disgust, sentimental in its excess, saps his initiative, breaks through his disguise, and alerts everyone to the danger he poses. In other words, Hamlet's "antic disposition," his pretended melancholy, amounts to nothing other than transparent exaggeration of his genuine contempt for a world he deems intolerably offensive. Yet the world offends because Hamlet's demands for purity are extravagant.

Beneath Hamlet's continual acerbic jests there is, as Claudius guesses, "something in his soul/ O'er which his melancholy sits on brood" (III.i.164-165). What most obviously preoccupies Hamlet's mind are his Christian beliefs. We are meant to see that Hamlet's melancholy broods on Christian doctrine, or more precisely, on a version—arguably a distortion—of Christian teaching. Claiming the authority of sound doctrine, Hamlet cultivates a philosophical desperation that undermines political dedication by calling into doubt the worthiness of temporal activity of any sort whatsoever. Shakespeare devotes much of the early and middle portions of the play to anatomizing a soul who espouses world-denying aspects of Christian belief while neglecting those Christian teachings that enjoin caring for one's sinful neighbor.

Besides regretting man's vulnerability to fortune, Hamlet's preoccupation with thoughts of moral weakness causes him to view Denmark as a discouraging setting for any endeavor. He laments the drunkenness and "levity" for which his countrymen are notorious, the tainted status of virtue even in good men, and what he considers ubiquitous hypocrisy ("I know not seems" he protests to his mother while accusing her and everyone else of false display). He deplores the human propensity to subject reason to passion, complaining especially of greed, lust, and woman's inconstancy. Of the three sources of evil traditionally recognized by Christians—the world, the flesh, and the devil—Hamlet expatiates on the flesh. *Flesh* is his favorite term of opprobrium. He employs the word both colloquially and as a philosophical term of art. Hamlet identifies sin neither with the worldly attractions of power and glory nor with the active rebelliousness of Lucifer, but locates wickedness in the sordid, half passive, ignominious weaknesses of the body. Chief exhibit in Hamlet's grievances against flesh is Gertrude. Having witnessed his mother's intemperance in her hasty remarriage, Hamlet flays himself with the idea of human vulnerability to lust, a judgment he projects onto a universal canvas. The generalizing tendency of his mind causes him to expatiate upon flesh whenever he speaks of humanity's chief limitation. We perceive this loathing of the body in Hamlet's first extended meditation, the soliloquy with which Shakespeare introduces his protagonist in the first Act. The imagery of that speech deserves some comment since it gives us insight into Hamlet's mind prior to the Ghost's revelation, insight that is into opinions most native to his character carried over from a time previous to the action of the play.

In voicing throughout his diatribe a hatred for everything associated with the body Hamlet introduces a theme upon which he continues to dilate throughout his various speeches. Editors debate whether his first adjective for the body should be construed *solid, sullied,* or *sallied,* but whichever of these emendations one prefers it is at all events a body too obdurate, besmirched, or impure that Hamlet objects to. The body prevents a desired liberation of the soul. Nothing other than Gertrude's subjection to bodily passion has prevented her from maintaining a proper widow's fidelity to a once beloved spouse. Hamlet complains that the vicious strength of lust has usurped "discourse of reason." Yet even when it is not leading us to intemperance the body in Hamlet's opinion humiliates us. Bodily corruption subjects human beings to chance, force, treachery, and mortality. His noble father has gone the way of all flesh. Corporeality stands convicted in Hamlet's opinion as the ultimate cause why the world appears an "unweeded garden" overrun by things "rank and gross." Rank flesh dominates completely, we notice. Hamlet imagines no flowers left among the obnoxious weeds. By rushing to the gross bed of Claudius, Gertrude has given proof that gross matter outweighs noble intentions. Spirit cannot withstand the urgencies of the glands. Whenever he is on stage, Hamlet inveighs against human corporeality. Most of his references to anatomical members are disparaging (e.g., "kissing carrion," "[Fortuna's] waist," "lap," "maid's legs," "candied tongue," "pregnant hinges of the knee," "damned fingers," "pickers and stealers" referring to his own hands, "my edge" referring to his sexual organ). Nausea directed against bodies shows through Hamlet's contemptuous "lug[ging] the guts" in speaking of disposing of the corpse of a man he has murdered (III.iv.213). Such loathing accounts for Hamlet's dwelling upon images of his mother's lovemaking with Claudius. A father promoting his daughter's marriage is in Hamlet's imagination a flesh peddler (i.e., Polonius). Hamlet also likes to imagine the indignities suffered by the deceased. Charnel worms fatten themselves on the decayed bodies of noble historical figures:

> Your worm is your only emperor for diet. We fat all
> Creatures else to fat us, and we fat ourselves for maggots. (IV.iii.21-23)

This resentment of the body continues to be Hamlet's signature emotion right through to the end of the play. Act V presents a Hamlet still descanting upon the indignities to which the greatest men are liable solely because they are fleshbound. In the Gravediggers' scene Hamlet remarks how once deceased Caesar's body undergoes a demeaning progress through the guts of a beggar or produces just sufficient loam to plug the hole in a barrel (V.i.191-203). He takes pleasure in observing that decayed skulls belie feminine cosmetics (180-183). In a sermon to his school friends he identifies flesh corrupted in death with the one inescapable limitation to which will be reduced all the ennobling faculties of reason, movement, and intellectual apprehension. Looking to the spirit, man is the "paragon of animals," but allowing for corporeality, man's "quintessence" diminishes to merely so much "dust" (II.ii.304).

Hamlet does not exempt his beloved from the dragnet of his resentment. Revulsion against the flesh finds an outlet in scurrilous language heaped on Ophelia. We hear this biting invective in the Nunnery scene and in the quips Hamlet utters during the performance staged by the touring actors. However ungracious, Hamlet's mistreatment of Ophelia is not inexplicable, given his reduction of moral evil to bodily inclinations. What one supposes to have been at one time genuine affection for

Ophelia gives way to cruel misogyny in Hamlet's reaction to the outrage done his sense of propriety by Gertrude's transfer of affection. Hamlet will not subject himself to such inconstancy as his mother has displayed. So he reverts to sarcasm in the love letter Polonius reads, i.e., "To the celestial, and my soul's idol, the most beautified Ophelia"(II.ii.109). Subsequently Hamlet takes his revenge on her by insulting the young woman with lewd innuendo.

Some commentators have argued Ophelia deserves Hamlet's rejection because, they conjecture, Hamlet detects Claudius and Polonius spying upon the couple in the Nunnery scene and infers Ophelia's complicity in plotting against him. Yet *prior* to this scene Hamlet has practiced deception upon her, and it appears more likely he now excuses harsh treatment of the woman he once loved because he feels entitled to revenge himself upon all women. Women are after all open to the charge of perpetuating human embodiment. Generating is a crime in his eyes: "why wouldst thou be a breeder of sinners?" (III.i.121-122). Because he condemns human sexuality in general, there is more than pretended irrelevancy in Hamlet's prohibition of any further marriages (143), for, if human beings did not generate, disagreeable bodily limitations would not be perpetuated in the race.

Connected with his revulsion against fortune, flesh, inconstancy, and hypocrisy we observe Hamlet's fascination with the notion of suicide. In the first, and again in the central of the seven soliloquies, Hamlet considers suicide an attractive escape from all the ills we endure from being creatures of flesh. This is evident when Hamlet itemizes his several reasons for preferring not to be. It is notable that in posing the question "To be or not to be" Hamlet hypothesizes a case for suicide on behalf of all men at all times. The grievances he lists are grievances not particularly pertinent to his present situation. He has not crouched under an oppressor, nor has he suffered the "proud man's contumely." Hamlet has inflicted but not sustained "the pangs of despised love." In his own person he has not had to put up with "the law's delay" or with insolent office holders, or felt the "spurns" heaped by the unworthy upon "patient merit"—unless imaginatively, this elegant prince has presumably never borne weighty physical burdens ("Who would fardels bear to grunt and sweat under a weary life?"). We conclude that instead of dwelling upon his actual pains Hamlet is here devising a justification for self-destruction that will have the widest conceivable application. He has cast a wide net absurdly hyperbolic and, indeed, tantamount to the claim that life is not worth the living if attended with any considerable misfortune. But then for Hamlet, as we have seen, to be confined to a body is itself an unacceptable affront to a soul that requires absolute purity. Suicide is Hamlet's revenge against the flesh. As he puts it, self-destruction promises deliverance from "the thousand natural shocks that flesh is heir to" (62-63).

Hamlet's preoccupation with suicide contrasts with the attitude toward self-destruction exhibited by Shakespeare's Romans. The suicides portrayed in the plays set in the pagan city and in *The Rape of Lucrece* exemplify extreme but defensible demonstrations of friendship or patriotism. Shakespeare's Romans destroy themselves when convinced they can by no other means preserve honor. Or, in Lucrece's case, the aim is to secure simultaneously fame and the public good. Hamlet on the other hand proposes a fantastic and unmanly escapist dream yearning to flee the general inheritance of humanity. In contempt of the human allotment he desires to shuffle off that burdensome life which he can only think of as a chain, a "mortal coil." Nothing in the nature of man or civil society seems of sufficient worth to convince Hamlet that he ought to accept Adam's legacy. Grudgingly acquiescent to a Christian law forbidding suicide, Hamlet perceives no justice in that law. Lucrece, acknowledging such a divine interdict but intent upon benefiting her country, follows a higher obligation and makes her suicide the means of ridding Rome of tyranny. She consults a sense of justice that proportions means to ends and prudently accommodates principle to circumstance. Once she comes to see her duty Lucrece is freer than Hamlet because she neither clings to life nor despises it. She is thus free to expend her blood in a public cause.

Hamlet by contrast expresses the sadness which has unmanned him for political action in a reply he mutters to Polonius when the courtier asks permission to depart: "You cannot take anything that I will more willingly part withal—except my life, except my life, except my life" (II.ii.213-215). "To be or not to be" manifestly is not the question. What to do about ridding Denmark of despotic Claudius is the question that should occupy Hamlet's attention. Yet to distract himself with such an irrelevancy is quite in character. The prince permits himself to be deflected from his political duty on principle, so to say. His philosophical reflections on the vanity of human effort have convinced him that striving is futile because no effort can improve a world held in bondage by the flesh. If the world is lost in any case, what matters Denmark?

What exactly has this metaphysical despondency to do with Hamlet's theological beliefs? We might conclude that Hamlet has interpreted the

Christian doctrine of man's fallen condition in the extreme terms prescribed by a Calvinistic insistence upon total depravity resulting from original sin. Reminiscent of this doctrine, Hamlet assures Ophelia that however we may overlay our inherited sin with graftings of virtue, our "old stock" will necessarily reassert itself (III.i.116-117). The metaphysician in Hamlet thinks of matter as principle of corruption while the moralist makes a case against bodily allurements. He distrusts physical beauty because it does the work of a pander degrading "honesty" to the role of a "bawd" and soliciting us with temptations to lust (III.i.109-111). The Augustinian and Calvinist notion of original sin holds that Adam's disobedience had two consequences: the first sin made his descendants subject to death and undermined the rule of reason over the passions so that man inclines to evil in the form of concupiscence or irascibility, lust or anger. Hamlet denounces our old stock on two counts: the body subjects us to death, weakness, excess, and it beguiles with the spurious bait of sexual pleasure compellingly attractive to our intemperate leanings. His father's fate has substantiated the first charge, his mother's inconstancy the second.

Martin Luther's teaching is also relevant to the theme we have been considering. In view of allusions to Hamlet's recent study at Wittenberg (Luther's academic stronghold) and to the quibble on "convocation of politic worms" (the Diet of Worms condemned Luther's doctrines), Shakespeare seems to have had Luther in mind as he created the character Hamlet. In his commentary on Galatians, Luther states that he finds in St. Paul's theology the essence of Christian teaching:

> Now the true meaning of Christianity is this: that a man first acknowledge, through the law that he is a sinner, for whom it is impossible to perform any good work. For the Law says: "You are an evil tree [Hamlet's "old stock?"]. Therefore everything you think, speak, or do is opposed to God. Hence you cannot deserve grace by your works. But if you try to do so, you make the bad even worse; for since you are an evil tree you cannot produce anything except evil fruits, that is, sins."

Luther represents himself as a faithful disciple of Paul in this extreme disparagement of the worth of natural virtue. Certainly Luther—and Hamlet—have seized upon one genuine theme of Pauline Christianity. This extreme depreciation of human effort is not Paul's only theme, but his preaching against the flesh may be the lesson best remembered by Christians who emphasize, as Hamlet does, the struggle of spirit against body.

In its most severe forms this war against the body's sinfulness produced a dualist mentality which in some sects could go the length of
extolling suicide as liberation and condemning marriage on the same
grounds as Hamlet condemns begetting children. The medieval Cathari
taught that the body was the prison of the soul. Hamlet's extreme asceticism is similar in temper. Given his sense of universal defilement associated with embodiment Hamlet might well endorse the prayer attributed
to the Cathari: "Have no mercy on the flesh born in corruption but have
mercy on the spirit held in prison."[5]

The state of mind Hamlet espouses presumably would threaten to
overwhelm any young man called upon to act in a world that seems unworthy of his exertions. But for a man nurtured on Christian teachings,
encountering evil poses the further problem of reconciling the existence
of evil with belief in a beneficent and omnipotent Creator. Although
Hamlet's skepticism of human goodness never expands into atheism, he
does imagine a complete disjunction between a God who is pure but
unapproachably distant and a world impure and unredeemable. So thor-
oughgoing is this denial of vestiges of God's goodness in creatures that
one may conclude Hamlet has combined Christian piety with nihilism.[6]
The nihilist holds the world as it is to be intolerable whereas the world as
it ought to be is impossible. Hamlet's nihilist convictions dishearten him
for any demanding deed that calls for deliberation or for any difficult
political enterprise. He cannot accept the limitations one must accept if
one is to achieve political ends, ends which by necessity are limited in the
good they accomplish.

Nietzsche, the connoisseur of nihilism, recognizes a kindred spirit
in Hamlet:

> While the transport of the Dionysiac state, with its suspension
> of all the ordinary barriers of existence, lasts, it carries with it a
> Lethean element in which everything which has been experi-
> enced by the individual is drowned. This chasm of oblivion
> separates the quotidian reality from the Dionysiac. But as soon
> as that quotidian reality enters consciousness once more, it is
> viewed with loathing, and the consequence is an ascetic, abulic
> state of mind. In this sense Dionysiac man might be said to
> resemble Hamlet: both have looked deeply into the true na-
> ture of things, they have *understood* and are now loath to act.
> They realize that no action of theirs can work any change in
> the eternal condition of things, and they regard the imputation
> as ludicrous or debasing that they should set right the time
> which is out of joint. Understanding kills action, for in order to

act we require the veil of illusion; such is Hamlet's doctrine....
(*Birth of Tragedy*, sec. VII).

Although Nietzsche considers Hamlet's nihilism to constitute a true perception of reality, Shakespeare's political understanding, evident not only
in *Hamlet* but also in the successful statesmanship of wise men and women
in the comedies as well as in *The Rape of Lucrece*, would seem to be
rendered impossible on the assumption that the dramatist endorses
Hamlet's philosophical desperation.

Shakespeare invites us to perceive the practical consequence of
Hamlet's spiritual disorder in a scene he places at the center of the play,
the crisis of Hamlet's happening upon Claudius at prayer in his chamber.
Killing the despotic usurper when he is caught thus in solitude would
fulfill the Ghost's command, save Denmark from further abuse, and because the circumstances afford secrecy, preserve Hamlet for his role as
the next king (Claudius has publicly declared his support for his nephew
in the next election [III.ii.328], and Hamlet, we are told [IV.iii.4], enjoys
the favor of the people). To a man disposed to view his situation politically from the vantage of a prince, coming upon unprotected, kneeling
Claudius might appear a providential arrangement. But despite his title
of Prince and king designate, and in contradiction to the expectations of
everyone in the court, Hamlet does not habitually view his opportunities
in the way proper to a statesman, and he does not so view them in this
instance. Hamlet can think of himself at this point only in the role of
instrument of unlimited vengeance, not as one who could be content to
secure a confined, political good. He decides, therefore, to delay the
killing until he may come upon Claudius in some act of sin that will damn
his soul (III.iv.88-95). The opportunity for a responsible execution of the
regicide once passed by will not offer itself again. Although Hamlet will
eventually destroy Claudius, the purge will take away Hamlet himself
and leave his country without leadership under the threat of foreign domination. Shakespeare invites his audience to deplore Hamlet's pious cruelty when passing over this opportunity for justice, Hamlet insists that
Claudius be consigned to hell when it suffices that he merely be removed
from Denmark. Hamlet's all-or-nothing moral absolutism here demands
a vengeance in excess of what justice requires because he conceives himself to inhabit a world so shot through with evil that nothing short of
ensuring the eternal perdition of bad men seems worth his efforts.

Lucrece requires no vengeance beyond eliminating tyranny because
Shakespeare's Romans do not depict human existence as a cosmic struggle
between benign and evil supernatural agents. But within a soul agitated

by dualist beliefs retribution becomes apocalyptic and boundless, rather than political and circumscribed. So Hamlet feels he must reach beyond the commission given by his father's ghost, translating that limited command into a plenary warrant from God designating him heaven's "scourge and minister" (III.iv.176). We must wonder whether the qualification accompanying the Ghost's charge—"taint not thy mind" (I.v.85)—ought not be understood as a warning against just the sort of presumption Hamlet here displays. The father's spirit evidently disapproves of the son's plan for engineering Claudius's damnation because when he reappears in the closet scene he rebukes Hamlet, reminding him of his "almost blunted purpose" (III.iv.112). The Ghost cares nothing for what happens to Claudius's immortal soul but only that the throne of Denmark be spared further dishonor. That a disembodied spirit may care more for the welfare of the realm than its living prince shows how far Hamlet has deviated from a proper view of his social station and his political duty.

Hamlet cannot enter upon a course of deliberative action because he has come to deprecate the ends which men pursue through their deliberate deeds. No longer confident of the choiceworthiness of love, political justice, or patriotism, he is left with no other impetus but the morally dubious motive of personal revenge. The same disposition towards cosmic resentment which has deprived him of interest in matters that ought to occupy a prince now makes attractive a revenge eternal in its effect. Such a revenge is only something to be dreamed of. Hamlet would never lay hands upon the murderer of his father were he not thrown into collision with Claudius by the series of unplanned events that constitute most of the action of the last two Acts.

Yet by the end of the play such a marked change of circumstance transpires—from Hamlet helpless in custody of Rosencrantz and Guildenstern to Hamlet seemingly in command of Denmark's future— so marked the apparent change that we may feel we are to infer some correspondingly thorough recovery on Hamlet's part. On at least the important issue of God's providence we observe that he does reverse his earlier cynicism. Does Hamlet then overcome his earlier self to succeed in discharging his obligation as a prince?

An answer to the question whether the play exhibits some heroic development in its protagonist depends upon one's view of the incidents extending from Hamlet's killing of Polonius to the scene depicting his own death; and, especially, the issue turns upon one's estimate of the degree of moral recovery conveyed by such actions as Hamlet's boarding the pirate ship and his fencing match with Laertes. A tendency among some readers to perceive a regenerated Hamlet in the final Act rests upon two items of evidence: Hamlet does slay Claudius; and he announces a new-found composure before the catastrophe signalized by his expressing his trust in heaven's supervision. C. S. Lewis, probably the best known of the exponents of the reading of a Hamlet redeemed, maintains that the speech to Horatio in which Hamlet makes allusion to Matthew's Gospel and God's care for sparrows is the "precise moment" at which a Hamlet who Lewis thinks has previously "lost his way" finds it once again.[7] Supposedly he finds himself when he gives over thinking and yields his will to God's direction. Critics who attribute a moral renewal to Hamlet generally conclude that events occurring after Hamlet's murder of Polonius certify the operation of a benign providence. This line of interpretation would make the play something of an heroic melodrama, taking the protagonist to the brink of damnation by despair, then pulling him back to regain faith, shoulder his responsibility, and thereby achieve his salvation. Hamlet near the end tells Horatio "the readiness is all." The decisive test of the authenticity of any supposed recovery must be with regard to that readiness which, as Hamlet maintains, is everything. How are we to understand his claim to be ready?

The context makes clear that Hamlet here means to assure Horatio that he is ready to die, a disposition which in itself would indicate no great change since Hamlet had said as much at the beginning of the play, and of course in two of the famous soliloquies he had desired to die at once. The issue in doubt throughout the play is more whether Hamlet can find the resolve to assume the responsibilities of life than whether he is prepared to escape the burdens of life by dying. The speech about special providence appears to be more hopeful than the earlier statements to the extent that it acknowledges God's disposing of a man's fate. Hamlet now conceives a God who has an interest in him and who will determine the time of his death according to that interest, whereas the Hamlet who admired the scathing reproaches spoken by the Player against indifferent divinity had seen no careful providence superintending human affairs and had evidently endorsed the Player's outrage over uncaring gods. The Hamlet of Act V appears to have risen above his earlier chafing against Fortune's tyranny.

Nevertheless we see no political benefit nor moral clarity emerging from Hamlet's trust in a hidden hand. His duel with Laertes comes about despite Hamlet's own misgivings and despite Horatio's advice that he decline the challenge. Hamlet answers both his own doubts and Horatio's with the speech about the fall of sparrows and God's care. Hamlet's reply is remarkable, however, for its supposition that the only issue at stake is his willingness to hazard himself. He seems to feel that he is at liberty to risk his life so long as he entrusts his fate to providence. But since he is a prince, Hamlet's part is to acknowledge that he holds his life in trust to his countrymen. For the welfare of Denmark depends upon his living on after slaying Claudius to set the country in order by his own rule. Because Claudius is killed in the course of the duel we might by a trick of hindsight mistake Hamlet's acceptance of Laertes's challenge as his embracing the means to come at the king. The final incidents, however, offer no indication that we are to infer such intent. Hamlet mentions no plan to Horatio, although after Osric's exit privacy allows him safely to do so had he conceived a plot. What he does say to Horatio moreover—that he ought to win at the odds (V.ii.200)—seems to establish an intention of taking the contest at face value, merely a gentlemanly exercise confirming a reconciliation with Laertes, though, given the hostility of the court, attended with a certain danger.

Hamlet's consent to fence with Laertes extends the sequence of occurrences in each of which he responds to someone else's initiative. At the outset of the play he is drifting back to Wittenberg despite having already conceived suspicions of Claudius. Quite apart from any effort on Hamlet's part to resolve those suspicions, a supernatural apparition sets him a new purpose. Thereafter he does nothing of consequence for two months. Just as his purpose seems to have dissipated, he hears of the traveling players and hits upon his "Mousetrap" performance. Then, despite his stated desire to "drink hot blood," he again loses his hold on the main point, passing by Claudius and indulging his resentment by playing the confessor to his mother so that the Ghost must reappear to remind him of his commission. Even then, the first mover continues to lie elsewhere than in Hamlet's deliberate will. He submits to being conducted to England, is saved by the improbable attack of the pirate ship, and finds himself pulled back into the orbit of the court by the chance encounter with the mourners at Ophelia's burial. Although Hamlet recites to Horatio a bill of particulars against Claudius (V.ii.64-66), concluding with the rhetorical question

> is't not to be damned
> To let this canker of our nature come
> In further evil? (68-70)

we recall that several times before he has protested with equal vehe-

mence an intent to revenge which he has not made good. Nothing thereafter indicates that Hamlet has taken upon himself the responsibility for
devising definite means for bringing down Claudius. "Readiness" may be
all, but Hamlet apparently is still not ready. Judged by its lack of practical
results Hamlet's newly espoused faith in providence no more promotes
responsible action than did his earlier despair. St. Augustine's exhortation to pray as if everything depends on God, while acting as if everything depends on oneself, is neglected by a Hamlet who has passed from
hatred of fortune to a quietist "let be" (V.ii.212) without acquiring the
balance of trust in God and self-reliance proper, one would suppose, to
the Christian virtue of hope.

From a political standpoint, one must conclude that Hamlet's announcement of trust in an all-disposing divine providence is in its effect
indistinguishable from the hopelessness he had earlier expressed when
he had exaggerated the sovereignty of fortune. Neither his doctrinaire
denunciation of corrupt nature nor his eleventh hour deference to providence suffices to produce the political deeds required of Hamlet. If we
understand the best of heroic purposiveness to be comprehended in the
prudent daring of a Lucrece or Brutus, we can see how Hamlet's Christian reliance on providence prevents him from reviving Roman political
virtue. Lucrece becomes responsible and prudently decisive precisely
when she realizes that she must not look beyond this world of human
interdependence in society to grasp the causes of virtue or the responsibility for crime. Hamlet, by insisting upon seeking beyond character and
choice some invisible supervening cause of human events, robs himself
once more of initiative. At the very moment he thinks he discerns such a
cause in heaven's ordinance, the audience knows that Hamlet will die not
by divine arrangement but as the result of Claudius and Laertes' criminal purposes abetted by Hamlet's own culpable passivity. The death scene
suggests that forbearing to act while presuming upon divine care allows
evil men to assume the direction of affairs. Hamlet's failure to discharge
the political obligation to which he has been called points up the significant difference between Lucrece's pagan regime, wherein moral responsibility clearly reposes in man, and Denmark's Christian order, wherein
an uncertain boundary divides human from divine government. This
ambiguity of jurisdiction, so to speak, has figured from the outset, inasmuch as the political question of how to oppose Claudius's despotism has
been muddled by the question of whether the Ghost speaks with Heaven's
authority or Hell's. Hamlet had then neglected the troubling yet soluble
political problem in favor of the impossible project of determining the

Ghost's veracity. Now, at the end, he prefers his theological musing to purposeful thought because he is never quite certain where God's plans leave off and his own ought to begin. Because Hamlet relies on supernatural authority to direct him he takes no thought for the ends of political life or for the statesman's art of fitting means (deeds) to ends (the good of the nation). For Hamlet, faith supplants prudence, except when despair displaces both faith and prudence.

To a point, then, the implicit teaching of *Hamlet* appears to coincide with Machiavelli's complaints against the politically enervating effects of Christian education. Lucrece's sense of honor serves justice better than Hamlet's version of Christian doctrine. Hamlet first concedes too much to fortune (much more than the half Machiavelli allows), then, at the last, too much to providence. That he agonizes in the first position but takes comfort in the second does not alter the conclusion that for the purpose of accomplishing justice both views are ineffectual. Shakespeare's portrayal of a country usurped by a murderer who prays to the Christian God and left in disarray by a prince who professes Christian belief suggests some sympathy with Machiavelli's arraignment of a Christian education which at the expense of the active promotes passive virtues. Shakespeare appears to give the charge specific point when he depicts the contrite but unregenerate Claudius at prayer, and the play appears in one respect to expand Machiavelli's complaint. Hamlet's distraction shows that irresponsibility is not confined to the meek. Instead, Shakespeare has exemplified in Hamlet's failure political virtue undermined not by the long-suffering humility Machiavelli decried but by an otherworldliness proud and categorical in its certainty that human nature has suffered ruin beyond the capacity of civilization to repair.[8]

It is proper to add, however, that Shakespeare's notion of a remedy would seem to differ from Machiavelli's. Machiavelli professed to find a cure in reviving ambition, making men once again "full of the desire for worldly glory" (*Discourses* II.2). Machiavelli's enthusiasm for strong adventurers such as Castruccio Castracanni, not to mention his approval of Caesare Borgia, makes one think he would sympathize with the self-assertive opportunist Fortinbras, and for the same reason that Hamlet comes to admire this captain of armies who allows no clog of justice to slow his ambition. The name *Fortinbras* ("strong arm") says it all. Machiavelli, who believes that strong arms are more important than good laws, would approve of the Norwegian prince's conquest of fortune. I think it doubtful Shakespeare encourages his audience to correct the weakness of Hamlet with the moral insensitivity of Fortinbras. His Lucrece and Brutus show us a better way, Lucrece by displaying a grasp of honor that entails more than mere ambition.

What then might one conclude about Shakespeare's relation to Machiavelli, about Shakespeare's effective Roman tyrant killers and his ineffective Christian regicide?

Shakespeare's standard of honor conforming to justice finds expression in the heroic integrity of Romans such as Lucrece and Brutus. Machiavelli's heroes are avid for glory but unscrupulous and not much concerned with arranging justice. Hamlet fails because, despising human capacities in general, he expects too little of himself in respect of securing justice. Whereas Machiavelli would loosen moral restraints, Shakespeare's play appears to intend a strengthening of Christian audiences by teaching the dangers of passivity incident to a version of Christian education, a familiar version yet only one of several. Shakespeare's remedy may look to alleviating defects of Christian education by offering as models of conduct public figures who combine patriotism, magnanimity, and dedication to those principles of natural right that unassisted natural reason can perceive. Hamlet probably could not learn from Machiavelli the one thing needful to retrain his melancholy spirit in a proper attachment to his role as prince, that is, he could not learn a regard for his countrymen and a zeal for justice. The difference between Lucrece or Brutus, on the one hand, and Fortinbras on the other, may correspond to the difference between the political standards of Shakespeare and those of Machiavelli. Christianity is not necessarily incompatible in Shakespeare's mind with love of honor, as the examples of his Christian monarch Henry Monmouth and of a number of his French and English noblemen suffice to show.[9] And, as the rarer example of Scotland's Malcolm indicates, Shakespeare can conceive a Christian prince who adequately combines love of country, resoluteness against tyrants, and prudence with a confidence that he will prevail by "the grace of Grace" (*Macbeth* V.viii.72). To more resemble Malcolm than the ineffectually pious Henry VI or the distracted prince of Denmark, Shakespeare may have thought his Christian audience required an education that would revive a proper care for things of this world. The teaching through negative example provided by *Hamlet* encourages audiences to a deeper regard for their earthly city than Hamlet could call forth from his world-weariness and contempt for the flesh.

Notes

A longer version of this essay appeared in John Alvis, *Shakespeare's Understanding of Honor* (Durham, N.C.: Carolina Academic Press, 1990), pp. 59-97.

1. *Discourses*, II.2.
2. My reading of *The Rape of Lucrece* is indebted to the thoughtful remarks on the poem offered by Michael Platt in his *Rome and Romans According to Shakespeare* (Salzburg: Salzburg Studies in English Literature, 1976), pp. 1-40.
3. My text throughout is *The Complete Pelican Shakespeare*, Alfred Harbage general editor (New York: Penguin Books, 1969).
4. *Discourses*, III.2.
5. Cited by Steven Runciman, *The Medieval Manichee: A Study of the Christian Dualist Heresy* (Cambridge: Cambridge University Press, 1960), p. 154.
6. Rebecca West, *The Court and the Castle* (New Haven: Yale University Press, 1957), pp. 27-28, has ascribed to the play itself a mood of unremitting despair:

> The evil in the world is not the product of the specially corrupt present generation, it has its roots in the generations that went before and also were corrupt; it has its roots in the race. There is no use pretending that we can frustrate our sinful dispositions by calling on tradition, because that is also the work of sinful man. This is the situation of our kind as it is shown to us in *Hamlet*, which is as pessimistic as any great work of literature ever written.... What excites Shakespeare in this play is the impossibility of conceiving an action which could justly be termed virtuous, in view of the bias of original sin.

West gives an admirably accurate account of Hamlet's outlook upon his world. It would be a true description of the moral scene Hamlet looks out upon, however, only were it not that Shakespeare causes us to suspect that his protagonist cannot conceive the particular virtuous action he is called to perform, precisely because he attributes too much to the "bias of original sin."

7. "Hamlet: The Prince or the Poem," in *Modern Shakespearean Criticism*, ed. Alvin B. Kernan (New York: Harcourt, Brace & World, 1970), p. 307.
8. Harold Bloom's extravagant tributes to Hamlet illustrate modern readers' and audiences' fondness for a character which evokes their sense of kinship with a personality constantly in revision of itself. Bloom thinks Hamlet has discovered authentic freedom by taking a provisional stance toward his every affection, allegiance, or (momentarily adopted) moral principle. Hamlet thereby provides a charter for anyone who inclines to address life as an es-

say in improvisation wherein sovereignty resides in autonomous will solely. Consequently Bloom can overlook Hamlet's political debits, or, rather, transmute these shortcomings into credits, since, in Bloom's view, they attest Hamlet's freedom to "transcend" political obligation. See *Shakespeare: The Invention of the Human* (New York: Riverhead Books, 1998), pp. 383-431.

Hamlet is indeed the Shakespearean play most symptomatic of modernity in that it enables us to appreciate why the modern imagination attaches to figures who are resolutely individualistic. The question the play raises remains, however, whether Hamlet exerts his attraction over the better part of our natures or the worse?

9. Henry Monmouth's qualifications as a Machiavellian prince have been demonstrated by Vickie Sullivan, "Princes to Act: Henry V as the Machiavellian Prince of Appearance" in Joseph Alulis and Vickie Sullivan, eds., *Shakespeare's Political Pageant: Essays in Politics and Literature* (Lanham, Md.: Rowman & Littlefield, 1996), pp. 125-152.

MACBETH AND THE GOSPELLING OF SCOTLAND

Paul A. Cantor

*I regard the bad conscience as the serious illness that [men were]
bound to contract under the stress of the most fundamental
change [they] ever experienced—that change which occurred
when [they] found [themselves] finally enclosed within the walls
of society and of peace.... Suddenly all their instincts were
disvalued and "suspended." ...They felt unable to cope with the
simplest undertakings; in this new world they no longer possessed their former guides, their regulating, unconscious and
infallible drives: they were reduced to thinking, inferring, reck-
oning, co-ordinating cause and effect...they were reduced to
their "consciousness." ...I believe there has never been such a
feeling of misery on earth...and at the same time the old instincts had not suddenly ceased to make their usual demands!
Only it was hardly or rarely possible to humor them: as a rule
they had to seek new and, as it were, subterranean gratifications.*—Friedrich Nietzsche, *On the Genealogy of Morals*

Midway through *Macbeth*, the newly crowned king tries to convince
some desperate men to murder his rival Banquo. Claiming that in
the past Banquo thwarted their advancement, Macbeth questions whether
the chosen murderers will take their injury lying down. More specifically, his challenge takes the form of asking them if they are prepared to
turn the other cheek:

> Do you find
> Your patience so predominant in your nature
> That you can let this go? Are you so gospell'd,

> To pray for this good man, and for his issue,
> Whose heavy hand hath bow'd you to the grave,
> And beggar'd yours for ever? (III.i.85-90)[1]

In Macbeth's remarkable use of the word *gospell'd* here,[2] we hear the noble warrior's contempt for Christian forbearance and the tame willingness to endure injury without responding. The murderers understand what Macbeth is getting at, and, realizing that their very manhood is being questioned, they reply accordingly: "We are men, my liege" (III.i.90).

Macbeth goes on to articulate the concept of manliness the murderers are alluding to:

> Ay, in the catalogue ye go for men,
> As hounds and greyhounds, mungrels, spaniels, curs,
> Shoughs, water-rugs, and demi-wolves are clipt
> All by the name of dogs; the valued file
> Distinguishes the swift, the slow, the subtle,
> The house-keeper, the hunter, every one,
> According to the gift which bounteous nature
> Hath in him clos'd; whereby he does receive
> Particular addition, from the bill
> That writes them all alike; and so of men. (III.i.91-100)

In its sense that all dogs are not created equal, this speech embodies the aristocratic or heroic conception of manhood.[3] Macbeth is asking the murderers: are you merely run-of-the-mill human beings or are you real men, men who know how to stand up for themselves? The distinction Macbeth is making is best captured in Homeric Greek, in the difference between the terms *aner* and *anthropos*.[4] The Homeric hero is an *aner*, a he-man, raised above the ordinary run of human beings (*anthropoi*) by virtue of his manly strength and courage. In Homer, the difference between the hero and the ordinary human being is often presented as the difference between two kinds of animals, like the contrast between noble and base dogs in Macbeth's speech, or even more like the contrast between tame and wild species drawn earlier in the play when a character talks of "sparrows" versus "eagles" or "the hare" versus "the lion" (I.ii.35). Macbeth sees a natural hierarchy among human beings: some are noble and some are base.[5] Taking the view that a noble man would scorn to receive an injury tamely, Macbeth tries to shame the potential murderers into doing his will. But he realizes that this notion of noble heroism may be challenged in Scotland. A new gospel is abroad in the land, which teaches a Christian way of life, a gospel of peace and humility, opposed to the way of life of the warrior.

Shakespeare develops the tragedy of *Macbeth* out of this tension between the heroic warrior's ethic and the gospel truth. The story of Macbeth gave Shakespeare a chance to portray a world in which Christianity has changed the fabric of society, but in which some characters still think back nostalgically to the time before their nation was gospelled. Shakespeare seems to have been drawn to the situation of characters caught between two ways of life, an old and a new. In his tragedies, he often chose locales that allowed him to portray the clash of ethical alternatives; he liked to set the dramatic action at a point of intersection, a place where two antithetical ways of life cross. The Scotland of *Macbeth* is such a border land. It seems to lie at the crossroads of two different worlds, poised between warlike paganism and saintlike Christianity. At the beginning of the play, the peace of Scotland has been shattered by attacks by more primitive forces stemming from the west and the north, from the Hebrides and Norway (I.i.12, 31). These soldiers are referred to as "kerns and gallowglasses" (I.i.13), archaic terms that suggest foreign and barbaric troops.[6] To the south of Scotland lies England, presented within the terms of the play as a more fully Christian land. In fact England is explicitly said to have a saint as a king, Edward the Confessor, who is repeatedly described in profoundly Christian terms:

> To the succeeding royalty he leaves
> The healing benediction. With this strange virtue,
> He hath a heavenly gift of prophecy,
> And sundry blessings hang about his throne
> That speak him full of grace.   (IV.iii.155-9)[7]

In the symbolic geography of the play, then, Scotland stands as it were midway between Norway and England, less barbaric than Norway but less Christian than England.[8]

This situation is similar to the symbolic geography Shakespeare creates in other tragedies. In *Othello*, for example, Cyprus stands as it were midway between the Christian civilization of Venice and the pagan barbarism of the Ottoman Empire, a situation that reflects the division within Othello's soul.[9] *In Hamlet*, Shakespeare's Denmark conveys the same sense of lying on the fringes of European civilization. To the north of Denmark lies, again, Norway, a land of warlike characters such as Fortinbras, and hence the source of the Homeric heroism of single combat. To the south lie the centers of sophisticated Christian civilization, such as Paris and Wittenberg. The geographic divisions in the play once again reflect divisions within the hero's soul. Hamlet is tragically divided between paganism and Christianity, especially when faced with the duty of revenge, a task to which the two ways of life dictate antithetical responses.[10]

The idea of geography as divided heritage permeates *Macbeth*. The Scottish characters in the play are on the whole presented as believing Christians. Christian expressions come readily to their lips, as, for example, in Macduff's report of the death of Duncan, when he speaks of how "Most sacrilegious murther hath broke ope/ The Lord's anointed temple" (II.iii.67-68). Macbeth himself clearly shows the influence of Christianity, as his wife notes when she is wondering whether he really is up to the challenge of becoming king:

> Yet do I fear thy nature,
> It is too full o' th' milk of human kindness
> To catch the nearest way. Thou wouldst be great,
> Art not without ambition, but without
> The illness should attend it. What thou wouldst highly,
> That wouldst thou holily. (I.v.16-21)

Lady Macbeth here thinks of her husband in the same terms he later applies to the murderers of Banquo; his compassionate religion threatens to undermine his heroic manliness.

But there are signs that the Christianity of the characters in *Macbeth* does not always run deep, or that it may be confused with older, pagan notions. Consider Macbeth's bewilderment at his inability to join the grooms in their prayers:

> Macb.   One cried, "God bless us!" and "Amen!" the other,
>   As they had seen me with these hangman's hands.
>   List'ning their fear, I could not say "Amen,"
>   When they did say "God bless us!"
> Lady M.   Consider it not so deeply.
> Macb.   But wherefore could not I pronounce "Amen"?
>   I had most need of blessing, and "Amen"
>   Stuck in my throat. (II.i.24-30)

Someone might offer this passage as proof of Macbeth's Christianity, but in fact it points to a certain superficiality in his embrace of the newer religion. He thinks of *Amen* as a kind of pagan talisman, a magic formula that can be mechanically invoked, even by a criminal in the middle of his crime. Macbeth would gladly take any benefits he might obtain from Christianity, but he does not fully accept the moral demands the religion makes upon its believers. At least Claudius in *Hamlet* understands that his deeds are incompatible with his attempt to pray like a Christian. But here Macbeth seems to reduce Christianity to a mere set of verbal formulas. His case suggests that Christianity has not completely triumphed in the Scotland of *Macbeth* and is in fact in competition with and threatened by other forces. In the minds of warriors like Macbeth, older pagan ideas still maintain their force, strangely mixing with newer Christian beliefs.[11]

This analysis of the basic situation in *Macbeth* helps explain Duncan's problem in the play. Duncan is trying to act like a Christian monarch in a country that is not fully Christianized and that thus retains a strong element of an older, savage heroism. He is obviously not a warlike king; when we first see him (I.ii), he is allowing his nobles to do his fighting for him.[12] When characters in the play speak of Duncan's good qualities, they never credit him with the kind of virtues associated with a king's military function. Rather they tend to speak of his generosity or, in a key speech by Macbeth, of his meekness and his ability to evoke pity (I.vii.16-25). In all these respects, he seems to resemble England's Edward rather than the bellicose king of Norway. By his own admission, Duncan is too trusting of humanity, blind to the ambition lurking in the hearts of his nobles (I.iv.12-15). Within the terms of the play, he is presented as an anomaly in Scotland.[13] All the other leaders in Scotland are warlike men, great field generals like Macbeth, Banquo, and Macduff. Only Duncan does not lead his troops into battle;[14] instead he must stand on the sidelines, receiving reports, asking like an outsider to the war: "What bloody man is that?" (I.ii.1). Duncan is crucially dependent on his great nobles to fight his battles for him and to stand up to the barbaric invaders.[15]

Hence Duncan's fatal error is not to recognize and acknowledge how weak and insecure his position truly is. The Scotland of the play is presented as a kind of elective monarchy, one in which the powerful nobles have a say in who becomes their king.[16] The Scottish King cannot be said to serve at the pleasure of the great nobles, but he is so dependent on their military power that he must constantly work to maintain their allegiance. Duncan's generosity with titles, honors, and gifts to his thanes is a way of dealing with this problem. But he makes one key error: he nominates Malcolm as Prince of Cumberland, thereby trying to ensure his

son's designation as the next king of Scotland.[17] Duncan acts as if he were
already living under a system of hereditary monarchy, as if he were in
fully civilized England rather than more primitive Scotland. By prema-
turely naming Malcolm as his successor, Duncan undermines one of the
holds a king in his circumstances has on his thanes. They might remain
loyal to him in the hope that he would eventually throw his weight in
favor of one of them succeeding him to the throne. Duncan's designation
of Malcolm as his successor proves disastrous as the action unfolds, pro-
voking Macbeth into murdering the king, rather than waiting for events
to propel him to the throne.

    Duncan does not seem to understand the political necessities of the
regime he rules. Moreover, he seems temperamentally unsuited to maintaining control of a land in which constant warfare has become a way of
life. The civil war in Scotland with which the play begins is testimony to
Duncan's failure as a king. Shakespeare found this point made explicitly
in his source in Holinshed's *Chronicles*:

> The beginning of Duncans reigne was verie quiet and peace-
> able, without anie notable trouble; but after it was perceived
> how negligent he was in punishing offendors, manie misruled
> persons tooke occasion thereof to trouble the peace and quiet
> state of the common-wealth, by seditious commotions which
> first had their beginnings in this wise.[18]

Holinshed blames the failure of Duncan's rule on his forbearance toward
his subjects. The very meekness of Duncan, which makes him admirable
as a Christian, works against his success as a king in a warlike society. The
idea that the ethical principles of Christianity might not always work well
in the rough-and-tumble world of Scottish politics is developed later in
Macbeth when Lady Macduff finds herself in danger even though, or
perhaps precisely because, she is morally innocent:

> I have done no harm. But I remember now
> I am in this earthly world—where to do harm
> Is often laudable, to do good sometimes
> Accounted dangerous folly. Why then, alas,
> Do I put up that womanly defense,
> To say I have done no harm? (IV.ii.74-79)[19]

This idea of a double standard, of a conflict between worldly and
otherworldly principles, is basic to *Macbeth*, often imaged, as here, in
terms of manliness versus womanliness.

The germ of this conception can be found in Holinshed's contrast of Duncan's character with Macbeth's:

> Makbeth [was] a valiant gentleman, and one that if he had not been somewhat cruell of nature, might have beene thought most woorthie the government of a realme. On the other part, Duncane was so soft and gentle of nature, that the people wished the inclinations and maners of these two cousins to have beene so tempered and enterchangeablie bestowed betwixt them, that where the one had too much of clemencie, and the other of crueltie, the meane vertue betwixt these two extremities might have reigned by indifferent partition in them both, so should Duncane have proved a woorthie king, and Makbeth an excellent capteine.[20]

By juxtaposing cruelty and clemency, this passage points to the contrast between the warlike spirit of paganism and the compassion of Christianity.[21] We are used to concentrating on the tragedy of Macbeth, but the play also presents the tragedy of Duncan, tragically caught between the more civilized notion of Christian kingship embodied in Edward the Confessor and the more primitive notion of the king as battlefield warrior, embodied in both Macbeth and the King of Norway.

This contrast in notions of kingship is expressed most vividly in Shakespeare's source in Holinshed by the traitor, Makdowald, who calls Duncan "a faint-hearted milkesop, more meet to governe a sort of idle monks in some cloister, than to have the rule of such valiant and hardie men of warre as the Scots were."[22] This passage may have suggested to Shakespeare the theme of the heroic warrior's contempt for Christian meekness. Makdowald's taunt to Duncan resembles the speech of the usurper York to Henry VI in one of Shakespeare's history plays:

> That head of thine doth not become a crown:
> Thy hand is made to grasp a palmer's staff
> And not to grace an aweful princely sceptre.
> That gold must round engirt these brows of mine,
> Whose smile and frown, like to Achilles' spear,
> Is able with the change to kill and cure. (*2 Henry VI*, V.i.96-101)

The contrast between Duncan and Macbeth recapitulates and deepens the contrast Shakespeare drew between the saintly Henry VI and the warlike Richard III in one of his earliest works (and his first study of tyranny).[23]

The outcome of *Macbeth* harks back to the result of the Wars of the Roses in Shakespeare's First Tetralogy. The destruction of the great aristocratic leaders in England, culminating in the carnage created by Richard III, made possible the centralizing of the English monarchy under Henry VII and the Tudor dynasty. Similarly in *Macbeth*, a sufficient number of potential rivals to the throne have been eliminated by the end of the play to give some plausibility to the idea that Malcolm may reign more peacefully than his father did. Such considerations might explain Shakespeare's dwelling on the moment when Malcolm attempts to reconstitute his feudal followers: "My thanes and kinsmen,/ Henceforth be earls, the first that ever Scotland/ In such an honor nam'd" (V.ix.28-30). The transformation of the thanes into earls seems to represent an anglicizing of Scotland, an attempt to convert a barbaric consortium of feudal chieftains into a comparatively centralized monarchy, in which all honors and titles now flow from the throne.[24] Thus, by inducing his enemies to call in English aid from the saintly Edward, Macbeth may ironically have completed the process of the gospelling of Scotland he scorns.[25] Despite his contempt for the overrefinement of the "English epicures" (V.iii.8), Macbeth ends up giving them a foothold in Scotland. Malcolm anticipates that the English aid will bring about the domestication of Scotland: "I hope the days are near at hand/ That chambers will be safe" (V.iv.1-2), and he strongly associates the English forces with the power of Christianity (IV.iii.189-92). Though Malcolm begins the play just as dependent as his father on help from his subordinates in warfare (I.ii.3-5), by the end he shows signs of having learned from Duncan's mistakes. In particular, judging by Malcolm's canny behavior with Macduff in Act IV, scene iii, he evidently has outgrown his father's overly trusting attitude. Perhaps Malcolm is ready by the end of the play to provide the synthesis of Duncan and Macbeth Holinshed projected. Having learned a certain toughmindedness from his enemies, Malcolm may be able to mediate between Christian and pagan kingship.[26] Nevertheless, in the main action of *Macbeth* the tension between these two worlds remains acute. Duncan, never realizing his errors, goes blindly to his death, but Macbeth has some sense of the peculiarity of his situation. Consider his speech when he is terrified by the appearance of Banquo's ghost at his feast:

> Blood hath been shed ere now, i' th' olden time,
> Ere humane statute purg'd the gentle weal;
> Ay, and since too, murthers have been perform'd
> Too terrible for the ear. The time has been,

> That when the brains were out, the man would die,
> And there an end; but now they rise again
> With twenty mortal murthers on their crowns,
> And push us from our stools. (III.iv.74-81)

The horror of the occasion calls forth from Macbeth a strong sense of the contrast between the past (the "olden time") and the present moment. He acknowledges that a kind of progress has been made in Scotland, a process of civilizing in which the Christian spirit has tamed the barbarism of its warriors ("humane statute" has "purg'd the gentle weal"). But Macbeth does not see this process as an unequivocal gain. And what troubles him about the new dispensation in Scotland is something specifically Christian: quite literally the new possibility of resurrection ("now they rise again"; see also III.iv.73-75). In this speech he is looking back with nostalgia to the pagan past, when a man, once dead, had the decency to stay dead.

Macbeth's reaction reflects the disorientation of the old-style pagan warrior faced with the new worldview and expanded cosmic horizons of Christianity.[27] He has never had a problem dealing face-to-face with a living human opponent. That is the sort of situation he has been trained to handle as a warrior. What he cannot deal with is some kind of supernatural apparition, a power not of this world:

> What man dare, I dare.
> Approach thou like the rugged Russian bear,
> The arm'd rhinoceros, or th' Hyrcan tiger,
> Take any shape but that, and my firm nerves
> Shall never tremble. (III.iv.98-102)

Nothing in or of this world could frighten the courageous warrior Macbeth, but forces that appear to come from another world terrify him, although as we shall see they also appear to touch—or perhaps even call into being—something deep within his soul. To be sure, one cannot simply equate supernatural apparitions with the force of Christianity; as Senecan drama reminds us, ghosts are possible in a pagan framework as well. Though Shakespeare evidently worked to reduce the element of the supernatural in his portrait of the early Roman Republic in *Coriolanus*, one way he dramatized the weakening of the old civil religion as the Republic waned was to emphasize supernatural forces in *Julius Caesar* and *Antony and Cleopatra*.[28] But even when they are confronted by ghosts, and genuinely shaken by the experience, Shakespeare's Romans do not react with the panic that seizes Macbeth. Brutus's cool encounter with the ghost of Caesar is representative:

> Bru. Art thou some god, some angel, or some devil,
>   That mak'st my blood cold, and my hair to stare?
>   Speak to me what thou art.
> Ghost. Thy evil spirit, Brutus.
> Bru.   Why com'st thou?
> Ghost. To tell thee thou shalt see me at Philippi.
> Bru. Well; then I shall see thee again?
> Ghost. Ay, at Philippi.
> Bru. Why, I will see thee at Philippi then. [Exit Ghost.]
>   Now I have taken heart thou vanishest.
>   Ill spirit, I would hold more talk with thee. (IV.iii.279-288)

Though at first frightened by the appearance of Caesar's ghost, Brutus quickly pulls himself together. His calm and collected response—"Why, I will see thee at Philippi then"—is a good measure of the moderation with which Shakespeare's Romans accept the intrusion of the supernatural in their lives. Shakespeare was aware that the pagan world allowed for the possibility of the supernatural, but, as he shows, the gulf between the natural and the supernatural was not as wide or as sharply drawn in paganism. Strictly speaking, one might even say that paganism predates the genuine and full distinction between the natural and the supernatural. Allowing for a continuum between god and man, with all sorts of intermediary figures such as heroes and *daimonia*, paganism does not tend to separate a divine realm from a human realm in the radical way that Christianity does, with its transcendent conception of deity and hence its sense of the unbridgeable gulf between man and God. This is admittedly a complicated issue, but with all the necessary qualifications being made, it is accurate to say that Christianity is distinctly more otherworldly as a religion than classical paganism. Macbeth reacts more violently than Brutus to the supernatural apparitions in his life because he thinks of them as causing a radical rift in his existence, marking a kind of epoch ("The time has been,/ That when the brains were out, the man would die"). In *Macbeth* Shakespeare explores what happens to a pagan warrior wrenched out of his narrow horizons and displaced into a Christian context, with its radical divide between this world and the next.

These speeches in Act III, scene iv highlight a peculiar fact about Shakespeare's Macbeth: for a courageous man, he is remarkably subject to moments of fear. He begins the play as a model of courage; no one could be braver on the battlefield. But in the course of the action, he is increasingly tormented by doubts and fears. Lady Macbeth states the paradox of his character succinctly: "Fie, my lord, fie, a soldier and afeard?" (V.i.36-37). Though basically a stalwart warrior, with his feet planted firmly on the ground, Macbeth finds himself living in a slippery world of ghosts and apparitions that haunt his waking hours and torment his dreams, leaving him in a confused state in which "present fears/ Are less than horrible imaginings," and "function/ Is smother'd in surmise" until for him "nothing is/ But what is not" (I.iii.137-142). Faced with a world where "the earth hath bubbles, as the water has" (I.iii.79), Macbeth constantly experiences the melting away of anything he thought provided a foundation for his existence. Shaken to the core of his being by the strange visions that come upon him, Macbeth is left at sea and wonders how his wife can keep her equilibrium:

> Can such things be,
> And overcome us like a summer's cloud,
> Without our special wonder? You make me strange
> Even to the disposition that I owe,
> When now I think you can behold such sights,
> And keep the natural ruby of your cheeks,
> When mine is blanch'd with fear. (III.iv.109-115)

Macbeth undergoes an extraordinary transformation in the course of the play, from a manly hero to what he himself describes as "the baby of a girl" (III.iv.105).

At the beginning of the play Macbeth appears to be the most admired man in Scotland. In the second scene, people are singing his praises, celebrating precisely his courage as a warrior:

> For brave Macbeth (well he deserves that name),
> Disdaining Fortune, with his brandish'd steel,
> Which smok'd with bloody execution,
> (Like Valor's minion) carv'd out his passage
> Till he fac'd the slave;
> Which nev'r shook hands, nor bade farewell to him,
> Till he unseam'd him from the nave to th' chops,
> And fix'd his head upon our battlements. (I.ii.16-23)[29]

Macbeth first appears in the play as a kind of Homeric hero, cutting his way through lesser men on the battlefield like a Scottish Achilles (the Homeric similes throughout this battle narrative give an epic feel to the passage).[30] In our first glimpse of Macbeth, he is hacking a man in half— and is being commended for it.[31] Even the meek King Duncan is favorably impressed by Macbeth's heroism, calling him "valiant cousin, worthy gentleman" and "noble Macbeth" (I.ii.24, 67).[32] Later in the play, characters view Macbeth as a bloody, cruel, violent tyrant, but at the beginning he is praised for the same savage qualities—as long as they are directed against Scotland's enemies. Unfortunately for the warrior, how he is evaluated depends on the context of his violence, whether it is perceived as in the service of his own community or opposed to it.[33] The epic language of Act I, scene ii suggests a situation typical of the genre. It involves a variant of the original epic conflict, what one might call the Achilles-Agamemnon problem, the dilemma of the legitimate king who is weaker as a military figure than one of his great warriors.[34]

But if Macbeth begins the play as a kind of Scottish Achilles, he certainly does not end that way. We cannot imagine Achilles plotting to murder Agamemnon in secret—if he decided to kill the king, he would do it openly. Achilles can be very cruel, but the *Iliad* builds up to the moment when he shows compassion to Priam. The movement of *Macbeth* is just the reverse—the hero becomes crueller as the play progresses. What accounts for this difference between Achilles and Macbeth as heroes? I want to make what will at first sound like a perverse argument, that the transformation of Macbeth can be traced to the impact of Christianity.[35] This point is, to say the least, counterintuitive: as a gospel of meekness Christianity ought to tame the fierceness and savagery of a warrior, not inflame it. Indeed we witness this process happening in Scotland; as we have seen, it may explain Duncan's imprudent clemency and seems to have provoked Macbeth's contempt for gospelling.

But now I am not examining the case of the warrior tamed by Christianity. Rather I want to consider the more complicated case Shakespeare is intrigued by in *Macbeth*: what happens when a warrior retains his martial spirit, and yet allows it to be redirected or reconstituted in a new Christian context? Macbeth stays a warrior, and even expresses scorn for the new religion of meekness. And yet he is secretly affected by it, secretly accepts its premises, almost against his will. Macbeth is not immune to the Christian critique of heroism and hence he cannot remain true to the old-style pagan ethic in its pure form. Consider the moment just before Macbeth's death when he refuses to kill himself: "Why should I play the Roman fool, and die/ On mine own sword?" (V.viii.1-2). Who taught Macbeth that the Romans were fools? My answer is: the Christian gospellers. Roman suicide was based on the principle that honor is more precious than life, and thus in certain circumstances a noble man would rather kill himself than live on in disgrace. To Christian thinkers, this principle was an example of pagan vanity, of placing the transitory value of worldly honor above the eternal value of one's immortal soul. Macbeth is obviously not approaching the issue as a theologian, but the way he abjures suicide and desperately clings to life does suggest something in him opposed to pagan attitudes.

What Macbeth has learned from Christianity is contempt for the transitoriness of pagan values and an appreciation of eternity. I am not saying that he behaves like a good Christian, in the way, for example, Duncan does. Rather he tries to remain true to a warrior's ethic, but he reinterprets that ethic with a distinctly Christian inflection, though this obviously involves a significant distortion of Christianity. Holinshed held out the prospect of a positive synthesis of pagan and Christian ethics, of combining "cruelty" and "clemency" and thus moderating the bad effects of both. In the figure of Macbeth, Shakespeare creates the demonic counterpart of this happy synthesis of pagan and Christian, a heroic warrior who turns tyrant in pursuit of a secularized version of the Christian Absolute.[36]

To clarify Macbeth's transformation of the heroic ideal, it is useful to contrast him with Achilles. Homer's hero is famous for having been confronted with a tragic choice between a long but obscure life and a brief but glorious one. His character is defined by his opting for the second possibility, and to many his decision has seemed the prototype of all tragic choices.[37] But what is characteristic of Macbeth is precisely his refusal to be bound by the terms of Achilles' choice. Macbeth wants to have the best of both worlds; he obsessively pursues the goal of a long *and* glorious life. He is driven by the idea that any glory is worthless to him unless it can be prolonged, perhaps forever (through his posterity). This is the way Macbeth covertly accepts the Christian critique of pagan heroism. For Christian thinkers, Achilles is the archetype of pagan vanity, willfully embracing glory at the price of his own transitoriness. Macbeth rejects this pagan foolishness. At the peak of his success as King of Scotland, he says: "To be thus is nothing,/ But to be safely thus" (III.i.47-48). This line is profoundly characteristic of Macbeth, and shows his peculiarity as a hero. He is an absolutist, with an all-or-nothing attitude; his achievement is worthless to him unless it is perfectly *secure*. Macbeth's scorn for the transitoriness of pagan values leads to a concern for safety that seems

unheroic by classical standards. One cannot imagine Achilles saying at
the moment of his triumph over Hector: "To be thus is nothing, but to be
safely thus." Achilles' scorn for his safety is the hallmark of his character
and his distinctive brand of heroism.[38] One can find no better measure of
the transformation of the idea of heroism in the figure of Macbeth than
his almost bourgeois concern for the security of his achievement.[39]

We can see the impact of the Christian context on Macbeth's thinking
in the famous opening of his soliloquy contemplating the murder of
Duncan:

> If it were done, when 'tis done, then 'twere well
> It were done quickly. If th' assassination
> Could trammel up the consequence, and catch
> With his surcease, success; that but this blow
> Might be the be-all and the end-all—here,
> But here, upon this bank and shoal of time,
> We'd jump the life to come. (I.vii.1-7)

The simple fact that Macbeth is thinking about the "life to come" immediately suggests his difference from a purely pagan hero. As Shakespeare
does in the key scene in which Hamlet is considering killing Claudius,
the playwright indicates how the expansion of Christian horizons to include an afterlife changes the terms of heroic action.[40] Someone might
immediately object that Macbeth's point in this passage is precisely that
he would like to "*jump* the life to come," to exclude thoughts of the afterlife from his deliberations. As in his later complaint about the dead coming back to life, he seems to long for the contraction of his horizons back
to pagan dimensions, so that he would only have to worry about what
happens in this life. But the very fact that Macbeth wishes to exclude
thoughts of the afterlife shows that Christianity has in fact altered his
manner of thinking.

Indeed, no matter how unchristian the object of Macbeth's thinking
in this soliloquy is, his thought processes display the influence of Christianity. Instead of unthinkingly plunging into action, he tries to analyze
his situation with an almost priestly dissection of motive and consequence.
The tortuous syntax of his speech reveals a mind turning inward, opening up its depths. If Macbeth is an Achilles, he is an Achilles with a conscience.[41] As is even more evident later in his anguished reaction to having murdered Duncan, Macbeth has become aware of the moral dimension of human action, even though he does not act morally. That is why

he strikes us as a more complex figure than a purely pagan hero. His exposure to Christianity has created a division in his soul, which makes it impossible for him to act singlemindedly or to face the consequences of his actions without flinching. The initial description of Macbeth on the battlefield might lead us to expect him to be a brainless fighting machine. Instead, in Macbeth's soliloquies in Act I, Shakespeare reveals a character with a richly developed psychological interior, torn by conflicting impulses and struggling with a nascent conscience.

Whatever else one may say about the impact of Christianity on the warrior hero, it gives him psychological depth.[42] The length, frequency, and convoluted syntax of Macbeth's soliloquies give him a complex interior that is lacking in any of Shakespeare's Romans. Even as thoughtful a character as Brutus, who at first is clearly troubled by the prospect of killing Caesar, is not anguished by his decision to do so. To be sure, Brutus pictures himself as undergoing a psychic civil war when trying to decide whether or not to kill Caesar,[43] but he never experiences the kind of inner division that tears Macbeth apart. Indeed, once Brutus convinces himself that he is justified in killing Caesar, unlike Macbeth, he never once wavers in his resolve, nor does he suffer pangs of remorse or even regret after the deed.[44] That is why Brutus is able to confront the ghost of Caesar as calmly as he does, whereas Macbeth is tormented by his visions of the murdered Duncan and Banquo. Despite his initial doubts, Brutus kills Caesar with a sense of moral conviction; by contrast, Macbeth must resolve to kill Duncan against his own moral scruples, and thus approaches the deed with a deeply divided soul. The complexity introduced into Macbeth's situation by the conflict between pagan and Christian principles in his soul is what makes him a profoundly tragic figure. A purely pagan Macbeth might have killed his king without any pangs of conscience; a purely Christian Macbeth might not have murdered Duncan at all; it is the combination of paganism and Christianity in Macbeth that produces his peculiar tragic situation as a murderer with a bad conscience.

Moreover, in analyzing Macbeth's "If it were done" soliloquy, we can see how Christianity has given him new desires and in fact transformed his ambition in a subtle but profound way. Although Macbeth appears to be rejecting "the life to come," what he is really doing is trying to gain here in this life what Christianity promises to believers in the afterlife, a kind of absolute perfection, an infinite satisfaction.[45] As he first reveals in this speech, Macbeth is questing for what I will call the Absolute Act, what he calls "the be-all and the end-all," a single deed that will give him everything he desires and give it to him securely and forever.[46] What gives him pause at this moment in Act I, scene vii is the consideration that no human act is entirely self-contained; every deed has consequences, and hence a misdeed may come back to haunt its perpetrator. Macbeth would have done well to heed his own warning, which turns out to characterize prophetically the course of his career in crime. But he cannot close his eyes to the tantalizing vision of the Absolute Act that will yield him complete and perfect happiness.

Thus Macbeth kills Duncan in expectation of gaining at one stroke all he desires, only to have his hopes thwarted, since once in power he finds himself exposed to a new sense of insecurity as a tyrant. But the futility of his quest for the Absolute Act does not lead Macbeth to abandon it; rather he tries to reformulate it. Instead of focusing on Duncan, he starts to think obsessively about Banquo, and concludes that the only obstacle standing between him and perfect happiness is his rival general: "There is none but he/ Whose being I do fear" (III.i.53-54); hence "his death" would leave Macbeth "perfect" (III.i.107). In his obsession with the royal succession, we can see the concern for eternity Macbeth has absorbed from Christianity. What troubles him is the thought that the Weird Sisters promised Banquo that he would found a "line of kings" (III.i.59). Macbeth cannot be content with having achieved his personal ambition of becoming king if it now appears to lead nowhere in the future:

> Upon my head they plac'd a fruitless crown,
> And put a barren sceptre in my gripe,
> Thence to be wrench'd with an unlineal hand,
> No son of mine succeeding. If't be so,
> For Banquo's issue have I fil'd my mind,
> For them the gracious Duncan have I murther'd,
> Put rancors in the vessel of my peace
> Only for them, and mine eternal jewel
> Given to the common enemy of man,
> To make them kings—the seeds of Banquo kings! (III.i.60-69)

In the most unchristian act of contemplating another murder, Macbeth thinks in Christian terms. He is tormented by the thought that he has given up his "eternal jewel" to the devil for the sake of Banquo's heirs, not his own. Once Macbeth has been told of the immortality of the soul, he cannot help conceiving of the issue of his happiness differently from the way a pagan hero like Achilles would. He comes to desire a perfection unimaginable to a pagan living in a world of finite horizons.

Having failed to satisfy his infinite desire by killing Duncan, Macbeth nevertheless feels that perfection is still within his grasp. All he has to do now is to have Banquo killed, together with his son Fleance. Shakespeare does not reveal the full extent of Macbeth's hopes until the second attempt at the Absolute Act goes awry. When the murderers are forced to report that, although Banquo is dead, Fleance escaped, Macbeth responds in despair:

> Then comes my fit again. I had else been perfect,
> Whole as the marble, founded as the rock,
> As broad and general as the casing air;
> But now I am cabin'd, cribb'd, confin'd, bound in
> To saucy doubts and fears. (III.iv.20-24)

This speech provides the most forceful expression of Macbeth's all-or-nothing attitude.[47] He is constantly searching for a kind of pure perfection, an analogue to Christian salvation; in its absence, he feels himself left with nothing, trapped in a form of damnation. The height of Macbeth's hopes is thus responsible for the depth of his despair. He desires something infinite ("as broad and general as the casing air"), but he discovers that every human act is finite, something is always left over, like Fleance, to provoke further consequences. Contrary to Macbeth's hopes, no single act can "trammel up" all the consequences and forestall the need for future action. Hence Macbeth's quest for perpetual satisfaction yields only perpetual dissatisfaction. As his wife painfully sums up his situation: "Nought's had, all's spent,/ Where our desire is got without content" (III.ii.4-5), and she correctly diagnoses her husband's problem as an inability to live with "doubtful joy" (III.ii.7). Yet despite the mounting evidence of the failure of his quest for the Absolute Act, Macbeth allows himself to be drawn into a series of deeds that only succeed in damning him further. Even toward the end of his life, when his world seems to be crashing down around him, he still hopes for some kind of enduring happiness and is willing to risk everything on one last gamble to achieve perfection: "This push/ Will cheer me ever, or disseat me now" (V.iii.20-21).[48]

This analysis sheds light on what is probably Macbeth's most famous speech, his response to the news of his wife's death:

> To-morrow, and to-morrow, and to-morrow,
> Creeps in this petty pace from day to day,
> To the last syllable of recorded time;
> And all our yesterdays have lighted fools

The way to dusty death. Out, out, brief candle!
Life's but a walking shadow, a poor player
That struts and frets his hour upon the stage,
And then is heard no more. It is a tale
Told by an idiot, full of sound and fury,
Signifying nothing. (V.v.19-28)

Struck by the profound nihilism of this speech, some critics have wondered whether to attribute this attitude to Shakespeare himself. But Shakespeare is careful to place Macbeth's nihilism in a specific context. Given what we have seen of his all-or-nothing attitude, it is not surprising that the collapse of his quest for the Absolute Act should generate this glimpse into a nihilistic abyss. This speech is surely not an expression of Christian sentiments, and yet once again we see how even in opposition to Christianity Macbeth turns out to be influenced by it. When he speaks of "the last syllable of recorded time," he clearly is no longer thinking in pagan terms, but is rather haunted by the apocalyptic expectations of Christianity.[49] Indeed in its feeling for time, this speech marks a turn from a pagan to a Christian outlook, as Macbeth learns to devalue this world from the standpoint of eternity.[50]

What is characteristic of Macbeth's words in Act V, scene v is that he speaks of *tomorrow* and *yesterday*, but he has no thought for *today*.[51] He has lost the pagan ability to take pleasure in the moment, to live happily in this world, without looking beyond its borders to eternity. Futurity has cast a shadow over his life, driving him to leave the past behind ("what's done, is done"; III.ii.12) and in the process poisoning the present for him.[52] The key to the transformation of Macbeth's heroism is his reorientation toward the future, brought about by the intervention of the Weird Sisters in his world, who in some way stand for the impact of the supernatural on human life and hence the subversion of the natural. Recall that when we first hear of Macbeth in the play, he is "Disdaining Fortune" (I.ii.17).[53] Like any good pagan warrior, at first he is not obsessed with the future but fights for the glory of the present moment, oblivious to the consequences for his safety. But by suggesting to Macbeth that there may be some providential order to events in this world, the Weird Sisters shake his faith in himself and in his own efforts, and awaken his longing to ally himself to whatever force in the universe represents the wave of the future. Lady Macbeth quickly picks up the same attitude: "Thy letters have transported me beyond/ This ignorant present, and I feel now/ The future in the instant" (I.v.56-58).[54] For both Macbeth and Lady Macbeth, the present moment becomes contemptible as soon as they think they can see beyond it confidently to a perfect future. Drawn inexorably into the future, Macbeth eventually sees all present moments voided of meaning, and, since in one basic sense life can be lived only in the present, this means that life itself loses all meaning for Macbeth.[55] His contempt for the "brief candle" and the "poor player" who merely "struts and frets his hour upon the stage,/ And then is heard no more" is one last reflection of the disdain for the transitory he has absorbed from Christianity. Ultimately Shakespeare shows that Macbeth's nihilism is the obverse of a kind of religious faith; this world becomes worthless to him when it fails to live up to an otherworldly standard of absolute perfection.

To understand more fully how Macbeth comes to be governed by a demonic parody of a religious faith, we must analyze the role of the Weird Sisters in the play. Of course, on the face of it, as witches, they appear to represent an anti-Christian force within the world of *Macbeth*. But although as "instruments of darkness" (I.iii.124) the witches must be viewed as enemies of orthodox religion, the principles in which they in effect instruct Macbeth are at least in one respect indistinguishable from Christian beliefs. What the witches teach Macbeth is after all a lesson in providence. The providential order they represent may be demonic and lead Macbeth to his damnation, but the fact remains that their prophecies embody for Macbeth a form of religious teaching, that earthly events are governed by higher powers.

As we have seen, Macbeth begins the play with the faith of a Homeric warrior—whether he succeeds in battle depends largely on whether he behaves bravely on the battlefield. But the Weird Sisters undermine Macbeth's belief that the outcome of his actions lies in his own hands, and teach him instead to rely on supernatural aid. As the play unfolds, Macbeth becomes increasingly hesitant to take the risks a hero normally accepts as a matter of course, and instead seeks guarantees from the witches that his success is assured because it is foreordained. One would expect that Macbeth's turn from heroic self-reliance to a faith in a providential order would lead him to act more virtuously in conventional moral terms. But in the paradoxical world of Macbeth, the hero's newfound faith in providence actually makes him crueller in his actions. As long as Macbeth believes that the outcome of single combat is a function chiefly of the behavior of the combatants, he acts nobly, as shown by the general admiration he initially evokes. But once Macbeth believes himself in league with hidden powers, he begins to act secretly himself, concealing his evil intentions behind false displays of good will (I.vii.82), working through proxies, and striking down opponents when they least expect it, rather than in honest open combat. Moreover, once Macbeth comes to believe that his victories are fated, he loses all restraint and becomes willing to do anything to achieve his goals, including murdering women and children. Macbeth develops a kind of fanaticism; he becomes so convinced that he is favored by providence that he comes to view his personal cause as universally valid (III.iv.134-35).

Thus the Weird Sisters, who seem to offer new power to Macbeth, in fact take away whatever power he originally possessed and turn him into a creature of their own ends. He thinks that providence is serving him, but in reality he ends up serving providence, or at least whatever order the witches represent. Macbeth's loss of freedom is reflected in the diminishing proportion of thought to deed that characterizes his behavior in the course of the play.[56] As we have seen, at first a significant expansion and deepening of Macbeth's consciousness occurs. He agonizes over the decision to kill Duncan, running over in his mind all the moral objections to the deed. Speaking of meekness and pity with respect (I.vii.16-25), Macbeth comes closest to espousing genuine Christian principles in this speech. Even once he has killed Duncan, Macbeth cannot rest content with the deed or put it out of his mind. Although it may be inaccurate to speak of remorse in his case, he is clearly troubled by what he has done and convinced that he will never sleep peacefully again (II.ii.38-40). The way his conscience plays tricks on him, making him see visions and hear voices, is one more indication of his transformation from a purely pagan hero. His behavior provokes a reproach from his wife, who wants to see him act like an old-style warrior again: "You do unbend your noble strength, to think/ So brain-sickly of things" (II.ii.42-43).

But the new interiority that has opened up in Macbeth eventually begins to close down under the pressure of events. To be sure, it is still evident when he is faced with the prospect of murdering Banquo. Shakespeare again gives Macbeth a long soliloquy before the deed, in which he reflects on why he must do it. And once Banquo has been killed, Macbeth's conscience wreaks havoc with his peace of mind, perhaps even producing the apparitions that haunt his banquet. Lady Macbeth once again tries to restore his heroic attitude by shaming him: "What? quite unmann'd in folly?" (III.iv.72). But Shakespeare introduces subtle variations into Macbeth's second murder, which suggest how his attitudes are changing. In considering the murder of Banquo, Macbeth dwells more on prudential than on moral considerations. Moreover, as he finishes his soliloquy, he has the potential murderers enter and indicates that they will be going over matters they discussed the night before. It is thus clear that even before the soliloquy Macbeth had already reached the decision to kill Banquo. Unlike what happened in the case of Duncan, this time Macbeth's soliloquy merely confirms a choice he has already made. Furthermore, his decision to hire murderers to kill Banquo suggests that he is trying to distance himself from the deed and perhaps avoid the fits of conscience his murder of Duncan provoked (unsuccessfully as it turns out). Macbeth seems to be reacting against the moral scruples that go along with the opening up of interiority in his soul. As the banquet scene confirms, the warrior wishes he could return to an earlier state of affairs, when he was a simpler man and remained undisturbed by the prickings of conscience.

Thus at the end of Act III, scene iv, Macbeth proclaims: "Strange things I have in head, that will to hand,/ Which must be acted ere they may be scann'd" (III.iv.138-39). Here we see Macbeth provoked into a willful contraction of his consciousness. Up to this point he has been characterized by the unusual amount of thought he gives to his deeds before acting (at least unusual for a warrior). Now he wishes to reverse this pattern: act first and then think about it. The new principle of interiority in his soul has clearly become painful to him, a burden from which he now wishes to escape. But the price Macbeth pays for this escape is his freedom. Reacting against the agonizing thought processes that have been going into his decisions, he starts to act mechanically, without thinking, and that means to act more brutally than ever before. The very fact that up to this point he has been deliberating at length about his deeds indicates that he has been free to act or not. But from this point on, he allows himself to be drawn into a pattern in which he reacts automatically to events, rather than planning them; thus he gradually surrenders his freedom of action.

When Macbeth is shaken by the news that Macduff has fled to England, he conceives the idea of what would today be called a pre-emptive strike: "Time, thou anticipat'st my dread exploits:/ The flighty purpose never is o'ertook/ Unless the deed go with it" (IV.i.144-46). This attitude follows from the Weird Sisters' success in increasingly convincing Macbeth that events in life are fated. If his destiny is already decided, then there is no point in Macbeth debating what is right or wrong for him to do; rather his one task becomes to try to figure out, with the aid of the witches, what is fated to happen next and act accordingly. Once he believes that he can have certain knowledge of the future, he comes to think that haste, and not due deliberation, will be the key to his success:

> From this moment
> The very firstlings of my heart shall be
> The firstlings of my hand. And even now,
> To crown my thoughts with acts, be it thought and done:
> The castle of Macduff I will surprise,
> Seize upon Fife, give to th' edge o' th' sword
> His wife, his babes, and all unfortunate souls
> That trace him in his line. No boasting like a fool;
> This deed I'll do before this purpose cool.
> But no more sights! (IV.i.146-55)

After debating at length killing both Duncan and Banquo, here Macbeth plunges precipitately into several murders, all of them crueller and more repugnant morally than his earlier deeds. But having had enough of moral scruples, Macbeth goes to the opposite extreme of unthinking action, which in this case leads him into indiscriminate violence.

One might be tempted to view this development as simply a return to pagan impulsiveness, an attempt to annul the new Christian principle of interiority. But lurking behind this speech is a model that cannot be traced to pagan sources. "To crown my thoughts with acts"—as several critics have noted, in this speech Macbeth is attempting to live out a dream of omnipotence.[57] He fantasizes that he need only think something and it will instantaneously happen, a pattern fully embodied only in the Biblical God. Just as he has been attracted to the Christian idea of eternity, Macbeth feels the pull of the Christian idea of an omnipotent God, whose thoughts translate directly into actions. As part of the absolutism we have observed in Macbeth, he now covets the omnipotence of the Biblical God for himself. Reacting against his discovery of his vulnerability as a mortal, he goes to the opposite extreme of wishing to believe himself invulnerable, a desire which makes him fall prey to the Weird Sisters' schemes. Once he places himself entirely in their hands, he is able to overcome his unheroic sense of insecurity and in fact develops a remarkable faith in himself as unconquerable. Toward the end of the play, in a reversal of the way he is portrayed in the middle, Macbeth begins to sound conventionally heroic again: "The mind I sway by, and the heart I bear,/ Shall never sag with doubt, nor shake with fear" (V.iii.9-10); he actually says: "I have almost forgot the taste of fears" (V.v.9). But the irony is that Macbeth's sense of absolute power comes just before his experience of absolute powerlessness.[58] Seeking to take total command of his world, he in fact quickly loses control of events, forced to watch his enemies seize the initiative, while he is reduced to waiting passively and

reacting to their moves, precisely because of his faith in the witches' prophecies (V.iii.2-7). In the end, he even loses his freedom of movement: "They
have tied me to a stake; I cannot fly,/ But bear-like must fight the course"
(V.vii.1-2).

As his speech in Act IV, scene i indicates, Macbeth repudiates thinking prior to acting in the hope of avoiding "more sights," that is, he does
not want to have to contemplate the moral consequences of his deeds.
Thus his speech fulfills a wish that both he and his wife express earlier in
the play—to be able to act without seeing, that is, without having to face
up to the consequences of one's deeds.[59] But the ultimate realization of
this hope is Lady Macbeth's sleepwalking: "to receive at once the benefit
of sleep and do the effects of watching!" (V.i.9-11). In Lady Macbeth we
see literalized what happens metaphorically in her husband's case. He
comes to sleepwalk through life, just going through the motions; his actions are provoked by his opponents' moves and lack any inner motive or
meaning, even in his own eyes. The ultimate result of the deepening of
Macbeth's consciousness is paradoxical—it leads him to act mechanically,
without consciousness. As we have repeatedly seen, the opening up of
Macbeth's consciousness causes a deep rift to develop in his soul, a painful division between what he wants to do and what his conscience tells
him is morally right to do. Though for much of the play he wrestles with
his new-found conscience, in the end he starts to repudiate it and all
consciousness. Troubled by what he finds in the depths of his soul—"full
of scorpions is my mind" (III.ii.36)—Macbeth searches for a way to heal
the rift in his consciousness and "raze out the written troubles of the
brain" (V.iii.42). But in seeking to extinguish consciousness, he leaves
himself prey to the unconscious forces in his soul, which make him act
more savagely than he ever did before. Chafing under the constraints of
a new morality, he eventually repudiates all restraints on his actions, and
becomes a slave to his basest desires. That is how his seemingly new-
found freedom turns into a new form of slavery.

In examining the impact of the Weird Sisters on Macbeth's thinking, we
have seen what he dimly suspects from the beginning and finally confirms to his horror—their effect is thoroughly ambiguous and equivocal.
As Macbeth himself says: "This supernatural soliciting/ Cannot be ill;
cannot be good" (I.iii.130-31). It is of course notoriously difficult to pin
down the exact role of the Weird Sisters in *Macbeth*. As the opponents of
the legitimate Christian forces in the play, they seem to represent a link
to the older pagan forces in Scotland, as was of course historically true of

witches in medieval Europe. But in many respects the Weird Sisters seem to be aligned with the tendencies that are leading Macbeth out of the pagan world—they concretely represent the impact of the supernatural, and above all they lead him to believe in particular providence.

Ultimately it is as difficult to place the witches squarely in either the pagan or the Christian camp as it is to place Macbeth. As we have seen, Macbeth is a strange hybrid, neither fully pagan nor fully Christian, but torn between the two worlds, combining aspects of both. In his case, Christianity does not, as it usually does, temper the fierceness of the pagan spirit, but paradoxically inflames it. Supplying an absolutism to Macbeth's pagan spirit, Christianity—or rather his distorted interpretation of it—turns him into a crueller and more devious figure. Convinced of the inevitability of his triumph, he lets nothing stand in his way, becoming a demonic parody of the crusading Christian warrior and hence a fiend in the eyes of the genuine Christians in the play. One might think that a combination of classical and Christian principles would produce some kind of higher synthesis, incorporating the best of both worlds. But Macbeth himself suggests the difficulty of synthesizing antithetical qualities: "Who can be wise, amaz'd, temp'rate, and furious,/ Loyal, and neutral in a moment?" (II.iii.108-9). If Macbeth achieves a kind of synthesis, he might be said to combine the worst of both worlds, pursuing pagan goals with a Christian absolutism or, alternatively phrased, pursuing Christian goals with a pagan ferocity.[60]

The witches are similarly hybrids, walking violations of any category one is tempted to impose on them.[61] *Macbeth* may seem to deal in sharp and well-defined polarities: good versus evil, Christian versus pagan, male versus female, supernatural versus natural, and so on. But from their first appearance, the witches work to break down any simple sense of binary opposition in the play: "Fair is foul, and foul is fair" (I.i.11). The way they violate fundamental category distinctions is the first thing Banquo notices about them: they "look not like th' inhabitants o' th' earth,/ And yet are on't" (I.iii.41-42). Above all, the witches seem to cloud the normally clear distinction between male and female: "You should be women,/ And yet your beards forbid me to interpret/ That you are so" (I.iii.45-47). The masculine/feminine dichotomy is unusually important in *Macbeth*, in part because it becomes aligned with the pagan/Christian opposition. The pagan heroic ideal is associated with a vision of manliness in battle, while Christianity is associated with a softer, sensitive, more feminine view of life. When Macbeth worries that the murderers have become too gospelled, he might as well have questioned whether they have become too feminized. As we have seen, the fact that they reply "We are men, my liege" (III.i.90) shows that they are aware that Macbeth is calling their manliness into question.

The issue of what it is to be a man is raised frequently in *Macbeth*— whether it involves acting solely like a male, true to the warrior's code of aggressive behavior, or whether the notion of manhood needs to be extended to encompass a feminine, sensitive side of human nature.[62] Lady Macbeth is able to taunt her husband into murdering Duncan early in the play by appealing to a narrowly masculine conception of manhood and speaking with contempt for compassion (I.vii.39-59), thus treating him as he later does the murderers of Banquo. But toward the end of the play, when Malcolm tries similarly to goad Macduff into savage action, the older warrior stands up for a broader definition of manhood as compassionate humanity:

> *Malcolm.* Dispute it like a man.
> *Macduff.* I shall do so;
> But I must also feel it as a man. (IV.iii.220-21)

We see here how complicated the masculine/feminine dichotomy becomes in *Macbeth*. Far from constituting a simple, straightforward opposition in the play, the boundary between male and female is always on the verge of dissolving, creating new hybrid forms. One of the signs of Macbeth's disorientation as a warrior is the degree to which he allows himself to be influenced by female forces—the Weird Sisters, of course, but also his wife, who plays a major role in determining his course of action. But even as the masculine is being feminized in the play, the feminine is being masculinized. This tendency is evident in the beards of the witches, or in Lady Macbeth's various attempts to act the part of a male, most fully demonstrated in her famous speech in which she desires to be "unsexed" and to exchange her compassionate femininity for a cruel masculinity (I.v.40-50). One cannot simply equate the masculine with the pagan in *Macbeth* or the feminine with the Christian. Nevertheless, the recurrent images of sexual ambiguity in the play, most fully realized in the Weird Sisters, suggest the larger point I have been making about Shakespeare's attempt in *Macbeth* to portray a world that is a hybrid of pagan and Christian elements.

One final aspect of the Weird Sisters' impact on Macbeth remains to be considered: the way they change his view of nature. As he is drawn into the world of what Lady Macbeth calls "metaphysical aid" (I.v.29), his increasing obsession with supernatural forces leads him to develop a contempt and even hatred for the world of nature. In part, this development reflects the fact that Macbeth's desire for the infinite leads him to despise anything merely finite in the world, and hence ultimately the natural world itself.[63] Shakespeare establishes a connection between Macbeth's desire for the infinite and his tyrannical nature. In the long exchange between Malcolm and Macduff concerning the character of the tyrant, infinite desire emerges as his distinguishing trait: "Boundless intemperance/ In nature is a tyranny" (IV.iii.66-67). Testing Macduff by pretending to be a tyrant, Malcolm accuses himself of "stanchless avarice," indeed an insatiable desire for wealth: "my more-having would be as a sauce/ To make me hunger more" (IV.iii.78, 81-82). He also presents himself as lecherous, and claims that his lust would brook no restraints:

> but there's no bottom, none,
> In my voluptuousness. Your wives, your daughters,
> Your matrons, and your maids could not fill up
> The cistern of my lust, and my desire
> All continent impediments would o'erbear
> That did oppose my will. (IV.iii.60-65)

As Shakespeare presents the tyrannical character, his infinite desire makes him fight against any limits set to his will.[64] Thus the tyrant ultimately finds himself at war with nature itself, since the very idea of a natural order is that things have natures which define their behavior, thus setting limits to their actions. Macbeth seems characteristically to long for the moment when "Nature seems dead" (II.i.50).

As Macbeth plunges deeper and deeper into tyranny, Shakespeare reveals the titanic egotism that fuels the tyrant's actions: "But let the frame of things disjoint, both the worlds suffer,/ Ere we will eat our meal in fear" (III.ii.16-17); "For mine own good/ All causes shall give way" (III.iv.134-35). Ultimately Macbeth's tyrannical ego leads him to challenge all the forces of nature and even the natural order itself:

> Though you untie the winds, and let them fight
> Against the churches; though the yesty waves
> Confound and swallow navigation up;
> Though the bladed corn be lodg'd, and trees blown down;
> Though castles topple on their warders' heads;
> Though palaces and pyramids do slope

> Their heads to their foundations; though the treasure
> Of nature's germains tumble all together,
> Even till destruction sicken; answer me
> To what I ask you. (IV.i.52-61)

This passage provides a profound insight into the character of Macbeth's soul and his tyrannical desires. His imagination leaps to picturing the dissolution of all order in nature, and that means particularly the dissolution of all natural boundaries. Macbeth's tyrannical soul cannot stand the way nature sets limits to all activity and especially to human desire. He would rather see the world in chaos than accept natural constraints on his will. Ultimately he rejects the idea that there can be any kind of order subsisting in nature, independent of human will. That explains his attraction to the idea of a supernatural order, the notion that what happens in the world is always the product of some will, even if it must be a sinister one. The more Macbeth feels in league with supernatural forces, the more tempted he is to look down upon the world of nature and view it as justifiably subject to his own will, destined to serve his purposes and his purposes alone.

Perhaps the most striking feature of Macbeth's speech is his curse on "nature's germains," the seeds out of which all the world of nature springs. He despises the generative power of nature, its fecundity. Ultimately Macbeth turns out to be at war with natural generation. It is no accident that his most horrible crime is the murder of Macduff's wife and children. But there is a profound irony in Macbeth's attack on the children of Scotland—his own marriage appears to be barren, thus leaving him without the heirs he needs to perpetuate his line and hence his achievement. Even the tyrant cannot dispense with the power of nature, for he needs it to generate an heir. Early in the play Lady Macbeth unnaturally tries to deny her role as a woman (I.v.40-50) and in particular lays a curse on her natural potential as a mother (I.vii.54-59). Shakespeare seems to be establishing a pattern in which those who curse natural powers will live to regret it, for nature will come back to take its revenge. Having tried to deny the womanly side of her nature, Lady Macbeth finds herself unequal to the aggressively masculine role she tries to play and her mind snaps in the process.

In Act V, Shakespeare brings in a Doctor of Physic to treat Lady Macbeth. Perhaps he was aware that the root of *physician* is *physis*, the Greek word for nature (related to the Greek word for *plant* and thus emphasizing nature as a generative power). The doctor diagnoses Lady Macbeth's problem as "a great perturbation in nature" (V.i.9) and supplies a formula for the fate of both Macbeth and his wife: "Unnatural deeds/ Do breed unnatural troubles" (V.i.71-72). The doctor suggests that, having turned against the natural order, Lady Macbeth can be helped now only by supernatural forces: "More needs she the divine than the physician" (V.i.74). Faced with the doctor's failure to cure his wife, Macbeth expresses his contempt for medicine: "Throw physic to the dogs, I'll none of it" (V.iii.47). Macbeth's rejection of the physician is consistent with the rejection of nature that has informed his whole career as a tyrant.

And yet in his attempt to reject the natural and embrace the supernatural, Macbeth turns out to be profoundly confused. The Weird Sisters prey upon his confusion in order to instill a false sense of security in him and lead him to his destruction. The riddling prophecies with which they deceive him build his confidence only because of his lingering faith in the power of the natural order. The prophecies suggest that Macbeth can be overthrown only by powers beyond the natural order, such as a man not born of woman. When Macbeth hears that he cannot be defeated "until/ Great Birnam wood to high Dunsinane hill/ Shall come against him" (IV.i.92-94), his reaction depends on his belief in the limits of the natural world:

> That will never be.
> Who can impress the forest, bid the tree
> Unfix his earth-bound root? Sweet bodements! good!
> Rebellious dead, rise never till the wood
> Of Birnam rise, and our high-plac'd Macbeth
> Shall live the lease of nature. (IV.i.94-99)

We see here how truly egotistical Macbeth has become. He expects everybody and everything to be bound by the order of nature with one exception: Macbeth himself.[65] As the last line in the passage shows, he is relying on the power of nature at just the moment when he conceives himself to be raised above it. To see how inconsistent his thinking has become, one need only note that here he is rejecting the possibility of resurrection that only two scenes earlier he himself had contemplated. Macbeth has become totally confused in sorting out the natural and the supernatural in his world. Having demanded to be above the limits of nature himself, he forgets that someone else might achieve the same power.

In the end it is purely natural forces that destroy Macbeth, even though the conclusion of the play is surrounded by a supernatural aura.

The prophecies suggest that only mysteriously supernatural powers could defeat Macbeth, but in the event the forces that triumph have simple natural explanations.[66] The man not born of woman turns out to be simply the product of a Caesarean section. And the miraculously moving forest turns out to be nothing more than a camouflaging maneuver. Having attacked the natural order, Macbeth finds himself ultimately defeated by it. And the deepest irony is that the Weird Sisters did not conceal his fate from him. As several critics have noted, the prophetic apparitions come with their own explanations.[67] The prophecy concerning the man not born of woman is delivered by a bloody child, suggesting a Caesarean section, and the prophecy concerning Birnam wood is delivered by a child with a tree in his hand, suggesting the exact manner of Malcolm's later stratagem. Macbeth's problem is that he does not look carefully enough at what the Weird Sisters show him; he only listens to what he hears and interprets the prophecies in light of his own desires, above all, his wish to be invulnerable and omnipotent.

Earlier in the play, when Macbeth sees the apparition of the dagger, he says: "Mine eyes are made the fools o' th' other senses,/ Or else worth all the rest" (II.i.44-45). This disjunction between sight and the other senses forms an important pattern in the play. Had Macbeth followed the advice of his eyes in this scene, he might have been spared destruction. His experience with the witches' apparitions suggests even more strongly that he would have been better off trusting what he saw with his own eyes, rather than allowing himself to be tricked into interpreting the revelations in light of his own hopes and desires. The ultimate trick the Weird Sisters play on Macbeth is to make him think that he is seeing with his own eyes when in fact he is interpreting what he sees in light of what he hears from the witches and their apparitions. As Macbeth finally comes to understand, the Weird Sisters only "keep the word of promise to our ear" (V.viii.21); perhaps the ultimate lesson Macbeth ought to learn is the difference between hearsay and seeing with one's own eyes.[68] One might sum up the Weird Sisters' strategy this way: awakening Macbeth's infinite desire and appealing to his dream of omnipotence, they make him long for a supernatural alliance and breed a contempt for the natural world in him. Thus they blind him to the power of nature, which eventually destroys him.[69]

No interpretation will ever seem fully adequate to the mysteries and paradoxes of *Macbeth*. But I have tried to show that the strangeness of *Macbeth*, the many riddles that have puzzled critics of the play, can in part be traced to the peculiar situation of its hero. Macbeth is in the odd position of a heroic warrior whose ambitions have been redefined and redirected along lines suggested to him by the Christian influences in his world. Faced with the Christian critique of the transitoriness of pagan values, Macbeth can no longer settle for the kind of glory that satisfied Achilles and all those Roman fools. In particular, under the influence of the Christian idea of eternity, Macbeth feels a need for something absolute in his life, something absolutely secure and absolutely lasting. Transposed into a world with the expanded horizons of Christianity, he finds a desire for the infinite awakening within his soul, which Shakespeare links with Macbeth's new form of tyranny and his new attitude toward nature as subject to human will. If one were to analyze fully Shakespeare's portrait of the transformation of the pagan hero into the tyrant of infinite desire, one would see that he was prophetically looking to the future; the tragedy of the Scottish warrior prefigures the tragedy of modernity. Indeed, if Macbeth could have found a way to translate his personal hopes for heaven on earth into a political program, into what we would call an ideology, he might well have served as the prototype of the distinctively modern tyrant.

Notes

1. All quotations from Shakespeare are taken from G. Blakemore Evans, ed., *The Riverside Shakespeare* (Boston: Houghton Mifflin, 1974). The original version of this essay was given as a lecture at the Carl Friedrich von Siemens Foundation in Munich on November 28, 1991. An expanded version was published in German translation under the title *"Macbeth" und die Evangelisierung von Schottland* by the Siemens Foundation in 1993 (translated by Anke Heimann and edited by Heinrich Meier). I want to thank Dr. Meier for the opportunity to lecture in Munich and for the original publication of this *Macbeth* essay in book form. A significantly revised version of this text appeared in English in *Interpretation*, 24 (1997): 287-318. I have revised the essay further for republication in this volume.

2. According to the concordances, this is the only appearance of the word *gospell'd* in all of Shakespeare.

3. For an insightful discussion of the concept of manliness in *Macbeth*, see José A. Benardete, "Macbeth's Last Words," *Interpretation*, 1 (1970): 63-75. For another good discussion of manliness in *Macbeth*, see Matthew N. Proser, *The Heroic Image in Five Shakespearean Tragedies* (Princeton: Princeton University Press, 1965), pp. 51-91.

4. On this distinction, see Seth Benardete, "Achilles and the *Iliad*," *Hermes*, 91 (1963): 1-5.

5. On this point, see Michael Davis, "Courage and Impotence in

Shakespeare's *Macbeth*" in *Shakespeare's Political Pageant*, ed. Joseph Alulis and Vickie Sullivan (Lanham, Md: Rowman and Littlefield, 1996), p. 221.

6. The terms are taken directly from Shakespeare's source in Holinshed's *Chronicles*; see Geoffrey Bullough, *Narrative and Dramatic Sources of Shakespeare* (London: Routledge and Kegan Paul, 1973), Vol. VII, p. 490 (all references to Bullough will be to Vol. VII).

7. See also III.vi.26-34.

8. For a similar analysis, see David Lowenthal, "Macbeth: Shakespeare Mystery Play," *Interpretation*, 16 (1989): 351. The best attempt I have seen to characterize the Scotland of *Macbeth* is by Wilbur Sanders in an imaginative essay entitled "*Macbeth*: What's Done, Is Done" in Wilbur Sanders and Howard Jacobson, *Shakespeare's Magnanimity: Four Tragic Heroes, Their Friends and Families* (London: Chatto & Windus, 1978); see especially pp. 59-65.

9. See my "*Othello*: The Erring Barbarian Among the Supersubtle Venetians," *Southwest Review*, 75 (1990), especially pp. 300-1.

10. See my *Shakespeare: Hamlet* (Cambridge: Cambridge University Press, 1989), especially pp. 54-55.

11. See Bob Stewart, *Macbeth: Scotland's Warrior King* (Dorset, UK: Firebird Books, 1988) on the historical Scotland of Macbeth: "Elements of this pagan quality to kingship remained in eleventh century Scotland, which had a curious mixture of Christian and pre-Christian beliefs and practices" (p. 13).

12. Holinshed speaks of Duncan's "small skill in warlike affaires" (Bullough, p. 490).

13. See Sanders, *Shakespeare's Magnanimity*, p. 69.

14. Here Shakespeare departs from his sources to sharpen the contrast. At one point Holinshed writes of Duncan: "he set all slouthfull and lingering delaies apart, and began to assemble an armie in most speedie wise, like a verie valiant capteine: for oftentimes it happeneth, that a dull coward and slouthfull person, constreined by necessitie, becommeth verie hardie and active.... the king himselfe governed in the maine battell or middle ward" (Bullough, p. 492).

15. See Sanders, *Shakespeare's Magnanimity*, p. 65. For an incisive critique of critics' tendency to idealize Duncan as a perfect ruler, see Harry Berger, Jr., "The Early Scenes of *Macbeth*: Preface to a New Interpretation," *ELH*, 47 (1980): 1-31. For further analysis of Duncan's problems and weakness as a king, see Graham Bradshaw, *Shakespeare's Skepticism* (Brighton, UK: Harvester Press, 1987), pp. 244-49 and John Turner, "The Tragic Romances of Feudalism" in Graham Holderness, Nick Potter, and John Turner, *Shakespeare: The Play of History* (Iowa City: University of Iowa Press, 1987), pp. 130-31, 137.

16. On Scotland as an elective monarchy, see II.iv.29-32 and Nicholas Brooke,

ed., *Macbeth* (Oxford: Oxford University Press, 1990), p. 74. On the complicated matter of the principle of succession in Scotland, see Bullough, pp. 431-32. Historically, Macbeth's reign marked Scotland's transition from an elective to a hereditary monarchy. See Stewart, pp. 8, 29-30.

17. For a contrary view of Duncan's policy, see Lowenthal, pp. 321-23. Turner, pp. 125-31, also develops a positive view of Duncan's kingship.

18. Bullough, p. 488.

19. For a good discussion of this passage, see Lowenthal, p. 331.

20. Bullough, p. 488.

21. Although clearly Shakespeare derived his sense of Macbeth's cruelty from Holinshed, the idea of giving it a specifically anti-Christian inflection seems to be Shakespeare's own. At one point in Holinshed's account of Macbeth, he writes that "he also applied his whole indevor, to cause young men to exercise themselves in vertuous maners, and men of the church to attend their divine service according to their vocations" (Bullough, pp. 497-98). This passage comes from a section in Holinshed about a period of ten years during which Macbeth ruled Scotland justly and well, a part of the story Shakespeare chose to suppress. In general, Shakespeare found a confused mixture of pagan and Christian elements in Holinshed's account of Macbeth and Scotland; the playwright worked to sharpen and develop the contrast.

22. Bullough, p. 489.

23. *Macbeth* also appears to be returning to Shakespeare's *Henry VI* plays in the way it considers the influence of women on politics, and especially the question of witches, as originally embodied in the figure of Joan de Pucelle.

24. On the historical Malcolm's "gradual but almost total anglicising of the country and its methods of government," see Stewart, p. 30. The importance of the transformation of thanes into earls is suggested by a passage in Hector Boetius's *The Description of Scotland* (which may well be one of Shakespeare's sources for *Macbeth*, since Holinshed included it as a preface to his history of Scotland). Boetius discusses the decline of the virtue of the Scots as they came to imitate the English, specifically in their handling of aristocratic titles: "Furthermore as men not walking in the right path, we began to follow also the vaine shadow of the Germane honor and titles of nobilitie, and boasting of the same after the English maner, it fell out yer long, that whereas he in times past was accompted onlie honorable, which excelled other men not in riches and possessions, but in prowesse and manhood, now he would be taken most glorious that went loaden with most titles, whereof it came to pass, that some were named dukes, some earles, some lords, some barons, in which vaine puffes they fixed all their felicitie. Before time the noble men of Scotland were of one condition, & called by the name of Thanes...and this denomination was giuen vnto them after their

desert and merit." See Vernon Snow, ed., *Holinshed's Chronicles: England, Scotland and Ireland* (rpt. New York: AMS, 1965; London: J. Johnson, 1807-8), Vol. V, p. 26. For a discussion of this passage, see Turner, pp. 123-24. As Turner points out, this passage in Boetius sheds a new light on the end of *Macbeth*, suggesting something negative about Malcolm's renaming of the Scottish thanes as earls. In general, Boetius's *Description* may have contributed to Shakespeare's fundamental conception of *Macbeth*. As if he were a sixteenth-century Walter Scott, Boetius contrasts a primitive and barbaric but austere and heroic Scotland with a civilized and sophisticated but over-refined and effete England.

25. Turner, p. 143, aptly characterizes Macbeth as "the heroic destroyer of a heroic age."

26. In a late exchange with Macduff, Malcolm indicates that he is at least aware of what a remarkable combination of virtues a true king must possess, in particular a synthesis of "mercy" and "lowliness" with "courage" and "fortitude." See IV.iii.93-94. For helpful discussions of Malcolm's role in the play, see Lowenthal, pp. 353-54 and Turner, pp. 144-45.

27. For a discussion of how Macbeth "is unnerved by what he does not understand," see Howard B. White, "Macbeth and the Tyrannical Man," *Interpretation*, 2 (1971): p. 149.

28. For a fuller discussion of this point, see my *Shakespeare's Rome: Republic and Empire* (Ithaca, NY: Cornell University Press, 1976), pp. 142-45.

29. On the importance of this passage, see Bradshaw, pp. 219-20 and Davis, pp. 219, 223.

30. On the "epic rhetoric" of I.ii, see Bullough, p. 426.

31. On the importance of this moment and Macbeth's "pagan lightness of conscience," see Wilbur Sanders, *The Dramatist and the Received Idea: Studies in the Plays of Marlowe and Shakespeare* (Cambridge: Cambridge University Press, 1968), p. 297. The peculiar phrasing—that Macbeth and Banquo "meant to...memorize another Golgotha" in this battle (I.ii.39-40)—lends a strangely anti-Christian feeling, and hence a pagan aspect, to this action. On the oddness of this moment, see Bert O. States, "The Horses of *Macbeth*," *Kenyon Review*, 7 N.S. (1985), pp. 56-58. On the possible implications of the Golgotha reference, see also Berger, p. 11.

32. For analysis of the complexity of this moment, see Bradshaw, p. 221, and James L. O'Rourke, "The Subversive Metaphysics of *Macbeth*," *Shakespeare Studies*, 21 (1993): 223-24.

33. See Berger, pp. 10-11, and especially p. 14.

34. For a general discussion of this theme in epic literature, see W. T. H. Jackson, *The Hero and the King: An Epic Theme* (New York: Columbia University Press, 1982). That Shakespeare may indeed have had Agamemnon specifically in mind when writing *Macbeth* is suggested by the fact that crit-

ics have found a number of verbal echoes in the play of John Studley's 1566 English translation of Seneca's *Agamemnon*. See Bullough, p. 452: "This tragedy of Seneca's seems especially to have seized on Shakespeare's imagination." The most remarkable of these verbal parallels can be found in the Act I Chorus of Studley's *Agamemnon*: "One hurlye burlye done, another doth begin" (Bullough, p. 523—Cf. *Macbeth*, I.i.3).

35. See Lowenthal's parallel formulation: "It is disconcerting to realize that Macbeth's Christian belief helps worsen his tyranny" (p. 348).

36. The phenomenon of religious wars, and especially the Crusades, shows that Christianity is not simply antithetical to the warlike spirit and may in fact be combined with it. Shakespeare explores the strange ways in which religion may supply motives for warfare throughout his history plays, especially in *Henry V*.

37. See, for example, David Lenson, *Achilles' Choice: Examples of Modern Tragedy* (Princeton: Princeton University Press, 1975).

38. The contrast between Macbeth and Achilles may seem to be blurred by the Greek hero's appearance in the underworld in the *Odyssey*, which would seem to undermine the distinction between pagan thisworldliness and Christian otherworldliness. But the afterlife Homer portrays is a pale shadow of this life, not a higher state as in the Christian vision. Far from being desirable, the afterlife in the *Odyssey* is so close to non-existence that Achilles says that he would rather be a slave on earth than rule in the underworld. As Achilles' case shows, unlike the Christian hero, the pagan hero does not take his bearings from the afterlife. When in this life, the Christian hero thinks longingly ahead to the afterlife; even when in the afterlife, the pagan hero thinks longingly back to this life.

39. See Mary McCarthy, "General Macbeth" in Sylvan Barnet, ed., *Macbeth* (New York: New American Library, 1963), p. 229: "A commonplace man who talks in commonplaces, a golfer, one might guess, on the Scottish fairways, Macbeth is the only Shakespeare hero who corresponds to a bourgeois type: a murderous Babbitt, let us say." Originally appearing in *Harper's Magazine* (June, 1962), this wrong-headed article nevertheless verges on interesting insights into *Macbeth*, though it loses sight of the heroic dimension of the play.

40. See my *Hamlet* book, pp. 43-45.

41. See Bradshaw's formulation: "Shakespeare's Macbeth is still the terrifying warrior—but a warrior with an intensely moral imagination" (p. 250).

42. See Bradshaw, p. 252: "The 'Christian', decidedly unclassical and unSenecan, character of *Macbeth* appears in its terrors, rather than in certitudes or assurances, and corresponds with that sense of the psyche as something stratified, vertiginous, which [Erich] Auerbach analyses in Augustine." See also p. 255: "Shakespeare has...sunk himself into the mindfalls of

Macbeth's anguished imagination.... We are...intimately involved in the inner workings and processes of Macbeth's thought and feeling; and that difference corresponds with Auerbach's distinction between classical and Christian modes of feeling."

43. See *Julius Caesar*, II.i.61-69.

44. One can grasp the difference between Macbeth and Brutus in the opening of their soliloquies. Whereas Brutus begins with the straightforward: "It must be by his death" (II.i.10), Macbeth immediately gets twisted up in the convoluted: "If it were done, when 'tis done, then 'twere well/ It were done quickly" (I.vii.1-2). I discuss the distinctive nature of the soliloquies in the Roman plays in *Shakespeare's Rome*, pp. 113-16.

45. See Maynard Mack's formulation in *Everybody's Shakespeare: Reflections Chiefly on the Tragedies* (Lincoln: University of Nebraska Press, 1993), p. 194: "Macbeth and his wife seek to make hereafter now, to wrench the future into the present by main force, to master time."

46. The best discussion I have seen of this pattern in *Macbeth* is to be found in Gordon Braden, "Senecan Tragedy and the Renaissance," *Illinois Classical Studies*, 9 (1984), 287-88. See also Terence Eagleton, *Shakespeare and Society: Critical Studies in Shakespearean Drama* (New York: Shocken, 1967), pp. 130-32. The use of the term *Absolute* may sound anachronistic in a discussion of Shakespeare, as if he were some kind of Elizabethan Hegel. But in fact Shakespeare does use the word *absolute* three times in *Macbeth* (I.iv.14, III.vi.40, IV.iii.38), and with something of the force the word was to acquire in German Idealism. Indeed, much of what I am arguing about *Macbeth* is contained in the movement it portrays between "absolute trust" (I.iv.14) and "absolute fear" (IV.iii.38).

47. Macbeth's speech offers an interesting parallel to Hamlet's lines: "O God, I could be bounded in a nutshell, and count myself a king of infinite space— were it not that I have bad dreams" (II.ii.254-56). As different as Hamlet and Macbeth are, they share the all-or-nothing attitude I have been discussing. See my *Hamlet* book, pp. 50-52. For a provocative discussion of parallels between Hamlet and Macbeth, see Harold C. Goddard, *The Meaning of Shakespeare* (Chicago: University of Chicago Press, 1951), Vol. II, pp. 110-111.

48. Macbeth's all-or-nothing attitude apparently even infects the murderers of Banquo, one of whom describes himself as: "So weary with disasters, tugg'd with fortune,/ That I would set my life on any chance,/ To mend it, or be rid on't" (III.i.111-13).

49. See also Macbeth's mention of the "crack of doom" at IV.i. 117. For the importance of the apocalyptic mode in *Macbeth*, see States, especially his characterization of Macbeth as "an apocalyptic personality: a man obsessed by finality, by absolutes, and by his bondage to time" (p. 58). See also White, p. 154.

50. For suggestive analogues to this process, see the essay "Gnosticism, Existentialism, and Nihilism" in Hans Jonas, *The Gnostic Religion* (Boston: Beacon Press, 1963), pp. 320-40.

51. "In a play which, from the premises of the plot, is Future-driven, Macbeth, especially, is one who cannot *be* in his Present." See Francis Berry, *Poet's Grammar: Person, Time and Mood in Poetry* (London: Routledge and Kegan Paul, 1958), p. 53. This brief essay on "*Macbeth*: Tense and Mood" provides an insightful analysis of how Macbeth's distinctive sense of time is reflected in the grammar of the play. See also Sanders, *The Dramatist and the Received Idea*, pp. 270 and 279.

52. An analogue of this aspect of Macbeth's tragedy is provided by the Porter in his paradoxical tale of "a farmer, that hang'd himself on th' expectation of plenty" (II.iii.4-5).

53. Similarly, when Macbeth first hears the witches' prophecies, he seems willing to accept the chanciness of the world order: "If chance will have me king, why, chance may crown me/ Without my stir" (I.iii.143-44).

54. On this point, see Mack, p. 192.

55. For a similar analysis, see Arthur Kirsch, *The Passions of Shakespeare's Tragic Heroes* (Charlottesville: University Press of Virginia, 1990), p. 95.

56. On this subject, see Timothy Fuller, "The Relation of Thought and Action in *Macbeth*" in *Shakespeare's Political Pageant*, pp. 209-18.

57. See, for example, Kirsch, pp. 94-95, and Turner, p. 138.

58. Cf. Turner's formulation about *Macbeth*: "the magical sense of omnipotence is haunted by its fellow-contrary nightmare of impotence" (p. 141).

59. *Macbeth*.   Stars, hide your fires,
    Let not light see my black and deep desires;
    The eye wink at the hand; yet let that be
    Which the eye fears, when it is done, to see. (I.iv.50-53)

    Lady Macbeth.   Come, thick night,
    And pall thee in the dunnest smoke of hell,
    That my keen knife see not the wound it makes. (I.v.50-53)

In both passages, the characters unconsciously reveal what they will in fact do, namely act blindly—act without fully realizing the consequences of their deeds.

60. For the idea that a synthesis of classical and Biblical morality might produce an ethic very different from either, see Leo Strauss, *On Tyranny* (New York: Free Press, 1991), p. 191.

61. On this point, see Lowenthal, p. 354.

62. For a thorough discussion of this issue, see José Benardete's essay.

63. In this context, Lady Macbeth's line about Banquo and Fleance is sug-

gestive: "But in them nature's copy's not eterne" (III.ii.38). Nature lacks eternity; like the pagan hero, nature appears defective in Macbeth's eyes when judged by the standard of eternity.

64. There are interesting parallels here to Plato's presentation of the tyrannical soul in the *Republic*; see especially 571a to 580a. The central parallel is the idea that in seeking to liberate his appetites, the tyrant becomes a slave to the force of desire in his soul. For a discussion of these parallels, see White, especially p. 145.

65. On this point, see Davis, p. 226.

66. See Lawrence Danson, *Tragic Alphabet: Shakespeare's Drama of Language* (New Haven: Yale University Press, 1974), pp. 138-39.

67. See, for example, Howard Felperin, *Shakespearean Representation: Mimesis and Modernity in Elizabethan Tragedy* (Princeton: Princeton University Press, 1977), p. 133, and Mack, pp. 194-95. Roman Polanski's film of *Macbeth* realizes this point in visual terms—Polanski intercuts a scene of a Caesarean section with the original prophecy of the man not born of woman.

68. Cf. Romans 10:17.

69. See C.S. Lewis' formulation of a similar point in a different context: "At the moment, then, of Man's victory over Nature, we find the whole human race subjected to some individual men, and those individuals subjected to that in themselves which is purely 'natural'—to their irrational impulses.... Man's conquest of Nature turns out, in the moment of its consummation, to be Nature's conquest of Man." See *The Abolition of Man* (New York: Simon & Schuster, 1996), p. 76.

Shakespearean Wisdom?

Michael Platt

According to Leo Strauss, the beginning teacher should assume that there is "one silent student in your class who is by far superior to you in head and heart."[1] Indeed, when one teaches a work of the wise, there in the classroom there is indeed someone by far superior to you in heart and in mind, namely the author. Such a discovery would transform a teacher of Shakespeare into a student of Shakespeare. Such a student would regard Shakespeare as one who says exactly what he means, every sentence, every word, every sound, rather than as one who is human and weak and for whom allowances must be made.

Such a student is not ashamed to read Shakespeare for the sake of wisdom. Yet high-hearted though he be, his endeavor will not be easy. For one thing, the wisdom such a student seeks is enigmatic. Is the wisdom of Shakespeare his wisdom or wisdom? Is the wisdom of Shakespeare the wisdom he shares with other wise men, say Plato or Machiavelli, or is it *his* wisdom as distinct from, or even opposed to, the wisdom of all others?[2]

And what about wisdom itself? Is wisdom impersonal, universal, self-same, and steadfast? Or is it particular, personal, protean, and scattered? Although it is not possible to settle such a question now, or perhaps any time, it seems better in the beginning to assume the latter answer, for it alone protects us from finding in Shakespeare, or any wise man, what we already very well know. When we compare what the wise say with what fools proclaim and villains insinuate, wisdom seems to be a single, mighty light, but when we compare what one wise man says with what another says, wisdom seems to be so many watch fires in the night.

With this in mind, let us examine ninety-eight words Shakespeare has left to us. Since these ninety-eight words are arranged in a sonnet, and since lyric poetry is commonly regarded, not without reason, as confined to private life, and especially to love, I must mention one thing before we begin reading together.

All of us can, if asked, tell the story of our lives. These lives are made up of necessity, accident, and choice, but the latter is decisive. However much we must acknowledge, or plead, that we were made by accidents and necessities, we know that we are made by our choices as well. How we choose affects the happiness and the worth of our lives. When we are young we ponder the paths which opportunity and reason present to us, and when we are old, we live at the end of the one path we have chosen.

Our lives, then, are an answer to the question, "What is the best way of life?" and since we share our lives with others, influencing them even as they influence us, our answer to this question affects public life as a whole. A people or a regime is known by the lives it publicly esteems and promotes. Athens, Jerusalem, Rome, Amsterdam, Moscow, and Manhattan—these are names for distinctive ways of life, and changes such as from St. Petersburg to Leningrad are revolutions.

The strongest souls may choose against the grain of public life, and perhaps the best way of life will always be against that grain, but it is not easy. Consider the difference between growing up now and growing up fifty years ago in America; then your fellow boys and girls expected to become men and women; and now the majority aspire to become Teenagers.[3] It is no wonder, then, that those who are concerned with the future of their country are concerned with poetry, in the widest sense, for poetry instructs more vividly than the laws, and it speaks especially to the young. Indeed, liberal republics such as our own are especially in need of poetry; for while our Constitution provides for the nobility we will always need to pass the blessing of liberty on to our posterity, it does not speak of it. This absence, which accords with the delicacy and with the precision of the Framers, was once amply supplied by nature and nature's God. In the interest of discovering what Shakespeare thinks of nature and nature's God, let us turn to his Sonnet 94.

THey that haue powre to hurt,and will doe none,
That doe not do the thing,they moft do fhowe,
Who mouing others,are themfelues as ftone,
Vnmooued,could,and to temptation flow:
They rightly do inherrit heauens graces,
And husband natures ritches from expence,
They are the Lords and owners of their faces,
Others,but ftewards of their excellence:
The fommers flowre is to the fommer fweet,
Though to it felfe,it onely liue and die,
But if that flowre with bafe infection meete,
The bafeft weed out-braues his dignity:
For fweeteft things turne fowreft by their deedes,
Lillies that fefter, fmell far worfe then weeds. [4]

The poem begins with "they" and it spends the rest of itself catching up with its first word. Yet we are not sure we want to share in the end of the chase. While this riddle attracts the mind with its graceful inscrutability, it chills the heart with its indifference. A nameless force seems poised in it. We want, and we do not want, to know who "they" are. Had the first line of the poem read:

They that have power to hurt *but* will do none,

we could breathe easy, knowing that no hurt will come nigh us, because "they" are moderate and restrained. But the poem's first line is not concerned with reassuring us. Instead of the considerate "but" it has the indifferent "and":

They that have power to hurt, and will do none.

It is not pity or kindness or compassion which restrains "they" from doing what they can very easily do. What is from the first, then, disturbing about "they" is not so much the hurt they might do but the contempt they must hold human beings in. They serenely disdain to hurt us, and by doing so they hurt us.[5] In "their" gaze we feel what is to be looked down upon, to be not even treated as a sport or an annoyance, let alone an enemy.

The rest of the poem will only increase this hurt, but at first we are allowed to fight back:

That do not do the thing, they most do show,
Who moving others, are themselves as stone,
Unmoved, cold, and to temptation slow:

The remainder of the first quatrain allows us to resist "them." We can defend ourselves from their serene disdain with indignation and disapproval. In the name of honesty we can be indignant with those who do not do the things they most do show, who are deceitful. In the name of integrity we can protest against those who deliberately mislead us with false expectations. In the name of feeling we can disapprove of those who are like stones, unmoved by moving things, and who insult living beings such as ourselves by seeming to regard living as a temptation. But our defense only gets us in deeper trouble. By censuring "they" we have only shown how right they are to disdain us, and the next stanza brushes aside our indignation effortlessly and therefore utterly. When we read:

> They rightly do inherit heavens graces,
> And husband nature's riches from expense,
> They are the Lords and owners of their faces,
> Others, but stewards of their excellence:

we know that all that we thought said in disapproval in lines two, three, and four was said in praise. Thus we discover how very different our view is from the view of the speaker. Sonnet 94 tempts the reader to indignation and then teaches him sternly that precisely such indignation is a small-souled evasion. Now we have nothing in reserve and this disturbs us even more. We are naked. Perhaps we are tempted to clothe our nakedness with irony, by claiming that the poem means the opposite of what it says, that when it seems to praise "they" it means to dispraise. Precisely by taking refuge in this comfort will the reader show how right "they" are to disdain such persons. This search for comfort in irony only signifies that there is something disturbing here. The disturbing thing seems to be that the "they" of the first stanza is the same as the "they" of the second stanza, that those who are described in terms which most human beings regard as terms of blame are unmistakably praised. Those who are cold, unmoving, and serenely disdainful are the rightful inheritors of "heavens graces." The stone that gives nothing and saves everything seems to be the peak of nature. Those who do not do the thing they most do show are praised as the lords and owners of their faces. It is the most ordinary and easy, almost irresistible, thing for human beings in the street to show in their faces some recognition of others, even strangers. On a country road even the man from the city responds to the greeting of the country walker. This sonnet tells us that all those who smile or nod in recognition of others do not possess their faces. Finding themselves on a country road, "they" would save all their "looks," all their faces, for themselves. Yet despite the fact that the chilly "they" are owners who never spend their wealth, "they" have "others" who are their stewards. We are puzzled; does "their" refer to "they" or to the "others"? Does the line "Others, but stewards of their excellence" mean that all others are stewards of their own, or stewards of the excellence of "they"? Either way, others are stewards; they do not really possess excellence; they only have it in the way a steward does, on loan and on terms and for the sake of a master? And either way, "they" are masters.

The sestet only adds to our difficulties. Having failed to understand the octet thoroughly we must now comprehend not only the sestet by itself but its relation to the octet. While still trying to understand the riddle of "they," we are faced with the new riddle of the summer's flower, the lilies and the weeds. It seems we are dealing with two riddles, two riddles with the same answer. But we can only be sure when we solve both riddles. Faced with such riddles, it is natural for the reader to find the final couplet as seductive and irresistible as a breath of air is to someone who has had his head held under water.

> For sweetest things turn sourest by their deeds,
> Lilies that fester, smell far worse than weeds.

We are comforted. How are the mighty fallen, at least in speech. Nevertheless, our feeling of dominion is short-lived; we have only to put our head back into the water underneath the final couplet to find ourselves as disturbed as ever. Reading Sonnet 94 is like gazing at a black hole you are fast falling into. Help!

When we need help, we should turn to others for it. Between us and Shakespeare there are many readers, and some have written about this sonnet. A good many of them resolve the mysterious figure in Sonnet 94 into a story they discern in the surrounding sonnets, a tangled story of love, of triangles 'twixt a poet, a beautiful young man, a rival poet, and a dark lady, a mix of ardor and lust, of inflamed yet disinterested respect and jealousy, of joy and of suffering.[6] These readers are not unprovoked by the *Sonnets*, and yet the stories they discern, the more clear they appear to one reader, the more they differ from the others, and also the more sonnets they leave out of the story, so many that some readers are provoked to reorder all the *Sonnets*. Yet even if most readers agreed on one story, that would hardly dissolve the mystery. As one reader acknowledges, "In its impersonality and detachment the sonnet [94] stands apart from the story; appropriately, for its resolution of ideas cannot be attributed to the poet who speaks almost every other sonnet, and its magisterial voice is not his."[7] In truth, Sonnet 94 stands out from the rest of the *Sonnets* like a soliloquy from a play. Moreover, unlike most soliloquies, this "soliloquy" is so lofty, thoughtful, and serene that it frames the speakers of the other sonnets as passion's slaves. It should not surprise us, then, that while most readers acknowledge Sonnet 94 to be uncommonly challenging, few try to interpret it. While all climbers feel challenged by the north face of the Eiger, few attempt it.[8]

More likely to help us, then, are those readers who concentrate on Sonnet 94. Still the most famous is William Empson.[9] According to him, the figure described in Sonnet 94 is the Prince as sketched by Machiavelli and portrayed by Shakespeare in, e.g., *Henry V*. Empson is careful to distinguish such a prince from both the fascination and the fright of popular reputation. He rightly sees that the figure in Sonnet 94 must be understood before it is praised or blamed. But, alas, there is no genuine help in identifying this figure as a prince. The "they" of Sonnet 94 cannot be either the prince according to Machiavelli or the prince according to Shakespeare[10], for this figure cannot be a prince at all. True, this being in Sonnet 94 inspires admiration and fear; true, he seems to prefer being feared to being loved; true, he seems capable of both force and fraud; but his shows are backed by no deeds. Indeed, he is forbidden any deeds at all, and a prince must be ever doing deeds and ever attending to them; to rule a polity he must attend daily to human affairs, and attend and attend to them, yet still not be done. A prince cannot leave ruling to his stewards, or captains, such as Fluellen. "They" are said to "inherit heavens graces," but it cannot be because they are founders like Moses, Cyrus, Romulus, Theseus, and the like. Being wholly without deeds, "they" cannot be political men at all.

When we need help, we should turn to others for it. Walter Kaufmann has done readers of this sonnet a service by proposing that nothing distinguishes Shakespeare from modern taste so much as his taste for nobility. This sonnet, he proposes, is a portrait of the magnanimous or great-souled man as Aristotle describes him in Book IV of his *Ethics:*

> A person is thought to be great-souled if he claims much and deserves much.... He that claims less than he deserves is small-souled.... Greatness of soul seems...a crowning ornament of all the virtues. Great honours accorded by persons of worth will afford [the great-souled man] pleasure in a moderate degree:

he will feel he is receiving only what belongs to him, or even less, for no honour can be adequate to the merits of perfect virtue, yet all the same he will deign to accept their honours, because they have no greater tribute to offer him. Honour rendered by common people and on trivial grounds he will utterly despise.... He... will be indifferent to other things as well. Hence great-souled men are thought to be haughty.... The great-souled man is justified in despising other people—his estimates are correct; but most proud men have no good ground for their pride.... He is fond of conferring benefits but ashamed to receive them.... He returns a service done to him with interest, since this will put the original benefactor into his debt in turn.... The great-souled are said to have a good memory for any benefit they have conferred, but a bad memory for those which they have received.... It is also characteristic of the great-souled men never to ask help from others, or only with reluctance, but to render aid willingly; and to be haughty towards men of position and fortune, but courteous towards those of moderate station...and to adopt a high manner with the former is not ill-bred, but it is vulgar to lord it over humble people.... He must care more for the truth than for what people will think;...he is outspoken and frank, except when speaking with ironical self-depreciation, as he does to common people.... He does not bear a grudge.... He is not given to speaking evil himself, even of his enemies, except when he deliberately intends to give offense.[11] (IV. 3)

For us moderns disdain for such a man is an easy thing; but unless we have read Plutarch's *Lives* with the ardor which burned in former ages, judging ourselves against a Lycurgus, a Caesar, a Coriolanus, unless we have read Plutarch as Montaigne and Rousseau did, we should disdain this disdain.

Nevertheless, Aristotle himself makes us think there must be something higher by spicing his portrait of the magnanimous man with details that make us smile and then look higher. The excerpts we quoted above were the selection of Kaufmann; now we must look at some of the things he chose to leave out. Towards the end of his portrait of the magnanimous or great-souled man, Aristotle speaks of the body and the gait of this man:

Further, we think of a slow gait as characteristic of a high-minded man, a deep voice, and a deliberate way of speaking. For a man who takes few things seriously is unlikely to be in a hurry, and a person who regards nothing as great is not one to

> be excitable. But a shrill voice and a swift gait are due to hurry
> and excitement.[12] (1125a12-17)

By speaking of the gait and voice of this man, Aristotle reminds us of
what our ancestors called deportment, what young Washington studied
in his maxims, and what today Henry Kissinger most practices, but also
what seems to us stiff and unnatural, and what we deride as the result of
pacing slowly before a mirror and taking voice lessons. Our vanity wears
a different mask. Were Aristotle sketching the hero of modernity, who is
no statesman, he would speak of the nervous subway-rider who may yet
be careful to display a copy of *Fear and Trembling* in his jacket pocket.
Yet, this description of the great-souled man's gait points to the fundamental tension in Aristotle's portrait. On the one hand, he describes the
great-souled man as concerned with honor (1123b17-23; 1124a5-19;
1125a35 and *passim*); on the other, he is concerned with something higher
than honor. When Aristotle writes,

> For even toward honor, his attitude is that it is not of the great-
> est moment, (1124a16-18)

he makes us ask what is greater than honor. If there is something greater
than honor, then there must be something greater than the man "primarily concerned with honor" (1124a5) whom Aristotle deigns to call "great-
souled." And when Aristotle says:

> He must be open in hate and open in love, for to hide one's
> feeling and to care more for the opinion of others than for
> truth is a sign of timidity, (1124b26-27)

he makes us ask whether truth is not something higher than honor, and
whether the truth-seeker is not higher than the great-souled man. And
when Aristotle goes on to say:

> He speaks and acts openly: since he looks down upon others
> his speech is free and truthful, except when he deliberately
> depreciates himself in addressing the common run of people,
> (1124b28-30)

he makes us think of Socrates and his famous self-depreciation or irony.
Again when the passage continues, it looks higher:

> He cannot adjust his life to another, except a friend, for to do
> so is slavish, (1124b31)

for friendship is in Aristotle's account of human things the highest human thing in man, though not the highest thing in man.

What is this highest human thing? While considering friendship between unequals, Aristotle mentions the gods and says that there cannot be friendship between men and gods, or rather between the human and the divine. He goes on:

> This raises the question whether or not we wish our friends the greatest of all goods, namely, to be gods. For [if that wish were fulfilled,] they would no longer be our friends, and, since friends are something good, we would have lost this good. Accordingly, if our assertion is correct that a man wishes his friend's good for his friend's sake, the friend would have to remain the man he was. (1159a5-10, translator's brackets)

That Aristotle understands this latter statement to be a non sequitur is shown by what follows immediately:

> Consequently, one will wish the greatest good for his friend as a human being. But perhaps not all the greatest goods, for each man wishes for his own good most of all. (1159a11-12)

It seems that there is a good, a great good, open to men whose possession would, however, erase their humanity because to possess this good would be to become divine. Indeed, there is such a good according to Aristotle and he speaks of it later in the *Ethics*:

> So if it is true that intelligence is divine in comparison with man, then a life guided by intelligence is divine in comparison with human life. (1177b29-31)

The next sentence reads as a response to the friend who does not want his friend to become divine:

> We must not follow those who advise us to have human thoughts, since we are [only] men, and mortal thoughts, as mortals should; on the contrary, we should try to become immortal as far as that is possible and do our utmost to live in accordance with what is highest in us. (1177b31-35)

Aristotle continues:

> For though this is a small portion [of our nature], it far surpasses everything else in power and value. One might even regard it as each man's true self, since it is the controlling and better part. It would, therefore, be strange if a man chose not to live his own life but someone else's. (1177b35-1178a3)

In reading Aristotle's *Ethics* so as to discover the highest types of men we uncover an ascending sequence. Very high is the great-souled man; higher still is the friend; highest of all is the divine man, the man who cultivates the divine in himself.

Do the portraits of these men and the relation between them help us to understand the kind of being Shakespeare describes in Sonnet 94? Let us examine them to see if any of them fits. Even the Kaufmann selection from Aristotle's portrait of the great-souled man discloses enough of Aristotle's intention to allow us to see that Shakespeare presents something far more exalted than the great-souled man. The beings he describes in Sonnet 94 are not concerned with honor and dishonor; they are not so dependent on others. For the same reasons that they cannot be the prince according to Machiavelli, they cannot be the great-souled man of *Ethics* IV. The friend too fails to fit what Shakespeare describes, for the friend stands on some kind of an equal footing with his friend. It is not clear that the being Sonnet 94 describes is a friend or could be a friend. He seems far more solitary and also far more self-sufficient. Yet he cannot be the philosopher or divine man as Aristotle speaks of him. The "they" of this sonnet are neither divine nor striving to be divine. Though they are mortal ("Though to itself it only live and die"), they are not in motion. They have no eros; neither do they lack any thing. They seem to be at rest and yet the cause of motion in others ("moving others" yet "unmoved"). As such they are more like the unmoved mover of Aristotle than anything else, but again with a disqualifying difference, for the unmoved mover is not a person, is not capable of deeds, and is not mortal. The same things disqualify the Aristotelian god, *nous* as described in *Metaphysics* Lambda. While *nous* is self-same, necessary, and the cause of intelligibility in all things, including the moving perishable ones, *nous* itself is neither perishable nor really an agent or doer, much less a creator like the mysterious Biblical god. *Nous* cannot do deeds and so cannot be tempted.

Has our reading of Aristotle been fruitless? No. By considering the great-souled man, the friend, the philosopher and *nous,* and by dismissing each, we have drawn closer to understanding the "they" of Shakespeare. It seems we must have something more than what pagan antiquity considers the highest or the highest human. We have searched in Athens, now we must go to Jerusalem.

Sonnet 94 itself points the way. When in the sestet it refers to the lily, it puts the reader on a holy path toward the Gospel of Matthew where Christ urges the multitude on the mount to imitate the lily. Later, at the end of his life, Christ will teach solely through a deed, one which will be fully understood by no one who witnesses it. By then disappointment with speech and disciples will have inured him to solitude. But now in the early part of his ministry he seems confident of the capacity of speech to teach and, indeed, seems to take himself most seriously in relation to the multitude.[13] It is in the course of addressing them that he refers to the lily. Like Aristotle he would have us liberate ourselves from mortal thoughts:

> Therefore I say unto you, Take no thought for your life, what ye shall eat, or what ye shall drink; nor yet for your body, what ye shall put on. Is not the life more than meat, and the body than raiment?
>
> Behold the fowls of the air: for they sow not, neither do they reap, nor gather into barns; yet your heavenly Father feedeth them. Are ye not much better than they?
>
> Which of you by taking thought can add one cubit unto his stature?
>
> And why take ye thought for raiment? Consider the lilies of the field, how they grow; they toil not, neither do they spin:
>
> And yet I say unto you, That even Solomon in all his glory was not arrayed like one of these. (Matthew 6:25-29)

Solomon is the magnanimous man in Biblical raiment; what Aristotle praises with qualification Christ does not praise at all. We must understand what Christ advises in the light of what he is. Christ is the lily; because he trusts in his heavenly Father, he need neither toil nor spin. So in asking the multitude to consider the lily he is asking them to imitate himself. As such a lily, he seems to resemble "they" in the sonnet. Indeed, the poem seems to be a deliberate commentary on Christ as we find him speaking here in Matthew.

The episodes that precede the Sermon on the Mount show us Christ, who is "to temptation slow," who is unmoved, and whose temptation is sprinkled with stones. In Chapter 4 of Matthew the Devil tempts Christ to make bread out of *stones*. A second time the Devil tempts Christ to cast himself down and see whether the angels will let his foot "dash against a *stone*." A third time the Devil tempts Christ; from a high mountain he offers him the kingdoms of the earth. To all these temptations, Christ responds in the same manner; he does not move. He is "unmoved, cold, to temptation slow." He is what he is by refraining from deeds; he refuses to perform deeds for the sake of showing who he is. In the end he disappoints nearly everyone, especially on the Cross. He will not be a Caesar. He will not be a David. He cannot be a prince. To do his greatest deed he must refuse to do any deeds at all.

By alluding to the lily of Christ, Shakespeare appears to indicate that of all previous accounts of a being who is both human and divine, Christ's comes closest to what he describes in Sonnet 94. Both are self-sufficient without being exempt from death. Still, we must conclude that Christ and his lily do not fit perfectly with Shakespeare's.

Consider Christ and his lily again. A thread running throughout Christ's teaching which he illustrates with the lily is the depreciation of thought. We are reassured that our Father in heaven provides for us. He takes care. We need only be. We need not toil and spin. The thought here depreciated is not only prudent thought, directed to securing daily needs, even daily bread. It is all thinking which might exalt us. We are asked whether we can add a cubit to our stature by thinking.

When we return to Shakespeare's sonnet we find a different appreciation of thought. True, "they" are not occupied by thoughts of raiment and shelter, but they do think. Of the summer's flower we hear that "to itself" it "lives and dies." That "to itself" is significant. "To itself" means thinking. The being described by Shakespeare in his sonnet thinks about life and death, and without considering either the comfort or the terror of the Holy Creator God known to Christ. This thinking lily seems not to know of any world elsewhere, not the Blessed Isles Socrates speaks of, and not the afterlife of heaven. "They" neither love, nor fear, nor trust in a heavenly Father.[14]

Shakespeare's teaching about talents and stewards also departs from Christ's (Matthew 25:14-30). According to Christ, those who put to work and increase what they have received as stewards will enter the Kingdom of Heaven; he who buries his talent is called wicked. But according to Shakespeare, he who hides his talent is called the rightful heir of heaven's graces;[15] by hiding he husbands nature's riches from expense.

Once again our search for a being who fits perfectly the riddle of Sonnet 94 has failed. We have looked to both Aristotle and Christ for help; we have looked to both classical pagan philosophy and to Christian Biblical religion to find some high being who will fit exactly what Shakespeare describes. Neither supplies us with the complete and precise answer to the riddle of Sonnet 94.

Yet the failure of our inquiry is not fruitless. We can reach a provisional view. The being described in Sonnet 94 seems to be a unification of what is high in antique philosophy and what is high in Christianity. Nevertheless, this unification is still mysterious to us. We know that it was the long task of the greatest minds for nearly two millennia to unify antique philosophy and Biblical religion. We know of the attempts of Augustine, Anselm, Maimonides, Thomas, Descartes, Pascal, Hegel, and Kierkegaard to unify philosophy with the revealed truth of Biblical religion. We know that these attempts contradict each other. We know that thinkers who deserve a hearing insist that the task cannot be accomplished without one party being subordinated to the other (Pascal, Kierkegaard, Hegel), and we know of the insistence that Christianity should have nothing to do with philosophy (Luther). We also know of the counter-insistence that philosophy should have nothing to do with Christianity (Nietzsche). Yet even for the most famous of those who say this, the task for the West still remains the unification of what is highest in antiquity and what is highest in Christianity; for Nietzsche himself speaks of the Übermensch as "Roman Caesar with the soul of Christ."[16]

Indeed, this enigmatic formula comes close to describing our provisional view of what Shakespeare describes in Sonnet 94. Yet since "they" of the sonnet are forbidden deeds, our provisional formula must be amended to: "Aristotle with the soul of Christ." Nevertheless, the way in which "they" are a unification of philosophy and Christianity, of Aristotle and Christ, is hardly clear. In truth, such formulas only show us that we do not yet understand what Shakespeare is talking about. To understand what Shakespeare means by uprooting his allusions is finally to understand what is strange and mysterious, and perhaps utterly new, by what is familiar. It is, then, but a higher kind of ducking from "they." We can only release ourselves from the grip of what is familiar by reflecting that if "they" are really familiar, then there would be little point in continuing our inquiry. If "they" are philosophers, then either Aristotle's or Shakespeare's account is superfluous. If "they" are Christs, then either the Gospels' or Shakespeare's account is superfluous.

The poem tries to release us from the grip of the familiar, both what is familiar in Aristotle and what is familiar in Christ, by taking us a long way, by taking us through the familiar until we see it as "familiar." The poem means us to misunderstand "they" as Aristotle and then as Christ so that we may begin to understand. It teaches us to put aside "what we already very well know." We must misunderstand and then understand that we have misunderstood before we can understand. Earlier when we found ourselves helpless, we said that it was natural to seek help from other readers and from their answers to the riddle of the sonnet. Now we must say that since we are without help, we can only turn to ourselves. With this thought, which the sonnet has forced upon us, we return to the sonnet.

We must ask ourselves whether Shakespeare needed to look back in the West to write this sonnet. Aristotle and Christ are present as allusions or hints only, while "they" are emphatically present. The "they" of Sonnet 94 are near to Shakespeare. He did not need help from elsewhere to describe what he describes. He needed only to turn to himself.

"They" must be dramatists. It is dramatists who do not do the thing they most do show. While presenting speeches, the dramatist does not speak. While putting forward persons, he is not them. While these persons do deeds, the dramatist does not. Yet it is precisely such persons, speeches, and deeds which move others. Through them the dramatist can hurt and please, enchant and perplex, subdue and ignite. His shows speak daggers to the guilty, peace to the just, and wonder to us all. We laugh and smile, and over the death of Cordelia even strong men (Dr. Johnson) weep.

Nor is the power of the dramatist limited to his immediate audience. Long after he is dead, his shows still hale men's souls out of their still bodies. The love of his shows and what they show can make friendships ("oh, you too?") and can go some way to knitting a nation together. According to Churchill, the English-speaking world is a world, in part, because of the reading of Shakespeare.[17] If so, then we must count the Germany of Schiller and Goethe a part of this world and remark the declining place of Shakespeare in the life of Germany. Nietzsche mentions him prominently once, with high praise, but otherwise ignores him. And, so far as I know, Heidegger mentions Shakespeare only once, perfunctorily.[18] In Heidegger his place is taken by Hölderlin, a poet who gives his people no vivid image of tyranny and the tyrant's soul, as Shakespeare gives us in Tarquin, Leontes, Macbeth, and Richard III.[19]

Yet, this sonnet suggests that the dramatist, while moving others, is himself unmoved, even cold, like a stone, and removed from human society, an unmoved mover, invisible to the many moved. For the dramatist need never appear in his works; while he presents the world and lets it shine in his shows, he may hide from his audience. It is in this way that "they," as dramatists, are the lords of their faces, more lords than lords, who ruling in society must appear in it. And what of all those who appear in the dramatist's shows? These actors lend their faces to the roles they play and for their faces are selected for their parts. To be who they are, dramatists do not need faces at all. These actors and others in the company are but stewards of the dramatist's invisible excellence. Drama is a most public art, and yet the dramatist need not be public. Drama lives in gregarious, conversing humanity and yet the dramatist dwells in solitude. Though no light casts so far, no one keeps the lamp that sheds it more under a bushel than the dramatist.

Yet according to Shakespeare it is solitary dramatists who inherit "heavens graces." They do so *rightly,* he adds. Apparently, it is possible to receive such graces without right, *sans droit.*[20] Not so the dramatist. That these graces are heavenly makes us wonder about God's grace; in any case, these graces that the dramatist has are not a free gift; they are *rightly* inherited. Such graces may stir wonder in their recipient, but not gratitude, for they are merited.

Apparently it is these graces that allow the dramatist to husband nature's riches. Nature throws up rich beings; they sprout, well up, reach ripeness, hold steady for a while, then wither and perish. It is the office of the dramatist's shows to preserve these riches from decay or use. To look at them, to make them visible, and to make their rich "looks" last a little longer is the dramatist's delight. Art is not a conquest of nature, either hostile, chaotic, or messy. Art fulfills nature by saving it from falling back into its invisible beginning. To husband is to farm and to preserve, to encourage and to keep.

The dramatist knows this and also knows the power his shows have to move others; through them he can hurt like a tyrant or please like a flower. Prospero puts on a show so as to marry his daughter happily, regain his crown, unite Italy, punish his enemies, and prepare for death. All is well. But Iago also puts on a show so as to break up a marriage, please his spleen, stir up Venice, and evade the thought of death. All is ill. It seems that both dramatists who smell sweet as a summer's flower and dramatists who hurt husband nature's riches. Poetic virtue need not coincide with moral and political virtue.[21]

The dramatist knows this, yet to himself he only lives and dies. Here we must be careful, for the line reads:

> to itself, it only live and die.

Shakespeare's choice of the subjunctive rather than the continuous present is more than correct, for it seems to emphasize, as an aorist in Greek might do, the compact, selfsame wholeness that we stretch out in the words "lives" and "living" or "dies" and "dying."[22] This flower knows that it dies only once and so he writes "die." He knows he lives only once and so he writes "live." He knows that living and dying are not separate and so he writes "live and die" together. The human unmoved mover is mortal. As dramatist he is unmoved mover; as man he is mortal. This conjunction is not adventitious; for it is mortality which makes the choice of way of life momentous.

What kind of way of life does the dramatist choose? It is one in which he makes shows. Or perhaps we should say he husbands, farms, and cultivates shows, for the emphasis here does not fall upon art as opposed to nature, say as material and form. As the sonnet shows, the dramatist knows of his shows and their effect, but their effect of sweetness, like the fragrance of the flower, is something which is *more* apparent to the summer or audience. Closer to him, in his solitude, is his mortality and his relation to nature as husbander. He himself is one of nature's riches and he is his own husbander. Indeed he does so in this very sonnet; this is Shakespeare dry and salted away, Shakespeare husbanded from expense.

Yet this dramatist is also warned of a grave temptation in this sonnet. At first it seems that this temptation is the temptation to do "hurt." But when Shakespeare adds the word "and" and not the word "but" to what follows, he dissuades the reader from concluding that the temptation of the dramatist is moral. To find out what tempts and what restrains the dramatist we must read the sestet

> But if that flower with base infection meet,
> The basest weed outbraves his dignity:

We do not know yet what base infection is, though we sense the vulnerability of the highest natures. When we read the conclusion:

> For sweetest things turn sourest by their deeds;
> Lilies that fester, smell far worse than weeds.

we learn the identity of the base infection; it is deeds. It is deeds that turn the sweetest things sourest. The lily will remain self-sufficing, an unmoved yet moving sweetness among men, only by shunning the base infection of deeds. What is permitted for weeds is a grave danger for the lily. In this sonnet Shakespeare the dramatist considers the life of deeds. He knows that it is a temptation and he resists the temptation. Does he mean the deeds of love elsewhere mentioned, and embodied in speech, in the *Sonnets*? Yes, he does mean them, and also the marriage and procreation therein mentioned as well. The being described in Sonnet 94 stands out from all that surrounds him in the *Sonnets*. The dramatist does not do any of the things the other speakers in the *Sonnets* do or would like to. He does not do any of the things he shows in his plays. Shakespeare does not do the murders his Tragedies show, enjoy the marriages his Comedies conclude with, and endure the tumults his Histories perform over and over.

Let us be clear: this means the dramatist resists the temptation to do good. Shakespeare could with equal rightness have begun his sonnet:

> They that have power to do *good*, but will do none,

Indeed, this meaning belongs to the full meaning of what he has written, since the power to do hurt necessarily includes the power to do good, or at least some power to do good.[23] By writing as he has written, Shakespeare has, as he knew, aroused fear and indignation in the reader. But by so doing he has also hidden the power of the temptation; it is much more tempting to do good than to do evil. The voice that says to the poet "you might do great good, you could really help us, won't you please?" is much harder to answer or ignore than the voice which says "you could really do some hurt." And yet, it seems that Shakespeare resists these pleas, even regards them as temptations. He may acknowledge that others have an obligation to do good and therefore to elect the life of deeds, but if he does he surely knows of a higher obligation, an obligation to put on shows, to remain cold and unmoved, to be a stone. He says such a person rightly inherits heaven's graces. Rightly does he husband nature's riches from expense. By forgoing the public realm, by not doing deeds, even good deeds, he saves himself and grows richer.

The depreciation of deeds is *a fortiori* a depreciation of politics. You may say that it is dangerous to depreciate politics, to turn the best minds and hearts away from caring for the world. Perhaps. Yet the greatest minds do so. The originator of political philosophy, Socrates, suggested that only if the city begs the philosopher to rule, should he consider doing so. Even Aristotle whose *Politics* dignifies the statesman still deems friendship more precious than justice, and ranks the vita contemplativa above the vita activa. And although He rendered a good bit of the world to Caesar, Christ showed in his refusal to rule it that there is something superior to the Caesarean world.[24] Is the city or world the worse for hearing itself so ranked by the wise? Surely it has been better served by the gentlemen and statesmen who knew that there is something better than themselves, even by those who felt forced to acknowledge it, than by those teachers, such as Machiavelli and his train, who tell princes there is nothing better than a prince.

Shakespeare is not, however, teaching in this sonnet; he is speaking to himself. To himself he is saying that the choice of his way of life excludes all others utterly. This is hard to take. We democrats, we who change professions four times in a lifetime, or we democratic souls who hammer in the morning, fish in the afternoon, and think we can philosophize in the evening, we do not like to be told that some lives require single-minded and exclusive devotion, which to interrupt once may be to lose forever. We do not like to overhear Shakespeare telling himself this in Sonnet 94. It is noble aristocrats, such as Pascal, who understand that there are different orders of things, that none can be substituted for another, that force can never do the work of beauty, nor beauty the work of reason, nor reason the work of charity.[25] And the Tocqueville who said he believed there would never be a Pascal in America, we tend to forget. The closest we may come to appreciating the severe precision of Shakespeare's thinking is in our Constitution's prohibition of serving in more than one of the separate branches of our republican government at a time and the adumbration of such separation in the Declaration, whose distinction of nature and nature's God, and its First Amendment consequence, is also fundamental to Shakespeare.[26]

Shakespeare knew he could not be a dramatist and a king. This is remarkable, when you consider how much this dramatist knew about being a king. As Shakespeare's portrayal of kings shows, he knew what it is to be a king; in imagination he was every one of the score of kings, from gentle Duncan, to bloody Richard, and up to glorious Henry, who flourish across his stage; their deeds, their speeches, their very souls, he knew; indeed, Shakespeare is like his namesake, Williams, in *Henry V* in being able to imagine the most solitary of a king's thoughts. Yet Shakespeare says to himself, "You may know what it is to be a king better than any king. Thus, by nature you may be more qualified to rule than any other man. Yet if you did rule you would not be the man you are. Merely by ruling you would lose and spend your rich gifts. If you are a dramatist, you must resist deeds, even the offer of a crown. And so, if someone should say, only when dramatists such as yourself become kings, or kings become such dramatists, will there be just rule on earth, you should not believe them."

A matching consideration, of the good of others, would seem to account for the fact that in his plays Shakespeare almost always portrays poets as incompetent in affairs of state (consider the poet in *Julius Caesar*). Shakespeare seems to have thought that dramatists will surely do only hurt by deeds, either when they choose the life of deeds or if they think of their dramas as deeds, as neo-classical Brutus does. It seems Shakespeare did not think poets are good at everything they know. How strange that knowing about practical things does not mean you are good at them. As if to know them well, you must not practice them at all. Such is Shakespeare's view, however. For him, although virtue may be knowledge, knowledge is not virtue. Shakespeare is unlike the philosophers, especially Plato, in whose agonistic dialogues the philosopher always wins the highest esteem, always turns out to be better at whatever the specialist he is talking to does, better at ruling than the rulers, better at speaking than the rhetor, rhapsode, or sophist, more enchanting than the tragedian, more disenchanting than the comedian, more courageous than the warrior, etc. Naturally, such a philosopher is always exhorting everyone, especially the gentlemen, to become a philosopher, to become like him. Not Shakespeare. Though he must know his way of life fulfills human nature as few others do, maybe as none other does, he does not exhort other humans to follow it. Thus, the little praise of his own way of life he put in his works is entirely inconspicuous.

There is, however, a grave consequence of this depreciation of deeds, and in *King Lear* Shakespeare has thought about it. To the Fool Shakespeare has given his own part, that of seeing truth and then speaking it aloud in the presence of the powerful. The Fool is permitted to do so only because he is not only powerless but regarded by everyone as desiring no power. In order to know whether he is loved, as much as to perpetuate his realm, the dying Lear seeks a similarly powerless condition. But the terrible consequence of this wish is that once you see the truth, you will, by virtue of your powerlessness, be unable to protect it. You will know the quality of love but be unable to prevent her being hanged, right in front of you. If, then, as a consequence of husbanding the riches of nature with dramatic shows, you come to savour and love these riches, will you not want to protect them? If so, you must have power. You must do deeds. But what if, by doing them, you must soon go blind? *Lear* suggests that one can either know the truth *or* protect those one loves, but not both. In his life Shakespeare may have been saved from this painful dilemma by the fact that his birth excluded him from high political office. Yet this sonnet suggests he had the strength to live with it. We may call this strength solitude, for while rare gifts put a man in solitude, they also give him the strength to endure it.

The solitary Shakespeare we find in Sonnet 94 allows us to understand both why his work is available to us through writings in which he never appears and also why his work is not better available to us. Is it not a powerful impediment to reading Shakespeare seriously that he seems not to have taken his writings seriously enough to make sure that we read an accurate text?[27] The narrative poems he published as a younger man show he could take the care to publish an accurate text. Perhaps those texts were prepared by the younger man in Sonnet 55 who thirsts for a more-than-marble immortality. The mature Shakespeare was surely careless. Thus, the *Sonnets* themselves seem to include unfinished work, Sonnet 99 for example, with its fifteen lines. Was Shakespeare proud of his workmanship? If so, then wouldn't he have held back the *Sonnets*? That they were not held back seems to mean he no longer cared to leave a good, or a faithful text. Unless someone else put them in print without his permission.[28] Setting that instance aside, what are we to make of the fact that many details, sounds, words, phrases and sentences, and even many scenes and some acts in his plays owe their exactness to the choice of later editors from the variant and sometimes flawed texts Shakespeare left unsuperseded by one he had perfected?

Indeed, others have had to be stewards of Shakespeare's excellence. We owe the preservation of some of his plays, the best text of others, and an arrangement that still guides our study to the First Folio, and the First Folio is the work of other men. Since these other men, John Heminge and Henry Condell, were his former associates at the Globe, since they seem to be his friends (he mentions one of them in his will), and since their prefatory advice "To the great Variety of Readers" shows a discerning respect for his quality, it is plausible to conclude that their work had his approval. Perhaps the exceptional accuracy of the text of the *Tempest* is his work, and perhaps its location at the beginning of the whole is his plan. If so, then why did he not get further with the work of editing? How many labors to discern his intention, how many controversies, and how many uncertainties would be spared us. Between Shakespeare's retirement from the stage and his death, there were three or four years, surely enough time to prepare a better text than the First Folio. Should the reader treat seriously what Shakespeare seems to have treated so casually?

I think so. The persons of both Christ and Socrates, mentioned earlier in our attempt to understand Sonnet 94, remind us that there are serious men who neither publish nor write. The impression of casualness which Shakespeare's texts give to us comes from a seriousness akin to that of Christ and Socrates. He is a man for whom there is more on earth and under heaven than publishing, even the publishing of what he knows has the power to help. To see the truth is higher than to speak it publicly. The latter is close to "deeds" and deeds are forbidden to the dramatist. For the dramatist, Shakespeare, publication is only the afterthought or unintended consequence of his primary intention, to understand himself and all others. For such natures, solitude is a joy. Perhaps it helps to think of a fountain. Its jet ascends and ascends, with no thought of the pool someone builds below, to catch its overflowing waters. It gives and gives and gives, without pity and without consideration. We can guess, on the basis of Sonnet 94, that writing was for Shakespeare first and finally an aid to thought. What he wrote were traces of an activity. Just as Friday in *Robinson Crusoe* did not intend Crusoe's astonishment at his human footprint in the sand—he was simply fleeing for his life—so Shakespeare did not intend our wonder when we come upon his footprint, Sonnet 94. If you enjoy running between the shadowy mountains and the echoing sea, you will not care to preserve your mind's footprints in the sand. It should not surprise us, then, that for the publication of his works Shakespeare is only somewhat more responsible than God is said to be for evil or for a world which includes evil.[29] Such "irresponsibility" teaches the responsible spirit in which one might read what he has left to us.

That Shakespeare had the most to say to other men is shown by his plays; that he had no *need* to say anything to them is shown by this sonnet. In it he speaks of himself, to himself, and for himself alone. His *Confessions* were addressed to no God; he published no fabulously autobiographical *Discourse of the Method* in order to mold an army of methodical readers in a war against nature; he needed not to set his life aright in the eyes of posterity with his *Confessions,* and his *Ecce Homo* is marred by no desire to be known. Augustine, Descartes, Rousseau, and Nietzsche, all lacked solitude. Shakespeare so little lacked it that he did not mind being mistaken for someone else. In Sonnet 94 be invites misunderstanding, and may even intend it; he writes so as to be taken for a cruel Prince, a self-important man, an Aristotle, a Christ, or an Aristotle with the soul of Christ, and elsewhere, in the Droeshout portrait, we see that he did not mind being taken for an idiot.[30]

The happy solitude of Shakespeare has, I think, something to do with the abundance of his works, so many persons, so many times, so many regimes. The immensity of that creation required that its creator be hidden. The greatest creators speak very seldom about themselves and then only in an enigmatic or shy manner. Only once in the Hebrew Bible does YHWHElohim speak of himself and then only in reply to a question. His "I am that I am" is as enigmatic to those who seek to understand Him as He understands Himself as it is satisfying to Moses. It should not surprise us that Shakespeare speaks seldom about himself and then only darkly. In Shakespeare as in Genesis creating means separating, and something is most a creature by enjoying the greatest separation from its creator. To his own works Shakespeare is a hidden God, hidden from his characters as much as he is hidden from us by them. To create all that he did Shakespeare seems to have had to hide himself.

Lest I be misunderstood, Shakespeare does not say he is a Holy Creator God. He only understands himself *in the image of* the Holy Creator God. To be in the image is not to be. Shakespeare's creating, more precisely his making, uncovers what is already there. Thus Sonnet 94 speaks of nature's riches; the "they" of this sonnet did not create nature or make its riches. Because Shakespeare cared for nature and its riches he failed to create them, knowing that to create them he would first have had to destroy them.[31] In this respect he is more like the God of the seven days of creation than the God of the forty days of deluge, who had to destroy in order to recreate.[32] Yet his "let be" to the grass, the sun, and to so many brave new females and males calls none out of nothing. Like nature's riches they seem already there and so Shakespeare's "let be" to them is an ardent beholding. That he could behold himself we know from Sonnet 94.

"Behold the man" were the words of a Roman beholding Christ; when Nietzsche adopted them as the title of his autobiography, *Ecce Homo*, he suggested he might be a Roman with the soul of Christ, for surely he was both beholder and beheld in *Ecce Homo*.[33] We might say the same of Shakespeare, but with a difference. Most of what Nietzsche says of himself suggests that had he written Sonnet 94 it would have begun "He who has power to hurt" or "I who have power to hurt." By writing "they" Shakespeare suggests that there have been, there are, there will be other "Shakespeares." Greater self-love hath almost no man. Certainly not Nietzsche.[34]

That the self-love of Shakespeare is truly generous we also learn from comparing his autobiography with Descartes'. Nothing is more prominent in *The Discourse of the Method* than the word "I." To this "I" God is, for example, an afterthought. Descartes' proof of His existence not only comes after his proof of his own existence but is impossible without it. Yet his famous *cogito ergo sum* is in the image of the willful God, for it is a creative deed as much as an argument. The bringing into being of the godlike thinking ego comforts the frail doubting "I" which it once was. Also comforting will be this ego's project, the methodical mastery of nature. Descartes is profound but ignoble. Since he could not be a man, he made himself into a god; since he did not recognize himself as one of nature's riches, he treated nature as an enemy. That our walk through life is hedged by painful mysteries like death was not unknown to Shakespeare, but he sought refuge in no resolute certainty, either Cartesian or revealed. Shakespeare was courageous. He was so because he was erotic. Yet his irony surpasses even that of the erotic Socrates for, as Sonnet 94 shows, he better ignored those who have no ears to hear from someone their superior in heart and in mind than did Socrates. Nor did he ever compromise his solitude with a public *Apology* or any last words. Yet in comparison to Descartes, Shakespeare and Socrates seem to be twin brothers, encouraging us to so love noble things that we become the riches that nature would have us sweeten into.[35]

Notes

1. *Liberalism Ancient and Modern* (New York: Basic Books, 1968), p. 9.

2. Most of his life Allan Bloom found in Shakespeare instructive things he had already learned from others, especially Machiavelli, but in the end, he acknowledged Shakespeare his superior in heart and mind; on his last book, see *The Review of Metaphysics* Vol. 49 (June 1996), pp. 913-15.

3. See "The Myth of the Teenager," *Practical Homeschooling*, ed. Mary Pride, vol. I, no. 2 (Summer, 1993), pp. 19-21, (reprinted in an appendix to Mary Pride's *Big Book of Home Learning* (1999) and my little book, "The Teenager and the West" (whenever it comes out).

4. Here I print the 1609 text from Helen Vendler, *The Art of Shakespeare's Sonnets* (Cambridge: Harvard University Press, 1997), p. 402; elsewhere I modernize the text only in spelling; for purposes of interpretation, the arguments for the original punctuation, for example in Percy Simpson's *Shakespearean Punctuation* (Oxford, 1911), prevail, I think, over my old friend Theodore Redpath's defense of modernizing for general readers, as in his "The Punctuation of Shakespeare's Sonnets," in *New Essays on Shakespeare's Sonnets*, ed. Hilton Landry (New York: AMS Press, 1976); the full notes and annotations of the New Variorum are well supplemented by later editions, e. g., T. Brooke (1936), W. Ingram and T. Redpath (1964), P. Booth (1977), B. Evans (1996), K. Duncan-Jones (1997), and H. Vendler (1997).

5. Cf. the beginning of Rilke's first "Duino Elegy."

6. How very tempting it is to push Sonnet 94 back into the story of the *Sonnets*, how violent the resistance to finding depths in familiar surfaces is,

I learned from the elders in one well-educated audience, in the spring of 1982; one stormed out at the beginning of the question period and others in subsequent weeks substituted indignant refutations for the great books in the curriculum (so I learned from two students a decade later).

7. As James Winny says, in *The Master-Mistress: A Study of Shakespeare's Sonnets* (New York: Barnes and Noble, 1968), p. 164 ff.

8. Though sophisticated, heavy with learning, and decorated with au currant allusion, Joel Fineman's long book on the Sonnets, *Shakespeare's Perjured Eye* (Berkeley: University of California Press, 1986) does not refer to Sonnet 94, and even J.B. Leishman's fine *Themes and Variations in Shakespeare's Sonnets* (London: Hutchinson, 1963), though elevated by a high appreciation of Rilke, does the same.

9. Empson's essay, in his *Some Versions of Pastoral* (1935), is conveniently reprinted in the Signet edition of the *Sonnets*, prefaced by W.H. Auden's fine essay, in my view the best introduction to the sonnets as a whole. Meriting praise are other attempts at Sonnet 94: Hilton Landry, *Interpretations in Shakespeare's Sonnets* (Berkeley: University of California Press, 1963), pp 7-27, who acknowledges greater remaining riches in the poem, and Philip Martin, *Shakespeare's Sonnets: Self, Love, and Art* (Cambridge: at the University Press, 1972), pp. 30-43, who has the strength to say, at the end of his reading, that more remains than he has understood. The intellectual challenge of this riddle is also appreciated in detail by Stephen Booth in his *An Essay on Shakespeare's Sonnets* (New Haven: Yale University Press, 1969) and in his edition with commentary, *Shakespeare's Sonnets* (New Haven: Yale University Press, 1977). By faithfully describing the confusion which the reader experiences, and by holding to this experience, he is able to recognize the simplifying comfort offered by the readings of others (Empson, Ransom, etc.). Here, however, his inquiry rests, for he believes that "one" cannot pass from experience to a coherent interpretation.

10. These two differ; for Machiavelli's true view of the relation of heaven's riches to the prince, one must note Moses and consider the Mosaic images in the last chapter of *The Prince;* for Shakespeare's view, see the present author's manuscript, "Shakespeare's English Prince" (1998: Accepted for publication in 1982, hindered in unquiet times by a dean, this manuscript could thus be revised, somewhat, and properly titled "Shakespeare's Christian Prince," providentially perhaps).

11. This quotation is taken from Kaufmann's essay. See his *From Shakespeare to Existentialism* (New York: Doubleday, 1960), pp. 1-24.

12. Here and hereafter I cite the Martin Ostwald translation (New York: Bobbs-Merrill, 1962).

13. Nietzsche, *Jenseits von Gut und Böse*, # 63.

14. Cf. Shakespeare's self-sufficient and self-loving "love and die" with Paul's

advice: "For none of us liveth to himself, and no man dieth to himself" (Romans 14:7 and ff.). Shakespeare seems to have been an "only begetter" instead of an "only begotten." See footnote 20 below.

15. Landry, mentioned above, stresses the parable of the talents, and thinks that Shakespeare agrees with Christ's teaching.

16. *Kritische Gesamtausgabe*, ed. Giorgio Colli and Mazzino Montinari (Berlin and New York: Walter de Gruyter, 1967-78), 7:2, 289; this leftover (*Nachlass*), belongs to the period Sommer-Herbst 1884. Elizabeth Nietzsche put it in her arrangement of the leftovers, ~~The Will to Power~~, as No. 983. The story of her fraud is told by Walter Kaufmann in his warning preface to his translation of ~~The Will to Power~~ (1968), thus my strike-through marks for this non-book. In fact, by the end of his last lucid summer, Nietzsche had given up all plans for such a book; see Mazzino Montinari, "Nietzsches Nachlass von 1885 bis 1888 oder Textkritik und Wille zur Macht" in his *Nietzsche Lesen* (Berlin/New York: Walter de Gruyter, 1982), pp. 92-119.

17. Winston Churchill, *History of the English Speaking Peoples*, Vol. II (London: Cassell and Co., 1956), p. 124.

18. "Hölderlin and the Essence of Poetry" in *Existence and Being*, intro. Werner Brock, (Chicago: Regnery, 1949).

19. Could a German fighting for Hitler in World War II quote Shakespeare, as Commander Gale did upon landing on the bridges just behind the beach at Normandy? "And gentlemen in England now a-bed/ Shall think themselves accurs'd they were not here," he said to his fellow volunteers. See Chester Wilmot, *The Struggle for Europe* (London: Collins, 1952), pp. 238-240. By the same token, one should ask: does not the way Shakespeare is taught in the West today obscure or ignore his political wisdom? (1998: Now such study is very "political," mostly by unwisely denying he is wise, and willfully asserting he is willful.)

20. *"Non sans droit"* was the inscription on the shield Shakespeare obtained for his family. Readers of the *Sonnets* have long been puzzled to know the identity of the "only begetter" referred to in the dedication and also the identity of "Mr. W. H." In the light of Sonnet 94, I would suggest that both riddles refer to Shakespeare who was the only begetter of the sonnets and was *Mr.* William *Himself*. (1998: In rereading Wilde's *Portrait of Mr. W. H.* I find the same suggestion, tossed off in an attribution to a "German commentator called Barnstorff," whom I feared to track down, lest I go the way of Cyril Graham, and some others, but have nonetheless found in the New Variorum edition of Hyder Rollins [Philadelphia: Lippincott, 1902], Vol. II, Appendix VIII, pp. 214 ff.)

21. It would seem that good or evil is added to the dramatist's power by the character of the dramatist himself. Yet there is perhaps this difference between the good and the evil dramatist, between Prospero and Iago: the former

understands himself better than the latter. Iago could not have written Sonnet 94, but Prospero could, and Shakespeare did. (See the final page of my dialogue, "Looking at the Body," *Hastings Center Reports*, April 1975.) In addition, Shakespeare warns, as Iago does only to deceive the more, that his art can deceive.

22. That Shakespeare did not have to employ the subjunctive for the sake of correctness but could, if he wished, have employed the present tense is supported by 2 *Henry IV*, I.iii.78: "If he *should* do so,/ He *leaves* his back unarmed...(my italics). See F.A. Abbott, *A Shakespearian Grammar* (New York: Dover, 1966), s.v.

23. As Hobbes says "Orators...though they have great power to hurt, have little to save." (*Leviathan* II, 19, 97) Likewise, one might say of political men, that they can do evil but only protect and encourage good.

24. As Leopardi noted, Christ was the first to speak of "the world." See "Only Christianity," in *Saints, Sovereigns, & Scholars: Essays Presented to Frederick D. Wilhelmsen*, ed. Fr. J. Lehrberger, R. Herrera, & M. Bradford (New York: Peter Lang, 1993), pp. 211-230.

25. Consider *Pensées*, No. 308 (Lafuma numbering).

26. In the Declaration, George III tyrannizes by trying to unite the legislative, judicial, and executive duties, while the Creator is worshipped for his legislative, judicial, and executive effects; for more see my "The Declaration of America." The first two parts of this account were serialized in *Practical Homeschooling* in the Fall 1998 and Spring 1999 issues; the whole is available on the Declaration Foundation website (www.declaration.net) and is the basis of *The Declaration and the Course of American Events*, a text for advanced home-schoolers, written with Richard Ferrier, prefaced by Alan Keyes, and also available on the same website.

27. I am thankful to Harvey Flaumenhaft for posing this question to me long ago.

28. See the acute remarks of W.H. Auden, on how unfinished as a group, let alone a story, the *Sonnets* are, in his preface to the Signet edition, mentioned above. Indeed, as Auden judges, Shakespeare may never have intended the Sonnets for publication.

29. Here I employ an expression I first heard from Leo Strauss in answer to a question I asked him about transcripts of his classes, which contain many errors. (The effort to improve them lapsed later with the early death of Herbert Storing.)

30. According to Nietzsche (*Ecce Homo*, "Why I Am So Clever," 4), Shakespeare was a kind of Caesar who suffered so much that he needed to be a buffoon. However, what Shakespeare shows in Sonnet 94 is a forbidding exterior that, as in Nietzsche, hides a "heart of gold."

31. Cf. Nietzsche to Jacob Burckhardt, 6 January 1889: "Lieber Herr Pro-

fessor, zuletzt wäre ich sehr viel lieber Basler Professor als Gott: aber ich habe es nicht gewagt, meinen Privat-Egoismus so weit zu treiben, um seinetwegen die Schaffung der Welt zu unterlassen" (ed. Karl Schlechta, vol. III, p. 1351). I have described the way Shakespeare's dramatic making contributes to his knowing human things and hence makes him resemble the creative and knowing God of the Bible in *The Seven Wonders of Shakespeare*, to appear in Rowman and Littlefield's Lexington series. The full account will require an interpretation of all the places in his plays where he shows men making dramas, especially in *Othello* and in *The Tempest*.

32. Cf. Zarathustra's celebration of his creating in "The Seven Seals."

33. See my "Behold Nietzsche," *Nietzsche Studien*, Band XXII: (Berlin and New York: Walter de Gruyter, 1993), pp. 42-79; reprinted with revisions in *Friedrich Nietzsche: Critical Assessments*, ed. Daniel Conway (Routledge, 1998).

34. Nietzsche's idea of the eternal recurrence of the same would require him to face the idea that there have been and will be other "Nietzsches" even with "this thought and these whiskers," but I have found no evidence that Nietzsche faced this thought in *Ecce Homo*.

35. This portion of my inquiry into Shakespeare's self-understanding began suddenly in a class in the autumn of 1971 at Dartmouth College, was renewed in a Freshman Seminar entitled "Making, Knowing, and Being" in 1975, and offered as a public lecture at Dartmouth in 1972, Harvard in 1974, Freiburg (im Breisgau) in 1974, Heidelberg in 1977, and the University of Dallas twice in 1978. I am grateful to my hosts and all those, especially students, who shared in this inquiry. (And to two readers of the published version, who sought me out, I am indebted for their friendship.)

SHAKESPEAREAN COMEDY AND TRAGEDY:
IMPLICIT POLITICAL ANALOGIES

Robert B. Heilman

Political subject matter is everywhere in Shakespeare's tragedies and histories. One can detect political implications even in some comedies. I could imagine dealing with *Love's Labor's Lost* under the rubric "The Politics of Young Love," and with *The Taming of the Shrew* as "The Politics of Matrimony." Both touch on the problems of a polity that comes into being syncretically and makes its constituents face diversities that could beget disruptive turmoil. Lest this seem, however, an over-handsome formulation of issues in a community too restricted to be a political entity, I will treat the two plays not as exemplars but as mild analogies of the political. *Love's Labor's Lost* and *The Taming* go comfortably together because they are complementary treatments of the matrimonial relationship. While participation in it rests on passion, some passions need, if not to be reduced to passivity, at least to be curbed or realigned. In Katherine the energy that has gone into an anti-social self-assertiveness—in our day Kate would go for any public disruptive tactics that would draw a television camera to tickle her ego—undergoes a redirection that makes it more adjusted to cooperation. Here, a male figure sees what is needed. In *Love's Labor's Lost*, a female figure, seconded by three others, sees what is needed. The four young scholars have suddenly fallen out of love with their learning and in love with four French charmers, and they want to marry them on the spot. But the charmers impose a year's delay, and what is more, a year of tasks that in spirit resemble the monastic triennium from which the lovers have apostatized (or defected, to use the political metaphor). Now what Berowne and his fellow-lovers have in common with Kate the shrew is the desire to impose emotion on others, to have feeling force action, to have hysteria make history. All learn the same lesson: a limiting of the will, a curbing of the ego—necessities for a bearable and durable life for all the members of the community. What the characters have experienced is not unlike a lesson in politics.

So Shakespeare has a strong sense of the claim of the larger order upon the individual. But he has no less strong a sense—and we may not notice this as readily—of the individual's tendency to assert himself in forgetfulness, disturbance, or even defiance of the order. More than that, Shakespeare's imagination tends to make the best case that can be made for the individual who wants to do it his own way. Such case-making leads readers at some times to come up with greater sympathy for the self-indulgent or self-asserting than the text as a whole warrants. Surely readers of *Love's Labor's Lost* tend to do two things: one, to applaud the quartet of scholars when they flee study hall for love, and two, not to notice that the girls really send the hasty lads back to a kind of study hall. And how fashionable it has become to suppose that Kate is not a shrew at all but a superior person who is victimized by a surly papa and a naughty little sister, who is driven to tantrums as tactics of the undervalued, and whose gestures of submission to Petruchio are a brighter woman's ironic triumph over a lout. Since the text can give a small push or two to such readings, these comedies can lead us in to the ways in which Shakespeare, in the politics of his art, can habitually give sympathetic understanding to individuals whose political direction is not entirely exemplary.

I want to widen out the context a little, first by a brief allusion to the spiritual journeys of Father John Dunne of the University of Notre Dame. Father Dunne's quest for understanding, if I do not misunderstand him, involves an imaginative entry into writings—myths, autobiographies, confessions—about and by figures outside Christianity, such as Buddha and Mohammed, and his full experiencing of "the way, the truth, and the light" as it is presented in those documents. Though the journey implies a return, the spirit that returns may not be the same, for the journey also implies an openness to the illuminations that may be encountered in these alternative visions of spiritual reality. Father Dunne accepts these disparate accounts as having a true role to play for the seeker grounded in another faith. My next allusion is anti-climactic, for I drop from the spiritual to the professorial. My own essay on comedy, *The Ways of the World,* is a report on the wide applicability of Anthony Burgess's definition of comedy: "acceptance of the world, of the fundamental disparateness of all the elements of the world." Acceptance is best defined negatively: it avoids the reflective styles of abuse, satire, and radical reform. Unless I am mistaken, there is an analogy between the theological journey which accepts the value of experience in alien domains, and the comic method which accepts the diversity of human conduct—i.e., that disparateness which we see as such because of our sense of the norms essential to order.

These different manifestations of openness to diversity, of the acceptance of disparateness, provide the largest possible context for Shakespeare's habit—and habit I take it to be—of seeing what can be said for virtually all characters, even those of whom it might be said that nothing could be said for them. Likewise he imagines what they can say for themselves, and how they can put their best foot forward, even a better foot than they might seem to have by their foot-locker. He can imagine the steadfastness with which they look at that better foot as if they stood solely upon it, and, as they thus give themselves the best possible standing, become plausible enough to stir some fellow-feeling in us. He almost makes cases for them. For instance, when I first gazed in awe at the exploding universe of Shakespeare interpretation, one standard view of Iago was that he was a career army man who had been deprived of preferment expected and due. His lines on this in I.i are credible enough to be convincing, even with professors whom we might expect to admire Cassio's theoretical training and hence to reject Iago's contempt for what he calls "prattle without practice." Such interpreters of Iago would presumably find Coleridge's "motiveless malignity" a rather fanciful imposition upon the positive facts alleged by Iago. To the positivist mind Iago has to have a police-department motive, and unjust failure of promotion seems quite impressive. Well, the point is only that, in imagining character, Shakespeare almost automatically includes the self-image by which men and women put the best possible light on the actions that they take.

One might say, "But of course, self-justification," and thus see only a commonplace phenomenon of personality. Shakespeare tends, however, not so much to let the self-justification become purely that as to allow the possibility that it may contain some justice. Shakespeare is not very much on the lookout for Tartufferie. For him, the case-maker may have something of a case. What is more, the case-maker may manage a very subtle style. He may not so much use words that glamorize a role as enact a role that has in it something honorable or admirable and thus deflect attention, perhaps even his own, from all that he is up to. To adopt or even seek a comforting or reassuring role may in itself reflect a moral or quasi-moral subtlety in personality. Edmund, for instance, is less gross than Goneril or Regan; he craves a philosophic buttress for his

scheme to get on, whereas their aggressive self-interest is more blunt. It
hardly seeks a doctrinal base.

Since a tragic hero is more complex than a melodramatic protagonist, whether virtuous or villainous, it is to be expected that tragic heroes
go beyond the single role, carrying at least a two-suiter of motives. Oedipus, for instance, is both the crudely passionate aggressor and the prin-
cipled and responsible detector of evil aggressions. The Shakespearean
tragic hero almost always instinctively seeks another role than that of
tragic hero. Tragic heroism imposes an ultimate burden or strain that
humanity, it seems clear, prefers to evade. The final phase of tragic experience is the recognition of what one has been up to—the anagnorisis, in
the traditional term adopted for this more specialized meaning, or self-
knowledge (that very familiar phrase at which one hesitates a little because for all of us it is more easily said than done and is therefore in
danger of sounding glib). We do not shrink from the hubristic aggression—the violence which is the actional symbol of inner arrogance—
nearly as much as we resist the acknowledgment of what we have done.
The acknowledgment is the final surrender of, or at least a major blow to,
the *amour propre* that wants to escape judgment by self and others. Pride
may go on after a fall. We resist, postpone, or translate into waffle-lan-
guage the statement hardest for us to make: "I did wrong"—the statement that rounds out the tragic role (or tragic rhythm, as Francis
Fergusson called it, defining its phases as purpose—passion—perception).

I have said that the Shakespearean tragic hero instinctively seeks
another role than that of tragic hero. As my friend Leonard Dean put it
some years ago, the tragic hero has to live in a tragedy, but he tries as long
as he can to live in a melodrama. The role he craves is that of melodramatic hero. Tragedy is the realm of good-and-bad; melodrama the realm
of good-or-bad. As melodramatic hero one can push out of sight one's
misdoing by claiming either as much good for oneself as one can or as
much bad for one's adversaries as one can. Thus he can be a unified
person, not a disconcerting mixture of well-intentioned man and hubristic wrongdoer.

The Shakespearean imagination, I have said, has a strong grasp of
humanity's case-making instinct—either in the rhetorical form in which
words give the best possible coloring to deeds, or in the dramatic form in
which a man's assumption of a creditable role defines him as favorably as
possible. Shakespeare's awareness of the human passion to pare down or
modulate self-confrontation has a strong influence on the major trag-

edies, that is, on the characterization in them. It is not that Shakespeare doubts the emergence of moral enlightenment or recovery, but that he has a keen eye for the human resistance to paying the moral price. I have only lately come to see that this perception of his is a regular element in his tragic imagination, and hence to believe that it affords a way of approaching some of the problems that the tragedies appear to offer. The major heroes exhibit different combinations of the capacity for self-seeing and of that resistance to it which I am designating by the somewhat short-hand term of "case-making."

Lear is the best rounded of the tragic heroes—best rounded in the sense that his powerful drive for self-exculpation is most fully balanced by his eventual coming to understand what he has done. On the one hand he seeks a self-protective melodramatic role: the role of innocent victim of Goneril and Regan, and also of righteous judge of them—really a double self-saving. As early as Act I, on the other hand, he is able to say of Cordelia, briefly and fleetingly, "I did her wrong." It then takes him hundreds of lines of violent censure of Goneril and Regan—in this he enacts a role of implicit self-exoneration—before he comes slowly around to the series of lines in Act V in which he can acknowledge that he must beg forgiveness of Cordelia. Begging forgiveness is the ultimate confessional and humbling act.

Othello does not come around nearly so fully. This may reflect a time-situation almost at the polar opposite of that in *Lear. Lear's* great error is a sudden action that opens the play, and hence Lear has maximum time to come to understanding. Othello spends more than half a play working up to his great error; he does not kill Desdemona until halfway through Act V, so that a minimum of time is left for his understanding what he has done. Shakespeare may be thinking that in so short a time no man can really come around adequately from the self-justification which is his instinctive first stage after the discovery of disaster. This hypothesis is consistent with the distribution, among speakers and things spoken, of the barely 250 lines from Desdemona's "second death" to final curtain. It takes 110 lines for Othello simply to realize the truth; Emilia dominates these with her attacks on Iago and Othello, and most of what Othello says is dull reiteration of Desdemona's alleged misconduct. When Othello at last sees that he has killed an innocent woman, there are just under 140 lines left in the final scene. Othello speaks not quite half of these—a meager space in which to articulate complex alterations in attitude or movements of personality. A few of his lines have to do with the facts, a few directly express grief for Desdemona, a few more attack Iago. In still more lines Othello calls himself names, refers sardonically to himself, seeks a weapon, accuses himself of a drop from past heroism to present pusillanimity, sees Desdemona as sending him to hell at the Day of Doom, and calls for theatrical punishments upon himself. These points, which occupy about two-thirds of Othello's lines, have rather the air of self-censure by one who has been tricked into a bad mistake. In one short speech he insists that he did "all in honor," and finally there is the famous death speech which mostly calls attention to his political and personal merits. He serves as his own character witness. It is true, of course, that he sentences himself to death, yet it is almost as if it were a penalty for a tactical or strategic mistake. At the same time he continues to think well of his honor. What he never gets said is that what his honor amounted to was arrogant and ruthless egotism, and that he committed a terrible wrong. In him, that is, we see the vigorous action of Shakespeare's sense of the ego's persistent reaching out for the formula that will put the individual in the best possible light.

While Lear and Othello both act, one in literal haste and the other in moral haste, Hamlet is the most famous resister of haste in all literature. While Lear and Othello both come to know, as their natures make possible, what they have done, Hamlet wants to know what he is doing before he does it. These differences go along with one interesting ground of resemblance. Othello does not claim outright to be an innocent man, but he does present himself as free of the wrong emotions that would make him guilty of first-degree murder. Lear inferentially claims to be innocent as long as he can, that is, to be an innocent victim of ungrateful daughters. Hamlet passionately desires to remain innocent. Perhaps he is nagged by doubts of his innocence; such doubts would help account for the denunciatory and self-righteous elements in his style (these elements are also strong in the rhetoric of Hamlet senior, and in Lear's language as long as he clings to his role of wronged parent). Be that as it may, Hamlet's longing to feel innocent is his form of the pursuit of self-esteem which Shakespeare regularly depicts in his tragic characters. Other heroes act wrongly and then clutch at innocence; Hamlet so clings to innocence that he hardly acts, even to effect a retribution that he makes seem virtually judicial. He does not bring himself to it; rather he brings it about, and in a way, I suggest, that might be devised by wily innocence plotting unawares. He carries out a series of antics—outcroppings, in part, of inner pressures—that generate enormous tensions; tensions generate Claudius's plotting of a "final solution"; the final solution generates chaotic brawling; in this, deaths are generated less by ordered intention than by scrambled contention and hot unscheduled lunges. Retributory homicide is accomplished without the guilt of planned murder, retaliation without loss of innocence. Besides, the plotting of a final solution makes larger and more solid the guilt of Claudius. The more substantial the guilt of the wrongdoer, the more substantial the innocence of the agent of right.

Hamlet's pursuit of a self-image is unique among these heroes. Lear's and Othello's ways of claiming a sympathetic esteem embody more familiar patterns—Lear's "I don't deserve such unfair treatment," and Othello's "I am better than I look." In *Macbeth* we find a different situation and, in the erring hero, a different style of salvaging an honorableness that can be a bulwark against denigration by self and others. (In commenting on *Macbeth* I am using a different perspective from that which I employed in an earlier essay.[1] Since it does not contain a *peccavi*, this section loses the advantage of a self-correction, which makes the voyeur in everyman feel like a moralist.) Macbeth's way of thinking well of himself, and of encouraging others to think well of himself, differs from the methods of the other tragic heroes: theirs are rhetorical, his is dramatic. They verbalize their cases; Macbeth enacts a role that can elicit fellow-feeling, applause, or admiration. It is not that Macbeth plays tricks to mislead moral pursuers; rather he instinctively follows a course that in its way is creditable enough to deflect attention from what is less creditable. The role that Macbeth creates and enacts is that of a strenuous, come-what-may, fear-quelling fighter against hostile no-mercy forces who hem him in and must kill him. (There is also something of this in Richard III.) He is so completely in the role of hemmed-in hero that his mind is wholly empty of any awareness of why he is hemmed in. Shakespeare focuses all attention on Macbeth agonistes, the heroic warrior against odds. Macbeth shows no fear when he calls on the witches and sees their apparitions; when they give him apparently bad news, he does not fold but takes fierce, indeed savage, action. He must go on, despite his wife's illness and death; despite thought of how wretched life is now when he receives only "deep" curses and what he sardonically calls "mouth-honour"; despite a desperate feeling of emptiness; and despite news of thanes fleeing him and hostile armies approaching. "I'll fight till from my bones my flesh be hack'd" (V.iii.32). Birnam Wood moves toward him— the miracle which has to seal his fate, but still he can cry, "Blow, wind! come, wrack!/ At least we'll die with harness on our back" (V.v.52). In one small sense he can even see himself as a victim, yet a victim who will fight rather than merely suffer: "They have tied me to a stake; I cannot fly,/ But, bear-like, I must fight the course" (V.vii.1-2). It's what "they" have done, without any glimpse of what he has done. He will not "play the Roman fool, and die/ On mine own sword" (V.vii.1-2). When he meets Macduff and finds that he was born by Caesarean section—a pretty tricky fulfillment of the prophecy of death by one not "of woman born"—he backs off only a moment from the fight that the witches' apparition has predicted will be fatal for him. Then he comes back: "I will not yield,.../ Yet I will try the last..../...Lay on, Macduff,/ And damn'd be him that first cries, 'Hold, enough!'" (V.viii.27-34).

We may say that Shakespeare knows that a man who does evil may be brave, assumes the palpableness of the evil, and concentrates on the more interesting problem of dramatizing the bravery. Or since Macbeth's way of meeting his troubles is an enactment of a hero's role, and since the hero in him has stolen the stage from the villain in him, we might say that Shakespeare lets Macbeth get away with it. However this may be, it is clear that in *Macbeth* Shakespeare is more than usually fascinated by the devices that men—men of punitive, revengeful, or ambitious violence—use to think well of themselves or present themselves as worthy of respect or sympathy from observers. The devices are not conscious tricks; rather they represent an instinctive working of emotions. Shakespeare seems to fall into so thorough an imaginative participation in these self-extolling or self-creating devices that his characterizations can take on some ambiguity. Some commentators write as if, in the beleaguered latter part of his life, Macbeth had transcended his past and were now only a figure of heroic valor. Richard II so manipulates the divine right that is his theoretical strength, exploits the pathos of his practical situation, and converts himself into a poetical contemplator, as to elicit from some readers a fond sympathy and almost an ignoring of the royal incapacity, the combination of weakness and willfulness that invites a take-over by any aspirant stronger on talent than scruple. Again, is Timon a truly generous soul who is a victim of ingratitude and whose only mistake is an excess of a virtue, or does he err much more seriously by unconsciously believing that friendship can be bought and by mistaking his rash payments for pure generosity? If it is the latter, Timon is practicing what we may call timony—that is, a secular simony, the purchase of good offices. Yet to some observers he seems truly generous, a pathetic victim of panhandlers. As is his wont, Shakespeare has imagined the best that can be said for him, and thus makes him ambiguous.

Now let me try to knit up or together several lines of thought that may seem tangled. The emerging fabric should have constant implications for political life, though for the time I leave them implicit rather than make them explicit. I started by suggesting an analogy among a kind of theological imagination, a theory of comedy as the acceptance of diversity, and the Shakespearean habit of finding the best that can be said for characters whose flaws are quite evident. My Shakespeare examples, it is true, have been mostly in the realm of tragedy, though I did start out with *Love's Labor's Lost* and *The Taming of the Shrew*. My dominant use of the tragedies reveals no desire to push a paradox—that one can use the spirit of comedy as a perspective for discussing tragedy; rather it enables us to see a common element in tragedy and comedy. That tragedy and comedy are related is an old truism; but people who utter it may speak with solemn vagueness rather than with useful precision. Let me try a concrete formulation of an attitude shared by tragedy and comedy: neither envisages the eradication of evil but rather acknowledges the inevitable imperfection of things, especially the imperfection of human conduct (and, as we have seen, Shakespeare's acceptance includes his extremely active understanding of what may be said for imperfect beings, or what these erring creatures may say for themselves). Clearly I am attributing to both forms a solid reality sense, which I need hardly note is an essential foundation of political life. Now the risk in such an attribution, indispensable as the reality sense is, is that it may seem to invest both generic forms with an anything-goes or whatever-is-is-right or even a wrong-always-triumphs version of despair. But this conclusion, though we must not ignore it, does not really follow. To have a sense of the unregenerate as a constant is not to deny the influence of the regenerative; to be aware of the fallen nature of man—I beg the fact or the nature of the fall—is not to declare that man never can be, or is, upright. In tragedy, what survives anti-moral conduct is moral awareness; it may have to struggle to regain its power in the human soul or in the human community, but it is never replaced by a general yielding to the non-moral that for a time seems to call the shots. In comedy, what survives is the social order; the essential processes are the embrace of better values by the more capable, the restoration of good sense in those who have acted foolishly, and the general application of amiable tolerance in place of retaliatory and reformist pressure. But these survivals that are characteristic of the two genres and that are essential to the enduring of a free society make no guarantee that there will not be further outbreaks of destructive arrogance or disruptive folly. Neither form ever says, "This will never do" or "We will change all that"; what each form says is, "This is the way it is," one with an "alas," the other with a smile.

Tragedy, we may say, invokes a sense of honor; comedy, a sense of humor. A sense of honor means the acceptance of imperatives that one may not ignore or violate; a sense of humor means an acceptance of disparates rather than an application of conformitarian or egalitarian imperatives. Both honor and humor involve risks. The code of honor of course runs the risk that honor may mean contentious self-magnification rather than self-subduing obligation. The humorous acceptance of disparates raises the nice problem of the borderline beyond which acceptance may seem to go much too far. Two Shakespeare comedies approach the borderline problem rather adventurously, coming up with different solutions that cause difficulties to many readers. One is the extraordinary grace shown to Angelo in *Measure for Measure*; the other is the rejection of Falstaff in *2 Henry IV*. Each play makes a decision that many readers would not make.

In *Measure for Measure* Angelo, an acting duke committed to reform, is so eager to purify Vienna that he invokes the death penalty against Claudio because Claudio got his fiancée Juliet pregnant. When Claudio's sister Isabella begs for his life, Angelo feels so strong a sexual desire for her that he promises to free Claudio if she will sleep with him. Isabella is horrified, but later agrees to this as part of another plot: substituted for her on the nocturnal assignation is Mariana, a girl whom Angelo had once jilted for dowry-failure. But after this sexual pay-off for his promised mercy, Angelo orders Claudio killed anyway. Happily the Duke whom Angelo is temporarily replacing is a full-time *dux ex machina* masterminding defensive actions: Claudio is saved, Angelo's vices are publicly revealed, and he is sentenced to death. But Mariana and Isabella both plead for him, and he and Mariana become one of three couples that constitute a final rich matrimonial harvest. The problem is that Angelo has been guilty of judicial harshness, lust, blackmail, and treachery, but by way of the penalty that seems required he has no more than a brief fright. In effect, the play accepts the actions of Angelo as if they were not vices but follies like pretentiousness or boastfulness. One way of reflecting our difficulty with this situation is calling this play a "dark comedy." As a matter of fact, the way things are handled is very much like that in the modern form which we regularly call "black comedy": its hallmark is the acceptance of the unacceptable. The fact that we have to come to terms with is that comedy always has within it the seed of black comedy; acceptance can easily drift into over-acceptance. There is no wholly objective line that bounds the realm of the acceptable. *Measure for Measure* is useful in its focusing attention on this problematic indeterminateness.

In Angelo Shakespeare seems to go as far as he can to see what can be said for a character of rather ample questionableness. In effect, we are still to feel the character to be "one of us" if his motives, however unlovely, fail to result in the injuries that he is willing to inflict on others. In Falstaff, on the other hand, Shakespeare seems uniquely to depart from the principle that we have seen him frequently use: here, as it were, he seeks out what can be said against a character who is so widespread a favorite that anything short of adulation seems almost indecent. Yet I doubt that Shakespeare is really doing a turn-about. It depends partly on where we start. Even if we think that Shakespeare thinks of Falstaff as primarily a clown and entertainer, still Falstaff gets a pretty large slice of the military pie, and then adopts a style there, and in his relations with creditors, that makes it difficult to think of him only as an innocuous funny man. But suppose Shakespeare, as I suspect he does, thinks of Falstaff as primarily a sponger, a cheat, and a racketeer whom we would hate to have to rely on in any situation at all. Then we can see Shakespeare as indeed applying his standard method of finding everything that can be said for him: Shakespeare has given him credit for so much amiable jesting, easy wit, parodic skill, and general showmanship that he has charmed most observers out of their usual sense of what is socio-politically admissible. For the new Henry V, whose youth has been rather clouded by his crony-hood, to continue an intimacy with Falstaff would be a ruinous symbolic act; this should be clear to sentimental Americans if they will bother to recall their immense and often savage displeasure at any peccadilloes in any White House attaché or habitué. Shakespeare accepts what the king has to do, even at the cost of the king's looking unfaithful and ungrateful, and he also accepts the fact that Henry V may do what he has to do not very gracefully or winningly. In Falstaff Shakespeare accepts the fact that irresponsibility and rascality need not be repulsive but can be allied with vast seductive charm; he also accepts the fact that there is a point at which charm can no longer bail out irresponsibility and rascality. The situation is analogous to that in tragedy: all that wins our admiration and sympathy for tragic heroes cannot save them from the outcomes implicit in their deeds. Whoever objects to the discarding of Falstaff by Henry V should also object to the fact that Macbeth is done in by a coalition of more conventional political types, and that suicide deprives the world of so glamorous a charmer as Othello. And if we seek a consistency within Shakespeare's comic practice that condemns Falstaff but rescues Angelo, it may be this: that Falstaff is essentially corrupt, but because he is great fun we ignore his corruption as long as it is not politically significant; while Angelo, who of course is no fun at all, undertakes evil acts which represent, instead of an essential corruption, the faulty resistance to temptation which marks all humanity.

Looking at the new Henry V, Shakespeare sees that a king may have to be royal rather than loyal. Not that being royal means per se being disloyal, but that the royal imperative is to be loyal to community rather than crony, or, in another idiom, to polis rather than pals (incidentally the reverse of the moral formula enunciated by E.M. Forster some years ago, presumably for political commoners rather than political leaders). Looking at royalty—that is, political leadership—in numerous plays, Shakespeare can use, with equal ease, either a tragic or a comic perspective. And in both modes he sees reality as a mixed, ambiguous affair: the catastrophes of tragedy do not mean a total loss of sustaining values, nor the Act V satisfactions of comedy an elimination of the dissatisfied and the disruptive. On the one hand, the sufferings of tragedy are counterbalanced by the survival in consciousness of the distinction between good and evil. Things do not get blurred, meaningless, or contemptible; in other words, as someone said long ago, the opposite of tragedy is not comedy, but cynicism. In comedy, on the other hand, the comfortable accommodations reached in later scenes do not guarantee or even hint at happiness for all forever. We stop at a moment of gratifications and peace, but its continuance, if not denied, is not predicted. Trouble and troubling characters are still alive and around, and even in the luckier ones, human nature still holds on. Despite a recent tendency to invest the dramatic romances with an aura of the transcendental or the paradisaic, even there, I think, we see more a temporary surfacing of good nature or good sense than the creation of a utopia or even the establishment of a truly better world. What I am getting at, in other words, is that the opposite of comedy is—to employ a term now made widely available by the writings of Eric Voegelin—the gnostic illusion.

If we can set tragedy off against cynicism, and comedy against gnosticism, we can see these generic modes as having in themselves some significance in the context of political order. It is just possible that in this context there is a symbolic significance in the writing of tragedy and comedy. Perhaps it would be saying too much to propose that the writing of tragedy and comedy is essential to a healthy political order. But the moods out of which these forms come, and which they may nourish, are desirable in, if not actually indispensable to, political order, for ominous threats to that order would lie in cynicism and gnosticism, i.e., on the one hand the sense that anything goes because all is corruption, and the opposite sense that all corruption must be eliminated and intramundane salvation be accomplished, obviously by whatever compulsions are requisite. Tragedy and comedy are different modes of reconciliation to imperfect actuality: tragedy sees wrongdoing instead of corruption, sees the cost, and sees the spiritual survival; comedy sees folly, messiness, and even scheming as incurably persistent, but not finally triumphant over the decency and good sense and even wisdom that humanity is capable of in its better parts and at its better moments. Comedy also sees that not all differences are differences between right and wrong.

Suppose we could imagine a polity in which all members were equally equipped with a tragic sense. That is, they would recognize their wrongdoings as wrongdoings, as their own, as voluntary, as of a moral quality not to be upgraded by causes and conditionings that the doer can allege, and as imposing a responsibility to be borne and exercised. Highly improbable, it need hardly be said. But were it possible, this situation would define a political order in which the institutional arms and organs could be minimized; we might even approach the deinstitutionalized community projected hauntingly on the screen of the ideal by anarchist visions. At least an immense machinery of justice would seem gratuitous. Still to be taken care of, however, would be all matters of policy. Here, perhaps, the comic spirit would be useful. The acceptance of fundamental disparateness is a definition not only of humor and of comedy but of politics, at least of democratic and pluralistic politics as opposed to ideological politics, which is humorless and gnostic and therefore dictatorial. Ideological politics is always a melodrama: our own virtue against others' evil that must be done away with. *Carthago delenda est*, with *Carthago* as the symbol of all that is different (there is a version of this in anti-Semitism; "Jew," Arthur Miller has said, "is only the name we give to the stranger"). American political activity starts as the melodrama: campaigns for office are strictly non-comic affairs of good guy vs. bad guys. Election over, the winners soon discover, if they do not already know it, that what they face is not so much bad guys as it is complex and diverse claims that have to be met by various styles of compromise and accommodation. They move from melodrama to the comic spirit: acceptance of the disparate. (This politicization of the literary is also a secularization of Christian charity.) The problem, as we noted earlier, is always the limit of acceptance, the point at which the disparate calls for distinctions rather than undifferentiating embrace, the point at which even those behind glass walls have to risk throwing a stone or two. Comic practice may provide a model: it does not assume a plurality of options to mean an equality among the options. It does not go for compulsory homogenization; one result is that it lets cream rise to the top. In effect, it judges: some courses, some situations, some individuals are more admirable than others. Prospero is the superior person in *The Tempest*, Hermione in *Winter's Tale*, Imogen in *Cymbeline*, and to go outside Shakespeare for a great example, Mirabell and Millamant in Congreve's *The Way of the World*. In comedy all survive, all get something; but the higher the quality of the individuals, the greater the achievement, be it in measurable things, in way of life, or simply in the esteem which we accord to the exemplary. In dealing with the difficult issue of quality and equality, comedy provides a theatrical symbolization of a basic political problem.

The mark of the achieved quality may be the denial or rejection of apparent advantage or profit. Prospero's abjuring of his magical powers, whatever it may signify in Shakespeare's own spiritual or poetic history, is implicitly a piece of political theory: man may work a political miracle now and then, but he is wise not to count on a regular intervention of the miraculous. In the long run, political life is a gamble with human nature, to be understood and dealt with as best one may by the more limited tools normally at hand. Timon exemplifies the worst way of dealing with human nature, and he brings out its worst side, for he denies it nothing that it wants or thinks it needs. His experience is a cautionary tale of the relationship between politician and public as we often see it now. The politician believes that he can win the love, and votes, of his district only by handouts, the universal yes and the district comes to believe that the handouts alone symbolize quality. The receivers become corrupt, and the blessed giver bankrupt; his corrupted pupils can interpret this insolvency only as a willful termination of the largesse which has become for them the criterion of merit and truth. The eponymous practitioner of timony took to a rather tedious misanthropy. The disappointed public man of our day (not to mention the market-eyed publicist fighting, he says, for our right to know) also turns moralist and writes a best-seller exposing vice in government men and agencies. Lear, however, did not make a quick quid exposing Goneril and Regan in print. He died too soon to enjoy that ultimate anodyne for, or spinal block against, the harsh pain of the *peccavi*—that anguish of self-acknowledgment which Shakespeare understood so well that he could not always make his characters fully capable of it.

Note

1. "The Criminal as Tragic Hero: Dramatic Methods," in *Shakespeare Survey: An Annual Survey of Shakespearian Study and Production* 19, ed. Kenneth Muir (Cambridge: Cambridge University Press, 1966), 12-24.

Transcendence and Equivocation:
Some Political, Theological, and Philosophical Themes in Shakespeare

Laurence Berns

Robert Heilman has called our attention to the remarkable self-justifications that accompany the self-assertions made by many of Shakespeare's characters.[1] Shakespeare provides his flawed characters not merely with excuses, but with powerful cases that must be taken seriously. Self-justification, Heilman says, reflects a certain "moral or quasi-moral subtlety in the personality." Edmund, Richard III, and Iago, who work out rationales for what they do, engage us in ways that Goneril and Regan cannot. Every clever villain is aware of the importance of morality and how it works for most other people. It is the morality governing his victims that he relies on for his own exploitations. But this is not yet self-justification. Intelligence seeks reasons and causes. The very intelligence that permits the intelligent villain to understand his victims and their situations well enough to exploit them, leads him to try to make sense out of his own doings. In the impressive self-justifications of tragic heroes like Othello, Lear, and Macbeth, what is especially remarkable is the combination of powers of self-seeing with a resistance to self-seeing that Heilman calls case-making. The final phase of tragic experience is the recognition by the tragic hero of what he has done, the submission of self to judgment. What makes the tragic character interesting and gripping is the struggle in his soul between considerable powers for self-seeing and a resistance to self-seeing that is rooted in motives, aspirations, and pride that in some important respects are noble.[2] The drama is heightened by the fact that what is contending with self-knowledge for the domination of the tragic hero's soul is a serious contender. Self-justification, Heilman suggests, is the tragic hero's instinctual first reaction to the discovery of the disaster he has wrought. What Shakespeare may be pointing to here is a peculiarly human principle of psychic self-preservation even more fundamental for human life than that simpler instinct for self-preservation that all animals are said to share. Self-esteem and pride may be indispensable for human life, for the animal in whom rigidity of instinct gives way to openness to the world and guidance through cognition; pride and self-esteem are indispensable for the animal whose instincts are keyed to (or "released" by) not rigid stimuli, but to how he understands and to what he understands of his world. Forced by nature to rely on his own cognitive powers, action and life are paralyzed if a man's confidence in the validity of his judgments about the world is destroyed.[3]

The subtlety and depth of Shakespeare the psychologist have often been praised. But Shakespeare is more than a psychologist, taking the word in its current narrow sense. The self-justifications put forth by his characters are rarely only self-justifications; they become statements about the meaning of the larger world within which the self finds itself, larger moral, political, natural, and divine orders within which the self finds its place. Part of what makes Shakespeare's tragic heroes great is that they are too intelligent, too large-minded, to be concerned only with themselves. The rightness and wrongness of what they do and say become associated in dramatically convincing ways with the truth or falsity of the positions they take on the meaning of the whole of human life, on nature, and on divinity. At the end of *King Lear* it is difficult to know what Shakespeare finally decided about the relation between morality, justice, and nature; but there is no doubt that the problem, the question, has been powerfully and clearly raised. In short, Shakespeare is a philosophic poet. Further, Shakespeare explores not only how different self-vindications entail different views about the fundamental nature of things, but also how such views and doctrines in turn affect and shape the different kinds of souls they come to inhabit.

Macbeth's way of self-justification, Heilman explains, is different from Othello's, Lear's and Hamlet's; it is dramatic rather than verbal or rhetorical. He instinctively throws himself into the position of the hemmed-in heroic warrior, so completely that desperate action keeps his mind from dwelling too much on what he has become. "To know my deed," he says, "'twere best not know myself" (II.ii.72). Supernatural forces, the witches, in harmony with his ambition lead him to the threshold of damnable and maddening murder. Is not his very piety, his belief in the supernatural, part of what opens him to the influence of the witches? "But wherefore could not I pronounce 'Amen'?/ I had most need of blessing..." (II.ii.30-31). Macbeth seems to believe in two worlds: this world and the world of "the life to come." Once he is convinced that he has given his immortal soul, his "eternal jewel," to the Devil (III.i.67), that he has damned himself in the other world, he seems to lose all sense of distinction between bad and worse in this world. "I am in blood/ Stepp'd in so far, that, should I wade no more,/ Returning were as tedious as go o'er" (III.iv.135-137). These beliefs are connected with "the equivocation of the fiend that lies like truth" (V.v.43; cf. V.viii.19-20, "juggling fiends"). "Equivocation" recalls the sublime Porter scene.

Through his Porter, Shakespeare comments on the action of *Macbeth* as a whole. Much drink, the Porter tells us, is an equivocator with lechery: it provokes desire, but prevents performance. Macbeth's belief in supernatural powers and, consequently, two worlds, is intoxicating drink. The witches hold out the prospect for thisworldly greatness. Christianity holds out the prospect of the life to come: an eternity of salvation or of damnation. But the actions required to assure him of what the witches promise destroy his hopes and prospects for otherworldly salvation. At the same time, his pious conscience and its concern for otherworldly immortality, for the salvation of his soul, prevent him from coolly and effectively going about the murder of Duncan; it causes him unnaturally to involve his wife in the murder. Her involvement and Macbeth's own maddening despair and behavior eventually lead to her derangement and death, cutting off Macbeth's prospects for children, perpetuators of his thisworldly greatness. His despair and madness cause him openly to overleap all moral bounds, gaining him infamy rather than glory and fame. Thus he loses the two main props to the quasi-immortality of "this world," children to perpetuate his name, and fame. Intoxicating incompatible hopes for "immortality" in both worlds prevent accomplishment in either world. His belief in the supernatural and two worlds equivocates with his desire for immortality.[4]

Earlier we spoke of supernatural forces in harmony with Macbeth's ambition leading him to the threshold of damnable murder. But, as Lady Macbeth well knew, there was only one appeal capable of getting Macbeth over that threshold, that is, the appeal to courage. Until Birnam Wood comes to Dunsinane and he is opposed by one not born of woman, Macbeth fights with the maniacal fury of one certain that he is backed by

more than natural forces. Faced by Macduff and stripped of his belief
in supernatural support, Macbeth falters for a moment, till Macduff
hurls at him the one charge capable of bringing him to himself, the
charge of coward. In what may be his finest moment, bereft of the
supernatural aid he counted on, Macbeth returns to the simple natural creed of the soldier: Courage is salvation, cowardice damnation.
"[L]ay on Macduff,/ And damn'd be him who first cries 'Hold, enough!'"
(V.viii.33-34). As José Benardete has pointed out,[5] that word "damn'd"
must be taken with utmost seriousness in this play. What Macbeth
does is horrid, and courage (if it still deserves the name) without justice must be condemned. Even as a fictional object Macbeth would
simply be disgusting, if we did not sense the presence of something
noble at the core of his being. Samuel Johnson, commenting on Lady
Macbeth at the end of Act I, said:

> She urges the excellence and dignity of courage, a glittering idea
> which has dazzled mankind from age to age, and animated some-
> times the house-breaker and sometimes the conqueror; but this
> sophism Macbeth has forever destroyed, by distinguishing true
> from false fortitude, in a line and a half;..."I dare do all that may
> become a man,/ Who dares [d]o more is none."[6]

Hamlet finds himself in a similar moral-theological predicament.
Unobserved, he comes upon Claudius praying. "Now might I do it pat"
(III.iii.73). But he does not kill him, because he wants him to suffer an
eternity of torment in hell, and is afraid that his dying in prayer has too
much "relish of salvation in't" (III.iii.92).[7] The audience and readers
learn that even on the basis of his own theological suppositions Hamlet need not have hesitated. For Claudius, on rising from his knees,
informs us,

> My words fly up, my thoughts remain below.
> Words without thoughts never to heaven go. (III.iii.97-98)

Since his words did not actually go to heaven, that is, were not true prayers,
Claudius would not have been saved. But perhaps there would have been
some reward for merely trying to pray? These are unsure and slippery
grounds to base practice upon. Here too expectations for the other world
seem to thwart accomplishment in this.[8]

In his self-justifications Hamlet so clings to rectitude and innocence
that he hardly acts. He justifies himself in Heilman's tantalizing phrase
by "wily innocence plotting unawares." Something of the wily side of

Hamlet's innocence may be seen in what Heilman refers to as his "denunciatory and self-righteous style." Throughout much of the play Hamlet would not act before he thought he knew exactly what he was doing: he seems to have had control over his passion for retribution. But did he have control over his passion to preach, his passion to punish with words? As he said, he wanted to "make mad the guilty and appal the free" (II.ii.590). Punishing souls, to speak roughly, is far more complicated and less sure than punishing bodies or taking life. The theological predicaments it has involved Hamlet in must have been part of the daily fare at Luther's Wittenberg.

In Richard II a similar conflict between practical accomplishment in the ordinary sense and a religiously influenced desire to reach souls emerges. Heilman notes that Richard "so manipulates the divine right...," so "exploits the pathos that marks his practical situation...as to elicit from some readers a fond sympathy and almost an ignoring of the royal incapacity, the combination of weakness and willfulness that invites a takeover by any aspirant stronger on talent than scruple." At those decisive moments when there still might have been some chance to save his throne Richard's passion to wrench hearts—in Heilman's words, to exploit pathos—takes precedence over any political instincts. It is not without irony that it is the Bishop of Carlisle who says:

> My lord, wise men ne'er sit and wail their woes,
> But presently prevent the ways to wail.   (III.ii.178-179)

Richard's transformation in defeat has been variously interpreted as religious, theatrical, and poetic transcendence. However true each of these interpretations may be, here we shall focus on the religious. Quotes from or references to the New Testament, speaking of Richard as of Jesus, abound as he goes down.[9] Richard does not seem to be torn by the theological predicaments, the thisworldly and otherworldly tension besetting Macbeth and Hamlet. Shakespeare's interest in this play seems rather to explore the effects of different Biblical models on different kinds of souls and on political life in general.[10] Bolingbroke uses Biblical language twice, once before all Richard's New Testament allusions and once afterward: both are from the more political Old Testament, where Bolingbroke speaks of himself as the punisher of Cain.

The politically (and matrimonially) debilitating effects of a certain kind of Christian piety are seen most clearly in Henry VI. Henry is incapable of taming and containing the disruptive and straining ambi-

tions in his court. The hardness and severity it would require are simply beyond him. He sees quite clearly how utterly unjust the attacks
on the good Duke Humphrey are. He compares Humphrey, the pillar
of justice and mainstay of his reign, to a calf being driven to the slaugh-
terhouse, and himself to the helpless mother cow able only to weep
and wail "her darling's loss." Rank injustice prevails. Henry prays and
weeps while his kingdom is torn apart.[11]

Prospero's abjuring of his magic powers, according to Heilman,
"is implicitly a piece of political theory," which signifies that in political life one cannot count on the regular intervention of the miraculous. Since the magic and miraculous in this play are presented as
man-made, and, if, as has often been said, Prospero's art is parabolic
of Shakespeare's art, the politics pointed to here could be thought of
as poetic politics. *The Tempest* might help us to see how the political
problem of the reformation of humanity is a political-theological problem, and why the problem is insoluble. In *The Tempest* we are presented with a broad, if not the broadest, range of human types, or
natures, with Prospero, Miranda, and Ferdinand at the top; loyal
Gonzalo (perhaps) next; Alonso, Sebastian, and Antonio following;
with Stephano, Trinculo, and Caliban at the bottom.[12] Each of those
within Prospero's island polity requires supernatural prompting, but—
this is the problem—a different kind of supernatural prompting.[13] What
is appropriate to bolster Ferdinand's and Miranda's nobility are beautiful, generous, and beneficent deities; for Alonso, Sebastian, and Antonio there are fearsome Harpies, ministers of harsh fate; for Stephano,
Trinculo, and Caliban, spirits in the shape of vicious hunting dogs and
goblins that can grind, cramp, and pinch. It would seem that each
type of soul, each nature, needs a different kind of religion, but the
political community is united through one religion for all. Is it possible to unify the whole and at the same time adequately to reach the
variety of important human types? Can religion fulfill its broad-based
political functions without, in that very fulfillment, producing significant private alienation? Back in Naples and Milan, outside the play-
house, as Heilman puts it, "more limited tools" must be relied upon.

Do tragedy and comedy have inherent political tendencies? Can the
question of freedom for poetry and art reasonably be separated from the
question of the effects of poetry and art?

Tragedy and comedy, Heilman tells us, both acknowledge the inevitable imperfection of things, especially the imperfection of human con-

duct. Tragedy warns us of the danger that the craving for distinction, that spur to excellence, can sometimes lead a man to transgress the bounds set by moral, political, and sacred orders, confounding *hybris* with heroic steadfastness. Comedy belittles disruptive and pretentious folly with anger-soothing laughter. The sense of honor invoked by tragedy runs the risk of being turned into self-magnification at the expense of principle. The sense of humor invoked by comedy runs the risk of extending the range of the tolerable too far. Falstaff, for all his charm, cannot be accepted when he is no longer inconspicuous, no longer on the fringes of society. Falstaff at the paradigmatic center of political and moral life, where the tone or style of society is set, is impossible for any lasting, not to speak of any decent, political order. The opposites of tragedy and comedy, cynic license and puritanical fanaticism, point to that decent reconciliation with imperfect actuality that the spirits of tragedy and comedy should foster: that is, a kind of Puritanism, but a purified Puritanism, Puritanism with a sense of humor.

Angelo in *Measure for Measure* illustrates what is problematic in Puritanism, that is, in immoderate Puritanism. Puritanical Angelo is set up by Vienna's Duke to reform the city the Duke has allowed to become licentious, where "Liberty plucks Justice by the nose." The Duke knows that Angelo "doth with holy abstinence subdue/ That in himself which he spurs on his power/ To qualify in others" (IV.ii.83ff.). The bitterness from his own frustrated lust, not unmixed with envy, spurs him on to punish those who do not abstain. His self-righteousness is increased by his fear of falling into temptation, that is, the more he feels tempted, the more severe, he feels, must be the deterrent punishment. The intensity of purifying zeal in such cases seems to be directly proportional to the strength of the illicit desires in the zealot's own soul, directly proportional to the difficulty he has in keeping them under control. His judgment is warped in the direction of severity by what he feels is required by example to frighten himself into abstinence.[14] This "comedy," which the disguised Duke of Vienna kept from becoming a tragedy, ends with perfect justice, both legal and natural justice, in marriage. Lucio, a dissolute gentleman, is forced to marry the prostitute who is the mother of his child; Angelo, who lusted after Isabella, who was too good for him, marries the less scrupulous, the lighter (V.i.22) Mariana; that highly refined spirit, the Duke, intends to make that highly refined spirit, Isabella, his wife. Moderate Puritanism, Puritanism with a sense of humor, may be represented by the Duke: he knows both how to use and in a way how to purify the

Puritan, Angelo. If, on the other hand, the Duke comes short of perfection by way of leniency and Isabella by way of severity, it would be through the blending of their virtues and the mitigating of their defects in their offspring that Vienna could hope to receive its perfect Lord.

The political effect of tragedy, Heilman suggests, is an enhanced sense of moral responsibility leading to a reduced need for police and punitive powers in society. Tragedy's typical theme, the fall of the noble, with its attendant pity and fear, tends naturally toward the generation of moderation, awe, and even a sense of sin.[15] The political effect of comedy is the rejection of ideological melodramatic politics, increased acceptance for democratic pluralistic politics of compromise: yet not an undifferentiating egalitarian compromise with anything and everything; merit is to be recognized, greatness acknowledged.[16]

Freedom for poetry and art has at least two requirements. One is, obviously, freedom from political control of literature and art. Such freedom provides important, but only negative, conditions for fine or great art: there seems to be little artistic difference between the sycophantic propaganda of melodramatic official art and the offensive propaganda of melodramatic art of protest. Although we cannot minimize the importance of removing official impediments to the possible flowering of great art, we must face the fact that most great literature and art have been produced under political conditions far more repressive than those that exist in the liberal West today. Enlightened despots have sometimes sponsored great art and unenlightened despots have sometimes not been interested enough to interfere with it.[17] It would seem to be impossible simply to identify the conditions of healthy politics and society with the conditions that make for great poetry and art.

It might be more salutary for us now to dwell more on the other requirement for freedom of literature and art: reasonable responsibility on the part of writers and artists for the moral and political consequences of what they produce. The greatest danger to freedom of literature and art in America today may come from what I would call the abuse of the First Amendment,[18] from what I spoke of before as extending the range of the tolerable too far. To the extent that free institutions are associated with men and activities which are undeserving of them, the will to preserve such institutions will naturally wane. The abusers of freedom are enemies of freedom no less than the tyrannically minded. What Milton said about the study of Aristotle's *Poetics* may also be said about the serious study of Shakespeare:

This would make them [students] soon perceive what despicable creatures our common-rhymers and play-writers be; and show them what religious, what glorious and magnificent use might be made of poetry both in divine and human things.[19]

Notes

1. In his chapter "Shakespearean Comedy and Tragedy: Implicit Political Analogies," above.

2. See Heilman's "'Twere Best Not Know Myself: Othello, Lear, Macbeth" in *Shakespeare 400: Essays by American Scholars on the Anniversary of the Poet's Birth*, ed. James G. McManaway (New York: Holt, Rinehart, and Winston, 1964), pp. 89-98. Cf. Laurence Berns, "Gratitude, Nature, and Piety in *King Lear*," *Interpretation: A Journal of Political Philosophy*, 3 (Autumn 1972), sections II-V; and "Aristotle's *Poetics*," in *Ancients and Moderns: Essays on the Tradition of Political Philosophy in Honor of Leo Strauss*, ed. Joseph Cropsey (New York: Basic Books, 1964), p. 82.

3. If this is so, and pride is a sin, no man is free from it. If, as St. Augustine says, there is no ground for human pride because all goodness comes from God, even those who are steadfast in glorifying God can take no credit for it. They can only thank God for the grace he has bestowed upon them. Shakespeare's *Troilus and Cressida* could be seen as an experiment in looking at the paradigms of heroic pride from a Christian perspective: the problematic elements of heroic pride interpreted through the filters of Christian sentiment are seen as deception and self-deception rooted in envy. Reason left to itself, however, would seem to distinguish between just or true human pride and false pride.

4. The equivocation theme enters most effectively but silently in the striking irony of II.iii.91-96, where Macbeth in an equivocating lament over Duncan's death "in a brilliant counterpart to the equivocation of the fiend that lies like truth...utters truth like lies." Kenneth Muir in the Arden Edition of *Macbeth* (New York: Barnes and Noble, 1962), p. xxviii.

5. "Macbeth's Last Words," *Interpretation: A Journal of Political Philosophy*, I (Summer 1970), p. 63.

6. *A New Variorum Edition of Shakespeare*, ed. H.H. Furness, Jr. (New York: Dover, 1963), p. 105.

7. The notion of the other world and the life to come can, evidently, arouse passions of revenge and hate to a supernatural pitch, as well as "immortal longings" for supernatural bliss and love.

8. Conversely, his actions in this world spoil his chances for the next. On the premises about heaven and hell that Hamlet takes so seriously in this scene, the list of lives ruined by his actions could weigh heavily against any easy entrance into heaven for himself.

9. I have counted eleven: III.ii.24, III.ii.60-62, III.ii.132, III.iii.85, IV.i.144,

IV.i.169-171, IV.i.239-242, IV.i.309, V.i.24, V.ii.23-26, and V.v.15-18.

10. Is the behavior of the followers meant in some way to reflect back on the models?

11. The other side of the coin, ethically and politically supportive Christianity, could, among other places, be studied in *Henry V.*

12. We have listed Caliban at the bottom, although a good case could be made for the superiority of his natural slavishness over the sophisticated slavishness of Stephano and Trinculo.

13. Cf. Plato, *Phaedrus*, 271b-272b.

14. This may, in part, explain why Angelo was chosen over Old Escalus to represent the Duke in his absence.

15. Cf. Berns, "Aristotle's *Poetics*," pp. 77-78.

16. But cf. William Hazlitt, "Coriolanus," in *Characters of Shakespeare's Plays* (1817; repr. London: Dent, Everyman's Library, 1906).

17. These arguments can also be extended to science and philosophy. Cf. *Discoveries and Opinions of Galileo*, translated by Stillman Drake (Garden City, N.Y.: Doubleday Anchor, 1957), pp. 59-72, esp. 65-68. Cf. also William Hazlitt, "Why the Arts Are Not Progressive—A Fragment" in *The Round Table* (1817; repr. London: Dent, Everyman's Library, 1936).

18. Cf. George Anastaplo, *The Constitutionalist: Notes on the First Amendment* (Dallas: Southern Methodist University Press, 1971), the references in the Index under "Obscenity" and pp. 771-774; "Obscenity and Common Sense" in *Human Being and Citizen: Essays on Virtue, Freedom, and the Common Good* (Chicago: Swallow Press, 1975); "Censorship," *Encyclopaedia Britannica*, 15th ed. (beginning with the 1985 printing), vol. 15, pp. 604-11; Laurence Berns, "Our Political Situation: Good Government, Self-Government and American Democracy," in *The Great Ideas Today: 1997* (Chicago: Encyclopaedia Britannica, Inc.), pp. 78-123, especially notes 13, 15, 24, 25, 28-31, 39, 51, 54, and 83; and Walter Berns, *The First Amendment and the Future of American Democracy* (New York: Basic Books, 1976), chaps. 5 and 6.

19. From his essay *On Education*.

INDEX